W9-DGJ-190

HUMAN
EXPERIENCE

THE ARTS
IN CULTURE

THE NOTEBOOKS OF PAUL BRUNTON
(VOLUME 9)

HUMAN EXPERIENCE

THE ARTS IN CULTURE

PAUL BRUNTON
(1898–1981)

An in-depth study of
categories thirteen and fourteen
from the notebooks

Published for the
PAUL BRUNTON PHILOSOPHIC FOUNDATION
by Larson Publications

International Standard Book Number (cloth) 0-943914-30-2
International Standard Book Number (paper) 0-943914-31-0
International Standard Book Number (series, cloth) 0-943914-17-5
International Standard Book Number (series, paper) 0-943914-23-X
Library of Congress Catalog Card Number: 87-81537

Manufactured in the United States of America

Published for the
Paul Brunton Philosophic Foundation
by
Larson Publications
4936 Route 414
Burdett, New York 14818

Distributed to the trade by
Kampmann and Company
9 East 40 Street
New York, New York 10016

88 90 91 89 87
2 4 6 8 10 9 7 5 3 1

The works of Dr. Brunton

A Search in Secret India
The Secret Path
A Search in Secret Egypt
A Message from Arunachala
A Hermit in the Himalayas
The Quest of the Overself
The Inner Reality
(*also titled* Discover Yourself)
Indian Philosophy and Modern Culture
The Hidden Teaching Beyond Yoga
The Wisdom of the Overself
The Spiritual Crisis of Man

Published posthumously

Essays on the Quest

The Notebooks of Paul Brunton
volume 1: Perspectives
volume 2: The Quest
volume 3: Practices for the Quest
          Relax and Retreat
volume 4: Meditation
          The Body
volume 5: Emotions and Ethics
          The Intellect
volume 6: The Ego
          From Birth to Rebirth
volume 7: Healing of the Self
          The Negatives
volume 8: Reflections on My
          Life and Writings
volume 9: Human Experience
          The Arts in Culture

CONTENTS

EDITORS' INTRODUCTION

This ninth volume in *The Notebooks of Paul Brunton* is an in-depth presentation of the thirteenth and fourteenth (of twenty-eight) categories in the personal notebooks Dr. Paul Brunton (1898–1981) reserved for posthumous publication. Both topics in this volume explore the spiritual demand to cultivate one's full humanity.

Part 1, *Human Experience* radiates the sun of spiritual meaning and purpose through the opportunities and vicissitudes of daily living. Throughout his long career of spiritual service, Paul Brunton constantly reiterated this theme: every human experience has meaning and is related to a universal purpose. He considered it "a paradox of the strongest irony that the place where we can best find the Overself [the individual link with God] is not in another world, but in this one, that the chance to grow enduringly out of darkness into light is better here."

The comprehensiveness of P.B.'s approach to full human development matured into an outlook that incorporates classical Eastern and contemporary Western ideas, yet transcends both in its universality and relevance for modern spiritual practitioners. Through it we can combine the best points of the mystical and the humanistic views.

Like a humanist, P.B. insists that spiritual maturity and integrity are best expressed through bringing tolerance, compassion, rectitude, and dependability into character and conduct. Like a mystic, he reverently acknowledges the benefic omnipresence of a greater God and the urgency of seeking ecstatic mystical union with it. Unlike the secular humanist, however, he does not extol the virtues of human character as a suitable *substitute* for conscious inner communion with diety; and unlike the majority of mystics, he does not return from his ecstatic raptures to declare either that everyday human experience is worthless illusion or more lovely than God intended. His rich, balanced, and thoroughly rational insight exposes and leads us beyond the various shortcomings of each of these points of view.

For P.B., a higher power has invested in us being, life, intelligence, intuition, and numerous other potential powers. Events and circumstances are intelligently ordered as opportunities intended to elicit our qualities and our exercise of those powers. Yet it is *we* who *choose* whether the qualities we respond with are positive or negative, whether the powers we actualize are used for good or ill. In the same moment that unalterable fate presents its stimulus, we exercise the freedom of our own personal response. The inner qualities we choose to align ourselves with, and express in our reactions to what life presents, indicate what is needed for the next step in our spiritual growth. In this sense life tests us, not to give us a grade, but to show us ourselves and the consequences of the self we have chosen. Through the consequences we learn the wisdom or lack of wisdom in our past choices and revise our future ones on the basis of what we have learned. It is a process of forming our own character, and in so doing, contributing to our collective destiny—that is, to what life can offer humanity as a world to live in *today*.

In this context of the interaction of self-chosen character and consequent circumstance, P.B. explores in chapter four various aspects of the present world-crisis. Though many readers may feel as we did for quite some time—that the material in this section fits more appropriately with the material in the third chapter of *The Negatives* (volume seven)—P.B.'s outline does indeed call for placing the world-crisis material in the context of *Human Experience*. In arranging the material to accommodate this outline, we have come to see the sense of doing so. We hope that readers likewise will see the usefulness of having been prepared for this world-crisis chapter by material in the preceding chapters of *Human Experience*. Nonetheless, there are significant points of overlap between the world-crisis material and *The Negatives*: we recommend that the two sections be considered together for a full view of P.B.'s thoughts on this subject.

While *opportunity* and *choice* may be keywords for Part 1 of this volume, *beauty* is unquestionably the keyword for Part 2. What *Human Experience* does for the cultivation of unassailable integrity, *The Arts in Culture* does for the cultivation of aesthetic refinement. In this section, P.B. reverently celebrates the role of the Beautiful in human culture, including subsections on the mission of inspired art, creativity, genius, and the relationship of art and mystical experience. Here he also comments on specific works in a variety of art forms that have special value for individuals consciously seeking spiritual inspiration.

We should point out that P.B. placed his observations on literature and the art of writing in three different areas of his notebooks. Some appear in volume 8, *Reflections on My Life and Writings*. Another portion of them appears in the final chapter of *The Arts in Culture*. The vast majority of them, however, went into a complete notebook separate from the 1–28 "Ideas" series. This third section is scheduled for publication along with other independent notebooks following completion of the "Ideas" series.

Editorial conventions with respect to the quantity of material chosen, as with respect to spelling, capitalization, hyphenation, and other copy-editing considerations, are the same as stated in introductions to earlier volumes. Likewise, (P) at the end of a para indicates that it is one of the relatively few paras we felt should be repeated here from *Perspectives*, the introductory survey volume to this series.

As this ninth volume goes to press, we would once again like to take the opportunity to acknowledge gratefully the dedicated and skilled assistance of many friends at Wisdom's Goldenrod and the Paul Brunton Philosophic Foundation. We also deeply appreciate and are continually encouraged by the support of a steadily increasing readership of *The Notebooks* worldwide. Further information about publication schedules and related activities may be obtained from the

Paul Brunton Philosophic Foundation
P.O. Box 89
Hector, New York 14841

Part 1:
HUMAN
EXPERIENCE

All the experiences which life brings us are meaningful. Let us use our intelligence and learn these meanings. For life is trying to develop that intelligence in us until she can make us aware of the highest meaning of all—the Soul.

The human situation is a paradox. We are at one and the same time inhabitants of a world of reality as well as a world of appearance. A true human life must embrace both aspects, must be spiritual as well as physical, must integrate the intuitive as well as the intellectual.

1

SITUATION

Daily life as spiritual opportunity

All worldly experiences may become doors to divinity if interpreted aright.

2

Human experience is our laboratory for higher experiment. The world is our school for spiritual discovery. The vicissitudes of personal circumstance are our field for ethical achievement. The great books written by illumined individuals from antiquity till today are our guides.

3

Those who complain that their opportunities for meditation, study, travel to India, and so on are nil, and that therefore they have no possibility of spiritual growth, need not despair. The common life regarded in an uncommon light, the ordinary activities engaged in from a different standpoint, become part of a spiritual path through which development is possible.

4

If life is a process of gaining education through experience and reflection, it is also a process of correcting errors and approaching truth, of clearing illusions and perceiving realities.

5

The ego naturally and understandably revolts bitterly against calamities which are put upon it by chance, by destiny, or by any other apparent cause outside itself. The quester must not accept this emotion but ought to separate himself from it. In this way he advances at a spurt on his quest.

6

Life presents him from time to time with occasions for improving character and strengthening its weaker places. But whether he accepts them as such, or lets his ego follow its habitual trends without opposition, is his choice.

7

The various experiences through which we have passed, reflectively and analytically instruct us; the immoderate desires we have checked repeatedly, strengthen us; and the wandering thoughts we have concentrated determinedly, tranquillize us. Life never runs to waste if it thus is attuned to the notes of this quest.

8

Life is our real school, for it provides the chance to acquire virtue and discipline evil, to nurture the mind and clarify its thoughts.

9

If he can bring himself to look upon events when they flow upon him as being intended to elicit his qualities and exercise his powers, and thus give him the chance to cultivate them, he will learn to acknowledge and accept the responsibility of choosing whether those qualities be positive or negative, whether those powers be good or bad.

10

No experience is a wasted one when it is treated philosophically, when not only its final results but every moment of it is used as material for his strivings toward the ideal and his understanding of the True.

11

No situation or circumstance is really counter to self-liberation. Each one may be used for enlightenment.

12

Here, in this physical world, the ego is put to school. Here it learns lessons, sins and suffers, yields to passion and then checks it, responds to intuition and is led upward.

13

All activities in the world are an opportunity both for self-study and for objective awareness of the self in each situation. An intensified longing for the way itself, rather than a too great concern with the particular steps along the way, will clarify these efforts.

14

The experiences of daily living in the world become, for the quester, occasions for working on himself, for co-operating with the World-Idea as it concerns himself.

15

When every situation which life can offer is turned to the profit of spiritual growth, no situation can really be a bad one.

16

The kind of environment in which he lives may hinder or hasten a man's mystical development, but every kind of environment can contribute towards his understanding of life and therefore towards his general spiritual development.

17

In the end each experience incites the living entity to unfold the powers qualities and characteristics already within itself but still unexpressed.

18

The whole of his everyday experience can be brought within the area covered by the Quest. Indeed it must be so brought if the self-division from which ordinary unquesting man suffers is to be avoided. The ills and calamities of life, as much as its joys and boons, will then contribute toward his understanding and growth.

19

Regarded in this way, every experience becomes an instruction, all life a spiritual adventure.

20

He sees in the end that all his life and business, relationships and contacts in the world really constitute a contest with his own self; that all have the forming and finding of himself as the ultimate result and ultimate fulfilment.

21

Life on earth for us is not to be a goal in itself, but a means to the goal. All its experiences are to be used to shape our character and increase our knowledge and, above all, to bring us nearer the discovery of, and identification with, our Overself.

22

Everything, every experience, good or bad, pleasant or unpleasant, may be turned into a pointer towards our true nature, a reminder of the high quest which all human beings are here on earth to follow, whether consciously or not.

23

Each experience of human existence offers at least one clue, generally more, to the hidden secret of being, the Overself.

Spiritual laws structure experience

24

If we accept the existence of a higher power behind life and the universe and if, further, we believe that infinite wisdom is an attribute of this power, then, finally, we must also accept life as we find it and as we humanly experience it.

25

There is no problem which does not carry within it a hidden meaning, no person associated with us who does not bear within himself a hidden message. As soon as we rise above the level of their appearance, and as long as we stay on that level, the problem shows us the way to solve it and the person plays his true note in the harmony of our lives.

26

It requires a strong faith to believe that even in the midst of the direst distress, of the gloomiest hardship, what happens is sanctioned by, and under the rule of, divinely ordained laws and that it has a rational and higher meaning which we should seek to extract and heed. Those who lack this faith bear strain-ridden faces that betray no inner calm. Yet it is only a single step to turn around and start the journey from inner wretchedness to inner radiance.

27

The penetrative mind of the deep thinker finds in time that life in this world is not only life in illusion but also in pain. Yet for him to stop with this discovery is to stop at an intermediate stage on the way to truth. He must travel beyond it and learn the hidden cosmic laws and thus come to understand the magnificent goal toward which all this passage through worldly existence is leading.

28

All the power behind the cosmos insists on meeting cause with effect, action with reaction, evil with retribution.

29

What controls the course of our lives? *Fate* is something which descends on us from outside ourselves and to which we have made no visible contribution—as in the death of a beloved one. *Destiny* is something which arises out of our own causation.

30

Throw out the idea of coincidence. Remember there is a World-Idea. There is meaning in life, in its events, happenings, karmas, meetings, and opportunities.

31

The troubles and inconveniences of life do not come to us without the knowledge and sanction of the higher power. Therefore they do not come to us without some reason.

32

The man who is ignorant of the higher laws, such as the law of recompense, may still display sagacity in certain situations if his character is good and his intellect sharp. But if they are not, then he will display only fatuity.

33

The central message of philosophy to the modern era is that man is not isolated but supported by a friendly power, not left in the dark but surrounded by helping hands.

34

There is a higher destiny behind all the experiences which the aspirant undergoes. Although purificatory work may at times have brought hardships to him and to those whom he loves, still he must recognize that it may also have afforded protection against dangerous possibilities from which he and they have been saved.

35

Knowledge is the crying need of the hour, knowledge of the higher laws governing the life and fortune of human beings.

36

The man who hesitates to accept the idea of rebirth must confess, in his frankest moments, that he cannot reconcile the sufferings around him with faith in a benevolent power.

37

The teaching of reincarnation, that every individual enters repeatedly a new life on earth, carries the sister teaching of compensation. The two constitute the most plausible teaching about the suffering of man which he has ever been offered. This teaching sets in place under universal law what otherwise seems mere chance.

38

The nearer he comes to this insight the larger is his acceptance of life. Each event is seen to be either inevitable, just, or right. No news is ever so bad that there is no good behind it. Less and less is he inclined to attempt to reform others or to meddle in their affairs. More and more he sees that there is wisdom and purpose at work in all happenings, and that the law of recompense never ceases to operate.

39

In the end, after so many births, all these experiences must lead to the mystical rebirth.

40

If you live in harmony with Life it will unfold in perfect sequence the exact experience which you need.

41

There is no situation in the life of a quester, no incident and no contact, which is not a parable to be penetratively read and its inner meaning adequately elucidated.

42

If he works faithfully on the quest, every experience which is essential to his inner growth will gravitate to him, every thing or person needful to his development will be drawn to him, subject to some synchronization with his personal karma. He, on his side, ought to welcome those situations which can be used to strengthen his inner life.

43

Nothing in his experience is to be condemned but everything is to be understood. It is there because its lesson is needed. Similarly, no one in his experience is to be despised but everyone is also to be understood. Each is there to test or tempt, to teach or uplift.

44

The friends of a man who was thrown out of work into unemployment asked, "Why should this evil happen to him? He is so upright in character and so scrupulous not to harm others. Yet he has been without work for the past three months and there is none in sight!" This is one way, the commonest way, of looking at the matter. But the habitual attitude towards events is often an inferior one. It is the ego's attitude. It is possible to regard unemployment from another and superior standpoint, a more impersonal and less egoistic one. For this question, like many others, is part of the larger and ultimate question, "Why am I here on earth?" Only when the answer to this second one is correctly found will the answer to the first one be correctly found. The unemployed man will see his situation not as an evil to be shunned but as an experience to be studied. If he does this calmly and properly, he may find that certain deficiencies in himself have to be supplied, or faults remedied, or capacities developed. With the acceptance of such a discovery, the lack of work will go and a cycle of more fruitful activity than ever before will come. For the Infinite Intelligence which placed him here also provided the necessary conditions for his existence. Where these conditions are not immediately favourable or discoverable, that circumstance does not nullify this statement, for then it is intended to educe his latent resources, to force him to make the efforts needed to develop his character and intelligence, to stimulate the growth of his energies, capacities, and qualities.

45

The fact that an event has happened or that an experience has arrived must have some significance in a man's life. It could not be there unless he had earned it or unless he needed it. If he is not willing to meet it from this approach and deal with its effect impersonally, he will miss most of its lesson.

46

The experiences which come to him and the circumstances in which he finds himself are not meaningless. They usually have a personal karmic lesson for him and should be studied much more than books. He must try to understand impersonally the inner significance behind these events. Their meaning can be ascertained by trying to see them impartially, by evaluating the forces which are involved in them, by profound reflection, and by prayer. Each man gets his special set of experiences, which no one else gets. Each life is individual and gets from the law of recompense those which it really needs, not those which someone else needs. The way in which he reacts to the varied pleasant and unpleasant situations which develop in everyday life will be a better index to the understanding he has gained than any mystical visions painted by the imagination.(P)

47

Every important event occurring to him who follows this path has an inner as well as an outer significance, for it traces back to a karmic origin which is specially selected to promote his self-knowledge and self-purification.

48

If he will look upon each situation when it comes as a new lesson to learn, or an old one to learn better, he will gain precisely what he needs just at the time he needs it. Books can only seldom speak with exactness to his personal condition, for they are written to suit too many individuals and they are too general to be quite pertinent to his own personal requirements.

49

If his growth requires a drastic change in his surroundings or his circumstances, be sure it will happen.

Experience as personal teacher

50

The whole world carries a message—nay, innumerable messages—to the man with ears to hear.

51

Every event, happening, and action-consequence carries its message to those concerned. Too often that message is the need of abandoning negativity or animality, of becoming positive or disciplined.

52

Some events happen to a man or some people come into his life to stand as symbols representing a truth of human existence generally, or a fact of inner life, or a principle of ethical, moral, or karmic law. The situation offers a lesson, or a warning, or an instruction or challenge.

53

Experience is apparently of value only insofar as it leads to thoughts about the experience, but actually it has another and hidden value—in the subconscious mind.

54

The education of self which is provided by experience is an almost subconscious process.

55

The lessons remain long after the problems themselves have died.

56

There is no school of philosophy where instruction is so regularly given as the school of life itself.

57

There is no substitute for personal experience, no more effectual way to learn the lessons of human existence than to see with one's own eyes and feel with one's own body. This said, philosophy neither justifies nor approves this way, but only explains why it is the commonest one.

58

Every generation must learn these lessons afresh, must find by its own experience that evil traits will invite the purgation of suffering. Technical advance can be kept for and maintained by the next generation, but spiritual advance is a highly personal and individual matter. It drops out again when the man himself drops out of circulation. This is why real historians who happen also to be deep thinkers tell us that mankind's moral nature changes only slightly during the centuries. The group has to learn its moral lessons all over again but some units in that group need not.

59

In life we learn that truth, principle, knowledge, or information best which we teach ourselves.

60

Reflection and imagination, analysis and anticipation, rightly used and harmoniously combined, can supersede experience. Indeed, they are forms of experience. But, being under our individual control and direction, they can be used as instruments to save us long-drawn and emotionally painful results.

61

Why should we individually undergo every possible experience? Can we not, by creative imagination, intuitive feeling, and correct thinking, save ourselves the need of passing through some experiences? This is so, but it is so only for those who have developed such faculties to a sufficient degree.(P)

62

Ironically enough, pain and suffering are not always necessary. But only the few understand this. They may learn quietly from philosophy within a few years what humanity at large must learn brutally through suffering, and relearn again in every epoch.

63

Experience is an expensive way of gaining wisdom.

64

All people are inescapably guided by experience. But the prudent man looks to other people's—especially the best—as well as his own, whereas the fool is limited entirely to his own.

65

He who will not heed the counsels of reason or accept the promptings of intuitive feeling will receive the less pleasant instruction of experience.

66

If a man feels that despite the dictates of reason he should embark on a particular unethical adventure simply to gain some sort of experience, and if he believes that this experience is a necessary part of the whole of his development, then let him go ahead, taste the bittersweet fruits of his actions, and learn at first hand why it should have been left alone.

67

What is demonstrated by observing contemporary life is that so few men are willing to take their lessons from the past experience of other men throughout history, that so many obdurately prefer to learn under pressure the hard way. The same foolish errors, the old pain-bringing sins are repeated monotonously and regularly. The cost of ignoring such experience is heavy. People are not teachable and their defects not corrigible by the gentle way. They will not absorb guidance from the interior sources of reflection or intuition or the exterior sources of preachment or observation.

68

It is true that wisdom comes with experience but that experience need not be gained at the cost of one's own suffering. It can just as well be gained by the observation of it in others.

69

Most people learn and can only learn by the method of trial and error— that is, by the method of experience.

70

Men are not left to depend for guidance only on what they learn by experience. What they believe by faith also guides them.

71

The art of living includes the arts of survival and social adaptation. In life, with its pleasures and miseries, its problems and mysteries, these arts must be learned from theory and practice, from surrender and compromise, from teachers and elders.

72

The truth starkly lights up certain situations, but it is equally valid to say that certain situations light up the truth.

73

They would not need to get any experience of the world without, if they would get sufficient experience of the world within.

74

All the experiences through which he passes, and many of those through which he observes others pass, should find their way after reflection and distillation into his wisdom.

75

The lessons of past experience are not enough in themselves to provide all the guidance needed for present living. We need also the ideals held up by intuition, the principles and ideas presented from within by the higher part of our nature, and from without by the spiritual teachers and religious prophets of mankind.

76

It is one thing to grope through life blindly and another to fulfil the law of our being *consciously*.

77

Where experience is extremely narrow, its deficiency may be supplied by reading, reflection, or intuition.

78

Only after he has fully tasted and long enjoyed the fruits of striving ambition and straining desire will he be in a position to assess their worth correctly. Only then will he be perceptive enough to consider the vacuity of his ephemeral life.

79

It is possible for man to learn whether a proposed course is wise or foolish, prudent or reckless, without having to wait for the testimony of events. In that case he must look for the counsel of spiritual teachers.

80

What he can teach himself from the pages of a book is one thing, and a very necessary thing, but what he can only teach himself from life's experiences is another.

81

He may learn this truth by reading someone else's ideas or reflecting on his own, by the arguments of logical thinking or the announcements of intuitive feeling.

82

Life and grief will teach a man through harsh tragedy what reason and intuition would teach him through tender pleading.

83

If they will not come to the truth by directly accepting it from the truth-seers, then they must come to it by a more roundabout and painful way.

84

Life is the real tutor; experience is the principal education. The voice of truth is within.

85

It is one thing to learn from experience, another to remember and not to forget these lessons.

Spiritual truth in practical life

86

A man's acts constitute the daily declaration of his faith. If he possesses spirituality let him demonstrate it by actual achievement. Action is to be considered the first criterion of philosophic achievement.

87

His fidelity to the Quest will be tested, both by specially critical periods and by everyday happenings. On the one side, temptations will call him; on the other, difficulties will deter him. Will he bend the knee before the world's idols? Will he stand strong amid the world's turmoil? Only when the hour of testing comes can he know.

88

The tests through which life itself outwardly puts him may seem appropriate or not but they contribute to the discoveries within himself, to the knowledge of his character, its strengths and limits, its belated ambitions and ludicrous self-deceptions.

89

I have tried to teach from the very beginning of my writing career—well before I went off to the Orient—and have repeated tirelessly, the close connection between spiritual *truth* and practical life, as opposed to spiritual imagination. I have insisted that the ordinary activities of everyday existence must bear the impress of this truth, that the inward light must shine in outward conduct. In other words, I tried to say that this is not a matter only for dreamers, useless to men and women who carry on the world's work, but a matter for all, whether they want to live in the busy world or in the cloistered monastery. Philosophy is for *use*. It is not a thing which is queer, outlandish, and entirely superfluous, as some think.

90

The beginner should look more to his outer situation and environment, for he is more affected by it; the proficient should look more to his inner reactions to situation or environment, for they then become his test. The role they play in his development depends on the stage he is at.

91

If, instead of bitterly resenting it, we receive the test in the right attitude or pass through the trial with the proper thoughts about it, we shall find when it is over that the experience has been of great value to us. We shall find that it has lifted us to a new and higher level of character, a new and truer conception of life. Our lower nature is weakened, our better nature strengthened. Our eyes are clearer. Our feet advance another step forward on the Quest.

92

Knowing that his reaction to whatever happens is even more important than the happening itself, he watches for hidden tests of his character and capacity. Whether he is coping with the problems of his work or moving in the circle of his family, he uses each episode or situation to prove himself worthy or to discover a weakness. In the latter event he will not become discouraged but will probe, analyse, plan, and resolve until he turns it into a new strength.

93

It is the unexpected situation, when there is no time to calculate a response or prepare a reply, that reveals what measure of strength we can rise to. It is in the sudden crisis—which is only a situation pushed to a complete extreme—when there is no chance to escape altogether or to evade partially, that what wisdom we have, or lack, shows itself.

94

Life with its variety of experiences is always testing him anyway, but it is when he is under stress that he is tested most.

95

Theoretical knowledge of the truth is not valueless. Its very presence, even if we fail to apply it, tends to irritate and impel us towards such application.

96

The test of bringing thoughts and theories, intuitions and revelations, to action is a means not only of expressing them but also of evaluating them. It is only by doing this, by bringing them face to face with the facts of life that he can learn what they are really worth or how they should really have been executed. Even though the opportunity to act wisely has been lost, the *knowledge* has been gained. Even though he may never be able to make use of it again in this lifetime, it remains in his mind and will enrich his later incarnations. Experience of the world, however studded with faults and mistakes it may be, must always complement understanding of life if he is to accomplish his fullest development. The abstract is man's left arm, the concrete is his right one. As he applies his ideas directly to the outward life, they become fruitful. Thus he is able to see for himself whether the fruit is good or bad, and to judge the tree accordingly.

97

These eternal truths must be brought down into his simple daily experience. Every act is to be done in their light, every thought held in their atmosphere.

98

If the practice of meditation is to be limited to recluses and the study of metaphysical truth confined to monasteries, then both mysticism and metaphysics will be in danger of becoming merely theoretical subjects. For active life in the world, with its problems to be grappled with and its realities to be faced and its temptations to be overcome, provides both a necessary testing-ground and a valuable expressional medium for mystical experience and metaphysical reflection.

99

The carpenter can bring his idea for a piece of furniture to the test by the simple act of making it. The quester can bring his understanding of the teachings to the test by trying them out in actual everyday living. Not before then can he conclusively determine how correctly he has absorbed them, or how utterly foolish and dangerously misleading they themselves may be. Here is the place of the physical plane and the purpose of physical action. Not before then can he have the certainty that they belong to reality, and not merely to his own or someone else's imagination.

100

When we understand it aright, each test is then seen not to be an ordeal to be shrinkingly dreaded, but a gate to be eagerly welcomed; and this is because it offers us the chance of a higher development, of an entry into a higher state of being and capacity.

101

Action is the best way to complete a thought.

102

An impracticable teaching is a defective teaching. What is unworkable in practice is untrue in theory.

103

The minor details which, in their numerous throng, make up most of our daily life offer a chance to express philosophy's wisdom and apply philosophic discipline just as much as the great ones.

104

It is largely through such spiritual trial and error that so many find their way through imitations, frauds, sterilities, and black perils to the authentic philosophy and the real quest.

105

Every new experience or new set of circumstances becomes his teacher. Every personal reaction to it becomes an indication of his spiritual status.

106

Sooner or later situations will form themselves which will remind him that only by enforcing the teachings in his own conduct can he get their benefits, only by applying them in deeds and linking them to daily living can he verify their truth.

107

Hardships offer tests but so do easier circumstances, although this is less plainly seen because the tests are so different.

108

The test comes when they find themselves in situations to which they are unequal.

109

The spiritual gains made in spite of the world's opposition and in its very midst will be solid durable and substantial. But the gains made in an ashram may be imaginary superficial and transient.

110

Awareness grows in silence, the test of it in activity.

111

What is its value for life? This is the test.

112

The result of his actions will tell him something about the ideas which led to them, about the truth or falsity, the rightness or wrongness, of those ideas. It will tell him whether his faith is well-placed or ill-placed.

113

The last test must still be how far he brings the truth into his life.

114

The troubles of a follower do not prove that the teachings have failed. They prove only that he did not actually follow them in reality, whatever else he may have done in appearance, that they were not active in his mind and heart and will, however much they may have seemed so in the sight of others.

115

When the truth alters his whole conception of life, penetrates his heart and stirs his will, it has become his own.

116

What he accepts as idea and principle must be applied to experience and sustained in action. Then, and then only, will it manifest itself in fortune and destiny.

Getting the point

117

Life does not tell us why we are here: we have to enquire of it, seek to understand it, and wait while seeking for the answers.

118

Every event in his life should be made to reveal its karmic meaning for him. He may not at first perceive this; time, patience, and tranquil invitation to his deeper being—best done after meditation, before sleep, or before rising—can help.

119

In some way this life is a charade, a play which is being acted out but whose meanings have to be inferred from given clues.

120

It is not the mere succession of events that make up the essence of a man's life: it is what he extracts from those events.

121

Every new circumstance or happening in his life has some message for him from the Infinite Mind or some lesson to convey to him or some test to strengthen him. It is for him to seek out this inner significance and to re-adjust his thinking and actions in accordance with it.(P)

122

"What is the Overself telling me through this experience? What does it want me to learn, know, do, or avoid?"

123

Many people read the lessons of their experience but alas! what they read is different from what is really indicated. Too often it is an egoistic distortion or even a gross falsification of the real lesson.

124

It is only if experience is correctly interpreted that it brings discretion, and only if thought is correctly reasoned that it brings discernment.

125

He should learn to profit spiritually and practically by all his experiences, the pleasurable as well as the painful, the gay as well as the grave. But he can do this only if he reads from them not what he wishes to read, not what will soothe or flatter his ego, but what is really their message and teaching. The unguided seeker finds it harder to succeed in this endeavour than his luckier fellow, but it is worth trying.

126

The undisciplined mind is easily misled.

127

It was because the Greeks knew that meditative reflection upon the meaning of tragic experience is less effective in the midst of it, while emotion is highly involved, that they avoided actual representation of the tragedy itself. The audience then received it only as an idea, not as a spectacle.

128

Reason alone may give him the truth about a situation, but personal feeling may give him a half-lie about it. Yet he will prefer that to the truth simply because the ego is being supported.

129

An experience involving suffering may not bear its lesson on its face—unless it has repeated itself so many times that the lesson is plain and clear. Although having a teachable and receptive mind will elucidate it more quickly, more often it is dark and obscure. There is needed something or someone to draw the line of connection between cause and effect. That something can be only the intuition, but how seldom is that achieved? That someone must be a teacher or a book.

130

He sees in the situation only what his bias permits him to. That is, he consciously or unwittingly excludes from sight those factors which he does not wish brought to his attention.

131

Those who have committed themselves to a particular belief, opinion, or theory may get back its mere reflection when they try to understand their experiences.

132

The profounder a truth the more it will be misunderstood and misapplied.

133

It is in the nature of human self-centeredness to appraise things, persons, and events only by the measure of satisfaction or suffering they yield. But such egotism hides their true nature and real value, and obstructs their power to bring about progress.

134

An experience may be wrongly interpreted so that little or nothing is learned from it, or, which is worse, the mind's error or heart's evil may be increased.

135

The worst misfortune is not to experience it but to misunderstand it, and consequently misinterpret it. When it makes us worse in character than before, less in faith than before, when it fills us with resentment bitterness anger or hatred, it is *we* who are injured and not merely our fortunes.

136

It is better, more prudent, more satisfying in the end to see things just as they are and not foolishly to imagine them in exaggerated, idealized, or wished-for forms.

137

We look only at the mere appearance of a situation or experience and expect to judge it rightly by that. The divine message it contains is nearly always a hidden one.

138

The ordinary person judges from the surface of things and at times is deceived in consequence. The seeker of truth must penetrate to the depth of things.

139

He should cultivate the habit of looking beneath the surface of many incidents in his daily life, both the important and the trivial, to determine the character of the forces they represent. Some show forth the good or evil within himself, or within others; all have some useful lesson to teach. Some, standing for the power of evil, ignorance, or illusion, necessitate constant watchfulness against temptations outside; others symbolize weaknesses inside that must be ceaselessly fought.

140

If he succeeds in keeping out of the emotional surface of his being the temptation to take his situation rebelliously, and penetrates instead deep down inside where he can take it resignedly, he will gain strength and feel peace.

141

The art of extracting a spiritual message even from the most ordinary circumstances is worth practising. But it can be done only if one lives in a certain independence of them, if while experiencing them one stands apart from them.

142

The aspirant lives a kind of double life. He sees all his experiences as personal events just like other men do. But he also sees them again as material for study: what is and what ought to be his reaction to them?

143

This is the double role he has to play: a looker-on at what is happening around him and an active participator in these events.

144

Where destiny compels us to follow an undesired path, to consort with undesired company, to work at undesired tasks, a special attitude must be created and kept until that particular cycle is ended. The experience must be studied philosophically—that is, impersonally—in the larger perspective of life's general meaning and our own character's personal needs.

145

If he is to learn the full lesson of his situation, he must not only examine and analyse it, but he must do so as if it were somebody else's.

146

It is not only a way of looking at life but also a way of participating in it.

147

Every circumstance or situation may be looked at from a higher plane than the merely animal or narrowly selfish one so that a higher benefit may be got from it. But this attitude calls for a willingness and detachment and courage which most people lack.

Sunshine and shadow

148

The misery on which the Indian mind likes to dwell, and which leads to the idea of escape from rebirth as the highest good fortune, does not obsess the philosophic mind. The latter does not deny life's brevity and tragedy, sorrow and pain, but at the same time it notes life's beauty and glory, joy and reward. In this it is very Greek. If the mysticism of India could be married to the sanity of Greece, a broader and better philosophy would be the offspring.

149

In youth we suffer from an unreflecting optimism or an unknowledgeable pessimism but the years correct that. After we have gone through enough experience, we know better how to be cheerful without permitting our optimism to obstruct our reasoning faculties and without permitting our pessimism to dominate during reaction to difficulties. We know we cannot afford the shallow optimism which thrusts the thorn aside and sees only the rose. We prefer to view the red beauty in all her brutality while enjoying the fragrance.

150

Neither suffering alone nor joy alone can educate his heart and develop his mind in the right way. Both are needed.

151

It is the ironic paradox of human existence that both suffering and joy can enable a man to pass to a higher plane. How is this possible? Suffering drives him to seek its own end, that is, to seek peace. Thus he is led inevitably and eventually to the quest of Overself. Joy draws him towards its source, which rises ever higher as it becomes more refined. Thus he is brought in time to recognize that the true permanent happiness is in the Overself. The urge to shun misery and experience joy shows itself on every plane and in every kind of condition because it is finally and fully satisfied only in the Overself.

152

Life is not all sunshine and no shadow, all fair sailing and no storm, all growing green-leaved trees and no decaying bare hulks. Both halves of each pair are found either side by side or alternate, and none is so far off that the other never appears during a lifetime. The complete optimist is as unjustified as the complete pessimist. This said, it is nevertheless true that personal realization of the higher truth does give a contented mind a perennial hopefulness and an inward security. All these combine and fuse into a quiet sort of happiness.

153

Human life brings inseparable anxieties along with its joys, dilemmas along with its successes.

154

Experience in the world at first satisfies his desires but later purifies him of them.

155

Hiding within our pleasures and lurking behind our possessions are their malignant enemies—change and death. Sickness trails behind the healthiest life and may one day catch up with it. Our joys are insecure, our loves and friendships ever open to separation and bereavement. We may try to ignore these facts by forgetting them but life itself will force us to remember them again. It is better to accept them frankly, even though we individually hope for the best.

156

The pessimism which Buddha taught in India as religion, the tragedy which Sophocles expressed in Greece as drama, should warn us that the human will cannot hope to achieve all its ends in a universe where fate has the greatest share of power and where that fate deliberately opposes itself to the realization of human happiness—I speak here not only of earthly happiness but also of spiritual happiness. The tragic element in our days is ineradicable. The hostile working of the cosmic laws is inevitable. Yes, life means struggle. Its satisfactions are often short-lived. The man who congratulates himself upon the joy he finds in it had better beware, for frustration and privation are even now travelling around the corner toward him. And the man who finds life wonderful had better keep his thought to himself, or he will tempt the gods to shatter his illusion with a more devastating blow than he might otherwise have received. What are the artificial pleasures of the modern age really but anaesthetics to hide either its boredom or its suffering, its emptiness or its discontent?

157

What is every man doing but trying to find his way toward the Happiness that intuition tells him is his birthright? His direction may be wrong, his mode of travel painful, but still—when his error is corrected and the means to his end altered—he will seek to be happy in the only way this is really and durably possible, for no other way will be left.

158

The adherents of sentimental sloppy-cults which refuse to see the dark sides of life but persist in seeing only the brighter ones, which find only Love in man and God, are practising an optimism which can never support them in their hours of severest trial.

159

He who hopes to find continuous satisfaction in any worldly thing, in any external creature, is either incapable of thinking deeply or inexperienced in the vicissitudes of living.

160

We ask for contradictory and impossible things—for instance, unchanging happiness in a changing world.

161

Pessimism turns life into a protracted funeral where we mourn our evils before their time. Such a doctrine can only be to the taste of morose minds.

162

Here, in this world, the human entity could not have come into existence unless it came in the form and way it did. This meant that the dualities of opposites must ever surround him, that the correlative of his happiness must be his misery.

163

A happiness which is gained at the expense of others will prove costly in the end.

164

The seeker should remember that it is possible to learn just as much from joyous, satisfying experiences as from those of suffering and frustration.

165

No experience is so pleasant that it has not a negative factor, nor so unpleasant that it has not a compensating one.

166

The egos attach themselves to one another, driven by the blind universal urges translated as personal "loves," passions, or needs. Glamour, *maya*, creates these attachments; but experience leads to awakening and, possibly, detachment, until *maya* operates again. So the drama goes on, repeating the old scenes, until awakening is finally carried to a deeper level and the truth seen at last.

167

In the world we find no perfect situation, look where we can. In the individual person we find no perfect character, behaviour, speech. There is no environment, no human arrangement, which is without any fault.

168

The same Greek culture whose architects gave us the chaste beauty of their structures, and whose philosophers gave us the Olympian serenity of their teachings, gave us also the horrors of tragic plays. It could not have attained the balance which it did if it had not so frankly looked life fully in the face.

169

The brevity of human life and the transience of human experience prevent the full realization of human happiness.

170

Life is a mosaic of brightly coloured pleasures and darkly coloured pains.

171

All life is tragic, as Buddha pointed out, and ends in frustration. It is only the degrees of frustration that differ with each individual's experience.

172

Extreme joy stupefies a man spiritually, as extreme misery paralyses him. Too much of either condition bars his way to the Overself since it prevents him from becoming interested in the quest.

173

The suffering which is attached to life may vary in extent and kind but it is missed by no one.

174

Life brings its joys and despairs and much of it is an oscillation between them, plus the long flat intervals separating the two.

175

Along with the mystery and misery of life, we must include its obviousness and gaiety to get a balanced picture.

176

Life, with its unfulfilled expectations, its unpleasant surprises, its slow disillusionments, is something we learn to bear because there are pleasanter experiences too or because the craving for existence is still not crushed.

177

The pains of childbirth come to the mother in spasms which strain heart, womb, and lung but which, coming between intervals of rest, are rendered more bearable. So the sufferings and troubles of a whole lifetime most often come in cycles and alternations which give rest from them or afford actual pleasure, and are rendered more bearable also.

178

What Buddha meant was that if life does not break your heart, it will at least give you plenty of frustrations.

179

The quest is a joyful labour: its glimpses afford a bewitching happiness. But it is not a blind labour. There are moments and moods when it acknowledges the suffering inevitably interwoven with human life, the sadness of some of the fundamental inescapable human experiences.

180

They want to keep their personal identity but they do not want to pay all the price for it. They want to keep the satisfactions but not the sorrows of earthly life: but the two go together.

Causes of suffering

181

The same God who gives you the inner peace of profound meditation gives you also the storm of outer tribulation. Why?

182

We suffer primarily because we have isolated our conscious being from the universal Being. Only when we renounce this isolation shall we be able to remove our suffering.

183

Pain and suffering belong to the worlds of limited being, not to the world of infinite being. If man has to endure them, it is because they serve to remind him of this, to warn him against self-deception and to arouse him to take the homeward path.

184

Men shut the door on their best self, and their best friend the Overself, and then wonder why they suffer.

185

We read past history and remember present history with the result that we stand appalled. Why all this tragedy and terror, blood and pain? It is not in God's will that the cause of this vast and endless suffering lies, but in man's flight from God's will.

186

It is this unconsciousness of his spiritual selfhood which is his worst calamity.

187

So long as men do not believe in the truth of Jesus' message, *"Seek ye first the kingdom of heaven and all these things shall be added unto you,"* so long will they grope blindly and suffer needlessly.

188

The more anyone resists the fulfilment of the higher purpose of his life on earth, the more suffering he creates for himself. It is the ego and the animal in him which instigate this resistance.

189

He pays heavily for this forgetfulness of his divine centre—pays in errors and sins, and in the miseries and sufferings which are their results. If the teaching had no other value than this one, to point out to him the need and worth of such remembrance, and the blessings which are its results, propagation of it as well as education in it would be fully justified.

190

The misdirection of energies, the waste of efforts, and the penalty of useless sufferings constitute the sad result of our ignorance concerning life's higher laws.

191

It is as if the higher law provides penalties for ignorance of it; as if the higher power, having given man intelligence and intuition, bids him find out the spiritual facts of his situation or take the consequences.

192

We have heard to the point of tiresomeness the one-sided statements which assert either, "We must blame ourselves for our troubles" or, "We must blame circumstances for our troubles." To get truth, bring the two statements together.

193

The root of most of his troubles lies in man's own psyche, the beginning of most of his distresses in his own thinking.

194

Our frail spirits fret at every handicap Fate puts upon us, forgetting entirely the far greater handicap of a mind bound with hard thongs to illusions.

195

The unenlightened mind sees in the shadows of existence only misfortune where the enlightened mind sees Karmic instruction and opportunity for self-improvement along with misfortune. When it is schooled both by experience and revelation to recognize and admit that its own mistaken behaviour has led to most of its misfortunes, to see the causal connection between personal wrong-doing and the penal troubles or sufferings which follow in its wake, it will act righteously through fear. But later, when it is schooled by subtler experience and loftier revelation to see the divine quest which life ordains it to follow, it will act righteously not from fear but through faith. When it comes to see or believe that most of its griefs are self-inflicted, it sees well.

196

To react to the pressure of suffering with blind resentment is the way of the ignorant. To study the nature of this suffering and learn its message, self-educating his character accordingly, is the way of the aspirant. He will understand that at some time, in some way, he broke the universal laws and inevitably brought this thing upon himself.

197

All experience shows what distress and misery often follow undisciplined passion and unruled feeling.

198

Suffering is the price of wrong-doing. Sin creates its own punishment. Prayer that has no higher purpose than to escape from the consequences of its own mistakes and its own ignorance is like an object standing in the sunlight which asks that its shadow be removed from it—it asks for the impossible. The proper way to separate sin from the price of sin is first, to stop sinning; second, to make all possible amendment and reparation; and third, freely to recognize, humbly to confess, and penitently to eliminate the faults of character which created the sin.

199

While he loves his chains, he must be prepared to accept without murmur the suffering they bring. Only when he loves freedom from them more will he have a right to resent the agonies they cause.

200

We build up mental pictures of what we want. When eventually they are fulfilled, we find the actualities to be accompanied by things we do not want, or to be so different that the happiness both they and the pictures promised is illusion. How much distress we could save ourselves if we could understand and accept the teaching that so many of our griefs are made so by our thinking, by our clinging to mental pictures and emotive thoughts when time bids us let go!

201

If he finds that his path is beset by opposition, his footsteps dogged by evil, he will learn to put himself on his guard against the shortcomings and imperfections which might bring victory to the enemy and failure to himself. He will accept the law that there can be no strength without struggle, but the struggle to which he is called is not with other men—it is with himself.

202

When a man has to receive and live for years with the results of his errors or sins, he is likely to remember them.

203

Only when he arrives at a clear understanding of himself, and especially a correct discernment of his follies and weaknesses, is he likely to arrive at the truth about the situations in which he finds himself and the cause of the troubles that affect him.

204

Events which are painful as well as unsettling may give him hours of anxiety. It is not enough to reach out only for spiritual comfort and peace in these situations; he must also constantly and rigidly analyse the causes of them *in himself,* the mistakes and weaknesses which led him into them, the lessons he needs to learn from them. He should carry out such self-examination quite calmly and impartially, taking care not to exonerate himself. He has to find out how far he himself has contributed to these situations even if the larger share comes from those offending him. It could be that he needs to understand that there is so much evil in this world and in people that he should keep his eyes open accordingly. He cannot take all people on their face value nor believe their words have much value if contradicted by their actions. He may have to develop critical judgement. Life brings contacts with people who show different and opposite facets of their character. Each type has its positive as well as negative qualities. The aspirant who is growing in sensitivity should keep away from those who show more of the negative than the other, who are unscrupulous, or who are emotionally unstable or physically dissipated. He should form no friendship or association with persons who are not clean, wholesome, honest, and stable. It is better to be alone than to get involved with undesirable characters. Having understood the needful lessons, he must resolve to govern his future conduct accordingly. Then and then only should he seek help and comfort through prayer and meditation. There will then be no need to despair, for these situations will work out in the end. If he adheres to right thinking he must accept them as working for his ultimate good.

205

Your suffering may be shortened or even ended if you will express the fullest self-inculpation and throw no blame for it on others. For their misbehaviour does not absolve you from the responsibility for your own.

206

He must thrust aside the unsatisfactory common habits—often unconscious but sometimes wilful ones—of overlooking mistakes, exaggerating difficulties, evading problems, excusing selfishnesses, explaining away failures, rationalizing evil conduct by shifting responsibility for his own shortcomings through blaming other people.

207

If a man will not take the trouble to discipline himself, then life, soon or late, will do it for him.

208

Life gives us enough problems from time to time without our own addition to them of still more which are self-created entirely.

209

If pain did not creep on the heels of passion, men would rarely desire to tame it, much less do so.

210

So long as we set up the goal of outward gain against the ideal of spiritual growth, so falsely and so unnecessarily opposed to each other, so long shall we continue to suffer.

211

A human existence cannot be separated from a painful and suffering one, however small its measure, so long as it is tied to the flesh or emotions.

212

Every tenant of the flesh pays a rent for the pleasure it affords him. He pays in limitations or infirmities, disobediences or pains.

213

After all their conniving and calculating, those who eat the coveted fruits of selfish ambition will have to eat along with it the fruit of their egotism, illusion, and passion.

214

While man identifies his highest good with momentary pleasure, he will continue to receive the educative experience of suffering.

215

If moral instruction and spiritual direction fail to lead a person on the right self-controlled course, then troubles, sufferings, shocks, and scares may have to do so. Sooner or later he will have to surrender himself to strict principles—the sooner the pleasanter in the end.

216

Years of error and suffering could have been years of success and peace if the man had known the principle of right thinking and right living. Wasted and spoiled years become so because of this first and fundamental ignorance leading to mistakes in judgement and sins in conduct. This is the reason why a man suffers and why he causes others to suffer.

217

Unless we learn something about how to live, or, rather, how not to live, we have suffered in vain. And this applies both to physical and to mental life. I like the words used by R.W. Emerson in conversation with a friend: "Why be sick, if to no purpose?"

218

In terms of lessons learned, no experience is wasted. All experiences contribute in the end. But because of the ego's reluctance to accept, many lessons are submerged until their cumulative effect pushes them into awareness.

219

Why should we be ashamed to learn new truths from life's experiences and, dramatically or slowly, to reverse our views in consequence? The answer is that the ego does not wish to humiliate itself, nor to inculpate itself.

220

The fortunes and vicissitudes of life have an educational value but if the conscious mind refuses to receive it, then the subconscious mind will have to do so.

221

He may undergo a vivid experience and yet seem to learn nothing from it. This may repeat itself several times. But on one of these repetitions the process of learning will start to actualize itself on the conscious level.

222

It is utter foolishness to bear in complete blindness, and with unlearning stolid apathy, the unpleasant results of wrong thinking or evil doing.

223

We suffer emotionally when our view of a situation is shown by experience to be self-deceptive. But if this view is itself involved in, and part of, our general view of life, then this disillusionment gives the chance to introduce a truer and higher one. Thus the suffering becomes its purchase price. But if we prefer to hug the emotion and refuse the lesson, we invite its recurrence at some future time.

224

Without the willingness to learn, all experience becomes doubly painful, although never futile. Without the willingness to apply what is learned, all experience becomes a source of inner conflict and self-division.

225

If a lesson has been learned so thoroughly that both character and outlook have altered in consequence, there is no necessity for the higher power which manages life to recur to it again.

226

Some sufferings entirely fail to improve character, so the sufferer continues to repeat and repeat the cycle of self-originating cause and painful effect.

227

We learn our lessons from suffering, it is true, but so inadequately that we forget them all too quickly. Out of this failure to comprehend life comes the continuance or recurrence of most human trouble.

228

When this curious feeling of having tried the same experiment or tasted the same experience dozens of times before in dozens of lives comes abruptly to the top of his consciousness, it is a warning not to waste his precious years in behaving like an ass—that is, not to let himself be tutored in the same lessons by the same disappointments again and again without end.

229

Even when extreme or prolonged suffering has forced a willingness to accept the peace of non-existence, a man cannot wrench himself away from his "I."

230

The result of wrong-doing will reach a man in the end and teach him the value of its opposite. If he stubbornly needs many lessons and many classes in life's school before he is willing to accept this value, the fact is regrettable and his suffering is inevitable.

231

A lesson which must be learned in the end had better be learned in the beginning. The price of lateness is multiplication of suffering.

232

Most people do not seem to learn at all the wisdom that life is trying to instill into them. Of the few who do learn, most learn either too little or too slowly or too late for it to be of any use.

233

They suffer but they do not learn. Yet this is true only of society as a whole, not of certain individuals in it.

234

Every experience carries its own lesson with it. But if a man is unteachable, through stubbornness or stupidity, through egoism or animality, he will not be willing or able to receive that lesson.

235

It is not enough to say that you have suffered. Have you profited from your sufferings? If not, all your weeping was useless.

236

Good fortune may put a stop to the suffering caused by ill fortune, but where the ill fortune has been the end-result of tendencies in our own character or defects in our own mentality or deficiencies in our own personality, these things will remain like seeds within us and will one day sprout again; then the ill fortune will reappear and the suffering with it.

237

The man who does not want to look at Truth because it is unpleasant hides from it or throws out the thought of its presence or excuses himself with sophistries and hypocrisies.

238

Stupid sincerity can go from one mistake to another, yet be none the less sincere.

239

If it were true that men gained nothing from self-earned suffering and learned nothing from it, that they went on making the same errors and committing the same sins again and again, then they would not be men but the lowest of the lower animals. The capacity to think distinguishes men from these creatures. It may be very feebly and most imperfectly used, but this capacity is still being used in some way. Such mental activity may lead to wrong results or to little results, but it cannot lead to no result at all. The conclusion is that if men do not learn from experience today—that is, in one lifetime—they will inevitably do so tomorrow—that is, in another and a later lifetime.

Different reactions to suffering

240

Some say suffering is ennobling, others say it is degrading. But if we look around us we shall see that both assertions are right in some cases, wrong in other cases. It does not have, and cannot have, the same effect in all cases.

241

Life for some is a slide to Hell, for others a bridge to Heaven.

242

The very struggles and sufferings which bring both practical and metaphysical wisdom to the mature and reflective person may bring evil emotions to the undeveloped and unthinking person. It is possible to read wholly opposing lessons from one and the same experience. Thus when afflicted by a common distress men rise to higher virtue or fall into deeper wrong-doing.

243

The same kind of shock experienced by two different kinds of men may have entirely opposite effects. The extremely materialistic may find the ground slipping under their feet and may feel, for the first time, the urge to seek spiritual help. The extremely unworldly may fall for the first time into a dark night which casts doubt upon the truth of their treasured beliefs and which drives them toward a worldlier outlook as being closer to the real facts. Great traumatic suffering, whether bodily or mental, points two ways.

244

Such is the intractability of human egoism that if suffering ceases too quickly he learns little or nothing from it. The old habits of thought and patterns of conduct will remain only slightly erased or else not erased at all. If suffering continues too long, it may arouse negative emotions of bitterness, resentment, anger, despair, apathy, or self-pity. Again little or nothing is learned.

245

If men suffer too much or too long, this drives them into being even more preoccupied with their ego than before. If they have to struggle continually for their livelihood, the same effect happens. Egoism is increased.

246

When suffering is too prolonged, too acute, or too large, it may induce a hatred of life and a longing for death.

247

Who shall blame them if the struggles, the frustrations, the difficulties, and the adversities of life become intolerable and leave them beaten, unable and unwilling to make any further effort?

248

Great hurts lead the perceptive to great surrenders but lead the unseeing to greater bitter blindnesses.

249

The tears of suffering may blind us to the truth behind suffering.

250

The passage from anguish of life to anger at life is often a short one.

251

Outward circumstances injure character for the weak man but improve it for the strong one. In the first case, the man lets himself be moved still farther away from his spiritual centre, but in the second one he moves closer to it.

252

Those who have had ample experience of the world may draw from it either despair and cynicism or advance in, and confirmation of, the Spirit's truth. For their capacity to learn correctly will depend on the extent to which they keep the ego out of the way.

253

What happens to him may tighten his bondage or, paradoxically, stimulate him to escape from it. The particular result depends on how satiated he is with this kind of experience.

254

What seems a wholly evil event to one man may seem a mixed good and evil event to another. The first man may see only that it brings affliction and distress. The second may see that it not only does this but also corrects error and checks weakness.

255

When a man is stretched on the rack of suffering, he may not be able to see or be willing to accept in his anguish its spiritual lesson.

256

Experiences take on their different private meanings in different men's minds. A public calamity may confirm the religious man in his belief that God's hand is behind history. But the same calamity may confirm the atheistic man in his precisely opposite belief.

257

Humiliation, which dwindles one man's stature, adds to another's spiritual opportunity.

258

Setbacks, and even more drastic shocks, may force a man to see what he could not or would not see before, and thus bring him into better balance. But, to the contrary, they may confuse and bewilder another man.

259

Intense suffering may dull the capacity for higher thought, as intense pleasure may lull it.

260

Experience, which gives the true quester fresh opportunities to eradicate errors, merely gives the foolish man fresh opportunities to repeat them.

Purpose of suffering

261

Philosophy does not ascetically applaud suffering and pain. It deplores them. In themselves, they are regarded as evils. It accepts them as good only when they succeed in bringing about a change of thought—a conversion of heart or an ennoblement of conduct.

262

Those who, like Gandhi, can find beauty in human suffering are welcome to do so; most of us cannot, but we may appreciate the values and
benefits it yields without enjoying such "beauty."

263

Since our faulty ways of thinking and living can be pointed out to us by
suffering and since we are thus given the chance to put an end to them,
does not suffering prove itself to be a useful part of the world-scene? Is it
not, at least sometimes, a friend disguised as an enemy?

264

No experience which turns a man more than before to recognition of
the truth and the sense of its worth is really an adverse one. Even though it
is a source of pain, it is still a step forward in his growth.

265

To the man on this Quest, the man willing to step aside from his ego,
earthly misfortunes may sometimes be seen as disguising spiritual blessings if they force him to fall back on the eternal truths and his own deeper
resources.

266

It is sometimes spiritually beneficial for a man to lose part of his wealth,
an official his position, a nation its empire. For then they may lose the
arrogance which too often accompanies these things.

267

Instead of complaining of difficulties, we should welcome them for the
opportunities they give us.

268

The error of thanking God for good fortune is that this forces us to
blame God for ill fortune.

269

When painful experiences are undergone by mind on the lower levels of
evolution, very little is learned from those experiences—and that little
slowly. When the same experiences are undergone by mind on the higher
level, much is learned from them—and learned quickly. This is because in
the one case there is no desire to learn the causes of that suffering, and no
capacity to learn them even when the causes are evident; whereas in the
other case, there is a keen desire to master the lessons and a prepared
attitude wherewith to receive them. When, therefore, the really earnest
disciple who has asked for a quickened advance on the Quest finds that all
kinds of experiences begin to follow each other for a period, he should
recognize that this is part of the answer to his call. He will be made to feel
loss as well as gain, bliss as well as pain, success as well as failure, tempta-

tion as well as tribulation at different times and in different degrees. He needs both kinds of experience if his development is to be a balanced one. But because he is still human, he will learn more from his sufferings than from his pleasures. And because their memory will last longer, he will not pass through this period of quickened experiences and extreme vicissitudes without much complaint. Each of those experiences represents a chance for him, not only to conserve what he has already gained, but to pass to a farther point where he can gain something new.(P)

270

The wine of wisdom is distilled in the grape presses of bitter agony. The best tempered steel comes out of the fiercest fires. If you have suffered more, you have learned more and may perceive more than others.

271

If Nature's way of evolution is cruel, it is also necessary. For the human entity would soon be led astray from its true path if there were no suffering to warn it of wrong direction, no pain to signal a disharmonious condition.

272

The sufferings which destiny brings us are not to be looked upon as punishment so much as instruction. They are intended to teach us right thinking and to turn us to right doing.

273

Lessons so painfully learned indicate that we are being nourished by truth.

274

All circumstances are used by the divine forces of evolution to develop the human soul and, distasteful though it is to us, suffering is one of the chief forces of such evolution. Humanity, having so deeply and so widely lost sight of the higher purpose of its life on earth, has had to undergo calamity and distress in consequence. To recall blind men and women to this purpose is a noble task and a compassionate duty for those who tread the path of philosophy.

275

Whatever difficulties we encounter in the course of a lifetime, we should remember that some reason has put them there: they are not meaningless. But whether put there by our own fault or by other people's fault, or by an implacable destiny, it is usually possible to extract profit from them, at the least, or to get through them successfully, at the most. Through the capacity they draw out, the power they develop, or the discipline and correction they impose, they can be made to yield personal advantage.

276

The impulses of Nature push men helplessly onward until necessity, suffering, reason, or aspiration forces them to make a stand and practise control.

277

The depth to be penetrated from the surface to the deepest layers of the human psyche is too great to be reached quickly without acute sacrifice and intense anguish.

278

The sugar cane yields its sweet juice only after it has been crushed relentlessly in a mill. The human entity yields its noblest traits and truest wisdom only after it has been crushed repeatedly in the mill of anguish.

279

He has the duty to learn why he suffers.

280

Environments which present no problems, relationships which bring no anxieties—these are pleasant circumstances and help foster pleasant qualities in us. But other qualities also need drawing out and developing and can be fostered only by tougher, even opposing, circumstances.

281

The extreme contemporary human suffering has also been an educational discipline in this wisdom. What men cannot yet receive with their conscious intelligence they are already receiving with their subconscious intelligence.

282

Suffering has a purgative place in the scheme of things. If in the earlier stages of man's growth it tempts him to seek relief in evil courses, in the later stages it presses him to seek out its real cause and final cure. Next it has an educative place for it leads him to analyse experience and learn to understand its lessons. Last it has a redemptive place, for it drives him to confess his weakness and seek mercy, grace, and help.

283

Every outward experience has its inward benefits, if only we will look for them with ego-free eyes. And this is true even when the experience involves suffering. Behind suffering we may learn to find some lesson to profit by, some purificatory discipline to be undergone, some ignored fact to be faced, or some wisdom to be gleaned.

284

If what he is undergoing is hard to endure, it is also an opportunity that will not recur again in the same form and under the same circumstances, an opportunity to master a special lesson or to arouse a latent energy or to work on a particular character-trait.

285

We ought not ask limited man to look at his painful predicaments with the same infinite tolerance that the higher power does. Only time, as it brings him to discover and desert the ego's outlook, can do that.

286

Pain lessens or even destroys attachment to the world and the body. Its misery is not all loss or waste. Attachments hold shut the door to heaven: when they are removed or reduced, we get the door to open much more easily.

287

Where suffering fails to detach us from the thing or the person outside us, from our body, or from the ego inside us, it fails to achieve its metaphysical purpose. To that extent it is wasted, even though the surface lesson it conveys, the practical purpose, is successfully achieved.

288

We must cultivate the philosophical spirit which seeks, through calm reflection, to learn and profit by the widest experiences and the commonest errors. It is important that disillusionment should not create bitterness, that we should blame no one but ourselves for our premature judgements. We shall be shamefully defeated in our quest of the Overself if the pain of our experiences makes us less generous intellectually when it ought to make us more so. Yes, our heart must not shrink; the more it has suffered, the more it should expand in forgiveness, in compassion, and in freedom from prejudice.

289

The quality of compassion presupposes the existence of some form of suffering toward which it is directed.

290

There is no situation so bad, no predicament so undesirable, no crisis so formidable that it cannot be transformed, either in its physical actuality or in our mental picture of it, into a good. But this requires a willingness to work upon it spiritually, that is, egolessly.

291

Perhaps more trials, more sufferings, will bring about the reformation of life and character which more preaching and teaching have failed to bring about.

292

Poignant suffering may foster profound thought.

293

Those who trouble to follow virtuous lives and ask why God should strike them down with some great misfortune or some grave malady and leave other uncaring ones unscathed, may find a possible answer in the idea of karma, but they will find a certain answer in the idea that their suffering is an ego-melting and ego-crushing process. Only after this experience is the truth about happiness revealed.

294

What else can be so beneficial and so necessary to him than an experience which tends to detach him from his ego? With some persons or at some times, it may be a joyous experience; with others or at other times it may cause suffering.

295

Every self-created unpleasant episode can be turned to constructive worth. It then becomes a disguised blessing if it arouses one to develop the qualities needed to overcome its painful consequences and to prevent a recurrence of similar episodes. It may sound a call to desert an old road of thinking and to discard an old way of living. It may even give a chance for a new man to be born.

296

Long ago Virgil believed that the agriculturist's troubles were sent to him by the powers that be to sharpen his wits. This view could be considerably broadened, if applied to life's troubles generally. They can not only sharpen wits, in the effort to overcome or evade them, but also nurture moral attributes.

297

Those sufferings which he brings upon himself will serve a useful purpose if they surprise him into discovering his inefficiencies and shock him into discovering his incompetencies. For after the first emotional wave of shame and the second emotional wave of despair have passed, he has the chance to set about putting himself right.

298

No man is so uneducable that suffering leaves no residue in his mind.

299

A member of the former Czech government, now imperilled anew in the Red blight which has fallen on his land, told me about his three-and-a-half years' suffering in the worst Nazi concentration camps. "Now, alas, I have lost the capacity to weep. My heart is tired, does not feel emotion. I have borne all and am above it all." Thus he had learned a forced detachment. Although it cannot be a durable one, some reserve will remain.

300

The aspirant who has experienced a great deal of suffering during his lifetime may be comforted by the thought that, undoubtedly, much unfavourable karma has been thus worked off. Moreover, such experiences lead to a better balanced personality, as a rule, which is as essential for the Quest as meditation.

301

If the aspirant could assume a perfectly impersonal point of view he would be able to see how much of his spiritual development he owes to the heartache, loss, and suffering which he once complained about or regarded pessimistically. He would then understand how these very factors have helped immeasurably to deepen his determination, sharpen his intelligence, and, above all, improve his character.

302

Disillusionment often breeds sourness and cynicism. But if it passes away it may leave true balance and philosophy.

303

Wisdom may grow out of anguish just as practicality may grow out of necessity.

304

A dangerous situation in which we become involved while dreaming may so frighten us as to cause us to awaken with a start. The situation is entirely imaginary, yet it is enough of itself to shock us out of the whole sequence of imaginary situations which constitute the dream life and into the relative reality of waking life. In the same way, the sufferings of earthly life, although ultimately just as illusory as the rest of that life, awaken us to search for reality that transcends it.

305

The world would like to settle down, but every now and then comes iconoclastic news which disturbs its comfortable rest in a most unwelcome manner. But unless the gods send things to stir up men, this rest is likely to pass into sleep and the sleep will pass into spiritual death.

306

When man becomes so engrossed in his own work and so entangled in his own creations that he does not know he is more than body, then life itself will one day jolt him out of his error. The body's needs, comfort, and surroundings must receive his attention. But they should not receive attention out of all proportion to their value. Is he here on earth for these things alone? Is the higher purpose of life to be entirely ignored? A sounder balance is required.

307

So long as the mass of men are contented with illusion and seek neither truth nor reality, so long will they be beset with adversities, dragged from pleasures, surprised by shocks, and tossed about from one birth to the next.

308

The shock of unexpected trouble may be followed by a mental awakening, may lead to the asking of questions about life and from Life. It stops the habit of half-dead, mechanical, routine thinking for a while.

309

The average man's mode of living becomes fixed by routine, by convention, and by the community. Unless he is an exceptional person, he is not particularly interested in teachings and counsel that directly oppose the desires, feelings, inclinations that he has come to regard as normal. No matter how true those teachings may be or how excellent the counsel, he will remain deaf to both until whipped into an about-face listening to them by sheer pressure of last-resort necessity, the desperate attempt to find relief or escape when all the usual channels fail him. Suffering becomes first his awakener and later his tutor.

310

Suffering assaults our shallowness and disturbs our ethical apathy.

311

If they are not born with the desire to pursue truth, meaning, and peace, men will not awaken until catastrophe comes.

312

Despite the imperfections and limitations of this earthly human existence, enough is caught and kept by it to provide a link with that invisible but little-known divine plane of being which is its source. It is this secret connection which pushes men to seek through their desires for happiness or pleasure, to pursue their ambitions or hopes until nothing is found except frustration. It is then that they can turn nowhere else except inward. For subconscious memory of the hidden link revives and points out its direction. So the true and final quest begins. Still only dimly aware of its goal, its power and beauty and serenity, he gets new hope, sometimes a gleam or two of true light.

313

You may have lost your long-held fortune, your wife may have shamefully betrayed you, your enemies may have spread false accusations against you, while your private world may have tumbled to pieces over your head. Still there remains something you have not lost, someone who has not betrayed you, someone who believes only the best about you, and an inner world that ever remains steady and unperturbed. That thing and that being are none other than your own Overself, which you may find within you, which you may turn to when in anguish, and which will strengthen you to disregard the clamant whine of the personal distress. If you do not do this, there is nothing else you can do. Whither can you turn save to the inner divinity?(P)

314

The presence of tears in the human constitution is another expression—remote though it be—of his divine connection.

315

Katherine Mansfield, the story writer, died early but not before she could write that the closing years of bodily suffering had changed her outlook on life. She had come from doubt about God to faith in God, from despair to a feeling that perfect Love behind the universe called for perfect trust from her. The tuberculous body, which had kept her so immobilized for so long a time, brought her nevertheless to a kind of meditation wherein she lay, feeling the stillness within grow more and more palpable and the aspiration to merge in it grow stronger and stronger.

316

Suffering forces man to pause on his onward way and reflect, however briefly, upon its cause, and search, however wrongly, for its cure. At such a moment he may be led to consider his life as a whole and so be led to the Quest itself.

317

When a man reaches the breaking point in his suffering, he is more likely to turn to the inner life. But when pleasure and health and prosperity fill the years, why should he?

318

His understanding of human misery and tragedy, their roots and growth, will develop with the quest's own development.

319

These sufferings cause us to seek relief and act as spurs to stimulate aspiration, as propelling forces toward spiritual efforts, as goads to drive us on to the quest. Without them we would live on the surface of things, squandering our energies on the petty, and tend to miss the true meaning of life.

320

The prophets and teachers may attract a man's interest in the path, but only misfortune and suffering will compel him to follow it.

321

The pressure of a difficulty or trouble for which no ordinary physical solution seems available has forced some people to seek an extraordinary solution. This has been their first introduction to a spiritual teaching, their first recognition that hard realism has failed them.

Transformation of suffering

322

The philosopher is quite capable of enjoying life even though he is deeply determined to realize life's highest goal. He is well able to get some fun out of life even though he does not believe with the thoughtless crowd that this planet was born to be an amusement park, or constructed as a dancing hall.

323

Philosophy is not darkly pessimistic and fatalistic, as a surface view makes some think. Nor, on the other hand, is it childishly optimistic and voluntaristic, as some mystical cults are. It takes fair and proper note of the real state of the world, refusing to be deceived by misconceptions and illusions or by wishfulness and egoism.

324

This is not to devalue worldly experiences but to look at them in a new way.

325

He who can rise superior to circumstances, crises, or vicissitudes is an admirable character, but we deem him hardly human. Thus have we hypnotized ourselves into a negative complex. But the really great ones are not supermen, they are truly men. It is for us to be what we divinely are; this the sages have perceived and accomplished.

326

We have to endure this ever-changing, unstable, and undependable characteristic of the world just as others do, but at least we are not taken by surprise and at most we can keep a kind of peace above it all. We have to face the brutal fact that life on this earth is not intended to afford lasting satisfaction or continuous pleasure—as so many used to think before the war—but our philosophical studies have prepared us to cope with it. Thus detachment becomes a part of our daily experience.

327

If the quest is good only for our brighter hours and not for our darker ones, it is no good at all. But if men desert it because of their troubles, then they have neither properly understood it, nor ever adequately followed it. For the quest is our best support when times are worst and emergencies are gravest.

328

If they have no assurance from within themselves, then they are forced to seek it from without; if the Overself's supporting intuition is lacking, then money and possessions, status and family must support them; if there is no faith that the higher laws by which they live will protect and care for them, then there must be fear that the world is a wild jungle around them; if they are unaware that at the very core of their being they are unbreakably linked with the World-Mind which is at the very core of the universe, then they have to tremble at the thought of their helpless situation when the great blows fall.

329

Should we not say with Plato that it is better to suffer wrong than to do wrong? The problem of suffering does not exhaust itself with its practical aspect. We have also to consider its metaphysical one. If we have the intellectual and moral courage to do this without the egocentric attitude and the surface emotionality which normally govern our approach to it, it will be possible to see it in a clear light. Such is the self-discipline which philosophy asks from its students and such is the emancipated outlook it gives in return.

330

We form different conceptions of the same event as we pass during life to various standpoints. Yet these conceptions will approach nearer to or diverge farther from the ultimate truth about it which philosophic insight would yield us. This is the worth of our passage through space and time, for it is bringing us to a standpoint beyond space and time.

331

Even if this philosophic attitude towards adversity and calamity did nothing more to change matters than to change his attitude towards them, it would have done enough. Even if it could not save him from the suffering they cause but enabled him to suffer with understanding, it would have done enough. Even if it only guided him to study his suffering and to listen to the message that it had to deliver to him, it would have done enough.

332

While he is a tenant of this body, so long as it lasts, while he finds himself in this world, receiving from it and giving to it, a man must pay due attention to care of the body and work in the world. This is his lot. If he becomes a quester, it still remains his lot. But his inner attitude to it will change, will be grounded on a higher level and ruled by a higher ethic.

333

He is to meet each experience with his mind, remembering his relationship to the higher self and, consequently, the higher purpose of all experiences. He is never to forget the adventure in identity and consciousness that life is.(P)

334

The philosopher will look his sorrows and troubles, his cares and burdens, in the face. He will not deny them. But he will not attach to them the interpretations which are commonly attached to them. Instead of lamenting his ill-fate, he will seek out the reasons why they particularly are present in his life. Instead of sinking into melancholy, he will remember that he is more than the ego, and refuse to let go of the peace that is behind and above it.

335

Will he accept also some disappointing, unpleasant, but inevitable oc-
currence just as calmly as a fortunate and pleasant one? Yes, he will,
perhaps a little sadly but not sadly enough to disturb his inner peace. But
knowing that the event itself is caused neither by the arbitrary fiat of a
personal God nor by the chance deed of his own self, he will seek to
understand its derivation and to trace the current of causation back to its
source.

336

He will then be able to take all the happenings of his life as divinely
preordained, to accept them without revolt as being perfectly right for
him.

337

Thus the very events and experiences of everyday life, which usually
involve a man more and more in egoistic outlook and worldly attachment,
usually involve the faithful philosophic student less and less.

338

A shallow person enjoys the acclaim of others: a profounder one couples
it with the critiques of his enemies. This is not necessarily because he is
humbler but because he is honester.

339

His must be a life guided more by principles than by circumstances.

340

The very situations which drag other men down become for him a
means of growth.

341

Insofar as the training gives him more discriminating judgement and a
better sense of proportion, it gives him more fitness to hold responsible
situations or to dispose of important matters.

342

When we learn to play aright this gorgeous game called life, to move
with a magnificent insouciance through all the glamours and repulsions,
the fears and tensions, which hold in thrall nearly all mankind, we find true
freedom.

343

Life may be hallowed or degraded or left just as it seems—commonplace and trivial. It all depends upon the attitude, the inspiration or lack of
it.

344

The thoughts we hold and the actions we perform are dictated in the
end by our attitude towards life.

345

If untoward circumstances obscure our pleasure in life and obstruct our aims in life, they also teach us something of the ultimate truth about life. If we react to them according to the blind instincts of the ego, they plunge us into greater darkness: if, however, we react according to the inner promptings of the Overself, they lead us toward greater light.

346

Karma is the precise result of what a man thinks and does. His reaction to events and situations is the precise result of what he is, his stage in evolution. Therefore, lesser reactions and hence better fortune can come only when he elevates his evolutionary status.

347

Your thinking will have its effect not only upon your inner character and outward activities, but also upon other people. This last is quite conceivable when we remember that telepathy is no longer a mere theory, but a proved fact.

348

How far does a man possess his external condition? He can do much in this regard but he cannot do everything, for obviously there are certain limits beyond which it is humanly impossible to go. The balanced fact is that Man's thoughts make his surroundings and his surroundings make his thoughts. When the materialist tells you that man is what his environment makes him and when the idealist tells you that man is what he creates out of himself, both are telling you the truth. But each is not telling you the whole truth. The philosopher must accept both apparently contradictory standpoints because he insists on seeing life whole, not in bits and pieces.

349

The philosophic man has to make up his mind that his attitude towards every experience counts more than the experience itself, that the way he thinks of it will either help or hurt his spiritual evolution. If his reaction to an event weakens his character and dulls his intuition, then it is really an evil one for him; if, however, his reaction is to utilize it for his spiritual growth, then it will in the end be a fortunate event.

350

If we bring a correct attitude to our life-experiences, they help us to gain greater inner balance and truer moral understanding. But if we bring the wrong attitude, then these same experiences plunge us into emotional unbalance and mental distortion.

351

Problems and troubles come to all alike at different periods of their incarnation, to the wise and the foolish, the passionate and the controlled, so that it would be futile to try to find one person who has never had them. But wisdom or foolishness will be revealed by the attitude, mental and moral, brought to deal with them, and by the dependence on self alone or on self and Overself together.

352
Outward changes for the better are almost always the result of improved inner conditions—that is, better, more inspired thinking, plus elimination of negative thoughts and actions.

353
He may react to the experiences of life and the course of events with either the animal part of his nature or the spiritual part. The choice is his.

354
The mental states and emotional moods that are strong and sustained within him are related to the events, environments, and situations which subsequently form around him.

355
The state of mind is not just a product of physical conditions: it is also a creative force which contributes toward those conditions. It is both a hidden cause and an evident consequence.

356
Beware of your thoughts, for when long sustained and strongly felt, they may be reflected in external situations or embodied in other humans brought into your life. But they cannot, of themselves and devoid of physical acts, make the whole pattern of your life—only the adept can do that. For other factors are also contributing, such as the will of God—that is, evolutionary necessity, or the World-Idea.(P)

357
When the sage looks back on the line of travel which brought him to this illumination, he sees how everything that happened could have been different only if he himself had been different. His sufferings could have been avoided, yes, but only by his being transformed into another person.

358
Assume attitudes that the spiritual teachers hold up as desirable. Put them into your mental and emotional picture. Carry them into your physical doing. For this is to be creative and to seize upon your own inherent possibilities by belief and conviction. What you believe must be really there and fully there, in the shadowy background of your mind as well as in the clear foreground. The faith must be intense, active on all levels of your being.

359
What happens to us is a continuing audit of what we are.

360

This declaration of the power of mental attitude to realize itself becomes invalid if the attitude assumed is a false one. We have no right to demand what we are not entitled to.

361

In their mysterious way these forces of destiny move in response to his inner needs as well as in reflection of his inner state.

362

He may transform opposition into opportunity simply by a change of viewpoint.

363

As this inner work brings about a change in his outlook, attitude, and especially consciousness, so a corresponding change or test in his outer conditions will, after some lapse of time, come about.

364

Strain and misuse of the mind create harmful habits. The one appears in tensions, the other in negative thoughts.

365

Each man responds to his surroundings and contacts, his experiences and fortunes in his own personal way. "As you are, so is the world," remarked the Ramana Maharshi at our first meeting.

366

Every important event or change in his life offers a challenge to meet it properly, which means philosophically. This applies, of course, equally to good fortune as well as bad fortune.

367

If you live *inwardly* in love and harmony with yourself and with all others, if you persistently reject all contrary ideas and negative appearances, then this love and this harmony must manifest themselves *outwardly* in your environment.(P)

368

Life is still the greatest of games a man can play. But he must play to win in every minute of it, with every move on the board. Every time despair comes and whispers to him, he should put cotton-wool in his ears. Man was born to master—not to be mastered. Faith can fight despair, and win, too. Let him look upon his difficulties not as stumbling blocks to trip him up, but as things waiting to be conquered.

369

Truth and love will conquer in the end—however far off that be—for they are deeply buried in the hearts of men and will be slowly uncovered by the instruction which life itself gives. We must acquire something of God's patience.

370

The human failing which makes so many worry and create avoidable mental suffering about themselves and about others, can and must be met by a strong positive endeavour to keep the mind in its highest place. It is not in the nature of our godlike inmost self to feel depressed, to suffer melancholy, or to express worry. If we are to turn to that nature as our true being and basis for living, we will reject these negatives.

371

Why add to any dark or difficult situation? Is it not enough to have to endure it that you must enlarge it by setting up the tension of your negative emotions or disturbed thoughts about it? Keep them out of it.

372

When he feels that his life is in the hands of a higher power, his fortunes governed by great laws whose ultimate intent is utter beneficence, his courage will be unassailable.

373

A time comes when we learn to stop worrying about ourselves, when we take the burdens off our shoulders and, in Jesus' words, "Take no thought for the morrow." We gain new fresh strength when we refuse to worry ourselves into misery, when the possible or impending troubles of the future are left where they belong.

374

But such calm does not mean he should do nothing at all about the situation. If it is going to affect his personal circumstances he may choose to take certain protective action, to avert or at least mitigate its effects, just as he may choose to put up an umbrella or wear a raincoat if the weather indicates the likelihood of rain.

375

This done, however, he still holds to his positive mental attitude, not only because he refuses to live with fear, but also because he refuses to become obsessed by the future and live in time.

376

Sometimes it is wise to follow Livy's counsel: "In great straits and when hope is small, the boldest counsels are the safest." Then the early manifestation of brief panicky fear will be followed by a new courage, despair will be succeeded by determination, weakness will yield to iron strength.

377

The anguish and cries of the ego in suffering are, to the aspirant, an opportunity and an inducement to make the great surrender and to rise to a nobler viewpoint. Giving way, in suffering, to negative emotions of resentment, anger, despair, and bitterness is very easy. The wiser attitude of doing all that can be done in a bad or difficult situation and then calmly accepting the issue is much less easy, but it must be attempted.

378

It would be easy to misconceive the philosophic attitude towards these negative feelings: anxiety, worry, fear, indignation, and righteous wrath. Philosophy does not teach us to avoid facing the situation or circumstance which gave rise to any of these feelings, but only to avoid the negative reaction to it. It tells us to learn all we can from it, to understand why it is there at all, to analyse its meaning and apply its lesson. Only after this has been done, and especially only after we have attended to the correction of whatever fault or failing in us helped to create the situation, are we advised to forget it, turn our face away, and calmly put ourselves to rest in thoughts and remembrances of the impersonal Overself. Only then is our sorrow and suffering to be discarded, and we are to recall that there is no room for despair in the truth. That reflective wisdom must be followed by courage and even joy.

379

The ability to hold on during a single dark period, when the frustrations and humiliations of poverty seem unbearable, may turn the fortunes of one's entire life for the better.

380

No animal except man lives in such constant fear, for no animal lives in the past, the present, and the future so much as man.

381

As soon as we succumb to moods of despondency, hopelessness, and helplessness, we are doomed. As soon as we triumph over them, we are saved.

382

It is not that he is required to be unwrung by calamitous events, or remain immune to them, but that after feeling the emotion he is to remember the Quest and try to rise superior to it.

383

When he is born again, adversity becomes an advantage, his evil hour becomes a good one. With it he lifts his drooping mood, whips his irresolute spirits, and instills perseverance into his arduous struggle.

384

We sometimes wonder whether we can bear more, but no experience goes too far until it crushes the ego out of a man, renders him as helpless as the dying person feels.

385

An American millionaire once told me how, in quest of making his living, he tried New York. The twenty-five dollars he arrived with went very soon and the penniless and friendless young man met with rebuff after rebuff. Came a time when he was almost starving, and he had to sleep out in a park because he could not afford a lodging-house. Finally his troubles and utter loneliness brought him to the horror of trying to commit suicide. But the strange hand of Fate sent someone to stop him; this very person who intervened was carrying the burden of still worse woes upon her back—but enduring them. When the young man heard of these from the lips of the woman who saved him, he realized as in a flash how unmanly it was for him to give up the struggle. So next morning determination took the place of despair. He started out again to look for work. He persevered so doggedly that the same afternoon brought him his first job.

386

Address to Muslim College, India:

You, young men, will sooner or later have to go out into the unfamiliar and sometimes unfriendly world to make your own personal careers. The change from the sheltered seclusion of college life to the open struggle for existence will necessarily be an abrupt one; the adjustment to the new conditions which will have to be faced necessarily a hard one. Moreover, the conditions in the world today are admittedly disturbed and unsettled. You are therefore likely to meet with many gloomy prophets who will tell you dismally of the difficulties of getting on and of the impossibilities of getting good positions. Let me warn you against these melancholy pessimists who paint only one side of the picture and wrongly regard that grey side as being the whole picture. There is another and brighter side which is equally deserving of your consideration.

You may have a discouraging time at the start. Opportunities may be few. But they are always there for the right men. So long as you nurse the unflagging spirit of ambition, so long as you set up a staunch determination to overcome the obstacles in your way, to master the difficulties that may surround you, so long as you say to yourselves "I will" and "I must" instead of "I won't" and "I can't," you will find yourselves on the highroad to eventual success. For sooner or later there are always openings for bright, keen, and determined young men. Why? Because the world wants such men.

If you will only remain faithful to the principles of truth, goodness, and unselfishness which are embodied in religion, you will certainly bring to your help heavenly forces which will ultimately assist you in your career. Do not be deceived by the cynical talk of superficial croakers. A man who lives according to these principles will eventually win the respect of society, and society in its turn will reward him with her gifts of place, honour, and prosperity. Therefore you should endeavour to cultivate an optimistic frame of mind; you should regard whatever difficulties the future may bring not as permanent setbacks but as opportunities to arouse grit and to enable you to show forth the powers inside you that can overcome them.

You should read the biographies of men who have risen in life from humble circumstances to high positions, as well as the biographies of others who were more fortunately born and, by their good character, developed capacity, and keen determination, have left their mark on history. What they have done some of you at least can also do, while all of you can certainly create a habit of looking to the bright side of life and thus make life easier both for yourselves and for others.

387

Our outer lives to some extent reflect the state of our minds. Many of the trials we have to bear would dissolve after we faced ourselves and removed the negative characteristics within our minds. But there are some karmic difficulties which cannot be altered, no matter how clear and pure the mind becomes.

388

When we are brought face-to-face with the consequences of our wrong-doing, we would like to avoid the suffering or at least to diminish it. It is impossible to say with any precision how far this can be done for it depends partly on Grace, but it also depends partly on ourselves. We can help to modify and sometimes even to eliminate those bad consequences if we set going certain counteracting influences. First, we must take to heart deeply the lessons of our wrong-doing. We should blame no one and nothing outside of ourselves, our own moral weaknesses and our own mental infirmities, and we should give ourselves no chance for self-deception. We should feel all the pangs of remorse and constant thoughts of repentance. Second, we must forgive others their sins against us if we would be forgiven ourselves. That is to say, we must have no bad feelings against anyone whatsoever or whomsoever. Third, we must think constantly and act accordingly along the line which points in an opposite direction to our wrong-doing. Fourth, we must pledge ourselves by a sacred vow *to try* never again to commit such wrong-doing. If we really mean that pledge, we will often bring it before the mind and memory and thus renew it and keep it fresh and alive. Both the thinking in the previous point and the pledging in this point must be as intense as possible. Fifth, if need be and if we wish to do so, we may pray to the Overself for the help of its Grace and pardon in this matter; but we should not resort to such prayer as a matter of course. It should be done only at the instigation of a profound inner prompting and under the pressure of a hard outer situation.(P)

389

Suffering and pain are parts of the divine pattern for human growth. They fulfil a wise and understandable purpose. But this does not mean that we are to look upon all suffering and all pain as necessary parts of that pattern. Some of it is avoidable and, to that extent, not necessary.

390

The more he remembers to think of asking what the divine intention is in these situations and hastens to co-operate with it, the sooner will they be rectified.

391

But even for those who lack the capacity to think for themselves or to intuit for themselves or to imaginatively work out the lessons of possible experience, God has still provided a way of avoiding pain. For He has provided the prophets and seers and holy messengers who point out the right way to think and live.

392

The lessons which life, guided by infinite intelligence and invested with infinite power as it is, seeks to make available to us through the turning wheel of destiny may bring suffering but they also bring the wisdom which will shield us from suffering in the future. This is possible only if we accept the suffering as self-earned, humbly study its lesson, and set to work on self-improvement. But if we are too proud, too weak, too foolish to receive the lesson, then the same suffering will reappear again and again in later years or later lives until we do. It will come as before through the same events, at the right time and in the right place. Whether it is life that punishes us through its eternal laws or we through our disobedience to them, we cannot dodge the step to be mounted.

393

He should begin by searching through his feelings to discover which one, if it exists, is the block to a speedier and favourable end to the trouble, which one is shutting out the forces of help, as well as which one is blinding him to the vital lesson behind the situation.

394

There is no permanent way of escaping difficulties other than the way of seeking spiritual realization. That is what we have really incarnated for. This may seem hard on us, but life on earth as it is known today is also hard for many people.

395

Those who turn cruel destiny or harsh accident to opportunity by taking a spiritual profit from it, abandoning natural bitterness and emotional rebellion, coming creatively in mind and positively in feeling to their suffering, thereby bring about its redemption.

396

If he remains true to philosophic principles in the various situations in which he finds himself, every so-called evil in them will be consciously turned to good.

397

Acceptance of suffering is sometimes a key to the way out of it. The greater the suffering, the greater are the possibilities of Peace succeeding it—provided that the lessons to be learned from it have been correctly interpreted and actively applied to daily life.

398

To see why our suffering is there and to know that it will pass gives us a great advantage over the ignorant who suffer blindly and forget its ephemerality; for it replaces rebellion and resentment with patience and endurance.

399

To *understand* the true cause of the trouble is already halfway to perceiving the remedy.

400

The wise man knows that suffering has been essential to his development and has helped him to learn certain lessons. When others fall into the same experience, therefore, he does not wish that they should not have it so much as that they should learn the lesson of it. It would be illogical to apply his wisdom in his own case but to withhold it in the case of others. If a sentimentalist says that because he feels sympathy for others, he wishes them not to suffer, then that is all the more reason—not less—for wishing them not to suffer blindly.

401

Where the understanding of life is deep and true, where the training of self for spiritual awareness has been long and earnest, men suffer less from their personal troubles than where these things are not present.

402

We may often escape the penalties which follow wrong thinking and evil doing only by altering the one and counterbalancing the other. But even such ameliorative measures must be taken in good time, or they will be useless.

403

The aspirant who heeds the injunctions of the Stoic sages and the Galilean preacher to dismiss excessive care for the external paraphernalia and possessions of life, who believes in and practises the doctrine of mental detachment, will not need to have forced upon him the physical renunciation and physical detachment taught in a more salutary and painful form by loss and misfortune.

404

From the first moment that we accept personal responsibility for our troubles, we take the first step towards relieving them.

405

To escape mentally into the past in order to take refuge from a present disagreeable situation may bring comfort but will not bring help.

406

The more he can inwardly free himself from the claims of his daily regime—that is, the more he can become emotionally detached from it and transfer his interest, love, and desire to the higher self—the greater will be his power to achieve dominance over undesirable conditions.

407

If misfortune is explored with understanding and its hidden message sought, it becomes something much more than an exercise in faith and patience, as the religious-minded would have us believe.

408

The wisdom that one is offered the opportunity to learn through experiences of suffering should lead not only to some self-renunciation, but also to some true self-humblement beneath the will of destiny, which has revealed itself as insuperable. Once he becomes inwardly submissive, he will find that time quickly heals its own wounds, and that a great peace will be bestowed on his inner life.

409

When one is sustained by truth and inspired by communion, the most bitterly discouraging experiences can be borne, examined, understood, and mastered.

410

Assets become problems by the fluctuation of fate. But problems can be turned into assets by the wisdom of man.

"Failure"

411

"Failure" is a tricky word. We often apply it indiscriminately upon hearing the glib voice of Appearance. Real failure is rare. He only has failed who has lost his soul. Such are hard to find, though millions today have chloroformed their souls.

412

Out of his own heart a man may seek guidance for his future. His former sins become his future teacher. His errors, once perceived, show him the right way. His thoughts, once overcome, provide him with new strength and new virtues. His trials, met and mastered, open new doors of consciousness to him. His weaknesses offer him a challenge and if he takes it up and if he uses his will to transmute them, he will be the gainer.

413

It was one's own ignorance and immaturity which made one act in a way which now seems very wrong and to be ashamed of. It is no use accusing oneself forever and ever of it. It is better humbly to distill its wisdom, gain its constructive teaching, and uplift one's character. For a man to accept himself as he is would be foolish counsel if he had nothing more than his sins and guilt, his ego and passions, his folly and stupidity. But it is because he has a deeper self—one that links him with the gods— that it can now become a wiser counsel. Let him take it now and work upon himself with this better self.

414

Frankly confess your past mistakes, then analyse and absorb their un- palatable lessons, and resolve to apply the unpleasant result to your future actions. This is practical wisdom. It may be a saddening procedure, and if it is to be an effectual one, it ought to be. But having done it, be done with it. Turn your face toward the sun of hopefulness. Remember the strength, light, and joy waiting to be drawn from your higher self.

415

If, in looking over the past, he feels shame over the crowd of his frailties, it is well. It is not good to forget experiences from which he has not thoroughly absorbed the lessons. But when he has done so, the sense of shame will depart and the sense of having been cleansed will take its place. He has been granted absolution, and may be at peace.

416

It is not always possible to judge appearances. There are failures in life who are successes in character. There are successes in life who are failures in character.(P)

417

If a man has failed in life, most likely he has also failed to look to his higher self for aid or guidance.

418

A man's personal history may teach him what it ought to teach him only as he is able to bring some part of his mind away from his habitual ego- standpoint into an unfamiliar aloofness.

419

No failure is to be considered a total one. All experience is tuitive, although the finest experience is intuitive. It is not necessary to get un- happy, morbid or agitated about a failure, although it is necessary to take its lessons seriously to heart.

420

It is not what the world calls success that philosophy endorses. A man may suffer the ignominy of defeat and failure and yet fulfil the highest function, the true purpose of his life. It is an ignorant and mean definition of success which ties it to social recognition and worldly prosperity.

421

A mistake comprehended as such may be the beginning of new wisdom.

422

One reason why we need at times to break away from the pattern of habitual thinking is that it is limited by our past experiences. This tends to keep us from our greater possibilities and to inhibit our true creativeness. If we were failures in the past, the auto-suggestion of failure in the future handicaps us and is eventually converted from thought to fact.

423

However much he may wince at the memory of them, he is answerable for his mistakes and should so regard many of the pains and penalties he suffers from. To the extent that he intellectually analyses the whole course of his conduct and comes to the right conclusion about it so as to discover where and how he went wrong, his anguish will be somewhat compensated in the end. To do this he needs to perceive those weaknesses in himself which led to his blunder and to set to work to eliminate them. If he omits this and merely surrenders to the emotional suffering, letting himself go into barren despair or falling into egocentric unbalance, he makes the bad worse.

Who has not made mistakes in the past? Wisdom lies in not making the same mistake twice. Situations which bring to the surface what might otherwise have lain hidden in his character and which put his quality to the test give him a chance to adjust himself accordingly. Every important event which leads to them has an inner as well as an outer significance, for it traces back to a karmic origin which is specially selected by the Overself because he is on this Quest to promote his self-knowledge and self-purification.

If he follows the deeper lead, these situations will surely work out for the best in the end, but if he follows the ego's lead, it may easily make a bad situation worse.

However the external situation develops he must cling to his ideals, to his faith in the higher power's intuitive guidance. In this way he does not depend on his own strength alone. At the same time, he can use all his human powers of judgement to fill in the details of what is necessary and right in his own personal behalf.

424

It is because all private history is never written that people unconsciously falsify it by looking only at a saint's moral successes and not at his moral failures. Did he never lapse back into a lower condition of mind, suffer uncertainties about what to do, or fall into despondency?

425

Human beings act wrongly or commit blunders sometimes. Mature human beings admit these failures but immature ones place the blame elsewhere.

426

If these things have humbled your self-love by showing you that the thing so much loved has its ugly blemishes, they have served a useful purpose. But you need not stay at this point. You don't have to moan over it for the rest of your life.

427

His past failures in human relations should be remembered with humbled, bowed head, and the lessons to be learned therefrom thoroughly digested. He should be grateful for this privilege of gaining self-correction.

428

To re-examine the events of ten, twenty, thirty years ago, much more to relive them, can only be justified if it helps to loosen one from the ego rather than fixing him more tightly in it. This requires a detached learner's attitude.

429

Failures directly contribute towards success, if he is wise enough to take their lessons so deeply to heart that his whole character undergoes a change in consequence.

430

If he has the sagacity to take in the sad lesson of these experiences and the practicality to turn it to moral profit, he is a true student of philosophy.

431

Hold no experience longer than its allotted time.

432

Listen to the message experience is trying to give you, then learn it and obey it.

433

Every situation which shows up the ugly results of his faults offers an invitation to repair them. Its profit lies in his egoless acceptance.

434

It is the business of intelligence to study the follies of misspent years, to reflect upon the mistakes of a wasted past, and to extract both warning and knowledge from such experience. If it does this, if it firmly resolves no longer to repeat endlessly those courses which bring loss and pain, it will lead the man to victory over failure. He may have made every blunder and committed every sin, but he can yet emerge triumphantly into peace.

435

But if man is to achieve this full welfare he cannot live solely on a negative wisdom, cannot be guided merely by the lessons gained from his mistakes. He also needs a positive truth to complement them.

436

If disillusionment is the prologue and substance of our lives, the cheering message of a mysterious Hope shall be its epilogue.

2

LIVING IN THE WORLD

A play of opposites

Is this a world of exile from our spiritual home or is it a world of education for our spiritual home? If it is the first then all experience gained in it is worthless and useless. But if it is the second then every experience has meaning and is related to this universal purpose.

2

The truth does not lie wholly with the Hindus, who liken life to the illusions of dream, nor with the Buddhists, who despise it as a burden and a misery, nor with the hedonists, who value it only for the pleasure it yields. Surely the truth must contain and reconcile all these points of view?

3

Where is the incentive to improve oneself or society, to make something of one's career, one's life, to be ambitious or enjoy art—what is there to live for if everything is illusion?

4

The value which so many put on life is paltry compared with its real value.

5

No man has any choice as to whether or not he should seek the kingdom of heaven, his higher Spiritual Self. Every man is seeking it, knowingly or unwittingly, and is preordained to do so. There is no escape. There is no satisfaction for him outside it.

6

It is not necessary to divide mankind into two categories—the believers and the infidels—for all alike are on this quest, only many do not know it.

7

The difference is that the seeker consciously enters on this quest whereas the ordinary man, although also pursuing it, does so blindly and un-knowingly.

8

Many persons mistakenly suppose that they have escaped from difficult problems by avoiding the environments or the individuals associated with those problems. This is mere escapism, useful as a relief but useless as a final and sole solution.

9

What matters is not only the quality of a man's consciousness but also the quality of his day-to-day living, not only the rare special mystical ecstasies that may grace his experience but also his relationship with the contemporary world and his attitude toward it. It is not enough to be a mystic: he cannot avoid the common road which all men must travel. In brief, can he be in the world but not of it? Can he sanctify the ordinary, the customary; those actions, this business, that very work for a livelihood; the contacts with family, friends, critics, and enemies? After all he is a *human being* with personal concerns; he cannot live for twenty-four hours a day in abstract ideas alone, or in religious withdrawnness: he has a body of flesh, a relevant duty or responsibility to perform in the world outside.(P)

10

To refuse to explore experience for its meaning by denying its very existence, merely because it is painful experience, is simply to evade the very purpose of incarnation here on earth. It is only by striving to understand the significance of what happens to us, only by drawing out the lessons of life from it, that the higher truth about one's self and about the universe can ever reveal itself.

11

Common sense is still needed here. We are in the body; we are surrounded by the world. It would be hypocritical to dismiss the first as non-existent and reject identification with it. And to talk as if one could even thrust the second away would be madness and self-contradiction.

12

It is utterly absurd to ignore the potent effect of one's surroundings, to try to put them aside as unimportant, to write them off in forgetfulness, to deny their existence as mere illusion, or even to consider such efforts as an indispensable part of spiritual training.

13

Our very existence as persons makes it necessary to give proper attention to the body and its needs, and to the worldly surroundings in which it lives. They cannot be dismissed, much less despised, without falling into an insane mysticism or an off-balance metaphysics.

14

Those who reject the external order of things are as foolish as those who reject the eternal order.

15

The unsolved problems which life in the world has brought him represent either debts requiring payment or weaknesses requiring amendment. If they are too much for him, flight to some peaceful retreat in Nature's green solitudes may offer relief—for a time. Such desertion of the world is not wrong, provided he uses it to help prepare himself for an eventual solution of the problems.

16

A reincarnated monk may tend to seek the haven of a cloister through inability or unwillingness to cope with a world which is admittedly difficult to cope with. Yet the world offers him an experience which may be just what he needs to draw out latent forces.

17

Life forces him to pay attention to the world: its denial in metaphysics or dismissal in yoga does not invalidate this necessity.

18

We must respect the facts of experience even though we try to transcend them.

19

It is not enough to look into himself. Even if he does find the kingdom of heaven there, Nature compels him to look out of himself too.

20

The worldly realities have to be recognized for what they are, treated with respect, and behaviour must be brought into accordance with them. What is the use of denying the world as "unreal," of dismissing the body as "nothing," as I have heard Indian mystics do, when all the time both are obstinately present to the senses and dominant in the mind? The world has to be dealt with, the body has to be tended, whatever views, opinions, or beliefs one holds.

21

Meeting the needs of physical existence is a justifiable and necessary duty if one is to survive. This involves realistic acknowledgment of the body's functions and practical connection with the world around.

22

It is not the goal to be unaware of the hard realities around him.

23

To throw away external experience is to throw away man's third-best tutor. Life also has its voice and speaks in this way to correct wrong theory and to discipline wrong action. The transcendental intelligence behind our personality has put us in this world neither to deny it nor to hide from it, but to accept it and learn its valuable lesson.

24

An intellectual recognition of the transiency of life is not the same as a temperamental despondency about life. The first may be allied with enthusiasm, serenity, and humour but the other may not.

25

If anyone feels the truth of Shakespeare's lament that "time will come and take my love away," if he complains that worldly transiency mars his pleasure in favourable circumstances, he ought also to rejoice that the same transiency mellows his pain in untoward circumstances, for time is just as likely to take them away too!

26

By abandoning so-called security, he finds a real freedom.

27

The very treasures for which they lose their ideals, their morality, eventually slip away from them, as if to teach a lesson.

28

During times of great suffering, he may best countenance his bereavement by taking it as a reminder of the transiency of earthly life, and of the necessity to cultivate the interior life of spiritual growth. By so doing, he helps himself and also others.

29

Man's life is not a static square: it is a turning circle. Change is either coming or leaving him at some point, in his mind, body, or circumstance.

30

It is in the nature of all things that they must perish, of all possessions that they must pass into other hands, of all desires that their satisfaction shall bring with it an accompaniment or a consequence that is not desirable. But to dwell only on this aspect is to become wrapped in negativity and obsessed by it.

31

All worldly happiness suffers from being incomplete and imperfect. Most worldly happiness is transient and unstable.

32

All mortal unions which begin in one year must be ended in another, must be divided after short or long time. One must learn how to stand alone if need be.

33

He must needs attend to the things of earth and self. But if he over-attends to them, if he dwells over-long in their midst, then loss, pain, or death will come to teach him the lesson of their transience.

34

The uncertainty of fortune and the brevity of satisfaction are two lessons of our time.

Status of the herd

35

We who are spiritually minded move against a background which is materialistic and uninspired.

36

The tragic antithesis between the divine and the material afflicts us at every turn.

37

Those who are seeking material fulfilment are at cross-purposes with those who are not; the one group is obeying the law of its being just as much as the other, yet they are moving in opposite directions.

38

It is not that they do not understand each other's tongues so much as that they do not understand each other's emotions. Such is the wide difference between men for whom the quest is nothing and those for whom it is everything.

39

The difficulties of being completely honest, truthful, and sincere, of keeping to idealism in a materialistic or mad world, afflict only the living. The dead are luckier. Not for them the compromises, the white lies, the half-measures, and the glib hypocrisies.

40

To recognize any situation as factual is one thing, but to reconcile it with spiritual life is another.

41

The quest's ideals draw him one way, the world's temptations pull him otherwise.

42

His problem is how to stay in the world and do the world's work without losing his spiritual integrity.

43

Down through the centuries there have always been men who made hearsay their truth, appearances their reality, and conformity their virtue. They are the gregarious many, the countless victims of those twin illusions: the ego and the world.

44

They are too concerned with earning their livelihoods, with the members of their families, and with attending to personal wants to bestow thought upon such abstract topics as life's higher meaning. They are not to be blamed but they are also not to be imitated.

45

There are millions of men and women living today whose whole conception of life is so entirely materialistic that they not only do not comprehend a spiritual conception, but do not even want to comprehend it.

46

They find a completely worldly life sufficient for their needs. They do not want, do not miss, and are quite indifferent towards spiritual things.

47

Most people react mechanically, not creatively, to surroundings and situation, events and persons. In this they are like children and animals, not like truly and fully human beings acting from knowledge and power.

48

The present state of the masses is hardly to be envied. Lives of humdrum toil, varied by a little sensual excitement, existences estranged from true happiness—the divine calm of the spirit is remote from them.

49

They readily fill all the day and even part of the night with activities intended to satisfy their worldly desires but grudge the few minutes required to satisfy their spiritual aspirations through prayer and meditation. Time, which is flowing like a tidal river through and away from their lives, thus carries them farther away from—and not nearer to—the higher purpose for whose realization they were sent into bodies on this earth.

50

Most men are enslaved by *things* and nearly all men by *thoughts*. They know nothing of the tremendous sensation of freedom which comes from the philosophic insight into both.

51

In the ordinary man there is no desire constantly to improve the moral nature, no hunger imperatively to enter the mystical consciousness. Spiritually, he is in a state of inertia, unwilling and unready to use any initiative in enlarging the horizons of the ego. Most, but not all, of this inner laziness can be traced to the fact that he is the victim of his own past, the prisoner of his own particular innate tendencies and habitual thinking. Nevertheless, the same evolutionary process which has placed him where he now is will also advance him to a higher point.

52

The truth is that few wish to trouble themselves with following such a way of regeneration, and most prefer the comfortable sloth of accepting their deficiencies as normal qualities of the human being. Therefore they allow one thing after another, one event after another, to detain them from making the mystical ascent and so waste a whole incarnation before they are even aware that it is wasted. Is their spiritual life to wait like a whining beggar on those intervals of leisure which a materialistic existence throws them like sops to Cerberus? Some aspirants have even turned away from the quest because other things claimed a stronger interest. Others have given up its goal simply because they believe it to be unattainable. And then there are those who are literally afraid of devoting themselves to the quest. It seems in their eyes to demand too much or give too little.

53

The first interest of the common people today is better economic conditions. The interest in religion, if it comes at all into their lives, is naturally somewhat distant from this one. The interest in mysticism, if it manifests in groups here and there, is still more distant from it. The interest in philosophy, if it awakens in a few individuals, is so far off from the interest in improving their lot as to be almost shadowy.

54

Those who are uninterested in any higher purpose, meaning, or activity which transcends their routine lives, who are spiritually unconscious, are to be neither condemned nor defended. They are simply immature.

55

In what way have the *basic* desires of people today changed from those of four, three, two, one thousand years ago? Shelter, food, sex, and clothes are still sought now as then. But the forms they have taken and the opinions or beliefs held about them have changed.

56

Man as a sense-bound beast is in conflict with man as a spiritual being.

57

Those who are satisfied to remain with their animal instincts form the larger group. Those who are struggling to advance beyond them form the smaller one.

58

Some say change systems if you want to improve men. Their opponents say change men if you want to change systems. Both state partial truths, both suffer from their limitation of refusing to acknowledge that the argument of the other side is essential to a complete judgement. The animal hungers and aggressive urges in human nature account for many or most of our more serious troubles: they cannot be altered as easily as we alter policies.

59

If men will not use their intelligence to examine and sift their traditional inheritances, social and individual, they must expect to suffer the sins of the fathers being visited upon the children.

60

Most are conventional; they do not like to appear unusual. They feel uneasy if they are with someone different from others. This makes them good citizens and communally helpful.

61

All these people have lost flesh-and-blood reality; they seem like marionettes, directed here and there by egoistic motives or animal reflexes in some cosmic play.

62

As they get more "civilized," their way of living gets more artificial, unnatural, and insensitive. How else explain the foods they eat, the noises they endure, the doctrines they espouse, and the tasks they toil at?

63

Theirs is the happiness of slaves and prisoners, slaves to the senses and prisoners of the body. It is the happiness of ignorance because it does not know what joy and freedom, what calm and beauty, lie beyond both.

64

Unfeeling toward these delicate vibrations, unaware of the nature of soul, they pass by the gate of the kingdom of heaven in ignorance of its existence and worth.

65

Caught up in all the trivialities of daily living, never having time for That which life is really all about, they should not wonder that their end is either a secret sorrow or a complacent self-deception.

66

The fact is that the truth has forever been open to mankind but man has rarely opened himself to the truth.

67

Of what use to offer the subtlest ideas and most refined sentiments of philosophy to crude, untutored minds which could see only madness in mentalism, only horror in ego-merger, and which responds so predominantly to animal instincts?

68

Our age is too ready with its cynicism, too sure of its materialism.

69

The man who has no awareness of his true self enjoys a certain sense of real living but it is largely a self-deceptive enjoyment.

70

Just because they move about and engage themselves actively they believe they are getting on, but that could be an illusion. Many get nowhere but find this out only when it is too late.

71

Modern man does not usually know that he is unwhole, divided in himself and ignorant of himself, and that the healing of this division is essential to health and happiness.

72

Those who respond to the dictations and commands of authority form the largest group—the masses. Those who respond to the directives of their intellect form the next one. Those who respond to their own intuitive determinations form the smallest group.

73

It is natural for a generation which thinks that being sophisticated means being intelligent to think also that being spiritual means being idiotic.

74

The average life is commonplace and repetitive; the average mind is inert and asleep.

75

They have no higher conception of themselves and hence no ideal to strive for.

76

This inner emptiness of their lives results in boredom, depression, irritation, and confusion.

77

Modern man lives in his body for material ends, almost independently of the rest of him. He has run his head into the noose of one-sided life.

78

To exploit the physical resources of Nature is not materialism, but to make such exploitation the chief purpose of human existence *is* materialism.

79

There is no peace in our restless daily existence, no poise in our restless minds and hearts.

80

We are wealthy in techniques and skills, poor in wisdom and insight. We have too much selfishness, too little goodness. Most of us are caught in a tangled web of activity, but few of us seek release from it.

81

If we examine the enormous volume of writing appearing in novel and play, film and radio, we shall find that two themes dominate. Scripts on crime or violence, sexual adultery or promiscuity, occupy more time than any other subjects. Sadism and salaciousness are human distortions, the development of animal attributes channelled through the human intellect—the very attributes which, as remnants of our prehuman stage of existence, are now in line to be overcome and eradicated if we are to conform to evolutionary purpose.

82

The fact is that most people are unacquainted with the mystical point of view, uninformed about mystical teachings, and unattracted by mystical practices. This is partly because there are few mystics in the world and not much reliable information about mysticism, and partly because the dominating trends of most people are materialistic ones. The values which they consider the most important are sensuous ones.

83

The contempt of mysticism prevails among so many who do not know what mysticism even means.

84

So long as human beings do not know and feel their real being within the greater being of God, so long will friction and hostility prevail among them.

85

Beauty is too noticeably absent from their minds, manners, and homes; truth is not an idea whose discovery would be exciting; goodness is taken for granted but only on the most ordinary bourgeois level.

86

All their ideas of truth are limited by the illusions, falsities, uglinesses, and weaknesses which limit and hold their own minds.

87

When Radhakrishnan was sent as the first ambassador to Russia of the newly created Indian Republic and presented his credentials to Stalin, the latter, on learning that his visitor was a professor of philosophy, answered, "We have to fill the people's bellies first, not teach them philosophy." This reminded me of Napoleon's visit to one of the Italian universities after his army had victoriously crossed the border for the first time by crossing the Alps. He went through some of the rooms in the university and came into one where a class was being taught. On learning that the students were being taught metaphysics he exclaimed, "Bah!" and went out. What is behind the attitude of those two men, Stalin and Napoleon, an attitude we often come across in less exalted circles? Is it not that people realize that a man who is hungry because of his poverty and inability to buy enough food is unlikely to be able to put his mind into the creation of art for its own sake or to think of lofty abstract ideas for their own sake with sufficient concentration?

88

Most people live upon the mere surface of their consciousness, knowing nothing of the great Power and intelligence which support it.

89

Those who are so immersed in outer activities that they have no inner life at all die before they are dead.

90

At one extreme are those who are held captive by convention; at the other, those who delight in flouting public opinion.

91

The common attitude regards that which is beyond a man's comprehension as being therefore beyond his concern.

92

The peasant mentality is a stable, solid, and reliable thing but it is unashamedly interested only in the smaller concerns of life. It would be openly materialistic too were it not for the inheritance of a conservative tradition of conformity to religion, strong but narrow, outward, and superstitious. That it has little time or use for culture is obvious.

93

All these people are trying to evade personal responsibility by finding someone else to make their decisions and be responsible for the results, someone behind whom they can hide from the world's stresses and under whose aegis they can shirk the necessities of thinking, willing, and experiencing.

94

Their need is for definite, invigorating ideas which will deliver them from wearisome perplexity and for an illuminating faith by which to live in a darkened world.

95

There is no inner aim, no spiritual significance, no worthwhile objective in their lives. They move through the years towards—nothing. They move from action to action without any consistency of principle. They grope through life like players in a game of blindman's bluff. They either do not know how to conduct their existence or else they fail to conduct it in the right way. In both cases they need help, guidance, direction. But unasked-for advice is unwelcome.

96

The conventional attitude which left Mozart to die in a pauper's grave but set up elaborate marble monuments to numerous mediocrities is not one to be admired.

97

It will not be by surrounding men with social benefits that they will take to the spiritual path. America is evidence of that. On the other hand, excessive deprivation of such benefits is equally an obstacle, for it continuously concentrates the immature mind on physical needs. What is needed, therefore, is a safe balance between these two extremes.

98

The masses should also be given what they inwardly need, not always and only what they demand.

99

It is often the minorities who hold the better views, for wisdom is not usually in the majority.

100

Today the mass-man resents the idea that anyone is better than he is, or entitled to more than he has. He demands equality in every way, from sharing responsibility to sharing rewards. Education, which was to have made him a gentleman, has missed the mark and made him a grumbling complainant, full of demands.

101

In ordinary times the less evolved masses were not pressed to accept a faith far beyond their mental reach or to submit to an ascetic discipline which they could not bear. But these are extraordinary times. The young postwar generation has an intelligence quotient nearly one-third higher than the earlier ones. The desire for knowledge is world-wide.

102

Their interests revolve only around themselves, or around those lengthenings of themselves called families.

103

The lack of time given in everyday living to religious devotion, let alone mystical practice, is partly responsible for the materialistic tone of society and, indirectly, for the moral degradation of society.

104

How few nourish their character on high principles, how many on cynical opportunism!

105

The masses float conventionally with the stream of religious authority; the individualized swim against it. The many merely echo what they have heard, like parrots; the few investigate it.

106

"There is nothing more absurd than to be of the same mind with the generality of men, for they have entertained many gross errors which time and experience have confuted. It is indeed our sluggishness and incredulity that hinder all discoveries, for men contribute nothing towards them than their contempt or, what is worse, their malice."—from *The Fraternity of the Rosy Cross*, 1652

107

They who reject the Quest live to no purpose beyond living itself, to no higher end than satisfying natural necessities.

108

They are unlikely to recognize a true teacher, much less respond to him.

109

Millions of people accept and hold certain beliefs because they get comfort from them, not because they have verified them and found them true. They are treating emotional pleasure as a better guide than rational judgement.

110

When life has cheated their hopes and illness has darkened their years, their shallowness and frivolity may appear insufficient and inadequate.

111

The soul-suffocating conditions of repetitive factory work creates not only an unhealthy boredom, but also an insensitivity to the finer things of life.

112

The lower self seems uppermost in humanity and directs its activities. The higher self is something unreal, remote, and impossible.

113

This blind unwillingness to see that man is more than his body has multiplied crime and dissolved virtue.

114

Those existentialists who find life meaningless must themselves necessarily become aimless.

115

They live for no worthy purpose, certainly for no high one, and so they live largely in vain.

116

Men of unlit minds will either humbly respect such a teaching or impulsively scoff at it.

117

The world is not ready for a fresh mystical revelation, not ready to follow a new religious seer, because it is not ready for a self-denying and flesh-denying life. It would not know what to do with such a revelation and it could not accept the discipline preached by such a seer.

118

What is it that motivates these people? First it is selfishness, second it is materialism, third it is inertia. But the selfishness is often masked under the guise of tradition, the materialism is often hidden under the form of religion, and the inertia is often covered by convention.

119

Where vulgarians throng to dance and barbarians eat corpses, there philosophy must isolate itself, withdrawn, while the karmic hurricane collects itself.

120

They are not sinners but mummies. Even sinners may be vital, may repent; but these are the dead-in-life, stiff with bourgeois hypocrisy and conventionality.

121

If they are without virtue, faith, moral principle, and God, the cause can be summed up as simple lack of interest in such matters.

122

In the end the psycho-physical progress of the mass depends upon that of the individual.

123

In the end society consists of its individual members. They are the materials out of which it is built. How then can it be better in quality than the general average of their individual quality?

124

In the past only a small number of persons had the interest, the equipment, or the time for such a quest. In the future there will be many more. But in the present, though the interest grows and the information swells, the limits remain.

125

The hunger for reality does not take a philosophical form in the less evolved herd. It may there take a political form, a social form, an emotional form, and so on. Only with the herd's own evolution will its awareness of the true objective evolve.

126

We are half-formed creatures, with only parts of us developed. The whole Man is yet to come.

127

Only when society reaches a higher level, when civilization evolves to a finer state than exists at present, can we expect that the proper respect and appreciation will be given to those higher truths literally shining with light to which only a comparative few give themselves.

128

If men do not have sufficient vision to see the importance of philosophy, that is not their fault any more than it is the fault of a tender plant not to be a mature tree.

129
Business can render honest useful service to society without falling into the absurd self-flattery and the blatant charlatanry of its publicity. Its easy ethical attitudes and easy surrender to economic pressures are responsible for the wholesale perversion of a profession such as writing. The advertisement which fails to go into hypocritical rhapsodies about some very ordinary product is uncommon. The advertisement writer who fails to hypnotize himself into seeing or imagining all kinds of exaggerated virtues about a product is uncommon. The advertised description which honestly tells you both what is right and what is wrong with the product is nonexistent. Such publication of the half-lie as if it were the whole truth, of the cheap and sensational or the exaggerated and misrepresentative, is another form of that crude immature culture whose world-spread is so rapid in our time.

130
Every important source of ideas, whether it be the press, literature, radio and film, the arts, or the schools and colleges needs to be brought into line with this ultimate purpose of moral and spiritual re-education.

131
The masses listen to scraps of news with eagerness as it pours out of the radio, as it is illustrated by the television, or as it is printed in the journals published every day. In this way their curiosity is momentarily satisfied, but only momentarily. It arises afresh day after day until it becomes a thirst.

There are two points of interest here which may not be generally noticed. The first is that curiosity is not all bad—it is a kind of caricature of the desire to know and to understand. It is related, if rather remotely, to that wonder which Plato said is a beginning of philosophy. The second point is that the satisfaction of continuing this curiosity scatters attention until the scattered condition becomes a permanent part of the mental character. Philosophy departs from this state through sustained interest in its study, concentrated practised attention in its meditation, and independent thought for its application in living. All these run counter to the scattered mental condition of the mass of mankind.

132
Most advertising depends on the power of suggestion, not on service. Therefore it is selfish, to some extent hypocritical.

133
The sort of journalism, and today even literature, which is mere backbiting gossip in print expresses the affinity of writer with reader; both fit this low plane.

134

The great technical advances which have been made in the past two centuries have not been made without cost. Before that period the psychiatrist was unknown because his service was not needed. Although man has done so much to improve his environment, he has also done much harm to himself. His nerve system and his muscular system are markedly weaker, his emotional nature more frayed and unstable, his faith in and sensitivity to the higher power markedly less.

135

Many of the forms of so-called progress which we have seen in the past century and a half were really corrections of the evils which the beginning of the Industrial Age had brought into being. They were not really new forms, real progress, but rather rectification of the wrongs we had done. Cities have grown immense in many countries, bringing many evils, difficulties, and problems which never existed before. The machine which can do so much to help us if used with wisdom and caution has become a Frankenstein. Chemicals have followed the same path in medicine and food, making it more difficult to get pure food, or to get well-healed without introducing new and hostile complications.

Of course, a world-wide spiritual awakening—by which I do not mean a merely religious awakening—could also remove the threat of self-destruction. But this century has been a period of challenge, and it is for the human beings to accept this challenge and rise to it positively if they want a positive result. So far we have seen mostly that the high degree of knowledge and skill which science has developed has been developed on a lavish scale financially for the weapons and instruments of destruction, and much less for pacific purposes.

If this short survey of the situation seems depressing, it will not alter the general structure of the World-Idea. The cycles through which we pass, the grim and the grand, must one day also bring us to a union of this high intellectual development exemplified by science with the less materialistic and gentler ideals which originally spread out from the East.

136

Progress must be meticulously and carefully defined as a theory, and the facts offered in proof of it must be as full and complete as possible, so that their adverse side may be included as well as their beneficial side—a point which becomes very obvious in the case of science. Therefore, it is not enough to point out the magnificent progress of technical, engineering, and scientific activities; there must also be a scrupulous examination of the pollutions and sicknesses, the dangers and hazards which they have brought into existence. The same critical examination is needed for the moral, the ethical, the religious, and the metaphysical progress of scholarly activities.

137

Without unreasonably rejecting the contributions of modern ways of living or the useful arts of twentieth-century civilization, or the practical techniques of science and industry, we may still refuse to let them dominate us to such an extent that the intuitive elements in human nature are overwhelmed and lost. We must complement and balance them.

138

The whirring machine is not a sin against life but rather a part of its larger fulfilment. For man cannot improve his intelligence without inventing machines. Ascetics, mystics, and sentimentalists who complain that the machine has maimed and killed should also remember that it has served and saved. And when the same people mourn over the lost Arcadian happiness of primitive mankind they might remember that men who lived in frequent fear of wild beasts and hostile tribes could not have been ideally happy.

139

We have done much to improve the architecture of a house but little to expand the consciousness of the person who lives in it.

140

If industrial civilization has enriched our outer life it has also impoverished the inner life. It need not have done so if we had brought about a proper equilibrium between the two and if we had done so under the light of the guiding principle of what we are here on earth for.(P)

141

We fuss about with so many things that we miss the fundamental and profoundest thing of all. Peace, inward beauty, and sanity are singularly absent from the mad, mechanized life of our large cities.

142

The victims of modern civilization are supposed to have more leisure. But do they really have it?

143

Mass-production of goods may cheapen their cost and thus spread their use, but this benefit is offset by the loss of the craftsman's skill, the artist's individuality. Everything has to be paid for, as always. We get nothing for nothing.

144

We live in a condition of spiritual languor, of lost spiritual vision, and decayed intuition.

145

Our mistakes have been to make the body's possessions and comforts, its machines and devices, so sufficient unto themselves that the mind's higher needs have been overlooked or brushed aside.

146

The discontent, rebelliousness, bitterness, and violence on the part of workers in industry which we have seen rising like a tide through the past century, in several cases ending in open revolution is not altogether or rather only a matter of more wages and fewer working hours. It is also a matter of the kind of work which they have to do. When men work *with* machines they get worked upon *by* the machines themselves, they begin to lose their humanness and become more mechanical. And if the work is a mere repetition of a previous operation done at speed—as we saw theatrically presented in Charles Chaplin's film *Modern Times*—the worker's situation psychologically gets worse. The dehumanization of large masses of people creates negative emotions and materialistic thoughts within them. This is not to say that the machine is an evil thing. It has its place, especially where it saves unpleasant, dirty, or fatiguing labour. This is only to say that it should be kept in its place and not allowed to overwhelm the worker inwardly.

147

It is less urgent to invent new mechanical devices than it is to correct old moral defects.

148

A wife and mother of three children who went out daily to work told me feelingly how much the automatic washing machine had meant to her in saved toil and time, how greatly it had relieved her from the dismaying burden of the family laundry. Here was a vivid and incontestable instance of machinery's positive value and necessary place in human life.

149

We have had proof enough that without a prior or accompanying spiritual growth, technical improvements lead to mixed evil and good results—with the evil ones always in excess.

150

We moderns have tried to make Nature serve our purposes. We have built a civilization on science and technology. But in the process of making material things our slaves, we have ourselves become slaves to them.

151

The present spectacle affords ironic evidence of the paradoxical nature of our vaunted "progress."

152

The products of applied science, the inventions of modern industry, and the energies which drive engines need not have evil consequences if they are used in inner freedom, not in enslavement.

153

The man of an earlier generation who looked through the slot of Edison's kinetoscope and was thrilled by what he saw would be pitied by cinema-audiences of the present generation for getting so much emotion out of so little an experience—such is the complacency bred by familiarity.

154

We live in an age of division of labour. It may make for industrial efficiency for a man to spend his whole life putting the heads on pins, but I fancy that he will be something less than a man at the end of fifty years. The artisans of old time, both in Europe and Asia, were equipped to practise all of a craft or even several arts at once. Moreover they created their own designs and then executed them by their own hands.

155

The machine may be used against men and women, as in war, or for them, as in peace. The ascetic notion, popularized by such men as Tolstoy and Gandhi, that it is necessarily harmful and always evil is unphilosophical.

Reconciling the mystical and mundane

156

Is it really necessary to choose between the way of the world, which leads to the possession of things, and the way of the Spirit, which leads to the possession of oneself?

157

Again paradox is truth. The brevity of life, possessions, beauty, and such is true and good reason to abandon all: world, love, and so on. But the opposite is also true. We can enjoy beauty, life, and all the rest if *detached*. So both sides *together* equal the whole truth. So I join no sect or teaching—alone.

158

In the true concept of spiritual life, there is plenty of space for the rational, normal, and practical life also.

159

To work effectively in this world of everyday without repudiating or forgetting the world of the Spirit—this is his duty.

160

This mystical preachment on the gospel of inspired action is written for those who find themselves tangled up in the affairs of this world and must make the best of it. I counsel them to make the best of it by making the better of their inner life. I suggest that it is better to aspire aright and rise spiritually than to remain like a stagnant pool. And I would remind them that their worldly work can be carried out on a basis of service plus self-interest, where now it may be carried out on a basis of self-interest alone; for to serve is to put the spirit in action.

161

It is not necessary to renounce life in the bustling world. It is necessary, however, to change its basis, to transform its character, to make it echo the voice of the Ideal, which is to lead us upwards towards better things.

162

The ugly way so many human beings behave is simply a revelation of the ugliness in human nature. The mystically inclined person may not like this sombre reality and may prefer a fantasy of how he would like them to be. Yet so far as his fantasy includes the picture of a divinity within their hearts, this is also true and is the bright reality which must be put into balance with the darker one.

163

He has to keep his feet on solid earth, but without letting himself get earthbound.

164

Instead of falling into the common attitude of classifying the natural everyday side of human nature as hostile to the mystical inner side, as an incompatible opposite, why not bring both sides together in harmony? This can be done intellectually by understanding mentalism, and emotionally by appreciating or creating inspired art.

165

We have to work with the actual but we can do so by the light of the ideal.

166

Wang Yang-ming maintained that wisdom and virtue could not be gained by meditation alone. He asserted that the daily experience of dealing with ordinary matters was also needed, provided that experience was sincerely reflected upon by conscience, reason, and intuition.

167

He need not seek flight to isolation or to monasticism. He can participate in the world's life without being soiled by the world's evil. He can continue to grow in knowledge of truth and devotion to the Good even in the midst of such profane activities. But to succeed in this a correct attitude toward them and toward their results must be acquired.

168

Living in the world as we are, having to submit to demands which the world makes upon us, we must learn how to deal with them in a correct way. By correct I mean in harmony with our inner goal.

169

The harder the situation is to bear, the more it should arouse a wise ambition in him to get out of it. Ambition requires, however, an all-around awakening and remaking of his personality. He can fight and be ambitious and yet hold on to ideals; there is no need to lose them. Balance is to be the ideal.

170

If he is to be in the world and of the world, he will still remain undeceived by the world.

171

Both attitudes are required for a proper result: the idealistic which looks to a new and better future, the practical which recognizes the limitations of its heritage from the past.

172

It is out of this new conflict in the personal situations through which he passes, the conflict between idealism's abstract call and actuality's practical demands, that he has the chance to discover his balance.

173

Only to the extent that a man can find harmony within himself can he adjust harmoniously with his world.

174

What is wrong if we claim some happiness from this world, provided we keep our balance, the heart anchored to an allegiance higher than the world, the mind always remembering for what it is really here?

175

Contrast remains the essence of all human experience.

176

A civilized life ought to possess better quality things—art, music, and literature, some touch of refinement somewhere, and a little basic knowledge of food values and perils, of personal hygiene and health preservation.

177

Precisely because it comes with the truth, because it is associated with the discovery of reality, the final phase of philosophy—*sahaja*—cannot be segregated from the business of living.

178

Each man finds what he is looking for, and the world is a mirror of his own self. The frog is lured to grovel in the mud surrounding a lotus whereas the butterfly is lured by the fragrance of the flower itself. The philosophic student perceives quite clearly that the lotus-flower of reality which looks so lovely in the bright gay sunshine cannot be separated from the roots which look so ugly in the black muddy slime. He makes a perfectly balanced adjustment to the world as he finds it, not merely as a concession to a compulsive environment, but because Philosophy does not stand aside from human needs nor remain unrelated to human affairs.

179

If his fidelity to worthy ideals remains through situations which test character and he reacts honourably to events which expose it, he finds that in the end his real welfare in the world also remains. Whether he is encircled by business affairs or pressed by everyday work or worthily consumes time in other ways, his lasting good will not suffer. Only the less important surface life may do so. Even there he may be saved from entering wrong courses.

180

It is a paradox of the strongest irony that the place where we can best find the Overself is not in another world but in this one, that the chance to grow enduringly out of darkness into light is better here.

181

This is the extraordinary paradox of the Quest, that it is a road leading out of daily life and yet far inseparable from daily living itself.

182

If he puts everything in its place—the lower and lesser things where they belong, the higher and greater ones above them—what has he to fear from the world? He can still remain active in it; flight will be unnecessary. If he does not forget the final purpose of all this worldly activity, that through the body's life and the mind's existence he may seek and find his true self, the Overself, the inner failure and superficiality of so many lives will be avoided.

183

It is needful to relate this earthly life to the divine one, not only in isolated sessions of meditation but also in the whole of the daily existence. When this is fully done the consequences are unpredictable, the effects on oneself and others incalculable.

184

The high moods created in meditation must be brought into contact with the personal daily life, must bear fruit there; and although this happens anyway quite automatically to some extent, it could happen to a much larger extent if turned into a conscious deliberate process.

185

This earthly life is the "narrow gate" which opens onto the kingdom.

186

Whoever lives in such a society, his heart in the Real, his mind in the True, is as much absent from it as he is present.

187

For sincere questers there is, or should be, an interest in life which grows with time.

188

It is here, in the ordinary and uneventful tasks of the day, that he may find just as much opportunity to practise nonattachment, to suppress egoism, and to express wisdom.

189

The flow of current events and the incidents of day-to-day living ought not be allowed to shake him from his stand in the truth. They give him the chance to view them metaphysically from the Eternal Now, and psychologically from the ideal Self.

190

"What is the path?" the Zen Master Nan-sen was asked. "Everyday life is the path," he answered.

191

We are told that economic necessities must be satisfied before spiritual ones. But why not both together, side by side, since there is no separation between them? The *way* in which we gain the mundane ends is always governed by our spiritual background.

192

Why do men embark on this quest? Is it not because it gives them hope? Here we should not confuse hope with optimism.

How to treat opportunity

193

Wisdom takes advantage of opportunity, spiritual not less than material, but foolishness neglects it.

194

It is of immense importance, whether in the internal spiritual life or the external worldly career, to cultivate the art of detecting, recognizing, and accepting opportunity. Two factors need especially to be remembered here. First, sometimes she presents her face plainly and unmistakably, but more often she presents two faces each equally attractive and each claiming to bear her name: or else she disguises herself under the garb of commonplace events and unprepossessing personalities. Second, she never repeats the same situation with the same chances in precisely the same way. With altered conditions, the same causes cannot produce the same phenomena. To miss those chances through ignorance or the blindness of unpreparedness, through logic's limitation or the dismissing of intuition, is to miss portions of success or happiness that could easily have been ours.

195

Understand that destiny often moves forward like a game of chess. If you cannot see immediately your way to success in a career or the solution of a problem, you should look for the first step in that direction. For only after that has been taken will the second show itself, and later the third, and so on. Learn to detect the *beginnings* of the way to opportunity, even though opportunity itself is still not visible.

196

The opportunity is unrepeatable and unreceivable in exactly the same way, for the passage of time—be it a moment or a century—has forced change on both the situation and the person.

197

In making a decision as to the kind of life he will lead, he has pronounced a judgement on the other kinds also. What happens thereafter will itself judge his judgement.

198

A single mistake in the rejection of an opportunity or in the choice of direction at a crossroad may lead to a quarter-lifetime's suffering. The student may quite easily discover by analysis the smaller lessons embodied in that suffering and yet may quite overlook the larger lessons, for he may fail to ascribe major blame to the early rejection or choice. He may still not realize how it all stems out of that primary root, how each error in conduct that naturally happens after it becomes a channel for a further one, and that in its turn for still another, so that the descent is eventually inevitable and its attendant sorrows become cumulative. Thus all traces back to the initial foundational error, which is the most important one because it is the choice of wrong direction, because such a wrong choice means that the more he travels through life, the more mistaken all his later conduct becomes.(P)

199

If he accepts the hand of opportunity when it is offered him, the effects will be favourable in every direction. If he feels the premonition that he is on the verge of a new cycle, and makes decisions or acts accordingly, the way into it will open out for him.

200

That man is immensely fortunate who is able to detect opportunities when they come and who, having detected, proceeds to take advantage of them.

201

What most people count as great misfortunes sometimes open the door to new opportunities, ideas, or courses of action leading to advantages that would not otherwise have come. It is wiser to defer an appraisal of such events until they have shown their results as a whole to a final view.

202

How little do we know that some small act, some minor move, may lead to consequences that open up an entirely new phase of experience.

203

If he acts too quickly on decisions made impulsively, he may suffer loss or hurt. But if he is overly slow to take action on decisions made long before, the consequence may be the loss of a good opportunity.

204

This situation has happened in the lives of many people. Where they have recognized its significance as a spiritual chance, everything thereafter went well for them, but where they failed to recognize it, everything went wrong, materially and spiritually.

205

If we do not make good use of our chances, they come to us in vain. If our opportunities are ill-used, they will not recur for a long time. Thus a life will teach us a better sense of values.

206

Situations develop where to take a certain course would lead to immediate advantage, and he may feel tempted to take it. But if, from the point of view of his spiritual growth, it is undesirable, what does he gain in the end?

207

Opportunities are not always recognized as such by the aspirant. He who expects them to come fully labelled for what they are falls into error. The difficulty which seems to retard his steps on the spiritual path hides within itself the chance to develop qualities and strengthen weak places.

208

What could be more poignant than the after-regrets at valuable opportunities thrown away through one's faults or missed through one's blindness?

209

Error begets further error, creates its own heirs. This is why the first step on a new course is the most important.

210

It is true that some opportunities by their very nature can come only once in a lifetime.

Seeking guidance

211

When a decision has to be made, and different sides of one's nature are pulling in different directions, creating inner conflict, bewilderment, and rendering a firm decision impossible, what is the aspirant to do? Find the true guidance? Let him first surrender the problems to the Higher Power. This surrender is best formulated through the medium of a heartfelt prayer in which there is earnest desire first to learn and then to accept the guidance. This must be done with the utmost concentration and sincerity, seeking to learn the Higher Will and being ready to abide by it even if it disagrees with personal desires.

After this is done, wait calmly for days or even weeks with faith that the solution to the problem will eventually come. If it does not come directly from within as an intuitive certitude, then it may come through some event or contact or as a distant trend forming itself in outward circumstances and pointing to a specific direction.

212

The need to guide his personal life more intuitively comes home to him after every major mistake has been committed and its effects felt. He sees then that it is not enough to calculate by intellect, nor feel by impulse, nor act on emotion, for these have led him to sufferings that could have been prevented, or caused other people sufferings that bring him regrets. He learns that it is necessary to listen inwardly, to wait in mental quiet for intuitive feeling to arise and guide him.

213

Success in the perplexing game of living is only possible when decisions based on balanced truthful thinking become easy and natural. But in turn, truthful thinking is only possible when every egoistic motive, every emotional weighting, and every personal wish and fear is removed from the thought process.

214

If a situation is fraught with anxiety and is also either unavoidable or unalterable, the first procedure is to organize all your forces to meet it calmly. The second is to call on the higher power for help by turning to it in relaxation and meditation.

215

However difficult the circumstances of his surface life may become, the student must cling to his faith that the Overself really *is*, and that if he seeks Its guidance It will lead him to the wisest solution of his problem. This does not necessarily or always mean that he should stop his own personal efforts. On the contrary, he should use his reason and judgement to the best degree of which he is capable, and also consult others who are more experienced or more expert than he is. But after he has done all that he can do, he should hand over his problem to the Overself. He must prove that he has really surrendered it by releasing himself from further anxiety concerning the outcome. He must be confident that the higher power, which is always with him, can meet his needs. He must be patient enough to wait and courageous enough to accept a solution which offends his egoism. Then, outer help or inner guidance or an answer to his problem will be forthcoming.

216

He must learn to depend on the infinite source of his being for everything, but only after he has done all that his limited mind and ability can do.

217

It is correct practice for a man to abandon his anxieties or fears and turn them over to the Overself, but it is incorrect for him to do so without or before analysing their nature, origin, and lesson.

218

The practice of trying, by "going into the silence," to rise above mundane difficulties *before* they are properly understood and *before* one's own responsibility for them is honestly assessed, is a premature one.

219

However harassing a problem may seem to us, if we can give up our egoistic attitude towards it, if we can keep the lower emotions away from it, the best possible solution under the circumstances will develop of its own accord. There is veritable magic in such a change of thinking and feeling. It opens the gate to higher forces and enables them to come to our help.

220

Each problem is to be solved by the simple method of turning it over to the Overself and then dismissing it from mind. The ego is faulty and blind; what it cannot solve or manage, the Overself can. But this method requires time and patience.

221

Sometimes the guidance will evolve naturally out of the situation, the circumstances, the events. He will then only have to be a spectator, but he must still supply the intuitive interpretation and recognition of this recognition.

222

Take your peril to the Overself, identify your real being with the Overself and not with the vanishing ego. Then you will be at the standpoint which perceives that you are as secure and safe as the Overself is. Hold your position as the final and highest one. Reject the very thought of being in danger. There is none in the Overself.

223

The problem which the ego has created for you but which the ego cannot solve for you will dissolve under the impact of the Overself's light.

224

He should make it an unfailing practice to turn inwards in moments of need for help and in moments of perplexity for direction.

225

No other act is so urgent or so important as this, to turn now in thought and remembrance, in love and aspiration, toward the Overself. For if you do not but turn toward that other and worldly act which is so clamant and demanding, you fall into a tension which may lead to error and consequent suffering. But if you do turn toward the Overself first and then act, you rise up to inner calm and consequent wiser judgement.

226

After he has meditated sufficiently on his problem, he should drop it from mental view altogether and wait, passively and patiently, surrendering it to the intuitive element within himself. If he can get deep enough, absorbed enough, he will touch this element and may instantly receive a solution from it. If he cannot, it will be necessary to try again another time, and perhaps even several times. Then, either in that passive contemplation or unexpectedly during the day, or abruptly on awaking from sleep, the elusive answer to his question may be presented to him as a clear self-evident fact.

227

Work quietly for a few minutes daily in handing your problem over to the Higher Power, confessing you have done what you could, and praying from the depths of your heart for the right solution. However, on no account dictate what that solution should be. Examine the lesson behind your sufferings in dealing with problems of the past, acknowledge the mistakes and repent them. Then wait and watch what happens during the coming weeks or months. The advantage of this method is that it "works"; the disadvantage is that it gives us what is best for our next spiritual step forward, which is not always to personal liking but is always for our best in the long run. The important thing is to adopt and maintain an attitude of surrender—not to another person but to the Overself—in the face of adverse emotions.

228

Without recourse to an experienced teacher it is going to be a longer and harder road than with it. For he will be compelled to find his way by a trial-and-error method.

229

It is not easy to know always what to do in certain situations, and this creates anxious states of mind and may lead to vacillating decisions. In that case it is better to make the experiment of waiting a little and praying to the Higher Self for guidance before falling asleep. Then, immediately after awakening, or rather in that brief state between sleep and waking, one should remain passive to whatever thought, message, or picture presents itself. This may require repetition day after day until the result is successful.

230

He must wait indefinitely until intuition supplies the needed answer or, if the matter is more urgent, wait only for a definite period and then review the situation again, ask humbly for guidance, and force a decision even though it is at risk.

231

Why fatigue yourself trying to make a difficult decision? Why not hand the problem over to the higher power, which knows better than you? Where logic fails to guide, surrender and intuition may take its place and prove their worth. Having turned the problem over to the higher power, just leave it to time. This does not necessarily mean you have nothing further to do. There may be action required, but in that case quietly await the signal or guidance: let it appear of its own accord in its own hour, meanwhile trusting yourself to the Power, giving your problem to its wisdom, and letting your destiny take its course under this new association.

232

One must be on guard against the ego. He should test his actions by their motives; let him ask himself whether his teacher would act in the same way. Seeking guidance should be combined with the active use of his own reason about any matter, because the highest reason coincides with the highest guidance. In financial matters, especially, he should make reason the touchstone.

233

He has to ask himself: What is it that the Overself is impelling me to do? The answer will hardly ever be a spontaneous one. He will have to wait patiently for days or weeks or perhaps months before it will be heard sufficiently clearly and definitely.

234

He may bring his problem into the presence of the Light, and seek guidance upon it. But he ought not to do so before first seeking the Light itself for its own sake. If he does, and makes the contact, it will throw his problem aside, and he must allow it to do so. He must be patient and let the matter of guidance come up later, or at another time.

235

Act neither too soon nor too late. Await the proper occasion with patience. Its coming will announce itself if you are sensitive to intuitional prompting. But if calculating doubt or emotional desire or other people's suggestions get in the way, you may misread the fitting time and spoil the opportunity.

236

If he will take the Overself's timing rather than his own, if he will cease struggling against this destiny and resign himself to it, he will begin to note and understand that many of the greatest events of his life have happened without his having any part in bringing them about.

237

To shirk all responsibility and get someone else to make his decision in a perplexing situation contributes little or nothing to his own growth, but to seek help from more experienced persons in making his decision is quite proper.

238

Often the guidance does not come till the time when it is needed, the answer to our questioning does not make itself heard until the eleventh hour. Until then we must learn to wait in hopeful patience and in trustful expectation.

239

It is a mistake to assume that the sought-for guidance must necessarily reveal itself in all its entirety and all at once. It may, but quite often it does not show more than the next step to be taken or the next truth to be assimilated. The later ones are then withheld until this is done. Why should they be given in advance before we have demonstrated our faith in the first lead already given and our willingness to put it into practice? Moreover, the proficient disciple must learn to live in the eternal Now and its resultant peace, not be anxious about the imagined future and its possible events.

240

At the moment of his greatest need—which usually means at the moment when a decision can no longer be deferred—the event will happen or the guidance will come which will show him the way out of his problem.

241

Only by the application of philosophic technique, referring every difficulty as it manifests to, and dissolving it in, the Infinite Mind, will it be possible successfully to handle such problems.

242

When confronted with an external situation which they are unable to cope with, some seek escape from the necessity of dealing with it. The philosophic method is to face and analyse the facts.

243

It is of practical importance in the affairs of his life not to enter any undertaking nor make a decision nor begin a day without first entering into a meditation. This will tend to introduce proper deliberateness and dismiss hasty carelessness from his decisions, to insert intuitive guidance into his activities, and to warn him against wrong enterprises.

244

The intuition may be slow in revealing itself but when it does the inner certitude it provides, the strong consciousness of being right, will enable him to act decisively and swiftly.

245

It is said proverbially that practice makes perfect and that habit makes easy. Certainly he who diligently cultivates the habit of relying on his intuitive forces for guidance and on his higher ones for courage, will do what he is bidden unswayed by his ego's criticism or other people's opposition. The worth of following such a course will prove itself by its results, for they will, in the end, promote the true happiness and real welfare of all concerned.

246

The history of his future will test his choices of the present and tell him whether they are wise or not. His mistakes will punish him, his right decisions reward him.

247

He will avail himself of the guidance of circumstances if he can detect the hand of the higher power in them.

248

If he turns away from his problem and to the Overself, the moment its peace is felt or its message of truth is heard, he may take this as a sign that help in some way will assuredly come to him.

249

He should not assume that the guidance must manifest itself in one particular way alone. On the contrary, it may come to him in a variety of ways, and may even be transmitted through someone else.

250

God may help us, or God's healing may come to us, indirectly. Instead of a miracle happening abruptly we may be led intuitively to the knowledge which, or to the person who, will reveal what we can do to serve or save ourselves. The end result may thus be the same as the miracle, but we shall have guided our lives toward it by our own informed effort.

251

As soon as he turns it over to the Higher Power to deal with, what is he doing? First, he is withdrawing the ego from trying to manage the matter. Second, he is placing the other person in the Overself's care or inserting the situation in the universal harmony. In the first case, management will no longer be limited by the short sight of his desires and the shallow penetration of his intellect. In the second case, the person will be exposed to the recuperative, renewing, and pacifying powers of the Overself or the situation will be benefited, through the mentalistic nature of the universe, in the best possible way for the ultimate good of all concerned in it.

This procedure is not the treatment suggested by rainbow-dreaming teachers, for it begins by noting the actual condition, however unpleasant or unhealthy that may be. It analyses by all the means within its reach the nature, the causes, and the effects of the condition: only then, only after this is done, does it turn away from miserable actuality and try to see the glorious ultimate ideality. From the moment that he consciously gives recognition to the Overself and its perfection, he opens the door to its forces.

252

If, while managing a situation, you are filled with anxiety or taut with tension, take it as a warning sign that you are managing with the unaided ego alone. That is, you have forgotten, or failed, to turn it over to the higher power, to put it in the hands of the Overself.

253

To become as a child, in Jesus' sense, means to become permeated with the happiness, with the joy, which a child's freedom from responsibilities and anxieties brings it. All problems being turned over to the higher power, the philosopher enjoys the same inner release.

254

The practice of turning to the Overself for relief, help, guidance, or healing in a grievous crisis is most effective only when, first, the will acts resolutely to put away thoughts of anguish, second, the turn is made swiftly, and, third, the will continues to keep the mind dwelling steadily on the benefic qualities of its sacred object, idea, or declaration.

255

He will not rigidly hold to any course of worldly action which he has charted, but will hold himself open to a change indicated by higher leading at any time. He knows that such an indication may come from within intuitively or from without circumstantially.

256

If it is a truly intuitive decision or choice, one of the signs validating it will be the feelings of satisfaction and serenity which immediately follow it.

257

If he has sought guidance through intuition or meditation but found only a barren result, he should watch whether circumstances themselves decide his course for him. If they do, it could well be that this is the outer response to his inner request.

258

While you are thinking about a problem and in search of an answer to it, you cannot get the intuition which is its true and final solution. But when you are no longer doing so, the answer appears. This happens with the genius during the interval between two thoughts but with the ordinary man during sleep.

259

The guidance, the message, the answer, the solution he seeks may come in different ways at different times. It may appear as a pictured symbol or be received as a mentally-thought sentence or flash through his consciousness as a self-evident intuition.

260

If he is seeking to solve a problem and receives as the fruit of his meditation a vague peaceful happy feeling, this is not necessarily the end; it often means that at a subsequent time he will receive a very definite solution, either from within or from without.

261

It is good for him to try the method of simple prayer for obtaining the illumination he needs upon the specific problems which trouble him. He may address prayer to whatever higher power he most believes in or to his own higher self.

262

If in doubt regarding any great difficulty, close your eyes, think of a master, silently call on his name, then patiently wait. The force using him may come to your help.

263

If the technique of turning a problem or situation over to the higher power fails to yield favourable results, the fault lies in the person attempting to use it, not in the technique itself. If he is using it as an attempt to escape from coping with the problem or as a refusal to face up to the situation, and thus as an evasion of the lessons involved, it will be better for his own growth to meet with failure. And even among those who claim to have perceived the lessons, they may not have really done so but may have accepted only what suited their egos and rejected the rest. The full meaning of the experience must be taken deeply to heart and applied sincerely to living before the claim to have learned it can be substantiated.

264

Counsel given in individual cases and isolated instances should not be taken always as meant for every case and for universal application.

265

Human beings are too varied for all to follow a single line. In personal temperament and moral character, in intellect and feeling, in aptitude and skill, differences are great enough to make necessary different prescriptions for the way of life.

266

The hardship, the difficulty, or the problem which he cannot meet by his own strength he may meet with the help of the divine strength.

267

Seeking help from the higher power need not mean turning away altogether from ordinary dependence on human power and skill.

268

Whatever outward changes he may find it desirable to make, or whatever decisions he may have to come to, he should do so in a way that will help him fulfil his high purpose, even while at the same time they take care of his earthly life. By attending to the deepest inner promptings that may come to him in moments of relaxed calm, he may get valuable pointers toward the best direction in which to make these changes and adjustments.

269

He will find that at the exact point in time and the essential point in place where his real need is, a way out or over or through his problem will appear. This is not always the point which this clamouring ego may determine it to be. Silencing the ego by going into the stillness within is the best way to draw this help.

270

Why should we bear all the grievous burdens of the ego? By turning them over to the higher self, not prematurely but after analysing their lessons and doing what we ought to, we gain relief.

271

With the onset of crisis or stress, trouble or calamity, he turns his mind instantly toward the Higher Power. This can be done easily, effortlessly— but only after long self-training and much practice in thought control.

272

He will not let others push him into activities that are not his duty or inclination; he is responsible for and must make his own decisions.

273

It is ironically paradoxical, this discovery that the very higher power to which we must turn in our helplessness is within ourselves.

274

Whatever the difficulty, you will certainly face it better and may solve it sooner if the ordinary approach through reason and practicality is controlled and illumined by the final approach through the higher self. This is done by dwelling on its never-leaving presence and healing power.

275

To lose one's faith in the higher laws and powers when the dice of destiny come up with an unfavourable number is not only a sign of weakness but also a sign that one's faith was incomplete. It has touched the emotions only or the intellect only but it has not touched both of them, while it has still to touch the will.

276

Although proper judgement may call for a particular decision, inexorable necessity may call for quite a different one.

277

There are certain periods in a man's life when he can find no help outside himself, just as there are occasions when help from others comes easily enough.

278

You are more likely to get light on your problem if you avoid getting tense or feeling frustrated about it.

279

The need to make a rapid decision may create panic in an uncertain mind. Here again the best counsel is to go into the calm Silence, push aside the insistent thoughts of pressure, and wait in patience for mental quiet to manifest itself. Then only can intuitive guidance emerge.

280

Bring your need, your problem, even your desire into the silence and let it rest there. If you do this often enough, it will be corrected for you should it be partly wrong, or totally eradicated should it be wholly wrong, or miraculously satisfied or solved should it be right for you!

281

He who, like others, looks to material things, but, unlike others, only as secondary to his dependence on the higher power, finds in experience his final confirmation. As Lao Tzu said: "The Tao knows how to render help."

282

Even where men are ignorant of the law of karma, the higher self provides warnings to them when they deviate from the right path; but, alas, they do not heed these delicate feelings which speak from within and are often called the voice of conscience.

283

When confronted with a troublesome situation, he must feel, "I, in my ego, can do little." The problem must be turned over to a higher power for solution.

284

He does not accept the situation in the merely fatalistic resignation which puts up with anything, but learns to live with it in living trust that the higher power will bring it to the best possible ultimate issue.

285

If he has done everything that is in his power, the results are not in his hands and must consequently indicate destiny's will for him. They do not belong to his own will and must be accepted by him. Time will show their wisdom.

286

On all occasions when the intuition's prompting is absent and the intellect's judgement is doubtful, prudence suggests a pause.

287

It is better not to act than to act prematurely, not to decide than to decide without sufficient reason or intuition to support one.

288

By giving himself more time to wait upon his problem, he may give himself an intuitive, and hence deeper, understanding of it than a merely calculated and shallower one.

289

Action taken prematurely under the pressure of need may turn a right course into a wrong one.

290

Timeliness is a necessary ingredient of successful action.

291

If he feels clearly guided to a mission which seems impossible, he may safely leave to the Overself the means of carrying it out.

292

So long as he fails to see that the answer to his problems is within himself, but prefers the glib and easy explanation that it is in his environment, so long will the problem remain unsolved.

293

In all critical situations, try to become very very quiet, seeking the help or guidance to come up from the deeper levels of being.

294

To say turn a situation over to the Overself is tantamount to saying turn it over to the Universal Power to deal with.

295

All questions can find some kind of an answer in this mental silence; no question can be brought there often enough without a response coming forth in time. It is needful to be patient and to have faith during the waiting period. The inner monitor is certainly there but we have to reach it.

296
Sometimes when every other road seems implacably blocked, the right road to travel is indicated.

297
He may be obliged by circumstances to follow a course of action that he might not otherwise have even considered.

298
At the very moment that any problem produces thoughts of despondency, turn that problem over to the higher power again, and try to remain inwardly calm.

299
They should heed the warnings of experience, the guidance of elders, the injunctions of religion; but they need not do so without having critically scrutinized and carefully weighed what is thus proffered to them.

300
Whatever is proper to a particular situation should be done; rules should not be followed blindly.

301
The arrogant do not seek help and consequently do not get it.

302
Can he put his personal problems, interests, or difficulties into the hands of the higher Power? This is both the first and the last procedure, but in between he may be led to call for the services of reason, observation, experience, authority, and specialized knowledge.

303
I have known questers who have reached a cul-de-sac when an intensifying problem finally entered the critical stage. Then, following this teaching, they decided to hand it over to the Overself entirely and be done with further cogitation and agitation about it. The tension came to a swift end, proving that they had really handed it over and were not deceiving themselves. They waited patiently for direction to be given them. Sometimes this came quickly, overwhelmingly, and clearly—sometimes it came slowly, gently, and weakly.

Worldly success

304
Despite Saint Francis, it must be stated that a wide observation and experience shows poverty to be not necessarily holy, nor prosperity evil.

305
The practicality of the ordinary common man is praiseworthy: it is not to be regarded as materialistic.

306

Efficiency in work and tidiness in homekeeping are not so materialistic as they sound. Even the mystic will benefit by them no less than the worldling, for they will save time which he can give to what he deems the more important activities of his life.

307

The problem of earning a livelihood under modern conditions and in harmony with the Quest's ethics is more complicated and less easy to solve for some people than for others. There are professions, occupations, pursuits, and trades which at times demand transgression of these ethics. If any general principles can be laid down, they are that earnings, profits, or dividends should be honestly made and that no suffering should be inflicted on any living creature.

308

It is true that more wealth means more opportunity and that this in turn, if rightly used, may lead to more wisdom. But it is not necessarily true that more wealth leads to more wisdom.

309

This foolish attempt to climb higher and higher in the Tower of Babel which they have built arises out of false notions of success and failure. They measure success by the conditions surrounding a man and assess failure in the same way. There is a harsh lesson that life will ultimately teach them—that there is no equivalent compensation for the loss of spiritual values.

310

The need of money is second to the need of good health, and both are second to the need of spiritual strength. All three are important, for most other desired things depend heavily on them.

311

If money occupies a large part of their thoughts, are they to blame for that? Life being what it is, necessity demands such attention, realism compels it. Only when higher purposes are displaced, neglected, or ignored because of this stress on the money-thought are imbalance and materialism produced.

312

The possession of money, as of power, is not an evil and may, by its wise use, be a positive good. But, by providing new temptations, it may also bring into activity weaknesses lying below the surface of a man's character.

313

Success can easily lead a man to failure if it becomes an intoxicant instead of a lubricant.

314

The man who is unwilling to put a deliberate restraint on his desire nature cannot possibly find peace of mind. Yet a noteworthy feature of life in certain Western countries is the encouragement of new wants, the stimulation by advertising and salesmanship of new hungers for possession.

315

The suffering of the rich cannot be put on the same level as the suffering of the poor, for the rich have compensations which are unavailable to the poor.

316

The search after happiness takes people to different activities and places, but rarely to the right ones. This is because they confound pleasure with happiness.

317

The ultimate value of all this activity in business, profession, politics, family, and so on is not in carrying them on successfully, but in using them to carry one's own mind nearer to enlightenment.

318

In a man's enthusiasm, which is so natural and so pardonable, for a great invention he has made or a great piece of work he may have done, he can become somewhat one-sided and indeed almost obsessed. Then it is good if he understands that it is necessary for him to restore the balance of his personality because it is unhealthy and unwise to stake so much of his happiness and thought upon what is, after all, a worldly activity. The frustrations and disappointments which may have been experienced in connection with his work will have carried this lesson behind them.

319

It is better for a man, as for a nation, to have less riches and more truth, than less truth and more riches.

320

Poverty is a stiff test of moral fibre.(P)

321

Being poor makes some men turn to materialism as the harsh real truth, but it turns other men to religion, as giving the consolation and support they need. Suffering of any kind and derived from any cause turns the sufferers either to or from a spiritual faith. It depends on several factors which it shall be in individual cases. We see this especially during and after a war involving the whole nation.

322

We still live in a world of slaves—slaves to money, to position that yields money, to things that cost money, to people who possess it. Money buys nearly all these things and persons. The sage is free in one way because of his inward indifference to money, and the millionaire is free in another way because he has all the money he needs.

323

Simone de Beauvoir: "Material independence is one of the necessary conditions for inner liberty." Is this true? Sometimes yes, other times not.

324

If it is for rich men to always learn the lesson that comfort does not mean happiness, it is for poor men to learn that simple living may go with a serene mind.

325

The businessman who is an adept at knowing how to make a living may be an idiot at knowing how to live.

326

What does all this extroverted activity or intellectual agitation mean, after all? It means that the human mind is unable to bear facing itself, looking into itself, being by itself.

327

The man whose name has become celebrated in certain circles, however limited, so that he is to that extent a public figure, must beware of the perils that beset his exposed position. He should especially be careful of those who try to draw him into confidential conversation in order to betray his confidence at a later date.

328

Every ambition achieved likewise means an addition to our troubles.

329

With conditions in the business world fostering the ego's over-growth as they do, I have often advised young men of exceptional talent engaged in or entering this world to make money quickly with the special purpose of escaping from it. Then they can give adequate time to the study and meditation and retreat they need for their philosophic interests. Thus they use their business career as an expedient, not to satisfy ambition.

330

Ambition is a good for the young man but becomes a bad when he overreaches himself. For then it is at the expense of others who have to suffer for it.

331

Does he really want the outer things for which he is striving more than he wants the inner qualities they are blocking?

332

He who gains a fortune is born again. He who lives in penurious squalor is as one dead. Those who despise wealth have never known it.

333

When men must struggle for their livelihood to such a degree that they have no energies and no time left for higher pursuits, it is futile to expect them to be fit for metaphysical study or mystical exercises.

334

Those Europeans who sneer at American dollar worship are really sneering at the effort to raise personal standards of living, to improve life on earth, and to provide the body with a worthwhile environment.

Independence

335

Despite Somerset Maugham's assertion that "there is nothing better than to be like everybody else," the commonly accepted and familiar view, the normal and ordinary way of living—these may have to be reversed when the truth hits one's consciousness.

336

Most people submit to the conventions and obey the unwritten laws which in the society or the community prevail at the time. The man who refuses to submit or to obey is manifesting either a disordered mind or an unbalanced temperament, or is showing personal courage in being loyal to a high idea or ideal at whatever cost.

337

We have no plaint to make against convention as such. Every arrangement for human living inevitably becomes conventional as soon as it becomes stabilized. Our plaint is rather against conventions which have become insincere, hypocritical, hollow, out-of-date, blind, or unjust.

338

He has to devise a way of living that will respect these principles without alienating him from the social world in which he has to live. The task may be an impossible one but he must try.

339

To live with men as one of them, yet not to live within their narrow limitations, is his duty and necessity.

340

Let others not mistakenly believe that he has adopted a non-cooperative attitude, has fled from reality, renounced a human existence in exchange for an illusory one in an imaginary world, or deserted the paths of sanity and reason. If he wants to live in comparative outer peace with them, he must make certain outer concessions. It is better to behave as unprovokingly as possible, to hide his deeper thoughts behind a screen, and to avoid being labelled as a religious fanatic or intellectual faddist. It is especially unwise to uncover one's philosophical thoughts before everybody. He must try to adjust himself smoothly to his environment. This is a hard task, but he must not shirk it and must do all that can be done in the given circumstances. He must fulfil his reasonable obligations towards society, must co-operate in turning the great wheel of human activity, must contribute his share in achieving the general welfare; but he should reserve the right to do so in his own way and not according to society's dictation. And because he has outstripped those around him in important ways, because he is already thinking centuries ahead of them, it is unlikely that he will succeed wholly in fending off their criticisms or even in avoiding their hostility. For with all his endeavours to placate them and with all his sacrifices for the sake of harmony, human nature being what it is—a mixture of good and evil, of the materialistic and the holy—crises may sometimes arise when society will attack him. If the inner voice of conscience bids him do so, then he will perforce have to make a firm stand for principles. It is then that he must summon enough courage to do what is unorthodox or to say what is unpopular and display enough independence to disregard tradition or ignore opinion. Up to a certain point he may walk with the crowd, but beyond it his feet must not move a step. Here he must claim the privilege of self-determination, concerning which there can be no compromise; for here, at the sacred bidding of the Overself, he must begin to live his own life. Consequently, although he will always be a good citizen he may not always be a popular one.(P)

341

Let us not betray the good that is in us by a cowardly submission to the bad that is in society.(P)

342

It is only the beginner who enthusiastically and indiscriminately discusses with friends, relatives, or strangers the new teachings or exciting truths which have only recently been accepted by him. The proficient student is also the prudent one. He restrains his feelings against the temptation of telling everyone everything. Thus his ego is checked instead of being displayed.

343

To make a public exhibition of asceticism, to display the peculiarities of one's soul always and everywhere, to cut oneself off showily from the common life, is to be not a spiritual aspirant but a spiritual egoist.

344

It is not in any arrogance that he must be true to himself against the pressures of society.

345

Every man whose activity brings him before the public—be he a politician, an artist, or a writer—becomes a target for gossip, and if because of his spiritual and cultural interests he lives a quiet, almost hermitlike existence, the gossip will turn to misunderstanding and criticism.

346

They see or sense that he never gives himself up entirely to the society in which he happens to be, that he keeps always a certain inward reserve and outward constraint. This puzzles, irritates, or annoys some, or arouses suspicion in others. Thus the seed of future hostility towards him is sown by their own imperfection.

347

The Silence which befriends him gives others a queer undesirable feeling.

348

He who is not content to follow the mob, who seeks to *be* an individual person and not merely appear to be one, needs strength and bravery to resist the mob's pressure.

349

If he insists on a way of life that is unconventional, he must accept the criticism which follows it. And if it is worthwhile he will pay this price quite cheerfully.

350

Among the traditions of Jesus current with Muhammedan mystics, there is one which mentions that the more people reviled him the more he spoke good of them. When one of his disciples complained about this as being an encouragement to them, Jesus answered, "Every man giveth of that which he hath." He who seeks to enjoy the smiles of truth must be willing to endure the criticisms of uncomprehending observers, the sneers of unbelieving ones, the frowns of convention, for he who is not prepared to conform must be prepared to suffer.

351

Mentally he may have to resist the ideas of the community in which he lives when they are thrust upon him through customs, conventions, conversations, and religion.

352

He has to contend not only with the foolishness of his fellow humans but also with the destructiveness of Nature itself, not only with the tendency of institutions and organizations to decline from their best to their worst, ending with the "letter" and losing the "spirit," but also with his own personal weaknesses and shortcomings.

353

Whoever rebels against the majority's view, whoever dares to think and speak independently, must be prepared to endure mental, or even physical loneliness.

354

Tolerance is needed if we are to live with even a minimum of harmony in society. To the philosopher it comes easily as a natural result of his development. But it need not be practised at the expense of the equally necessary attributes of prudence and caution. There is a point where it must stop, a point where it leads to greater evil than good.

355

But be warned that the same power which, *on your side*, brings you into a goodwill relationship with all people also isolates you from them. For it withdraws you from the herd's narrow outlook and petty interests to seek higher aspirations.

356

Independent judgement is an asset if it is sufficiently well-informed—if not, then it may be a liability.

357

He endeavours to live his own life in his own way, as much as circumstances allow and prudence dictates.

358

Where he knows that other persons will not be sympathetic to these teachings, he will be prudent to remain silent about them. Where his friends know of his own interests and disparage them, he will be wise to avoid futile arguments.

359

When he is in the crowded city he will keep himself inconspicuous, lest he draw other men's attention to himself, and with that their thoughts, impinging on his sensitive mind and disturbing its calm.

360

He must not be afraid to be in a minority of one. Millions may be arrayed against the Idea in which he believes. It is easy then to conclude that they are right, he wrong.

361

With those whose minds are shuttered, it is foolish to enter into any discussion, even if they try to force it (in order to show how foolish you are to hold such views). One might as well speak out of the window to the empty air, so it is better to save breath.

362

To live in the world by the higher laws a man must keep it at a certain distance. This may not be flattering to the world but it will give him more serenity.

363

He learns not to waste time arguing about his beliefs or views, not even to explain them to those who merely wish to air their hostility and criticisms.

364

He will have to put up with unthinking and ill-formed opposition from his environment, from friends and family alike. They may become openly alarmed at his deviation from the so-called normal but really abnormal standards which rule them, take fright at symptoms of purification which may develop, and cry out about his impending illness or dissolution and other imaginary disasters. Others, more indulgent, will tolerantly smile at his eccentricity, his fanaticism, as their prejudice will name it. But in the sequence, if he demonstrates the obvious benefits of his reform by abounding health, vigour, and cheerfulness, this opposition may die down and vanish.

365

If it be snobbish to prefer the best in spirituality, in culture, and in art, then we must accept the abusive term of snob.

366

The world is apt to regard these self-improvers as smug and complacent, selfish and conceited, and the world is sometimes right. But it is also sometimes wrong.

367

Just or humble people admire and respect moral superiority, but the others are provoked by it into hostility, for, whether consciously or unconsciously, they recognize that it shows up their own shortcomings. Jesus whipped the moneychangers out of the temple, but the rabbis put them back again and put Jesus on the cross.

368

Pythagoras, gentle compassionate apostle of the bloodless diet, killed by the Crotona mob, had to die for venturing to show a higher ideal—just as Socrates died for shaming his jurors with their inferior ethical standard. Plato was driven into exile for more than twenty years because he dared to teach truth. Above all it was Jesus, put to death for endeavouring to show men a kingdom not of this world, the kingdom of heaven. Thus the roll of light-bringers could be extended: those deprived of life and those persecuted but left to live, and those who escaped despite opposition. How low the level from which the half-animal men have yet to rise!

369

People like to be regimented, so the odd man who abhors mediocrity is himself abhorred. No one may appear different from the mass except at his own peril.

370

It is inevitable that the thoughtful will move ahead of the mass of public opinion. But they must beware and restrain themselves—not too much but also not too little.

Effects of environment, change

371

The belief that a change of city or land may lead to a change of mental condition is not altogether without basis, even though we still take the ego and its thoughts with us wherever we go.

372

Travel is worthwhile if one can visit the man who can make a contribution to his inner life.

373

There are situations in life and associations with persons which try patience. There are environments which appear to imprison him. The natural impulse is to run away from them or to resist them in bitterness. It may be well to avoid continuing the experience if he can. But let him enquire first if he has gained from it the hidden lesson and profited by the hidden opportunity to grow.

374

When a set of physical circumstances or a personal association becomes a source of strain rather than of pleasure, he may consider withdrawing from it. But this consideration should be governed by wisdom, detachment, and impersonality.

375

If changing an environment, residence, association, group, or situation is an attempt to escape the problems of oneself, no betterment can result from it. But if there has been a sincere and sufficient attempt to change oneself while in that environment, then the move may prove helpful. It is a fact that the man who is willing to try will find that even where he cannot master himself just where he is, if he continues his efforts unabatedly, destiny will unfold a new and different set of circumstances or environment where the fruits of his efforts will more easily and more quickly show themselves.

376

He cannot prevent himself taking an interest in his worldly welfare, for he has a physical body and is planted in physical surroundings. To pretend otherwise is either to repeat, parrot-like, what he has heard or read, or it is to be a hypocrite, or it is to exhibit the phase of temporarily insane unbalance which some seekers pass through at one time or another. His spiritual aspirations are blocked, hindered, helped, or promoted by his external circumstances. To see the truth of this, it is enough to take a single aspect of them—the social one. Is it of no concern to him, and will it be all the same in effect, if he has to spend the whole of his life with materialistic men and women who could not even understand what the quest means, or with those who are very far advanced along the quest? Will he not profit more by the latter contact?

377

The consciousness of race acts as a handicap to and throttles their ambitions and suffocates much that is good in them, but, on the other hand, to others it acts as a spur and develops ambition. Why does he continue, for the years of life left him, to put up with the annoyances of being despised by one neighbour and rejected by the other? If people place so much value, on a man's colour and so little on his character, if the mere accident of birth—and he has to be born somewhere, unfortunately!—is to be the sole criterion of one's value without regard to personality or soul, then the quicker he shakes off the dust of this place the better. Why does he tolerate such stupidity? Why not go to some country where there is less or no colour prejudice?

378

Mental attitudes are generated by circumstances, events, and historic changes. They are often what they are precisely because of where they are and what has happened to them.

379

Whatever stays in existence too long begins to assume attributes to which it is not entitled. For it seems completely necessary, quite unchangeable. Its power becomes absolute. Thus the past, so rich a storehouse of guidance, warning, interest, and wisdom when studied with fairness *and in full freedom*, becomes a tyrannical despot. If we are to find its best values and its greatest usefulness, we should take time off occasionally to forget it, to be detached from its rule, and to regard our way of life differently— thus changing our standpoint and its landscape. These periods may be short ones, but their fresh experiences will bring in some corrective balance, their new habits will improve us or widen outlook. Thoughts and things, principles and institutions will be measured, tested, weighed, and revalued.

380

A new occasion offers a fresh start, an attitude which need not be conditioned by his previous ideas.

381
When they are exposed to quite new environments where the opportunities and temptations are also new, it is quite possible that traits of character hitherto undisplayed and even possibly unknown to the persons themselves will respond and appear.

382
Although it is ultimately true that the inner work is the one thing that is necessary, it is sometimes immediately true that a geographical change, or an environmental removal, or an occupational transfer *is* necessary if stagnation is to be avoided.

383
Those who make their home in one place follow the norm; those who live itinerantly do not. If those in the first and by much the larger group have the advantage of stability and the reputation of respectability, those in the second and smaller group gain a kind of autonomy. Among the first are the bourgeois and the professional; among the second, the gypsy and, until lately, the Mongolian and the medieval friar and the Indian *sadhu*.

384
The nomad without a fixed home has to accept the uncertainty and unfamiliarity which accompany each new environment.

385
When the pressures of competition and the kind of people in the environment make a man's moral values wobble, it is time for him to reconsider his situation, perhaps time to leave for other environments or to change the nature of his activity.

386
It is true that there are conventional, narrow, and stiff people who travel like suitcases and learn nothing from their travels. But it is more true that most people absorb something from others and are liberalized by contact with foreign lands.

Cultivate an active attitude

387
Philosophy does not reject human experiences, but it does not yield recklessly to them either.

388
The student should live each day by itself, doing his duty as it arises from the demands of routine existence and accepting its responsibilities; he should leave the future to itself. If the day is lived by the spiritual principles he has learned, tomorrow will automatically take care of itself.

389

He is not asked to admire an attitude towards life which involves weak acceptance of misfortune or helpless submission to unpleasant surroundings. There is nothing spiritual in such an attitude.

390

Hope is the scaffolding of life. But unless the hands go out in action we may stand upon it forever yet the building will never be erected. That is why we who seek for Truth must work interiorly and work intensely amid the common mortar and bricks of mundane existence. Our dreams of a diviner life are prophetic, but we turn them to realities only when we turn our hands to the tasks and disciplines presented by the world.(P)

391

We are in rebellion against all these miserable advocates of the cause of misery who lean weakly on the worn-out excuse of God's will being behind everything and who therefore advise man to do nothing. We have raised the banner of rebellion against all those escapist mystics who defend "do-nothingism" as a rule of life when confronted by world-misery, merely because they themselves feel the bliss of inner peace; against all those Oriental religionists who defend it because they have made a dogma of the unalterability of karma; against all those unscientific metaphysicians who defend it because they regard every painful event as the expression of divine will and wisdom when it is so often the result of human will and stupidity; and against all those monastic hermits who find specious explanations for allowing others, who toil in the world, to wallow in ignorance or to agonize in suffering. The peace felt by the mystic is admirable but it is still a self-centered one; the karma propitiated by the religionist's prayers is ultimately self-earned and therefore must be self-alterable; the divinely ordered events of the metaphysician could not have happened without man's own co-operation. Those who remain inert in the presence of widespread misery often do so because they have not experienced it deeply enough themselves. The innate foolishness and disguised indolence which bid us always bear karma unresistingly and unquestioningly as being God's will, although advocated by so many Indian mystical advocates of lethargy, are denied even by a great Indian seer like the author of the *Bhagavad Gita* and by a great Indian moralist like the author of *Hitopadesha*. The first proclaims to a bewildered seer, "Action is better than inaction." The second, in a discussion of fate and *dharma*, affirms, "Fortune, of her own accord, takes her abode with the man who is endowed with energy, who is prompt and ready, who knows how to act."

Both Indian books quoted here were written by mystics. Yet they reflected this same superior standpoint. Why? Because their authors were philosophical mystics. There is thus a vast and vital difference between the attitudes of unreflective ordinary mysticism and philosophic ultramysticism. Anyone whose mind is not too bemused by personality worship and authoritarian prestige to see this difference may now appreciate why philosophy has a contribution of the highest value to make in this sphere.

392

The circumstances of his outer life must affect the condition of his inner one. But this is true only to the extent that he admits or counters them by his mute acceptance or dynamic resistance.

393

He can let the experience act as an alibi to give way to some weakness or he can use it as a spur to arouse some latent strength. He alone can cross the abyss between these alternatives.

394

When confronted by a formidable situation involving human weakness or expressing human evil, he will choose to affirm silently some great eternal truth covering the situation rather than letting himself be discouraged by it.

395

There are times when boldness is better than caution, when loneliness is preferable to society, and when emotional numbness is more proper than emotional sensitivity. The occasion, the circumstance, the timing are what then matter most.

396

To perform any action in the best way is to aim at the least strain and the most effectiveness and the greatest economy of movement.

397

The occasion, the event, the place, and the person contribute their influence and affect one man more, another less. But if aspiration is to come nearer to achievement, if he is not to be satisfied with a merely ordinary *inner* existence, then there is a point beyond which he cannot afford to let conditions impose the decisive factor, the determining fiat.

398

Neither the over-cautious nor the under-cautious attitude will suit this quest: a delicate balance moving between the two extremes, adjusted by timeliness and circumstances, will help more and risk less. This means that he will not be afraid of using his own initiative yet will be careful enough not to meddle in activities unsuited to him. Decisions have to be made, actions have to be done, and these depend in part on his own characteristics, in part on the outer scene. But personal reactions to life out in the world are intertwined with the quest, even coloured by it. So the Middle Way will show its presence and results in *both* areas.

399
His objective is to let a situation command him when it is wisdom to do so, but to take command of it when it is not.

400
There are times when adverse destiny becomes too much for him. It is then that a humbling acceptance of things as they just have to be is useful.

401
When we learn to accept the terms of our own limitation, and go along with them, we not only gain greater peace but also get more effective action. For to live in impossible unrealizable dreams is to end in futility.

402
When confronted by hard inevitability, it is more prudent to bow your head than to bang it.

403
You may accept the inevitable with bitterness and resentment or with patience and grace. Mere acceptance alone is not sufficient.

404
The indifference toward unalterable or the resignation to unavoidable suffering preached by so many prophets was not preached merely as an idealistic fancy, but, in most cases, as a realizable fact out of their personal experiences. Admittedly, its accomplishment is quite hard. For it depends in part on a complete concentration upon that which suffering cannot touch—the hidden soul. But this is not to be confused with a defeatist fatalism, a false resignation to God's will, or a harsh asceticism.

405
Holding the attitude that God is Supply makes us at one with the Psalmist who sang: "The Lord is my Shepherd, I shall not want," but it does not exempt us from doing our share of the necessary work.

Relations with others

406
The situation of the human being, neither animal nor angel but stretched out somewhere between both, is unique.

407
A forest ranger who had spent his life in intimate contact with wild nature, animals, and trees then retired to city life, whereupon he made a caustic remark which contained a great indictment. He said, "Hell is people." This thought is curiously like that expressed by one of the characters in a novel by Henry James. A man who was dying said to a visitor, "I think I am glad to leave people." Now what is implied by these two statements? It is not that human beings become a source of torment or of suffering to other human beings. Put in the way these two persons have put it, it is of

course not wholly accurate and needs qualification. It would be more correct to say that too many people cause too much trouble for others. If we ask why this is so, we must admit that humans are a mixture of bad and good and that it is only a minority which is striving to strain out the good and to discard the bad.

408

Whoever has dealings with others cannot afford to ignore the double nature of human nature. Failure to recognize it leads to confusing consequences. Looking neither for the good alone nor for the bad alone, but remaining emotionally detached during such an act of recognition, is a philosophical attribute. He who possesses it may hold no illusion about the mixed motives in others and yet still practise goodwill toward them. This must be so, for the primal source of all Goodness inspires him daily and constantly to hold to this practice.

409

Few people are all good or all bad. Few have motives which are not double. This is not to doubt their sincerity, but to explain human nature.

410

This is the final vindication of the practical truth that you must deal with human nature as it is, not as you would like it to be or as you imagine it to be. The man of today lives, moves, and has his being in his personal ego and will continue to do so until he has learned, grasped, thoroughly understood, and completely realized the truth of the illusiveness of the individual self. Until that happy day arrives, it is far wiser to take a human being as he is and simply to place checks and restrictions upon his egoism.

411

We take people too much at their surface value, their present position and possessions, not reckoning the truth that unless we get first into the sphere of thought wherein their minds move, we do not really know them and their real worth. The superiority of the man must in the end triumph over the inferiority of his position.

412

We mean so well but act so ill.

413

Nature has made no two human beings alike. However much he may share his views and life with another person, each man will have his own individual differences in thought and conduct. Hence attractions and repulsions, frictions, and misunderstandings will sooner or later arise between men. Perfect harmony with everybody and in everything on this earth is an unrealizable dream.

414

But this said, we must also accept the higher fact that beneath the egoic differences there subsists the Overself's unity and it is our sacred duty to realize it inwardly while tolerating difference outwardly.

415

It is not necessary for the aspirant to seek frantically any new outward relationships to things or people; these should and will evolve naturally, so to speak, from his own growing spirituality. "Seek ye first the kingdom of heaven, and all these things shall be added unto you." By denying the ego and by frequent meditation all things are influenced for him in ways he cannot now realize. As he directs his mind and heart to the Overself, his character, his disposition, even the outer contacts and relationships will become attuned and re-adjusted.

416

It is better to leave past personal history where it belongs; the attempt to revive old relationships is a misguided one; it becomes either a nuisance or a failure.

417

He will learn to measure the worth of another man or of an experience by the resulting hindrance to, or stimulation of, his own growth into a diviner consciousness.(P)

418

He may find himself planted by destiny among people with whom he is ill at ease, leading to tensions in himself and perhaps in them. Since he has not chosen this mental and emotional arrangement, there is probably an opportunity in it to work in an unaccustomed way on himself for his ultimate self-improvement.

419

It is easy and common to blame others who cross our path or belong to our surroundings as being the provocative cause of our irritability or resentment. But if we forgive them instead and hold them in the thought of goodwill, not only will our relationship with them improve but we ourselves will profit exceedingly.

420

Where a wrong is done us by someone generally we may be sure that the experience represents the expiation of a wrong which we have done to someone in a past incarnation. It is useless to cry out against the injustice of the injury when the cause lies deep within our own history. It is best to put aside the natural feeling of resentment and, understanding as well as we may what it is we are expiating, take its lessons to heart.

421

However virtuous our intentions, we not infrequently work harm to others. This shows that it is not enough to be good. Wisdom must direct our goodness, must bestow on us the capacity to foresee what is likely to ensue from our actions.

422

Every person who is important to him, every relationship that arouses emotion or thought is there for a meaning.

423

Our relations with other persons can produce deep joy or utter misery. If the second result is brought about, we need to amend our thinking, for however wrongly another person may behave there is some reason why he was chosen by destiny to let us feel the painful effects of his behaviour.

424

It is not hard to understand that the varied events of life which destiny fashions for us are devised to develop us by affording the range of experience which educes the response of our thoughts and feelings. But it may be much harder to understand that even the living creatures who enter our range of experience have entered for the same evolutionary purpose. The men women and pet animals who extract affection or aversion from our hearts, calculation or argumentation from our brains, unwittingly serve that purpose.

425

Society exists for the individual. Its high and hidden purpose is to make perfect the men who compose it. This is not to say that it exists for the exploiters and the parasites.

426

If each person could look at his own life not only in an impersonal way but also with philosophic insight, he would perceive the meaningfulness of the happenings in his life, of the relations with other persons, and even the larger backgrounds themselves. All served a higher purpose or fulfilled a higher service, leading him from half-animal to truly human being, or obeyed a moral law such as karma.

427

The more he behaves with kindly qualities towards others, the more will their behaviour towards him reflect back at least some of these qualities. The more he improves his own mental and moral conditions, the more will his human relations bring back some echo of this improvement.

428

Those who claim service of humanity as their only motive lay themselves open to suspicion. Outside the few who have transcended ego—the very few—it is ordinarily the case that every service has to be paid for, and that none is *really* free.

429

We need not be afraid to help others because we are afraid to interfere with their karma. Reason must guide our sympathy, it is true, and if our beneficent act is likely to involve the beneficiary in continued wrong-doing or error it may be wiser to refrain from it. It is not generosity to condone his sin and to confirm him more strongly in his foolish course. But the law of karma can be safely left to provide for its own operations. Indeed it is even possible that it seeks to use us as a channel to modify or end this particular piece of suffering in the other person. To refuse to relieve suffering, human or animal, because it may be an interference with their karma is to misapply one's knowledge of the law of karma.

430

We do not love our neighbour as ourself for the simple reason that we cannot. He loves himself quite enough anyway and does not need our addition. But, this said, we are ready to serve him amicably.

431

When a man's conduct is incorrect, it is sometimes wiser to stop further efforts to help him on the outer plane—however much we feel sorry for him—and let him learn the bitter lessons which he needs.

432

If people would only take care of their own business and let other people mind theirs, there would be less friction in the world and more peace between the nations. The late Bernard Baruch, American financier and presidential adviser, said on his ninety-fourth birthday that the greatest lesson he had learned during his very long life was to mind his own business. For the Quester, with his special aims higher than the ordinary, it is even more advisable not to mix himself up *unnecessarily* in other people's affairs or destinies where he is not really responsible for them.

433

The best way to help the other person who is in trouble is not to get swept away by his feelings and emotions of suffering. It is enough to register them at the moment of meeting, but thereafter one must stand detached if real help is to be given from a superior source. Real help is not sentimentality.

434

Weighted down with the burdens of his own unsolved problems as he is, he will add those of other people at his peril. Only when he has shown himself competent to master his own will it be time to tackle theirs and will he be in a position to do so effectively.

435

It is not that he seeks non-involvement in, or becomes indifferent to, other people's problems, but that theirs, and his own, are now seen from a higher vantage-point and a wider perspective.

436

He will rarely interfere with those who are happy in their opinions.

437

Although he may often see the straight line between cause and effect, between shortcoming in character and trouble in circumstance, he may find it better to practise a prudent reticence. Few like to be preached at.

438

When he travels away from his home, he should go humbly, as a seeker, to learn and not to teach, to meet inspired souls and gain their help rather than to meet students and offer help to them.

439

Over-anxious solicitude for family relatives may not always be helpful to them.

440

Whoever gets caught in the misery and unhappiness and self-pity of a person in distress and lets himself remain in that depressed condition, cannot render as much help—if any at all—as the one who is detached, imperturbable, but compassionate.

Marriage

441

Because the philosophic outlook is all-comprehensive, because it excludes nothing, it must include both the celibate and the marital condition. It recognizes that each has its hour and place in an individual's life.

442

If one man thinks he can get along better alone, he is quite entitled to his view and it may be that his quest requires it. But if another man thinks otherwise and seeks the companionship of marriage, he too must be granted the right to follow his particular expression of the quest. Neither one is an absolute. The married man is not in any way relieved of his responsibility to seek and find physical control, just as the celibate man is not relieved of responsibility for mental control. Nor does this apply only to aspirants. The same liberty must also be granted even more—and not less, as so many misinstructed beginners believe—to men of attainment, masters, and all who have finished their quest.

443

Marriage is not inconsistent with the philosophic path, but it often is with the mystical path.

444

There is no reason to feel that love for a marriage partner is at variance with efforts toward self-evolvement. In its best sense, mutual love is an aid for both to progress and develop as individuals.

445

There is certainly no bar to the highest spiritual attainment through marriage. If the greatest sages of the past have been single (or have lived as single men) this was not because marriage would have interfered with sagehood—for it cannot do so—but because they wanted to keep the external life as free as they could in order to carry out their work as fully and as freely as possible.

446

The necessity of achieving mental harmony and union of ideals in marriage counsels great caution in selecting one suited to be a life-companion. A wrong decision in this matter may be disastrous in every way, whereas a right one will be helpful in many ways.

447

Marriage is a most important matter, and is not to be entered into without a sufficient period of waiting: both persons are better able to check the wisdom of the step in this matter. If it turns out to be the right step, the time-test will see its survival and greater chances for happiness. If it is the wrong step, a feeling of uneasiness will soon develop—proving that the marriage would be based on physical infatuation, and thus could not ordinarily be other than short-lived and unsuccessful.

448

Those on the quest need to know each other quite well before marrying. This means they need to know the other person's negative as well as positive characteristics. Then they have to decide whether they are able and willing to spend the rest of their life living with those negatives, that is, whether the positive qualities which attract them are strong enough to overbalance the opposite ones.

449

It is the duty of married questers to teach one another. This not only includes the teaching of what each has learned of truth from guides, books, and life but also the pointing out of characteristics which need correction, nurture, development, or eradication. Who else can know these details so well as the person who is the life partner, the constant observer of the other's actions, the intimate sharer of thoughts and moods? But such pointing out must be done calmly, impartially, lovingly, or it will fail in its purpose.

450

There are many who will deem the philosophic attitude a callous one. This is partly because they misunderstand it and partly because they identify themselves too strongly with their emotional nature. It is inevitable that, with the growth in philosophic understanding and practice, the affections grow larger and deeper too, while their visible demonstration becomes calmer and more equable. Since philosophy is more concerned with realities than with appearances, more concerned with being than with seeming, merely conventional responses in emotional speech and expected action mean less to its practitioner than the silent inward existence of love. He does not feel any need to give continual evidence of what he feels in order to reassure the other person, who unconsciously fears that love may pass away at any time. Nor does he want to take such possession of the other as never to allow her to leave his side, always holding her in a narrow, confining domesticity.

451

It is certainly possible for a married man to attain enlightenment, for historic records supply the proof. My own contacts with both Oriental and Occidental illuminati confirm it. But it is possible only if his marriage is more than a mere animal mating. How far this discipline should go will depend on how far he wants his enlightenment to go and how much he is willing to subject himself to the necessary conditions. Marriage, like other normal human relationships, need not be denied if a man is ready to take the chances and risks it involves and if he chooses a partner who is likely to promote his quest rather than obstruct it.

452

The married relation offers an outlet for human affection and human tenderness. In this sense it becomes one of several opportunities which life offers for the disciplining of the ego. This applies both to the daily throwing together of two human personalities as well as to the consummation of the marriage in sex.

453

The serious obligations and powerful distractions which come with marriage constitute two of the reasons why celibacy has so often been recommended or enjoined for those who would scale spiritual heights. It is held that if they are to gain the leisure and strength needed for such climbing, worldly ties must be loosened and animal feelings must be controlled.

454

A sage's marriage cannot dim to the slightest degree or in actual fact whatever goodness or purity he may have, except in the eyes of those ignorant of what sagehood essentially is.

455

If marriage is taken to be a license to be sunk in sensuality then it is certainly a bar to this quest. But if it is recognized as a call to self-discipline, just as freedom is in a different way, it need not be so.

456

Young people, whose heads have been turned and whose emotions have been titillated by the romantic drivel of so many foolish novels and so many fantastic films, are likely to have exaggerated ideas about the happiness which can be derived from sex, courtship, and marriage. That is, they see only the bright side and do not know that a dark one also exists.

457

It is not enough for two persons to get married because they love one another. They must also suit one another.

458

It is wrong for fanatics to condemn marriage, for it may provide a person with the means of working out the psychic and moral problems with which he or she is faced.

459

That is a worthy love worth finding which enables both the man and the woman to grow and fulfil themselves. But that is mere passion, a poor substitute for love—and sometimes not even that, but mere social or economic convenience—which maims and cripples the inner being of one or the other person. A marriage in which wife or husband is spiritually suffocated is an undesirable relationship, a waste of precious, unregainable years. Yet fear of all the risks and troubles which a break would involve embalms the situation, when faith in the power of Life (God) to support and provide for a right decision would bring growth and fulfilment.

460

Immature persons can only make a marriage that is itself immature.

461

Where there is an element of doubt concerning a marriage problem, it is better to wait before plunging into action, to ruminate over past blunders and profit by them. The issues may slowly become clearer. If it is right to marry a particular person, the sense of rightness will remain and increase. But if it is wrong, then either the feeling of such wrongness will slowly manifest itself or the person will be taken away or some other hindrance will block this action. This refers, of course, only to one who is under direct guidance of a master or directly intuitive to his higher self.

462

Marriage is a risky experiment for those who have any degree of advancement along the path. The conditions under which it may succeed are hard to satisfy, but occasionally such successes occur. The higher degrees of the Quest call for a total renunciation of everything earthly, animal, and human. This must be inwardly attained, it must be real in thought and feeling, after which it does not matter whether or not there is outward renunciation in any direction. A mere external asceticism solves no problems but it is helpful to beginners. That other self of the aspirant which is his divine soul will, as and when its presence becomes vivid and intimate, become also the Most Beloved. No man or woman could give him its equivalent in satisfaction, however much he loves and however much that love is returned. He may marry if he wants to, but it must be with the clear knowledge that marriage is unable to yield him more than second-best happiness.

463

It is excellent to look for a mate among those with the same spiritual ideals and educational status as yourself, but it is not enough. What about physical fitness, hygiene, and compatibility? What about emotional harmony, blending, and suitability?

464

A man who marries a girl less than half his age inevitably becomes a father figure to her. It is not fair to her nor prudent of him to enter into such a marriage, even if she ardently desires it.

465

When a husband informs his wife that he has decided to find his happiness elsewhere, she can fight to hold him against his will—which is pardonable—or she can accept it because she thinks of his happiness first and her own second—which is divine. Time is the only healer of her wounds but they will surely be healed. When the storm of hurt feelings goes completely, a great peace will arise in her. Then she will see that she did the right thing to gain her own happiness too, quite apart from doing the right thing as a seeker.

466

Whether one sort of breaking marriage can be mended depends on three factors: the actualities of the wife's character, the possibilities of her husband's character, and the predestined fortunes of both. Such a situation needs generous forbearance, foresighted patience, deeper understanding of human nature, and, above all, emotional self-control. The suffering wife should secretly pray for her husband's spiritual welfare, not hysterically and sentimentally for his return to her. Let her be assured that if she can bring herself to adopt an unselfish attitude in this matter, if she will repay evil deed by good thought, and hurt feeling by forgiveness, she will not lose in the end.

She must not waste her strength in emotional self-pity, but rather try to build up a reasonable attitude. And if she is a quester, she must not forget the lesson behind her marital experience of not staking all her happiness on somebody else. She must first look within for it, and then only can others give some of it to her. She herself must make the most important contribution to her own happiness.

467

When a separation, divorce, or break-up of relationship comes between two persons—be they friends, spouses, or associates of some kind—it may appear sudden in happening but it already exists on the subconscious plane. The event merely brings it to the surface.

468

If a man is single or a widower, it is understandable that feelings of loneliness will often enter into his consciousness. But the aspirant must remember that it would be unfair both to a prospective partner and to himself to enter into an unsuitable marriage. It would only hurt him and bring unhappiness to his partner. His emotion needs to be disciplined, and he must wait for a partner suitable to his development and aspiration. If he has already had the marriage experience, he should consider seriously whether he really needs to remarry at all. He should weigh in the balance, from the standpoint of his own personal character and circumstances, whether its advantages and limitations outweigh the advantages and limitations of devoting the remainder of his life entirely to the quest of truth. The married life is compatible with these spiritual objects but not easily so.

469

Socrates once declared, "I am a man and like other men a creature of flesh and blood." He was married and had three sons. Yet this did not prevent him from attaining a lofty wisdom and the highest intellectual clarity and magnificent moral rectitude.

470

If marriage is regarded as a sphere of self-discipline—and especially of that discipline which seeks to transmute and absorb the sex urge—why should philosophy object to it? For parenthood will then become a means of honourable service, not a gutter of grovelling sensuality.

471

A simple equation will clear the sentimental nonsense which hazes the whole subject. How can two imperfect creatures give one another a perfect happiness?

472

One proof that marriage is no bar to enlightenment was reported to me at the time of writing this paragraph. A young married woman in the condition of early pregnancy with her second child had been practising meditation for short sessions at irregular intervals, as her circumstances did not offer opportunity for more. There was a feeling of frustration and nothing came out of the practice. One night she had retired to bed but not yet fallen asleep. Suddenly, without any preparation or warning, a mystical experience rapidly developed and lasted for about one and a half hours. "It was the most beautiful condition I have ever known—utter fulfilment, peace, contentment, and love for all," she described it.

473

For young people under twenty years of age to undertake the risks of emotional romantic marriage without consultation with, and respect for, older and more experienced persons, is somewhat improvident. To do so with little acquaintance and knowledge of one another is still more improvident. And without accurate horoscopes plus knowledge of each other's spiritual status, the risks keep increasing. Too often the young fall victim to lust, which is taken to be sufficient basis for marrying.

474

No human relationship, not even the most romantic of marriages, is always and continuously free from its jarring moments, its boring ones, or its annoying ones. The two members have their limitations; they are still finite and, in some ways perhaps, frail human beings. They still make mistakes sometimes and are sorry for them afterwards.

475

It is only romantic fancy or wishful thinking which creates the common belief that there is only one person who is suited, made, or fated to marry some other particular person.

476

The solemn man and the frivolous flighty woman are fit mates for marriage provided they are not extreme opposites. Temperaments may oppose, but must not be too extremely opposed. The finest successes of Hymen come from the coupling of circumferential opposites who possess a central unity. This cryptic phrase calls for interpretation.

477

The need of a mate is only an idea after all. Treat it as such and you will be better able to control it.

478

If he is on the quest, he will at least take care that she only shall be invited to share his life permanently who is not only in harmony with his temperament and aspiration, but also aware of his defects and limitations.

479

The finer side of marriage—companionship, partnership, affection, and considerateness—is not less important than the sexual side.

480

The woman who is to mate the evolved man should arouse a love for which body and mind, heart and intuition are all in perfect accord. This is an ideal, of course, and he may not be able to find its realization. But at least he will know in what direction to seek.

481

Marriage would then be allowable but restricted to the twin purposes of providing companionship, with its mutual service, and furnishing physical bodies for a few incoming egos of spiritual seekers. This form of modified marriage would reject lust.

482

Children born from such a consecrated marriage will necessarily be superior children—not in every way, but in some special way, and certainly in fine moral character.

483

The craving for a mate of the opposite sex is the unconscious feeling of the need for someone to balance him. It may, and does, get mixed up with other needs, but this fundamental one remains.

484

So many couples are yoked but not united, married but not mated.

485

That there is a connection between romantic delusions and subsequent neuroses (usually after marriage) can often be seen. This was also seen by ancient classical philosophical writers. Marriage can become a monotony, perhaps a boredom. Where has the romantic love gone? How much better would all have been if both had looked at, the realities from the beginning? If the facts of life are looked at, the romances change their appearance: they are mostly not eternal, often changeable; the beauties fade away, the ecstasies turn to pain or worry, the attractions to repulsion. In short, the end is disappointment. The deification of the allegedly loved one may be changed to its opposite—vilification—so self-deceptive is the whole experience in many cases, so misunderstood are the physical symptoms and so adolescent are the emotional ones.

486

Marriage is as much a partnership as any business one is.

487

The marriage which is either unsatisfactory to one of the partners or unhappy for both of them may always take a different turn if regarded from a different viewpoint—a higher one.

488

Women have too often allowed financial necessity to cause them to enter an ill-suited marriage, as men have allowed sexual difficulty to cause them either to do the same or to evade any marriage at all.

489

Tibet's most famous guru, Marpa, was happily married. Not all the most esteemed gurus and not all the best disciples are necessarily bachelors.

490

It is said and sedulously propagated by married couples that the bachelor is a selfish man. The truth is that a married man is not less selfish. His wife and children are merely extensions of his own ego.

491

Socrates suffered from a scolding, nagging, and bad-tempered wife. One day she gave him a farewell parting by pouring dirty water on him from an upper storey while he was in the street. This caused his friends to complain to him and ask why he endured it. Instead of complaining, he pointed out to his friends that this gave him the impetus, and provided some of the means, to become a philosopher.

492

In its highest meaning, love is simply mental and emotional empathy.

493

Marriage brings about an interfusion of destinies and auras which may have important consequences. If the partner is actively opposed to the ideals and ideas of the quest, the aspirant will find it much more difficult to follow its star, if not be indeed completely halted for a time.

494

To flee into marriage in order to escape from loneliness is not the highest motive for marrying, although often a common one.

495

When the student who is truly seeking to make progress on the Quest is confronted by an obvious failure in daily life—in marriage for example— he or she must realize there is a karmic lesson involved here, one which has not yet been properly learned. It would be extremely unwise for such a person to contemplate marrying again, before the important meaning of the message has been thoroughly taken to heart. So long as there remains any uncertainty in the matter, so long is it best to wait. Time alone is lost by such waiting, whereas the mistake of venturing blindly into another marriage might cause far greater grief. Guidance will come to the troubled seeker if he or she prays for it—and is patient.

496

When one has suffered through an unhappy marriage, a second venture into matrimony should be approached with utmost caution. If one has any doubts whatsoever, it is best to wait. It is the duty of each to be certain that it is the right step. A little patience is all that is needed. Even in the case where both individuals are students on the Quest, and are anxious to follow it together, waiting will only confirm their hopes and strengthen their chances for happiness.

497

The difficulties of rearing children, the irritations of family life, and the monotony of much married existence are problems which most people have had to face at some time or other. They must be mastered, however, for one cannot desert duty without suffering pangs of conscience. This mastery calls for much endurance and more gritting of teeth, but the road can be smoothed greatly if he will try to cultivate something of that spirit of inner detachment which the Overself is seeking to impart. To be able to stand aside from the self occasionally, to treat his problems as though they were someone else's, and to refer them at critical moments to a higher power for solution, is of enormous benefit in every way. In this connection one should read chapter 11 of *The Secret Path*.

498

The wife of one who seeks to follow this Quest has the opportunity of bringing a happy future to herself in helping to bring it to him. She also may walk beside him on that greater path of spiritual attainment to which all are dedicated. She will then get from marriage not only what she hoped for but much more besides.

499

It has been said in *The Quest of the Overself* that a married couple should grow together in companionly worship of the Light. If they do this they have found the basis of true marriage, successful marriage. In India a newly wedded couple are pointed out in the sky at night, by a Brahmin priest, a star called "Vashistharundhati." It is a pleasant little ceremony and supposed to be auspicious. For Vashistha was a great sage who lived thousands of years ago, Arundhati was his wife, and their marriage was a model of its kind in perfect conjugal happiness, wifely devotion, and mutual spiritual assistance. The ancient records link this star with this couple in their legend. Now the invention of the telescope has enabled us to discover that this star, which is the middle one in the tail of Ursa Major, or the Great Bear, is really a double star; that is, it consists of two separate stars situated so close to each other as to appear a unit to our naked eyes. Moreover, it is also a binary star; that is, the pair revolve around a common centre of gravity. Can we not see a wonderful inner significance in the old Indian custom? For the marital happiness of Vashistha and his wife was due to their having found a common centre of spiritual gravity!(P)

Politics

500

The wider our experience of this world, the more must be our realization of the truth that it is the spiritual outlook and moral attitude which really determine a society's socio-political form and active course.

501

Every problem that harasses mankind today was first born as a spiritual problem and only later grew into a political or economic one.

502

Unless there be a change of moral ground, a shift of ethical standpoint, a new spiritual approach, the hopes aroused by political changes, shifts, and innovations will be false ones.

503

Like Lao Tzu, Socrates held a low view of politics. He did not believe it had any room for complete honesty, justice, and truth. It was a clash of egos and a struggle for power. His opinion of the multitude, their ethical standards and quality of correct judgement, was equally low. But he believed it possible, given enough time, to lift them up and persuade them to follow better ways. This was, however, a matter for working upon a few individuals at a time, not publicly and politically but privately.

504

The thing that really matters in the life of a nation is the quality of its leaders, the character of those who guide its destinies. Young men may not realize that enthusiasm alone is not enough, that character always does and always will count, that he who fits himself for greatness will see whole kingdoms delivered into his hands. Inspiration brings fortune in its train and inspired teachers will always rise.(P)

505

When those who occupy high position, who rule, lead, advise, instruct, and inform, are unfit for their position and lack the needed qualities, attributes, and consciousness, then society falls into disorder; its levels get mixed up so that words, names, designations, and terms become empty, distorted, or misleading. And as a result of the disorders which break out, violence, hatred, and even wars—civil or international—afflict the world.

506

No system is likely to be better than those who administer it, while it *is* likely to be worse.

507

It is no adequate reason for the continuation of a bad system to say that there are good people working under it. They would work all the better under a good system.

508

Rudolf Steiner rightly taught that the true spiritual things could flourish only in freedom and that they need to be self-administered, independently of the state or political interference.

509

Where groups, sections, classes are unable to co-operate for the common welfare, which includes their own, then only ought a government step in to control them—not before.

510

If the world fails to stop another world war from eventuating, it will be because highly centralized government is as much a colossal failure as highly organized religion. Some organization in both spheres is inescapable, but it is also destructive of their true purposes when carried to an autocratic point.

511

The Western world needs a third economic form, one that will make a place for the spiritual purpose of living. Communism will never do it; capitalism has the chance to do it, although it has yet to make use of its chance. With all its faults, capitalism does possess a moral code of sorts whereas communism possesses none. From this lack comes the worst that could befall a people unfortunate enough to be the victim of communism's promises.

512

The third economic form will arise not only through the two older forms first modifying and then synthesizing one another, but also through the imperative needs of our own time forcing our inventiveness and creativeness to add their special contribution.

513

Why not accept different forms of ownership within the same national organization? Why not let public socialism and private capitalism compete with each other? Why force all people within a single ill-fitting form?

514

No two people are alike in mental reach, moral stature, technical gifts, and practical capacity. Many differences of thought, character, capacity, and physique exist and will always exist because the variety in an infinite universe will always be infinite. There are no two things or two creatures alike in Nature and consequently there is no equality in Nature!

515

All men are not born equal in ability, and any state built upon the thesis that they are is built upon a false foundation. However, all men should receive equal good treatment and equal opportunity; but that is a different matter.

516

Democracy is not the ideal form of society, but when a hierarchy becomes rigid and selfish, it is just as imperfect, just as much a failure.

517

There is far too much friction, abuse, recrimination, and even hatred among the members of the different political parties in many countries. All these are negative qualities and therefore represent a negative aspect of democracy. They are of no help in any way to the people, yet so long as democracy lasts there is no likelihood of their being eliminated.

518

A culture like democratic culture which brings knowledge and information to the masses but fails to bring them refinement of manner or taste or speech and also fails to lift up their moral standards is a very incomplete one.

519

People nowadays speak of democracy in the same reverent way as formerly they used to speak of aristocracy and of monarchy. In each of these three cases we will find that such forms of government and civilization had both a good side and a bad side and when the bad side became too heavy then the old form began to decay and eventually to be destroyed. We all know the merits and advantages which the waves of democracy have spread around the world, but what about the demerits—such things as coarseness and shallowness, ill breeding and vulgarity, obscenity and tawdriness in art?

520

Politicians—more interested in their own careers than in sincere public service, ambitious to gain their personal ends, unwilling to rebuke foolish voters with harsh truth until it is too late to save them, forced to lead double lives of misleading public statements and contradictory knowledge of the facts, yielding, for the sake of popularity, to the selfish emotions, passions, and greeds of sectional groups—contribute much to mankind's history but little to mankind's welfare.

521

The pooling of common ignorance in democratic debate does not remove that ignorance.

522

The multitude has the least capacity for truth, the lowest moral and intellectual development, the shortest sight into consequences. Mass rule leads downhill.

523

It is proper and kind that the proletariat should have their claims and demands heeded, that what they call "social justice" should be adequately available. But it is wrong to heed only theirs and ignore other classes, especially the middle ones.

524

If you want the best—that is, a meritocracy based on quality—then you must abandon democracy based on quantity.

525

If we need a higher class, an elite, let us have it. But let it be based on merit, on outstanding contributions or services, not on the accidents of birth, position, money—and let its members be themselves, not labelled with gaudy titles which make spineless people fawn like sycophants in their presence. In this Aquarian age, archaic hereditary dressed-up aristocracies posturing theatrically have no place.

526

The business of minding our own business comes first, that of attending to our neighbour's comes next. The need of understanding the truth about ourselves is much more important than that about others. Our own endless political worry is one consequence of being too concerned with somebody else's political duty.

527

Since all men are obviously not equal, it would be unwise to give all men equal rights. But every help and facility ought to be given to enable those who want to improve themselves to do so.

528

If authority has judged wrongly, misused power, or served selfish interests, these things should be scrutinized, plainly seen for what they are, and correction or reform demanded. But these are insufficient causes to reject all authority altogether. For when it is the voice of the accumulated experience, mental and physical, of many centuries, it has something to offer that is worth at least unbiased examination. But when it is unscrupulous, barbarous, or tyrannical, then it justly earns the nemesis of rebellion.

529

When Plato came to comprehend that politicians could not improve the character of the people by their activities, when he saw that politics did not conduce towards pursuit of the good, he gave up meddling in it altogether and turned in another direction.

530

He must allow others the same liberty of thought which he asks for himself, the same freedom of expression and the same right to a private opinion, but these liberties are valid only so far as he seeks the common welfare along with his own. If the others do not do so or do so under the form of dangerous illusions which are harmful to society, then he has a right to ask for restraints to be put upon them.

531

The lack of personal integrity, the satisfaction with paltry triumphs over other politicians, and the misuse of words to their almost utter falsification help to explain why modern democracy, with all its benefits and achievements, has led in the end to a chaos and a menace which darken the whole world.

532

If suitable conditions and helpful environments do not exist in a society for enabling the higher purpose of life to be fulfilled, for encouraging the studies and practices of philosophy, for preparing a way of life suitable for religious devotion or seeking truth, that society is materialistic. A wiser government and people will try to establish the proper conditions to lift the whole nation and to make arrangements that will meet the outward needs while not obstructing the inward ones as they do so, to create more opportunities for those who wish to answer life's spiritual call and improve themselves.

533

The failures of democracy are evident enough, and not at all surprising when it allows the same political power to a simpleton as to a sage.

534

An incursion into active politics by a man who is neither ambitious nor naïve, who is sincere, honest, and really seeking to serve the common welfare, must in certain countries end in dismay or withdrawal, disillusionment or cynicism at its corruption or hypocrisy.

535

It was not merely because a people needed a leader that the institution of monarchy came into being. It was also because they needed to develop the quality of veneration, to acknowledge that there was someone or something higher than themselves. It was only another step from looking up to a king to reverencing the highest power—God.

536

If the World-Mind governs all things and all beings, if this is the monarchy of God, then the monarchy of earth would be the best form of government through being in conformity with it. The king's title would not only be a worldly honour, but also a spiritual one. Monarchic authority would be a sacred copy of the divine pattern. The democratic distribution of power to each person equally would be the very contrary, hence an impious and atheistic act. "The divine right of kings" would then be a phrase full of meaning, truth, justice. All this has validity only if the monarch is himself in harmony with God, if his character reflects God's goodness, if his intelligence expresses God's wisdom: otherwise it falls to the ground. All this implies that the king is truly inspired from above, is fully aware of his Overself. If he is not born so, his duty is to strive to acquire this condition as quickly as possible. If he is unable or unwilling to acquire it, then there is no justification for a monarchical constitution's claim to superiority over a democratic one!

537

It is safer to entrust the welfare of a nation to the co-operation of its best men than to a single man, however wise well-meaning and honest he may be reputed to be. History and experience offer the best practical test of this statement's truth, but the doctrine of the relativity of ideas also underlines it.

538

It is not generally known that Ben-Gurion, the former president of Israel, was for many years closely interested in the study of Indian philosophy and in the practice of hatha yoga. Perhaps the broadening effect of his study tempered his attitude towards his country's enemies and uplifted his aims for the nation? In an interview he once said, "The chief danger facing Israel is not Arab hostility, it is Levantinism—we must not go in for pure commercialism. We must make this country a centre of culture and education."

539

The mistake which so many monarchs fell into, and which led in the end to the virtual downfall of monarchy, was that they regarded their subjects as persons to be exploited rather than as persons to be served.

540

The principle of adoption seems less faulty than both the principles of monarchy and republicanism. It allows the existing ruler to choose his successor, provided the Senate confirms his choice. None of the three systems is perfect, but this seems to offer more than the other two.

541

Society begins with the individual, goes on through him, and its higher purpose is fulfilled in him alone. Political thinkers, guides, and leaders who reject this truth will never escape from the immensely difficult problem into which their half-true, half-false concepts must incessantly lead them.

542

We do not find in authentic history any reliable record of sage-kings, although myths of prehistoric China speak of them. Perhaps the nearest to this ideal combination of knowledge, wisdom, goodness, and power appeared in persons like Ashoka of India. Certainly with such government many problems and evils associated with familiar forms—such as democracy, aristocracy, monarchy, and dictatorship—would vanish.

543

We have to restore the supremacy and demonstrate the practicality of the moral ideal in both political and economic affairs.

544

Those who shout constantly for freedom need to be reminded of its corollary—responsibility. If they use their freedom to behave antisocially or destructively then they are no longer entitled to it.

545

Those who demand freedom most, the violent revolutionaries, may be the least free even when successful, for they are slaves to their own violence, to the passion which propels them.

546

Plato's striking assertion that "until philosophers are kings or kings philosophers cities will never rest from their evils—no, nor the human race" is often quoted and indeed is provocative enough to be worth quoting. But its exact truth is open to question. For if the great prophets like Jesus and Buddha, invested with higher power in virtue of their special missions as they were, could not make a single city rest from its evils, not even all their followers, how is it possible that men not so invested could do so? What they could unquestionably do would be to limit the area and strength of those evils as well as to provide conditions which would tend to discourage their future growth. Just as the world was saved by the work of Jesus and Buddha from becoming measurably worse than it did become, so would it be possible for the king-philosophers to bring about a similar result in their own ways and lands.

547

The rancours of politics do not breed the calm judicial atmosphere in which problems are best solved.

548

It was insane to allow freedom to those who seek to destroy freedom.

549

To make the destiny of all the men women and children in any land depend on the whim of a single individual who has shown no sign of special fitness for such responsibility, no moral or mental superiority, no administrative skill or personal courage, is to combine folly with injustice. A would-be ruler—be he king or commoner—must prove his worth or go.

550

Independence is for those who are worthy of it. Freedom is for those who can be trusted with it. Without such fitness both drift into anarchy.

551

The hypocrisy which stains the United Nations is visible and notorious, at least to those who know a little of what goes on behind the scenes. Peace does not come out of moral insincerity. Nor does fear provide a permanent foundation for it, however large atomic bombs may become. Peace has vanished too many times in the past simply because it cannot stay too long out there in the world when it is not present in here, in men's hearts. History has tried all the varied forms of government and still has not solved its own problem. The way is known but the will is feeble.

552

It is not enough to agitate for public socio-politico-economic reform without, at the same time, seeking for private and personal reforms.

553

Statesmen who possess competence but lack character may be able to serve their people in some ways but will dis-serve them in other ways.

554

Beware of politicians. The more they protest their devotion to ideals, the less should they be believed, even though by constant repetition of glibly spoken words the belief is now theirs too.

555

We have seen many politicians appearing on the world stage in our lifetime and appealing to narrow human selfishness, but few wise statesmen.

556

Each political party represents some sectional and therefore selfish interest. No party seems to reconcile these conflicting interests by seeking the welfare of its nation as a whole.

557

Although I do not hold with a hereditary aristocracy and a hereditary royalty and would prefer to favour a meritocracy, one must live among the masses in the midst of their commonness and vulgarity and semi-animality to understand why the higher classes insist on separating themselves from the lower ones.

558

The notions of democracy lead people to delude themselves about facts which stare them in the face. The masses form a lesser breed of human beings and no amount of political propaganda can alter the fact that there are individuals who belong to a superior breed.

559

Lycurgus, the wise statesman, in the constitution he drew up for Sparta, counterbalanced power: the Senate against the people, the king against both.

560

Most people are the victims of suggestion and are easily impressed by (and deceived by) appearances. They confound bigness of size with greatness of soul; they call that nation "great" which has a big empire, often won by ethically dubious methods. A big pack of wolves is not something to admire or respect.

561

That government will do better which combines the vigour of youth with the knowledge of age.

562

Fitness for high social rank or public office is not necessarily transmitted by heredity, but if the parents already possess it, their offspring is more likely to receive the kind of upbringing which will favour his acquisition of such fitness. This is one argument for caste. But the numerous failures show that no guarantee is possible.

563

"Who should lead the leaders?" asked Emerson.

564

It is natural for a politician to operate for the benefit of his own nation, even to the detriment of other nations, to blind himself to their rights in the effort to secure such benefit.

565

Those who believed that human goodness would automatically follow economic improvement and political reform have had their complete refutation in recent history.

566

Those who believe that the United Nations should still be kept despite its imperfections ought to read Shirley Hazzard's full documentation of its uselessness in her book *Defeat of an Ideal*. The harm done by this dangerous and hypocritical piece of self-deception outweighs the good.

567

Reactionaries have been responsible for much human misery but then revolutionists have been responsible for just as much.

568

One danger of these fanatical movements is their gradual erosion of conscience and their rationalized eradication of pity. This they justify, and cover up, by pleading "political necessity." In the beginning they take a man of high ideals, through which they attract him. In the end they have degraded him into a monster of cold-blooded heartlessness.

569

If the United Nations is to be renovated inwardly, the precondition is to regenerate it outwardly by bringing it back to its proper home—small, pacific, neutral Switzerland.

570

The subterfuge and intrigue, the selfishness and double-talk, the manipulation and friction which come with democratic leadership in the political party system, inhere in the system itself. For politics is a struggle for power.

571

The firm idealist who scorns compromise and the bold reformer who scorns discretion have their place in society, to which indeed their very stubbornness acts as spur or goad.

572

No one who accepts philosophical principles could also accept the political doctrine which denies spiritual values, cancels human rights, advocates the conferring of arbitrary totalitarian power upon the small group, and uses violent, unscrupulous, and ruthless methods of achieving its aims.

573

To achieve prominence is one thing but to achieve power is another.

574

The clash between totalitarian ideologies and democratic ones, between humanistic and religious ones, between intellectualist and intuitive ones, has created a void in modern cultural life which can be adequately filled only by philosophy.

575

Bolivar, the great South American liberator, died disappointed and said that to serve the people was to plough the ocean.

576

Oscar Wilde was not led only by his customary habit of exaggeration to observe that "those who try to lead the people can do so only by following the mob." Follow the career of most politicians and the truth in his statement will become clear.

577

Spiritual aristocrats are disdained by the democrats and communists of today. They feel no need for deriving support from spiritual sources. Men may talk of unity and write of brotherhood, but they still work to exterminate each other.

578

They have all been tried, these different forms of government—monarchy, oligarchy, democracy, and despotism—in some century or some country, and in time they have all been found wanting. The notion that one or the other is an advance is falsified by history.

579

How right was the Russian writer Maxim Gorki: "It is necessary to lift oneself above politics. Politics has always a repugnant character because it is inevitably founded on the lie, the calumny, and violence." One could add "cynicism" and "hypocrisy."

580

Rasputin was not the only evil genius around the ill-fated Russian czar. There were others, chief of whom was Badmaev, a Tibetan black magician and witch-doctor. There were also several mystical idiots.

581

With his pure love of truth, the genuine philosopher is politically nonpartisan. He does not tie a political name-tag to himself for the reason that he wishes to be scrupulously honest in his attitude, which means that he wishes to see all around a problem whereas a party view is one which wishes to see only a single side of a problem—the side which best serves its own selfish interest or best pleases its own irrational prejudices.

The problem of what path social advance shall take is complicated and a successful solution is hard to come by. The desirable is not always the practicable. And because the rightness of the solution of a particular social, political, or economic problem must rest ultimately on its philosophic sanction, let economics not be too proud to take counsel from philosophy, which seemingly lies outside its province but actually lies deep within it. Inspired forethought is our need. Philosophy is alive and can contribute something here in its own way. It is perfectly relevant to the grave issues of today and indeed of any day. Philosophy can offer a statesman the right general attitude to take when confronted by situations, events, and problems. It does not offer him the particular policy he should follow in each case but rather a serene light which can illuminate every human and social problem. Nobody overnight becomes an encyclopaedia of all human knowledge or an expert economist or an expert agriculturist simply because he becomes a student of philosophy. It is unable to provide a blueprint of a new world order with the ease with which an engineer's draftsman might provide a blueprint of a new machine. For you cannot deal so easily with uncertain human factors and intractable human selfishness as you can deal with wood and steel. But it can indicate the direction in which the new world order must travel if it is to travel rightly. And that is all we propose to do here. We decline to predict what world order is going to arise during the next decade. But we can indicate the principles of wise or foolish actions and safely venture to say that such-and-such results will occur if you follow or obey these principles. Philosophy can advance only general proposals, a broad ideology upon which practical endeavours should be based. How these principles are to be applied and the technical details to which their elaboration will lead are matters which must be left to the experts themselves. It is not philosophy's task to supply detailed plans but only to supply a few fundamental principles upon which those plans may be worked out by specialists.

582

Men of fine sensitivity and high ideals do not usually feel at home in the atmosphere of active politics. They would need pressure or persuasion before acceptance of such involvement.

583

Do not look for political success in a man who is cultivating the sagacity which discriminates between appearance and reality, who is practising goodwill unto all, who would serve all sections of the community rather than the narrow selfish interests of a single one, who is swayed neither by the plaudits of the crowd nor by the censure of parties, who rejects from his speech the double-talk and hypocrisy which are such virtues in the political profession.

584

The unethical degradations which admittedly exist in the business, political, and social worlds cannot be made to disappear by running away from them but rather by the uplifting influence of individuals with superior personal character entering into them.

585

The world needs less politics and more spirituality. Politicians deal with effects and do not go to the ultimate root of most matters, that root which lies in human ignorance and sinfulness. However, politics plays a necessary part in modern life. It would be impossible in this era to do away with it anyway. The remedy is to purify, uplift, and inspire political activities. This can be done by those who have attained some spirituality, through their descent into the arena, if they feel suited to it.

586

It is not for us who are called to the philosophic work to meddle directly in the turmoils of politics, for usually such effort leads to nothing and brings the philosopher criticism or persecution. If, however, he has some useful ideas to contribute, it is better to do so indirectly, through other persons, than to directly get into the action himself.

587

We cannot legislate the human race into a change of heart. But we can legislate conditions which will be less obstructive to such a change than existing conditions.

Education

588

In its readiness to heed the new evolutionary impulse affecting the human ego, the twenty-first century will reorient the spirit behind the educational system.

589

The next century will not support an educational system which encourages cruel competitive egoism in place of co-operation among pupils, which freely punishes them because it rarely understands them, which sets up examinations as a criterion of culture when they are merely criteria of cramming, which tyrannically attempts to mold all minds alike to the same degree within the same time instead of making allowances for ability, individuality, sensitivity, tendency, and difference of innate capacity to progress, which overdoes its tougher disciplines and underdoes its gentler ethics, which worships the dead past and remains superciliously irrelevant to the contemporary scene, which vainly loads memory instead of stimulating and satisfying curiosity, and which has no place for a few minutes of mental quiet in its daily progress.

590

It is the first and fundamental business of education not to stuff the mind with memory-taxing catalogues but to train it to think rightly; not to ignore inherent defects of character but to correct them; not to set students adrift on the sea of adolescent or adult life without an accurate chart but to supply it. If any system of instruction does not do this, then whatever high-sounding names it may bear it is certainly not education. How many have found that their education did not begin until the day after they left school or college?

591

The next century will affirm that a true education must include spiritual education, that without its presence in the curriculum, pupils will step out of school into life only half-educated and only half-prepared to meet its struggles. It is not only a well-informed mind that education should develop but, just as much, a sensitive and balanced one. An education which leaves a man completely ignorant of his higher nature is surely not a finished one. He should leave the classroom with a mature approach towards the major experiences which he is likely to get. And how can it be called mature if he has not developed a mature understanding of himself, with a resultant mature handling of himself?

592

Education ought to be a threefold affair: the acquisition of information and knowledge, the acquisition of skills and training for a livelihood, the improvement and refinement of the quality of the human being. Under this last head I put spirituality.

593

Education should not be just for training the workings of the mind, giving it sufficient information: it should also be for making a finer person and a higher character.

594

There are certain influences upon children's early years which are too important to be left to chance. So much of their characters and happiness, destiny and health depends upon their experiences during those early years. It is the duty of those who control homes, organize schools, and lead churches—all three—to give children some help in shaping a proper outlook in life, some knowledge of the higher laws, some guidance in simple meditation practice.

595

To give full freedom to the young—whether infants, teenagers, or those near adulthood, whether in home upbringing or educational arrangements—is to abandon wisdom, prudence, and practicality. Their possibilities of losing their way, making mistakes, and harming themselves and others are merely increased.

596

The young must be taught to govern themselves, and how this is best done. They must be instructed in the higher laws and especially the law of consequences, so that they may avoid punishing themselves. They must learn the power of thought, the harm of anger, the benefit of surrendering the ego. They must regain the old-fashioned virtues of good manners, tolerance, and respect for the older generation.

597

If education were touched with spirituality, in its real and not sectarian meaning, the teenager would grow into maturity under influences and in surroundings which would improve character, discourage bad tendencies, instruct in basic higher truths, and train in controlling one's own mind.

598

Who can measure the great tide of unnecessary misery which the examination system has brought into being amongst children? The child who has made a poor show feels that he has brought down upon himself the displeasure of his parents, the ridicule of his schoolmates, and the dissatisfaction of his teachers. Nor is this all. Failure to pass this torturous ordeal creates inferiority complexes, anxiety neuroses, emotional warpings, and torturing fears which may mar the child's entire adjustment to his life afterwards. Moreover, the competitive character of his experience tends to arouse jealousy and even hatred for the more successful children.

We have made a veritable fetish of competitive examinations. Students are not really taught; they are not allowed to study in the true sense but are forced to cram books and notes. The examination system inevitably forces them to become mental automatons, whereas a less mechanical system would encourage them really to learn. Pupils who cram their heads with "stuff" and merely repeat it in examinations do not necessarily develop their minds. The ultimate goal of education ought to be not learned pedantry, not the gaining of a diploma or degree, but the understanding and mastery of life. The mere stuffing of information should be quite subordinate to this goal.

The coming education will be based on new and higher principles, its efficacy tested less by the miserable system of competitive academic examinations which grade powers of parrot-like remembrance than by powers of enlightened intelligence. The general outlook of whole nations will be healthfully altered.

599

It may be that in the hard world outside school walls and college precincts, public examinations play too useful a part to be discarded; but in the gentler world within these walls and precincts it should surely be enough if scholastic merits were evaluated on the basis of past records of work done, enthusiasm shown, and interests manifested, records kept for this special purpose. The elimination of the competitive system need not mean the elimination of measurement of progress. Marks, percentages, and form-gradings have their practical worth so long as they are not used to play off one pupil against the others.

600

Anyone may launch himself on the sea of life without having learned navigation, without having been equipped with the needed training, knowledge, and qualifications which fit him to assume life's responsibilities—be they choosing a wife, rearing a family, following a profession, or keeping his body healthy. A true education would prepare the young adequately from kindergarten to university in the art of how to live. The prevalence of so much avoidable distress, misery, ignorance, and evil shows up this lack. But the teachers, the masters, and the professors themselves need to be taught first.

601

An education which does not end in some spiritual understanding and some moral elevation is incomplete and imperfect. But this cannot be accomplished within the customary school and college periods. The higher education of the human being can begin only after his mind has matured and only after he has had some social experience—that is, in adult life. This is why it is equally important that grown men and women should go on learning, should never cease to be students, and should turn the experiences of life into lessons.

602

An education which teaches people to think, but only to think materialistically; to live, but only to live for the old ideas which have brought civilization to the verge of destruction; and which entirely fails to teach them to intuit, is an imperfect and incomplete thing, or rather a subtle illusion.

603

The school which omits any mention of the Quest, the college which gives no hint of the higher consciousness in man, the university which lets philosophy remain an unknown, disregarded, or merely speculative subject—these do not adequately fulfil their function of preparing students for life in the world outside their walls.

604

That education is incomplete which does not instruct men in the art of spiritual communion, which does not teach them the need to and the way to control thoughts, which carries them through a course in physics but fails to continue into metaphysics, which informs mind but does not reform character.

605

Going to school is one thing, getting educated is another, although they coincide at times. Learning from a teacher is preparation. Learning from life in the world is observation. Learning from oneself is intuition.(P)

606

We live in an age when false statements are passed off as true ones and when deceptive values are passed off as real ones, when the dissemination of knowledge is getting more and more into the hands of those who are themselves too young to wisely instruct the young, too unbalanced to help the characters of the young, and too theoretical to be able to pass on really practical information which will help their students.(P)

607

It is not enough for parents to protect a child—they should also encourage and stimulate it to awaken spiritually.(P)

608

Good manners should be taught in school from the most elementary to the highest university level, as was done in China when Confucius' influence was predominant.

609

Promptings to righteous living need not depend on the commandments of supernatural revelation alone. Religion ought not to be the only guardian of moral values. Education should also fill this position.

610

It is not enough to provide a young person with a technical education which will enable him to earn his living. There is also the question of what he is living for. Is his life to have any higher quality and value? Is his mind to have any higher awareness than a merely animal one?

611

The young are not usually taught that negative thoughts and feelings may bring suffering and trouble to themselves and those in their environments. Still less are they shown how to avoid, discipline, or sublimate such thoughts and feelings.

612

Children imitate their elders as far as they can and to a limited extent. If, therefore, parents want better children—better in behaviour, in character, in themselves, and in their relationships with others—then they must set constructive and desirable examples.

613

The conditions which surround a child, an adolescent, and a young adult during the period of preparation for responsible existence are very important. The impressions and suggestions, the training and forming he or she receives from them contribute heavily toward the final personality. Parent and teacher are giving forth more than they know.

614

Our universities turn out educated people in ever-increasing numbers, but they do not necessarily turn out wise people.

615

Why should the universities teach only the humanities and the sciences, but fail to teach a single student how to become a full human being? Why do they not impart the only science which deals with THAT WHICH IS? How many have told me that during the few minutes of a short Glimpse they feel that more worthwhile knowledge came to them than they gained in all their years of formal education in school and college!

616

"The academic people think they know everything already," Jung once said sarcastically. To which I would add: that is because they have never recovered from the effects of education. The higher the education the harder it is to recover.

617

It is clearly the parents' duty to transmit to their children enough moral values to protect them in later life. But if the children, through the inheritance of unruly tendencies brought over from former lives, reject those values, the parents are blocked in their well-meant effort.

618

The individual character grown upon the tree of rebirth must appear by maturity—indeed it begins even to show in the infant—and no mother or father, however loving, can stop the process. But both parents can do much to bring out the better characteristics and to weaken the worse, just as a conscientious gardener can assist his plants.

619

What does it mean to be a human being? The *full* answer to this question is not taught to the young (as it ought to be) because few parents, teachers, and religious ministers really know it by experience.

620

To educate is to elevate; if a school or college fails to do this, its balance has been overthrown, its work has become one-sided. And if a church, temple, or synagogue fails in its worship to generate reverence towards the unknown God, rather than to things, it also is unbalanced.

621

The young are either uncertain, if they are modest, or too certain, if they are arrogant. In both cases they have yet to learn how to separate fact from opinion—a faculty which may come only after long development, or even not come at all.

622

No system of education can be a complete or an adequate one if it omits to teach young persons how to meditate. This is the one art which can assist them not only to develop self-control and to improve character but also to master all the other arts through mastery of concentration. When their minds have been trained to concentrate attention well, all their intellectual capacities and working powers attain the most individual expression with the least effort.

623

The loss of influence by the priests has been balanced by the increase of power by the educationists. It is the teacher who should give us what we cannot get from religion. But does he?

624

So long as the young are falsely taught to identify the historic greatness of a nation with the successful aggressions of that nation, so long will violence, crime, and selfishness spoil their characters.

625

Where is the practicality of an education which lets the young enter life only half-ready at best? For they know only one side of the universe—the physical; barely two-thirds of man—the physical and the intellectual parts; and little or nothing of the divine in man and universe. How little they know, for instance, of the troubles which passion, when unbridled and ungoverned, brings them. This does not refer to the physical troubles nor even to those of human relationship, for these are visible enough, but to the unseen psychic troubles inside themselves.

626

The education which fills mends and exercises bodies may suit its purpose, but the education which, in addition, inspires is infinitely superior.

627

An upbringing which supplies children with no truth, light, virtue, or faith in the higher power behind the universe, which passes on to them no spiritual help or strength, is reproachable.

628

An education worthy of the name would fearlessly include comparative religion. If it taught nothing more than the folly of intolerance, it would do much; but it does more—it helps the search for Truth.

629

Although this argument applies only to a part of the question where education in philosophy is concerned, to this partial extent it does pertain:

"If we think them (the people) not enlightened enough to exercise (power) the remedy is not to take it from them but to inform them by education."—Thomas Jefferson, 1821

630

Education will place less emphasis on selfishness-breeding competition between individual scholars and more on tolerance-breeding progress of all the scholars. It will cease basing itself on the old error that all of them start alike and equal, and begin to base itself on the older truth that all of them start at different points and unequal grades. It will be more effective because it will recognize the operation of this universal law of repeated embodiment through successive earth-lives and hence recognize that unrestricted competition in the schoolroom is a cruel and unjustifiable thing.

631

Equality of opportunity is something which the modern demand for social justice is achieving rapidly, but this ought not to mean that children with more developed minds or higher evolutionary status should sit alongside those with less developed and more primitive minds in the school.

632

True education will nurture noble character rather than egoistic calculation, foster sharp intelligence rather than routine memory, train the student to the kind of technical work he or she likes to do and can do, and teach things of lasting value rather than force useless ones into the mind.

633

The futility of our lives is partially exemplified in our preparation for them, for our education attacks every problem but the most important: How to live? In the feverish overdoing of contemporary body-worship, too much time and honour have been given to sport and athletics. A transfer of some of this energy to the development of higher things has now become overdue. We must first decide what the primary object of education is to be. Does society thrive best on the information it has crammed or the virtues it has displayed? Should it not rather possess both while placing its emphasis on the second?

634

The young masses need to be taught the significance of courtesy, the importance of good manners, the value of refinement, long before they are taught the name of Chile's capital city.

635

Insofar as young men and women in their twenties behave like immature adolescents in their teens, with lamentably low standards of conduct, their upbringing is faulty and their education incomplete.

636

That is no bringing up of children which fails to bring them up to seek betterment of self in the inner sense, to admire virtue, strengthen character, and improve manners.

637

To be properly educated it is not enough to be well-informed and well able to think; one's potential talents and faculties should be brought out and developed. Such an education, although it begins with a school, can only continue all through a lifetime.

638

Any education that does not teach us the truth about ourselves, about the world, and about life is mis-education.

639

What is the use of educating so many young people's heads when we leave their intuitive natures absolutely untouched, uncultivated, and unused?

640

There is no true growth in our institutions because there is no true growth at the centre of our being.

641

Let religion learn to adjust itself to science and let science learn to adjust itself to philosophy, and let art learn to adjust itself to all three. Then we may look hopefully for a true education in our schools and colleges, a true life in our homes and workplaces.

642

If the young are not brought up to behave in a civilized manner, they are not properly brought up at all.

643

Higher education is necessary if we want to cultivate the higher mental faculties. The ordinary and elementary kind of education does not do this.

644

We are not sufficiently informed about the meaning of life and not sufficiently concerned with the purpose of life. In our ignorance we deify the machine and destroy ourselves. In our indifference we lose all chance of gaining peace of mind.

645

It is a striking comment on modern university campus activity that the students of ancient India were forbidden to take part in worldly affairs. Such activity properly belonged to the next (householder) stage of their careers when, instructed spiritually and morally in duties and obligations, they could take a constructive role in society.

646

The process of education never ceases, for beyond kindergarten and college there is the school of life, and everyone must attend it whether he likes it or not.

647

It is a widespread error which says that young birds who have reached a sufficient age are pushed out of the nest by the mother so that they may learn to fly of their own accord and live their own independent lives. This happens only in the case of the eagle and the swallow. Almost all other birds, when they are fully fledged, get out of the nest by their own power, persuaded partly by hunger because the food is no longer brought to them and partly by the persuasive inducements of the mother's call from a nearby point.

648

Each of us has been endowed with intelligence, determination, and ability, so that we may use these in order to grow spiritually—and to learn how to properly care for ourselves and others.

649

If in their public contacts with others they behave like half-savages; if they eat corpses as if they were half-cannibals; if they sneer at real art and support a meaningless coarse and ugly pseudo-culture of half-barbarian tastes: then after leaving university, college, or school they ought to go elsewhere to correct or complete their education.

650

We see young men sent out from the seminaries, ready to become ministers of religion. It is presumed by them and certified by their teachers that they see the truths of religion and will impart them. It does not occur to them, much less to their teachers, that they have been blinded, that they see only other men's opinions and beliefs, put into hard dogmatic form.

651

Education possesses a magic which we cannot afford to despise. What Hitler did to the hearts and minds of millions of young Germans through his grip on the system of public education was a miracle only to those who do not understand how amenable the young are to the influence of instruction and to the ideas sown in their minds. The war will not have been utterly valueless if it teaches the world to divert some of the money which has hitherto been spent on armaments into the channels of education.

652

Education cannot transform a child into what its former earth-lives have never made it, but a spiritual education can certainly modify its baser attributes and enhance its better ones.

653

Education will recognize that the study of philosophy should occupy the last and highest place in a complete course. But it is precisely this study which our present education sees no use for. The young need philosophy no less than the old, for on the threshold of starting life, with its varied possibilities and hard problems, they feel how useful some guidance can be. The time to save a man is not in his old age, after he has lived, but in his young age, before he has lived. It is then that he is most susceptible to moral guidance, most suggestible by nonmaterialistic teaching, and most imitative of good conduct. Later is often too late. The idea and practice of spiritual development ought to be introduced into the schools and colleges. How to do this and not be blocked by obstacles offered by sectarian religion is the biggest problem.

654

The world will change, and change for the better, when we put our schools in order, when we educate our children less in geography and more in unselfishness, less in history and more in high character, less in a dozen other subjects and more in the art of right living.

3

YOUTH AND AGE

Reflections on youth

Among the young there is a section which, if it could be convinced that there is a higher purpose in life, would respond to the call. There is also another section which would not respond because it is stupefied by life, passion, and, especially, negative feelings.

2

Young persons, whose enthusiasm is fresh and whose minds are open, especially need to become convinced by these teachings. In this way they would not only lay one of the best possible foundations for their future, but also be of the greatest possible service to others.

3

The young do not know, but some among them want to know. They want to know why they are here and what is the purpose of their lives, how they are to conduct themselves, and whether or not there is a deity. But for all this they need guidance and they need instruction. They come more quickly with faith to a teaching than their elders do, and that which could be their uplift could also be their downfall. For they are more easily misled than their elders. Those who know and can ought to do something to assist them.

4

Those who come to this quest in their early years—with all the hopes, enthusiasms and energies of youth—are lucky. But they have also the naïveté, inexperience, imbalance, and unrealistic expectations of youth.

5

A new type of youngster has been coming into incarnation since the war—or rather types, for there are good, bad, and mixed among them. They are different from the earlier generations. Here and there one finds open minds with wider outlook who are seeking Truth and that are not limited to their background, their environment, or their traditions, but imbued with a willingness to look to the Orient also.

6

Youth rightly refuses to be overwhelmed by tradition but wrongly refuses to take up its share of tradition.

7

Contemporary youth has been born into a world where for the first time they can see as a definite possibility destruction of life upon this planet, including human life everywhere. Inevitably and naturally they protest, some very violently, against this immoral misorganization which their elders have brought about.

8

Those of the young who fiercely reject all restrictions which hamper their freedom because they want to be themselves, to keep their individuality, are right in a blind unseeing uninformed way. They are free to be their *best* selves. Until they recognize this truth they need control, from within and from without.

9

Youth would be better advised to sift out and preserve whatever spiritual values may be found in the past and combine them with the best material values of our own day.

10

The young have had courage and honesty but in losing faith they have lost discipline and replaced society's old follies with new ones.

11

To young idealists it is among the important things in life to seek for its secrets, to question why they are here, and not to stop until there is some kind of answer.

12

Somewhere between youth's vital exuberant faith and age's blasé withered sleep there is the right attitude. Somewhere there is a state of mind which lacks youth's faculty of self-deception and rejects age's pessimistic summing-up of it all.

13

With the young, theories necessarily take the place of experience; with the old it is the reverse; with both there may be a foolish unbalance.

14

Although I deplore the condemnation of everything bygone, everything old, which is indulged in by so many of the young today, I agree with them that new times may bring new forms of inspiration and that the Truth, the Reality, does not necessarily have to be tied to tradition or look heavy with age or be stiff with the shapes given to it by our forefathers; it can be new, fresh, vivid, original. I include under this heading not only religious and metaphysical matters, but also artistic ones.(P)

15

Too many of those who rebel against the old forms, whether of society, art, thought, or politics, demand new forms vociferously—but why should the new be worthier than the old? It may be, but it is not to be welcomed merely because it is new. It is to be welcomed when it gives a chance to be better than the old.

16

The idea of authority is hotly contested by the young, who fail to see that it is just as necessary as the idea of non-authority or freedom. This is true whether it is imposed on us by the higher laws governing existence or by other persons who are qualified to do so or even imposed by ourselves in the form of ideals and standards.(P)

17

Where traditional views no longer conform to contemporary knowledge and needs, adaptation, sometimes even reform, must be brought in wisely. The older persons, fearful of change, resist it. So the pressures of life use the younger ones, who are more open to it but who often move too hastily, too far, and too unwisely. But they are a necessary counterbalance until a new generation arises which learns, accepts, and understands the World-Idea and seeks to live in harmony with it.

18

In the end it will be to the good that so many of the young are scrutinizing the values and institutions of the society in which they are born, that they are asking troublesome questions, and that they are concerned with the ultimate ends of all these activities. Most of us who were born in an earlier generation may deplore and criticize the violence, the folly, and the unbalance with which this re-examination (and its accompanying protests) is being made, but the need to explore new ways is plain.

19

It is when he is close to the period of puberty that these oppositional tendencies get strong enough to plainly assert themselves. From then on, the presence of inner conflict is felt as a feature of the moral character.

20

Of what use is it that a young man shall have the admirable strength of a lion if he also has the stubborn foolishness of an ass and the undisciplined passions of a goat? Balanced growth is better.

21

Life is stretching before the young person as a wonderfully interesting adventure, and the future is his chance to bring out all that is best in him.

22

The eagerness to acquire social position and to accumulate worldly possessions is more likely to be found in younger than in older persons.

23

The young feel too fresh, too alive, to concede that they also will grow old, feeble, haggard.

24

That period when he is half-youth, half-man is a dangerous one for a growing person. For the passions of anger and lust appear but the reason and willpower wherewith to control them do not yet develop.

25

If the young are to judge aright, they must call in and consider the experience and intellect of the old to help them. This does not at all mean that the old are to judge for them. On the contrary, the young are entitled to criticize severely and scrutinize cautiously whatever advice they receive. Too often, the old have lost vision and dropped idealism. Too often, only the young possess these important attributes.

26

While young, their minds are conditioned by the limitations of their elders, by the moral level of their times, by forceful appeals to passion and emotion uncountered by reason or experience.

27

The young wish to free themselves not only from outworn ideas and modes, which may be a good move, but also from what they consider outworn virtues, which may be a bad one. The qualities of character and the patterns of behaviour which society esteems are not all to be rejected.

28

The young experimented with turning their inherited way of life not only upside-down but also inside-out. The results have taught them to be cautious.

29

Some of us have gone a little way beyond the cup of youth, but have not gone so far as to taste the bitterness that rises into the life of all who desert the simple instinct of reverence which walked beside them in the childhood years.

30

The young advance eagerly toward the embrace of life, the old withdraw from it.

31

As the old questions about existence—whether of man, the universe, or God—clamour in the mind for answers, a conflict goes on inside the young and educated about what they are to do with their lives.

32

The proper attitude for a young person not too far from the threshold of adulthood is to keep his mind open, not shut in dogmatic slogans, too often themselves the result of half-true, half-false suggestions received from other minds.

33

It is one of the special services of youth to prod its elders into action, and to spur a trend or reform into faster pace.

34

It is particularly the young who ought to feel the wish to better character and ennoble life, the desire for self-improvement.

35

It is right that a young man should want to rise higher in his chosen career, should struggle for the best and strive for the Ideal.

36

The young are more likely to hold these new ideas and generous ideals, and hold them enthusiastically. They are virile enough to count action as a twin inseparable from thought.

37

Authority, against which the young rebel, has its place however much those who filled that place in the past abused it and misused it.

38

Past traditions may contain knowledge based on experience: they should be scrutinized, sifted, and tested, not ridiculed and rejected merely because of age.

39

It is a valuable part of a young person's earlier life to seek out the adept and the sage, to take advantage of the opportunity of sitting in contemplation with them, and to question them about the Way and its Goal.

40

The young experiment, seeking thrills, excitements, adventures—using the body, the passions, imagination, drugs, sports, contests, music, and noise. A few respond to worthy ideals, others to debased ones. The greatest adventure—the quest—has its adherents too but too often they are led into semi-lunacy.

41

Driven by passion and deluded by romance, the young will have to drink their wine and have it turn sour on them often, until they weary of the repetition and turn away to a correct balance.

42

These young dissenters from the establishment, whose methods procedures and practices are so often naïve childish and amateurish, are yet in a number of cases pioneers of new ways to come, of the movement towards the Overself. On the other hand, among these dissenting groups there are others who manifest evil characteristics and instead of leading towards the spirit, they are leading towards degradation and materialism.

43

Too young to understand either himself or the world, too inexperienced to perceive the illusions and traps in life, he easily falls victim to powerful leaders who are really misleaders or to agitators whose aims are solely destructive or to religious prophets whose person and message are half-insane.

44

Only stupid or insensitive persons will use a right saying such as "clothes do not make the man" to support an action such as wearing trousers with one leg black, the other white. Such bizarre dress may be fashionable among certain members of the younger generation today, but it is also expressive of unbalanced, bizarre minds.

45

If we want to win the young to any cause we must appeal to their emotion and imagination, to their capacity for enthusiasm, and to their willingness to make experiments.

46

One may admire those young people who refuse to fall into line with those modern ways of earning a livelihood which they call "the rat race" and who prefer to drop out of it. But merely to drop out in a negative way and do nothing further or constructive about the situation is no advance on the conformists and leads to sloth or idleness. Others have tried to organize the dropouts by groups, into communes where they practise co-operative living. Most of these have a short life and are then abandoned, but at least they represent an attempt to be constructive. All this shows that a new kind of economy is needed but has still to be found.

47

It is to be hoped that many fine young people who are facing great hardships will become the pioneers of that new age of practical spirituality which advanced spirits ardently desire to see inaugurated.

48

We all laugh at the tradition that the man of self-supposed or obvious genius must make tracks for Chelsea if he lives in England, or for Greenwich Village if he abides in the United States; must wear his hair a little longer than the Philistines, knock his head daily against a garret ceiling, and be satisfied with bread and cheese until Fortune picks him out as her favourite. We laugh at this, I say, yet the young man may not be such a fool as we commonly think. That rich and rare enthusiasm of his youth may come from Something higher than his conscious self; these brave, if bitter, fights with a mammon-centered civilization may receive urge and stimulus from the Spiritual Warrior within.

49

Sometimes, if guided by real inspiration, naïve innocence and high-flying idealism marry successfully; but more times, if they are inspired by emotion alone and are quite irrelevant to the facts of a situation, they do not.

50

Philo sadly noted that only a few of the young men of his time took philosophy seriously enough to heed its counsels and study its wisdom. True, they often went to lectures (since this was in Alexandria), but, he complained, they took their business affairs with them, so that what they heard was not listened to properly or, if listened to, was forgotten as soon as they made their exit from the hall.

51

The human being cannot be kept forever in the child state, neither physically nor mentally, neither in the home nor in the church. This must be recognized if we are to have fewer problems, less friction, more understanding, and more harmony.

52

There are shortcomings in every area of society. But this is not reason enough for joining the ranks of those who would precipitate chaos, destroy society, and, they fondly hope, start afresh. Students who follow such leadership would find themselves, in the end, completely misled. For what would follow would not only be a new and equally large set of shortcomings, but a cruel tyranny which would necessarily enforce the changes. But this is no excuse for society to remain static, to resist the penetrating renewals it needs.

53

Throwing away the accumulated knowledge, the truths, the skills, the quality, the forms, and the values inherited from the past, merely because they are traditional and aged, does not necessarily provide the young iconoclasts with creative power and inspiration.

54

Their elders do not move quickly enough to alter society to youth's satisfaction—hence its violence. But it is the elders who have the experience, judgement, knowledge, and power, even if they lack the will. Change will come, but the two classes must get together if it is not to come through catastrophe.

55

The culture, the education, the arts and styles—yes, it must be said, even the religion—inherited from the past belong to the past. The young need a new world, a better one, a new way of life and thought, even a new diet in food and drink.

56

Our sympathy goes out particularly to young seekers. They are perforce inexperienced in the ways of the spirit and the ways of the world. They are often bewildered by the contradictions and differences between schools of thought. Their enthusiasm is warmer and their idealism more generous, which makes them more liable to errors in thought and blunders in conduct. Their need of guidance is both evident and urgent.

57

The Stoic teaching that passion should be controlled by reason does not appeal to today's younger generation. But its merit remains.

58

These young street-hooligans who "cosh" harmless old people or rob small shopkeepers with violence are savages dressed up in the garb of civilized beings. But they have not even the advantages of tribal laws and taboos and standards that savages have, for they have no upbringing, no manners at all.

59

It is the lot of most young people either to be wanting to enter that transitory emotional condition which is falling in love or to be trying to.

60

The Angry Young Men, who write bitter pieces about squalid environments and personal frustrations, see no spiritual joy in life, no divine harmony back of the universe.

61

The young, with their passing enthusiasms, their undiscriminating evaluations, and their unconsidered decisions, should avoid irrevocable commitments.

62

Misled by coarse materialists into hatred, violence, and destructive activity, the idealistic young fall into error and confusion.

63

In today's world, adolescents have a confused and sometimes even dangerous outlook. Not a few new excitements come into their being; the taste for emotional, intellectual, physical, and sexual adventure disturbs their balance.

64

Do not ask from a child the intellectual comprehension which only a grown-up person can give.

65

It is good that the young are trying to work out ideas and paths for themselves. We must praise their independence. But it is not good if they express smart cynicisms at the expense of their elders merely because of the difference in age. It is worse if they make savage attacks on others who follow traditional, orthodox, or conservative customs and, especially, conservative good manners.

66

The limited character of the conditions under which most humans have to live and the adverse character of so many of the experiences they meet with, the millions of hearts filled with tormenting restlessness and frustrated longings and the millions of heads filled with uncertainties and strivings, the inescapable orbit of pleasures followed by pains and of attractions succeeded by repulsions, preclude the attainment or retainment of real happiness. The unsatisfactory final character of life's pleasures and the disappointments in the expectations it fosters are not so apparent, however, to the inexperienced young as to the well-experienced aged. Nevertheless, we have yet to meet the man, however young and enthusiastic he may be, who is fully satisfied with what he has got, or who is not dissatisfied because of what he has not got.

67

"O son, though thou art young, be old in understanding. I do not bid thee not to play the youth, but be a youth self-controlled. Be watchful and not deceived by thy youth." This advice is from *Qabus Nama*, an eleventh-century Persian book of conduct. It was written as instruction for his son by a prince on the southern shore of the Caspian Sea.

68

We elders have something to learn from the younger generation today, as they have a lot to learn from us. It is among them that sympathetic reception for higher knowledge is mostly found today.

69

A time comes to turn from youth and become a man, to put aside sloppy sentimentality and look at the hard realities which must be lived with.

70

It is proper for the young to be ambitious, to develop their potential capacities and improve their personalities. But they should not be left with the idea that this is all that life requires from them.

71

There is both good and bad in the spirit of revolt which so many students show. The good is a challenge to seek truth, an alarm to wake up from moral sleep and mental sloth.

72

Youth—and in some cases it extends into the thirties—with its inexperience, naïveté, imaginativeness, romanticism, and immaturity—easily falls into illusion, glamour, or a sloppy sentimentality.

73

What the young do not know is that while they may revere or worship some older person for a special talent, or romantically fall in love with some girl for her beauty, to live with the one or the other in close association for many years may prove an unpleasant experience.

74

He is too fastidious to accept the unwashed dirty clothes and bodies, the jerky slangy careless speech, the crude, often rude, arrogant ill-bred manners of the boorish, without some feeling of repulsion. After all, even Lao Tzu was a protester, but he still remained a refined gentleman in manners.

75

Once past the age of puberty, it is to be expected that young persons want experience, for they know that this is the period of initiation into life's possibilities and of preparation for adulthood. But through their very ignorance they fall more easily into the lures of drugs, promiscuity, alcohol.

76

They know what it is to be young. They do not know what it is to grow old.

77

But the generations move on and these young persons will become old ones.

78

If he has a protest to make, let him do so in a civilized manner. Being young does not excuse him (any more than does being old) from the requirement of normal decency, that he conduct himself properly when among others, with some measure of self-control and self-restraint.

79

The ancient civilizations of China and India traditionally respected, even venerated, the aged. Such was the high value assigned to experience. But modern civilization has reversed this attitude, denounced its older generation, and let its younger ones take the lead. The less experience, the more honours! The defiant ones, the angry ones, the rebellious ones, shape our thought, clothes, ideas, manners, morals.

80

Youth with its vigour gets needed action, with its hope formulates needed changes.

81

The young man who has not yet been ambushed and captured by ambition and sensuality is susceptible to enthusiastic idealism.

82

Neither a tame conformity nor a wild rebelliousness is helpful to most youths.

83

If the young lack the quality of reverence, is it not because nothing and nobody within their experience so far has seemed worthy of it?

84

If so many young people reject the moral codes which they have inherited as well as the social aims which are put upon them, it might be worthwhile for society to practise some self-criticism.

85

It is the instinct of the young to seek satisfaction of their passions and emotions untempered by caution and undisciplined by prudence.

86

I am with the young in their revolt against the limited concepts of a civilization which does not know or care about the dangerous and undesirable goal toward which it is moving. But I leave them when they become either parasitical drifters, unkempt and unclean, or violent destructive protesters who naïvely imagine that anarchy and chaos will automatically be followed by a state paradise.

87

The picturesque appellation of American slang to these young fugitives from the whole educational-economic system—"dropouts from the rat race"—implies a mentality of negative criticism of modern society which usually is sterile. Such persons take as alternatives an aimless existence of drifting, hitchhiking, drugs, sex, petty theft, or other things. *Sadhus, fakirs,* monks, nuns, and hermits may also be fugitives, yet their reaction is positive and affirmative. They have replaced the lost aim in life by what seems to them to be a higher one, by the cultivation of the soul, by the labours of self-purification and holiness or by the exploration of the spiritual consciousness. Some even devote themselves to the service of humanity in some form. All accept, at least theoretically, a moral restraint absent in the other group.

88

If the irate youngsters among us feel so strongly that they have something to give society in leading the way to reform or renovation of varied activities, we ripened elders have also something to give—what they lack but what their proposed changes need. We know for a start, what is impracticable. We know, where the pitfalls are. We know the difference between well-conceived proposals based on the facts of life and the other kind. We have learned, or had to learn, to live in society with responsibility.

89

The young need guidance, it is true, and so need to accept the authority of elders who have had more experience until they can replace it by their own. But they ought not claim this freedom prematurely or in its totality when they are only partially ready for it.

90

Whatever a man's work be in the world, whether he be close to the earth—and hence Nature—or far from it in an office, his life was never intended to become trapped only in that, concerned only with that. In a confused way, half-blind but instinctive, this is one of the promptings behind the violent protest and even rebellion of the postwar youth.

91

Let the mass of those who disagree with society's goals and ways protest in their own young rebellious manner, but the better-balanced will not turn to such destructiveness. They will set up a constructive attitude, a positive manner, and produce practical affirmations rather than sterile negations.

92

Today the adventurous young are uncovering the texts and truths which lie outside the boundaries of official schooling, but they are also—alas!—wading into marshlands where dubious practices and cults take their energies and minds.

93

Balance is a quality which youth seldom shows yet sorely needs.

94

The younger generation not only insists on understanding but also on feeling. Hence their interest in psychedelic drugs.

95

We see the young too often misled into embracing erroneous, distorted, or illusory ideals. It is pathetic, but they are usually too insistent on buying their own experience so they must pay the price.

96

People talk of the innocence of a child, but some children are so vicious that they will pull the wings off a captured fly.

97

The young are easily caught by superficial slogans and illogical arguments because they lack the patience, the balance, and the mental equipment to look beneath slogans and arguments.

98

The young are tired of bloodless sermons and dead observances—they demand living truths.

99

To deny the worth of traditions altogether, as young rebels and protesters, wrongly in some cases and rightly in others, so often do, is to deny the value of the very things whose use makes the denial possible: the experiences, skills, crafts, creations, knowledge, labours, and environments now inherited.

100

There is too much destructive criticism among younger people, too little positive thinking, too much scavenging and debunking.

101

A stirred and awakened section of the people, mostly young, protest against the pollutions of air, earth, water, and food we suffer from. What of the degradations of character too?

102

The demolition of society is sought by communists; of the materialism which supports both capitalist and communist societies, by idealists. For materialism, especially when allied to technology, mutilates the human beings caught in it.

103

We make so many mistakes, especially when young, through sheer inexperience that it is not fair to ourselves to accept the blame for them.

104

Our generation has seen many women and young men come nearer their own. It was right and reasonable that masculine tyranny should go and that senile governance should be overthrown. This long overdue and much welcome advance is admirable, but it does not justify going to the farther extreme of romantic idealization of anyone and everyone merely because he is young and she is a woman. The danger of this species of thinking and this course of action, which have always led in the end to disaster, is that they still infatuate young, shallow minds. From the silly notion that the old would make no mistakes, we are in danger of swinging pendulum-like to the equally silly notion that the young can make no mistakes. Nearly all the leaders of Nazi Germany were young men. Yet the mess into which they got their own country and indeed all Europe was unparalleled in history.

105

The younger generation, which mistook its cynical sophistication for wisdom and its exuberant worldliness for realism, got unwelcome shocks and unpleasant surprises when it had to face the war.

106

The wild feelings which make these young people sneer at the pursuit of virtue and applaud the practice of violence spring from their lower nature.

107

Humanity is not so enlightened in our times that it can afford to dispense with the best thoughts of former times.

108

In an atmosphere of world unrest, religious dryness, political selfishness, and sexual saturation, it is not surprising that so many of the young go intellectually astray and get morally lost.

109

The miserable mental confusion of so many young rebels is pathetic, but it is also perilous to society. Apart from a minority of intelligent idealists, who sooner or later separate themselves individually from their mixed-up contemporaries, the others are neurotic and irresponsible drifters, dirty in clothes and bodies, compulsive and impulsive, victims of false teachings or hallucinatory ideas. If this was truer of the 1960s in America it is still true in other countries.

110

It is out of their despairs and disillusions that some of the young have turned to violence.

111

If this hostility of the young is allowed to proceed to its extreme point, not freedom but chaos and anarchy must be the consequence.

112

It is absurd for the young rebels to try to sever themselves completely from the past. It simply cannot be done. The attitude which they should adopt is to take what is worthwhile from the past and discard the rest. But the influence of the past is present, whether they want it or not. Change is governing every phase of life, every period of a single lifetime, and every phase of this planet's history. Unless this is recognized and reckoned with in our practical dealings, we are bound to suffer because of our attachments to objects, things, persons, and ideas.

113

The young person today standing on the threshold of adulthood should use this propitious time to analyse past experience for its practical and spiritual lessons; also to formulate ideals and aspirations, as well as plans for future life. Such mental pictures, when strongly held before the mind's eye and taken as subjects for concentration, have creative value and tend to influence physical conditions. They should be accompanied by silent, heartfelt prayer for strength, balance, wisdom, and guidance.

Reflections in old age

114
Old age is a time to gather up one's good points, one's few strengths, as squirrels gather their food for the coming winter.

115
The young do not know the melancholy ponderings on the brevity of human experience which come to the generation whose time is nearly run out, or the subsequent futility of all those ambitions which drive men through the vital years, or the final emptiness of all those fleshly experiences which titillate the senses. Buddha has persistently emphasized these frustrations in his teachings, yet it is the need and work of a philosopher to come to terms with age, to accommodate more equably the other things in his life.

116
Age slows down the energies and withers the ambitions; too often it halts the aspirations.

117
Cynicism comes easily to the old, idealism to the young, but one day—in a later incarnation perhaps—both may learn that they cannot have life on their own terms: destiny predominates, for there is a World-Idea and a karmic adjustment.

118
In the evening of one's life, there should be the proper attribute—dignity.

119
Aged people discover not only that the world does not want them, but also that they do not want the world. The withdrawal from one another tends to be mutual. I speak, of course, only of those who keep to Nature's rhythms, not of those modern creatures who ignore its message that age is a time for reflection, not bustling action; for severance of attachments, not for clinging harder to them. This artificial juvenility which they affect would have been pitied by Manu, the ancient Hindu lawgiver, who allotted four age-periods to each human life, the last for concentration on spiritual concerns.

120
It is questionable whether the young are able to judge values correctly. But then it is equally questionable whether the old, in their smug complacency, are *willing* to judge them correctly.

121
There is a healthy, wise, and necessary conservatism and a stuffy, stupid,

and obsolete conservatism. The distinction between them must be kept clear.

122

If the years bring him a larger outlook, as I feel they have brought me (and I am nearer seventy than sixty), old truths come alive with new meaning.

123

The dogmas learned in youth may enter into the revelation learned in maturity.

124

Those whose good fortune has given them enough to satisfy many desires ought not wait for old age to see how these satisfactions were passing and uncertain. They ought to do the heroic thing and detach themselves from the desire while there is still vigour in their feeling and their will.

125

The old find themselves beyond the reach of passions and the touch of mad impulses. For many there is peace and for some almost a candidature for saintliness.

126

Old infirm people who become weary of the body and hence weary of themselves have no way out except the larger identification with something larger than the body self.

127

An intuitive wisdom may come with the years, which will serve better than calculated information.

128

Who, in a lifetime's history, fell into no indefensible activities, avoided all bad judgements, and made no serious mistakes?

129

Red passion cools with greyed age.

130

The withdrawals from activity and worldliness which he refuses to make willingly at the behest of reason, may have to be made unwillingly with the coming of age.

131

The elderly who have come at last to accept the unlikeable fact of their age, but who do so with rebellious groans and emotional melancholy, learn by bitter experience in every department of their existence that it is a fact which cannot be ignored.

132

Among the benefits of old age is the fact that one can look back and try to comprehend what one had to do to uplift oneself in this lifetime. While one was involved in the experiences, their real lessons were too often obscured by unbalanced emotion or blocked by fast-held ego.

133

The instinctive urge to go back home after a period of absence comes to young children and to old men. Not only is some comfort expected there, but also a kind of safety, a form of security. It might even be called a private refuge from the all-too-public world.

134

Why go back to the hopes of youth—however exciting—if their cost is the deceitful illusions of youth?

135

Plato suggests the age of fifty to be a suitable turning point for a man to pass over from mere experience of life to constant meditation upon the higher purpose of life. Cephalus, the patriarch in Plato's *Republic*, was glad to be free from the lusts of youth, which he denounced as tyrannical, and to be in the state of relative peace which, he asserted, comes with old age.

Youth cries out for romance and love. The silencing of that cry naturally and properly belongs to age. Yet it seems a pity that this early enthusiasm and tumultuous energy, which could in most cases partially and in some cases even wholly be devoted to the quest, should not be so used.

Youth is progressive, age is conservative. Both tendencies are needed, but they are not needed in equal proportions. Sometimes the one should be emphasized more weightily, sometimes the other.

Those who have reached the middle years are likely to know more about life than those who have not. They are certainly more capable of sustaining attention and concentration than callow youths. Hence they are better able to receive the truth and to accept the value of philosophy than the young. Old age ought to become the tranquil period which ruminates over the folly and wisdom of its memories; it is to reflect upon, and study well, the lessons garnered from experience.

Why is it that elderly persons tend to become more religious as well as more sickly than younger ones? All the usual answers may be quite correct on their own levels, but there is one on another and deeper level which is the ultimate answer. The life-energy of the Overself flowing into and pervading the physical body begins, in middle age, a reaction toward its source. The individual's resistance to the attack of disease is consequently less than it was before. His interest in and attraction to the objects of physical desires begin to grow less, too, while the force that went into them now begins to go toward the Overself. When this reversal expresses itself in its simplest form, the individual becomes religious. When the energy ceases to pervade the body, death follows.

136

There is a pattern of growth in all the different parts of a human being. If man reaches his physical maturity in the twenties, he reaches his intellectual maturity in the thirties, emotional maturity in the forties, and intuitional in the fifties. This is one of the reasons why those who are really interested in religion and mysticism come so largely from the middle-aged and elderly group.

137

It was formerly believed that one advantage—or disadvantage, depending on the point of view—of old age was the reduction or even disappearance of youthful passions, especially sexual passions. But this is true in some cases, not in others.

138

Men are apt to complain of old age: Buddha even listed it as one of the sights which set him on his course to search for a way out of life's suffering. But there is one advantage of being an old man: one will not easily accept illusions for the sake of their false comfort.

139

The disadvantages of being a celebrity, the fatuity of worldly honours, are more likely to be recognized by the old than by the young.

140

In old age he accepts the need to release himself from ties which formerly held so much interest for him, but now assume the shape of burdens—or else of obligations for which the strength is lacking.

141

Those who have reached the seventh decade of life and fulfilled the biblical span of years have usually suffered enough troubles and calamities to become somewhat dulled by the suffering when a new trouble appears. It does not have the same force, the same weight as the others. The reaction is slower and less; their feelings may perhaps be translated as: this is part of human existence, this too may pass.

142

Just as sex makes him delight in the flesh, so sickness makes him repelled by it. Out of the balance which is struck between them, he may glean a truer understanding of life. Hence it is the wisdom of the Universal Mind which places sex commonest in the early part of his earthly existence and sickness commonest in the later part. If men and women take to religion or reflection in their middle years, it is because they have by then accumulated enough data to arrive at better attitudes or juster conclusions.

143

In a young man ambition is a virtue, but in an old man it is a vice.

144

It is to the chronically infirm and the rapidly aging that moments or moods of the futility in life come all too often. It is not only the consequence of disgust with their general condition. It is also the beginning of a forced almost Buddhistic reflectiveness. For questions come with the condition. What is the use of going on with such an unsatisfactory condition? It serves no purpose useful to them or to others. This dissatisfaction becomes the source of their much-belated look into the meaning of life itself. Hitherto their interest was not so wide nor so deep: self, body, family, possessions—such was their limit.

145

Look at the last cycle, the last years, of a fully ripened man. Clemenceau took to Vedanta as did Jung, Thomas Merton to Buddhism.

146

He reaches with old age less cynicism than the refusal to accept illusions.

147

Bernard Shaw somewhere insists that all men who are over forty— presumably with the exception of himself—are scoundrels. Perhaps. But they are also potential philosophers. For I do not believe that it is possible to arrive at the breadth and depth, the balance and perception, which must mark the approach to philosophy, before that age.

148

Year after year it all recedes, the expectations and the dreams, until desires diminish and ambitions fade.

149

The closing years of life should bring a man to recognize its moral affirmation, if he failed to do so earlier.

150

When our eyes are focused too closely on our experiences, we are apt to distort or exaggerate them. But when we can see them from the distance afforded by later years, we can take advantage of better perspective and thus gain a truer sight. This is one value of ageing years.

151

With the years moved over a man's head into old age, regrets, confessions, and disheartening recognitions are less reluctantly forced from him.

152

In passing through the last season of the body's life, the chill winter of old age, he passes through a series of deprivations and losses. If in the past he thought too optimistically of life and enjoyed the body's pleasures, now he is forced to revise his views and redress the balance.

153
Looking back on the past years, be they thirty or sixty, all seems now a dreamlike experience.

154
Another disadvantage shared by some old people is loss of continuity of consciousness. This shows in failure to concentrate attention or remember names, and inability to hold the full length of a sentence in mind.

155
If the body did not wither or fail us in our needs, this could be such a beautiful time, with all the fullness of art, culture, intellect, even spirituality within our understanding. But the snows of old age are falling; and soon . . .

156
The tendencies of the period take a man along with them, the atmosphere absorbs him, and it may not be until middle life when time, experience, maturity, suffering, disillusionment, and revelation have done their work that he comes to realize what has happened to him and asserts his spiritual independence.

157
The prospect of becoming too old to stir out of the house, or too ill to stir out of bed, too helpless to depend on their own efforts, frightens prouder souls.

158
So many persons of my generation have passed on that it is hard to remember which ones are still living and which are not. It is all a grim reminder of my own precarious position. The menace is countered by two qualities the years have taught me to seek: resignation and calm.

159
I am too conscious of belonging to a generation widely different from theirs, alien in too many ways from theirs, so that as old friends die off or move into distant silence I do not venture to replace them. Solitude surrounds me more and more, but I accept it contentedly.

160
Cicero tried to console the aged by writing a very lengthy essay counselling them to ignore their difficulties and pointing to the compensations they possess. But I suspect that most of the readers it is intended for will be more irritated than helped, more annoyed than comforted, by its somewhat unconvincing pages.

161
Old age brings its infirmities and enfeeblements, its humiliations and lonelinesses, its feelings of being useless and being unwanted.

162

Those who feel the hopelessness of old age probably outnumber those who reconcile themselves to it resignedly.

163

Adolescents have more of the joy of living and particularly express it through song and dance. Old age has more of the burden and misery of living.

164

There is a lack of *joie-de-vivre* in old persons and an abundance of it in young ones. The feeling of getting near life's greatest ordeal is not pleasant and is even depressing.

165

Certain undesired features attend human life on this earth in every land and among every people. Birth and growth are followed by the ageing and slowing-up processes which culminate in death. Parting from those we love and association with those who are disagreeable are forced on all of us at some time.

166

Life, which too often seemed like a comedy in the past, may seem more like a tragic futility in the dismal last period of old age.

167

Sophocles, in his calm, wise, but afflicted old age, wrote, ". . . at the end Age, housed with sorrow, claims us," and also, sadly expectant, "At last, to make an end . . . the dance done, every guest has gone, save Death, the one last friend."

168

The old, the elderly, and even the middle-aged become subject to anxieties pertaining to health or fortune, relationships or events, which the young seldom have. If it be true, as Cicero asserted, that age gives them the peace of freedom from passions—which if true is only partially so—then the price has to be paid in the currency of these anxieties.

169

Age brings loneliness and lowered vitality. Friends move away, fall away, or die off, and their reassuring nearness is no more. Stairs become harder to climb, streets harder to walk. Life seems futile: a heavy fatalism settles over the will.

170

A death of someone loved or respected may come as a shock, but time dwindles its force, resignation lessens its sadness.

171

It is the testimony of all experience that good fortune and misfortune are intertwined. Those who do not see this when young will discover it later, for good and ill appear at separate times often, but together when old. Life is thus a paradox, but also a series of compensations.

172

This increasing loss of memory which afflicts so many elderly people need not be a cause of emotional depression, as it so often is: we have more likelihood of some measure of mental peace when the burden of unneeded or excessive memories falls away. It is something for which to be grateful.

173

If age makes more people more rigid and less doubtful about their opinions and beliefs, it makes a few humbler, questioning.

174

The pathetic bleakness of old age is balanced by the wisdom of experience. The pleasures of the senses may be less, or even no longer, available. But the fruition of knowledge is.

175

If the elderly man is to be saddened because the energy and enthusiasm for his best actions lie behind him in the past, he is also to be gladdened because the impulsions toward his worst actions lie there too.

176

Every period of life, from childhood up to old age, has its limitations, its lacks and deficiencies, but it also has its compensations. If the old have unhappy periods because of their infirmities, the young have unhappy moods because of their uncertainties.

177

For those without a higher viewpoint, the prospect of old age is a difficult one. The clever attractive modern cosmetics may take the years off a woman's appearance but they remain—oppressive and disturbing—within her consciousness. Early enthusiasm for living must, in the end, give way to a saddened recognition of our mortality. Reflection warns both woman and man of the frustrations awaiting human desire, but it also tells them of the compensations. These, however, must be earned. Foremost comes peace of mind.(P)

178

It is not pleasant to reach old age. One tires easily—not only physically but also mentally—and one begins to weary of the routines of merely living, performing similar acts day after day. I speak of course of the average person, mass humanity—but one who has kept his mind alive, alert, eager to know, learn, and understand, who has developed his inmost resources cultural and spiritual, can never get bored.(P)

179

It is true that a wider and longer experience than the average may toughen a man's will and harden his standards, but it also softens his sensitivity and opens up higher values—*provided he lets Nature do its work on him.*

180

Those who pass through life untouched during all those years by any sense of the mystery at its heart are to be pitied.

181

Any man who has reached the middle or late period of his life has reached an age when the most important activity he can undertake is to try to fulfil as much as possible of the higher purpose of his life on earth. The basis for this activity must necessarily be self-improvement, the building of character and the overcoming of the ego.

182

In the end, when all this agitation seems to have been for little more than keeping the body alive, the failure to fulfil any higher purpose will bring sadness.

183

The vivacity of youth may turn in time to the serenity of age, but only for those who have let life teach them and intuition guide them, who have observed their fellows and studied truth's texts and humbled themselves before the Overself. The others gain little more than the years, the infirmities, and the sadnesses.

184

Instead of wasting time excessively on sad recollection of vanished years, elderly people can use it for comforting meditation on life's highest meanings, and especially on one of the highest of them all: *MIND is all there is.*

185

With the years—the world being what it is and human beings what they are—experience often turns this idealism of the young into the disillusionment of the middle-aged or the cynicism of the old. Only a coming into awareness of the higher spiritual nature can balance and correct this condition with the higher truth of the World-Idea, thus renewing hope and giving peace.

186

There is no finer or more fitting way to spend time during the evening years of life than in turning the mind toward reflection and then stilling it in the Silence.

187

If those whom good fortune has given leisure fritter it away in personal or social trivialities, then the passing years will bring them no nearer the kingdom of heaven but only nearer to regrets at its inaccessibility.

188

Alas! for the uncaught intuitions and the undeveloped perceptions—our past is littered with them. How hard to see, how easy to remain blind!

189

He who is at the beginning of old age should have seen enough of life to know what is most worthwhile. He should hold on to the Intangibles; better still, remember what he really is—such stuff as gods are made of, immortal, timeless, watching the dreamlike show of this world. Let him stay where he belongs—high above the puddles that surround him, the midges that bite him—and be serene.

190

Deterioration of the body moves in as middle age moves out. This may encourage the kind of pessimistic view which Buddha held in India, the author of Ecclesiastes in Israel, and Schopenhauer in Germany, and turn the mind toward spiritual consolation and spiritual seeking. If it does not, it may even have the very opposite effect.

191

"If you have peace of mind, contentment, old age is no unbearable burden. Without that, both youth and age are painful," said Greek Sophocles to a much younger questioner.

192

The fresh vital enthusiasm of youth passes implacably with the years. We are left like drooping petals. This is the sum of our history, as Buddha noted, but the unloveliness can be borne if we find the heavenliness of inner peace.

193

When we contemplate our remote actions we may regret them, or when we remember old views we may disown them. For it is in the nature of man to change as he gets older.

194

He learns the lesson of the relativity of all things, especially human things. Time is the great scene-shifter. From careless vivacious youth to fussy stiff old age, the perceptions change, the objects thought about change, as the ageing process creeps in, settles in, bringing new problems.

195

To the young we old people are complete foreigners. Neither our ways nor our thoughts are theirs. More, they are not interested in us at all, hence make no effort to understand. This is not a criticism for, in return, the old behave towards the young in exactly the same way.

196

Too well we of the older generation understand youth with its follies and frailties; too seldom does youth understand us.

197

The need today is for young men with an old outlook and for old men with a young outlook.

198

The moral errors of the naïve and inexperienced young are understandable, although perhaps not excusable; but those of the middle and older years are unpardonable.

199

The effect of age on the mind is as various as human beings, but there is a general effect which is common to most persons.

200

Our elders are worthy of respect, but their counsel is worthy of heeding only if they are old in soul as well as body, only if they have extracted through many lifetimes all the wisdom possible from each one. Experience without reflection misses most of its value, reflection without depth misses much of its value, depth without impartiality may miss the chief point. For all our experience, our life in the body and world, is a device to bring out our soul.(P)

201

The mere number of years of existence is not enough basis on which to judge a man's wisdom. The body's age is quite separate from the soul's.

202

If it be true of some persons that wisdom comes with age, it is also true of others that wisdom departs with age. The years may settle a man's mind with great rigidity in early errors, so that he becomes unteachable.

203

It is said that time brings a man more wisdom. This is often true but it is also sometimes false. If he is unwilling to learn from his own experience, if he is unteachable by observation of others, if he does not see the pitfalls in good fortune and the values in bad fortune, then time will bring him not more wisdom but more foolishness.

204

Too many men have grown old without growing up.

205

It is said that old persons like to indulge in personal reminiscence. This would be useful if they did so to learn the lessons enclosed in it, but this is mostly not the case. Their memories of the past are only a clinging to, or bolstering of, their own egos.

206

If experience makes you bitter or cynical, smug or selfish, then it has served you ill. The passing of years can teach wisdom but only if you receive their message aright.

207

As past success recedes into memory with the years, as he finds himself moving toward the last farewell, what can support him? All three—past, present, and future—become a passing spectacle. He can rest in none of them. The thought that all are thoughts in the end is saddening and not sustaining.

208

Every man over a certain age is under sentence of death. Some men below that age are equally threatened. Should not both groups be sobered enough by such a remembrance to ask, "Why am I here?"(P)

209

The dying autumn leaves induce sad thoughts such as: we are only passengers travelling through this world.

210

When we older men add up the years gone beyond our reach, and estimate the number of those that may still be left for us, the shock may induce us to put our lives on a newer basis. What better way than to cast out all acidulous dismal negatives, to ally ourselves only with sunny cheering positives?

211

The older one gets, the quicker time seems to pass by. And for a really elderly person, the few short years which seem ahead become calls to urgency, responsibility, and spirituality.

212

At the end of many years, after passing through many varied experiences, as we draw close to the terminus of life, we realize that we have not altered our character in fundamentals. We know then that many lifetimes may be needed to change ourselves.

213

Only the young are capable of a strong passion for truth but only the old are capable of living by it. This is the irony and the tragedy of the Quest.

214

The time at the disposal of an old man is too short to make himself over again, however repentant he may be, but it is not too short for him to do the one thing just as needful, if not more so. He can hand this problem, just like any other hard problem, over to the higher power, and let the past go. It will then no longer be his anxious concern.

215

It might be well for us to realize that our present earthly arrangements and possessions are all provisional; they do not possess immortal life. We slip easily into the misapprehension that the things which surrounded us when we were babies must consequently continue to surround us when we are old men and women.

216

Time takes it all away—the strength from man, the beauty from woman, life from both.

217

If time has confirmed his early faith, it has rectified his early errors and shown his deficiencies. If it has proved the correctness of some important intuitions dating back to inexperienced years, it has forced him to undergo certain profound changes of view which were received from outside and accepted then.

218

Alas! that a man *begins* to get a sense of right values too late to make use of them, that he learns how to live only when he is preparing to make an end of living itself.

219

Even the harshness of personal bitterness tends to diminish with ripe old age as the man sees and feels how his own life is so diminished.

220

These facts—the shortness, the transiency, and the instability of human existence—become more and more apparent as youth and the middle years depart, leaving men unconsoled, sadder, and, if they are willing, wiser.

221

The limitations and finitude of human capacity sadden him, the brevity and transiency of human satisfactions sober him.

222

The seemingly deplorable tragedy of life is that by the time we really begin to understand what it is all about, materially as well as spiritually, it is time to make our exit.

4

WORLD CRISIS

Crisis and visible effects

The intellectual event which announced the opening of the modern era was Francis Bacon's publication of *Novum Organum*. The age of hearsay, guesswork, and fumbling ignorance was rung out in the search for facts and the sharp reasonings of science. The religious event which announced it was Martin Luther's proclamation of independence which he nailed on the church door at Wittenberg. The age of soul-crushing churchianity and sanctified superstitions was rung out in the recognition that the only representatives of Christ are those who do what he taught. The historical event which announced its arrival in the clearest possible words was the French Revolution. The age of feudalism and slavery was rung out in blood and tears. The industrial event which announced it was Watt's invention of steam engines. The age of hand power was rung out in factory whistles and whirring wheels. Thus this momentous epoch, which is beginning to witness a veritable reconstruction in human existence, struck down the human arrogance which barred its way and broke through the human ignorance which failed to perceive its inevitability.

The widespread character of the present world ferment proves that it is a historical necessity and that a new epoch is about to dawn. For the generation which grew up after World War I grew up also in search of a fresh ideal. What happened here yesterday and what is happening here today has surprised and stirred before. The human race is indeed at a fateful turning point of its history. The shape of its physical, mental, and moral life for at least the next thousand years has been and is being effectually decided by the meteoric decade in which we live. Every successive stage of the immense drama which has unfolded itself before our eyes has proved this.

2

No crisis which humanity has faced in the past is comparable with the present one either for spiritual gravity or physical consequences.

3

When we speak in our writings of the war's general effect, we refer not only to the period of actual fighting but also to the confused periods of so-called peace which precede and follow it. It is only for the sake of literary convenience that we lump the three periods together, either under the short term "war" or under the more descriptive term "world crisis." This preamble will help to make clearer our point of view.

4

"Crisis" is derived from the Greek word meaning "to decide." I fitly used the term in the title of my last book [*The Spiritual Crisis of Man*— Ed.] because a decisive turning point had been reached in human history, forcing two alternative directions for an inescapable movement.

5

The crisis which has been growing within humanity will open completely in this century. It is an inner crisis, and its meaning is that humanity can go no farther in its downward path into the lust of the senses and the intellect into the forgetfulness of its innermost divine soul, without the most dangerous consequences to its future, without losing the very thread of the possibility of one day recovering its spiritual memory. In today's world there is such indifference to the things of the spirit, such moral lethargy, that the higher power is forcing us either to call a halt or to perish.

6

We see before our eyes that the world is changing, that society is moving, and that men and women are debating most things and affairs as never before. Some of this is bad, some good.

7

Our times are noteworthy for their supreme suspense, for the unpleasant chaos which grips now a country and then a continent, and for their state of continued crisis.

8

Everywhere frictions and oppositions prevail between groups, classes, religions, races, and the upholders of different political, moral, social, or aesthetic ideas. This ferment of questionings and disputes, attacks and revolts, only underlines the need to invent a new civilization.

9

The overpopulation explosion is worsened by the exhausted soil, the poisoned environment, and, worse, the poisoned mental and emotional climate. The crisis I alluded to in *The Spiritual Crisis of Man*, written more than a quarter of a century ago, has not only worsened but spread everywhere.

10

A civilization which has magnificence without significance cannot endure. Its very lack of soul is as much a threat to its existence as the tail of a burning comet could be to our own.

11

The situation has not improved with the years; it has deteriorated. This alone should be interpreted as a warning that the road taken was a wrong one and that fresh thinking is needed.

12

Lunacy and violence are not the only things in modern life. They are present, but the ferment and discussion of new ideas, the interest in the knowledge and betterment of life are also there.

13

The meaning of our age puzzles the thoughtful man and perplexes the religious one.

14

A static condition of society has never really existed. Change has always been there, even if slight and unnoticed. The struggle between orthodoxy and heterodoxy, old orders and new ones, has never come to an end. But today we have not merely changed, we have rapidly changed. The transitions are sharper and quicker.

15

No other epoch of history ever offered so much opportunity to create a worthwhile everyday life for all humanity. No other ever delivered so terrible a warning about the results of failure along with the opportunity.

16

Time flies so fast these days that no matter how much one does, too much is still left undone.

17

The pain of humanity in world war is appalling in its scope and depth. It is not possible for the limited human mind to take in more than a tithe of it and still retain its sanity. As a matter of fact, millions of people are today mentally unstable as a result of these events.

18

That we live in an age of insecurity is evidenced by the flourishing business done by those who profess to foretell the future. Astrologers and clairvoyants abound in the larger cities.

19

The vogue for fortune-tellers is natural during a period of widespread unsettlement and warlike upheaval. Continental Europe experienced a similar vogue during the Napoleonic period.

20

We live in a society driven by compulsive restlessness, knowing no peace either on its surface or at its centre.

21

People feel the confusion and unrest of our times and need someone to help or some book to guide them to the Truth that God exists and that the divine existence can be made to uphold their individual lives.

22

A fuller realization of the horrible nature of the world's crisis than that experienced by the masses—constant thought about it and acute sensitivity to it—has deeply affected a small minority of mystics, writers, artists, and religious fanatics. This has paralysed their ambitions, frozen their creative powers, petrified their hopes of happiness, and nullified their zest for living.

23

Amid the perplexities and monotonies, the wars and calamities of our times, some may well ask themselves whether what they do in life is worth doing at all, whether it is all futile or worthwhile.

24

Never before have there been seen so many evil tendencies and yet so many idealistic ones as in recent years. This commingling of extremes, or rather conflict of extremes, is a characteristic indicator of the forces loose among us.

25

There is uneasiness in every land, even alarm in some lands. There are fears and crises, anxieties, and menaces everywhere.

26

Most people who are at all thoughtful or sensitive have the feeling that they are living today in a squirrel's cage. The free space in which they can move physically is extremely limited. They constantly find themselves stopped short by its bars, in whatever direction they may turn. For world conditions dominate national conditions and thus predetermine everybody's future as they have never done in the past. Mental freedom is hampered by individual helplessness in the face of humanity's dismal condition.

27

In these tragic times, men have not only public anxieties pecking at their minds, but also the personal problems resulting from them. The future is so doubtful and confused that the very thought invokes worry and incites fear.

28

But if pessimism can be rejected, optimism cannot be justified.

29

Spiritual teachings of doubtful quality are well mingled with the others of much higher value. The confusion of the two has always been present but hardly ever has it been so great as it is at present.

30

Unbalanced religious theories and personalities and materialistic dogmatic slogans abound today. They are signs. There is more ferment on both sides than ever before, more violent discussion of such ideas, more verve in the interest shown.

31

Bernard Shaw once put forward the theory that this planet is the lunatic asylum for the whole solar system. Nobody took his theory seriously, and everybody complimented him on his wit and humour. I, however, have long held a kindred theory that the human race is evolving from insanity to sanity and that except in a few rare individuals—the sages—it is far from the goal. The dangers of expressing this view are such that I have hitherto held my tongue along with the view itself. To question the mental status of so many millions of people would have been an open invitation to be incarcerated without delay in an institution for the mad. But I am at last emboldened to say all this because a scientist, Dr. Estabrooks, a professor of psychology at Colgate University, has pronounced a similar judgement and even dared to put it into print.

32

The widespread area and enormous volume of pain and sorrow which have made themselves such front-rank features of human life in this generation have also made more people think about this side of the problem of their existence than ever before. The pain of the body, the sorrow of the emotions—these two dark shadows of their lives have been the subject of terrible contemplations for millions of suffering men and women. It has been hard for many of them to sustain belief in divine goodness, or at least in divine mercy. The optimistic blindness to plain appearances which would say with Browning that "all's right with the world" and see only the truth, beauty, and goodness everywhere, the intellectual one-sidedness which would prefer to hide from unacceptable realities, must have received a severe jolt in many parts of the world during the war.

33

The mood of total pessimism may easily be engendered in those who concentrate on the state of crisis which has held the world for several years.

34

This much is certain, that the crisis situation does not permit people to stand mentally still. They are compelled to form views and make decisions about the direction they want to take. These experiences of crisis or war become, in their totality, the door opening to a new era of thought for many persons. Some seek new paths to spiritual salvation and are prepared to welcome unfamiliar and unorthodox influences.

35

The realistic view has become so unpleasant that worldly minded people look for some able leader and spiritually minded people look for some inspired prophet, both groups seeking from him a message of cheer or hope about the world crisis and the war's menace.

36

The immense industrial expansion which has taken so many millions out of the open spaces of nature and cramped them in town apartments has also stimulated their intellects.

Causes, meaning of crisis

37

It is not only a spiritual crisis for mankind but also a spiritual opportunity.

38

The nations need collective outer peace, but men themselves need personal inner peace. The two are related.

39

The sufferings imposed by the last war were terrible, but those who found a deep religious or philosophical support within themselves were better able to meet them. In the coming age which will dawn soon, the working classes will come into their own, culturally speaking. It is therefore important that they should learn to understand the inner significance of life and not be led by merely superficial doctrines. The ultimate purpose of life here on earth is a spiritual one, and this must be remembered.

40

Any new order which offers to fill stomachs and actually empties hearts is but a mockery and a danger.

41

If we are not to be obliterated, a new way out will have to be found. The political way is a failure. It has been tried since the last war, and the nations have not been able to get any agreement, much less harmony, on the disputes that divide them about particular places or peoples, or on those that ought to unite them, like stopping nuclear tests and achieving disarmament. But the political way is not the only way, as the political leaders naturally and pardonably believe. There is an alternative one—the spiritual way. Jesus showed it to us and Buddha stated it. At this late hour, it is indeed the only practicable way. Any other will lead inevitably to obliteration, because it will fail to lead to peace. The divine law which controls destiny points brusquely and uncompromisingly to this single path. If we fail to obey, the punishment will be severe. If we heed it, the consequence may be unpalatable in the beginning, but it will be sweeter in the end.

42

The world crisis as a sign that mankind is passing through a spiritual turning-point includes truth-seekers also. It is time for them to stop living by other men's spiritual experience and to start living by their own.

43

Let us not waste time looking for a mastermind to straighten out the tangled threads of human misery with magical overnight suddenness. The conversion of mankind to better ways, like everything else which is worth having, must be worked for and won.

44

Through all this range of experience, human consciousness is evolving, is coming closer to the level where it will be able to take the next step forward and upward. This can be a false pretentious "mind expansion" got artificially and perilously through drugs, or it can be the real thing.

45

It is needful to note also that the forces which are operating are altogether beneath the face of the human psyche. There is a deep incentive in the inner being of modern man towards a more conscious, more illumined life.

46

Only the unveiled perception of what is going on in the interior world of man's being can render plainer the answer to the riddle of the twentieth century.

47

The spiritual awakening can come to mankind only as it comes to individuals—after it is strongly desired by the individual himself; and it will be desired only when all other desires have been tried and found wanting.

48

A sage, looking at the world-situation today, might declare that its issue will be neither all black with evil nor all white with good. New elements wearing both these colours will begin to appear, but the balance which will be struck between them is not easily predictable. The tremendous tension within the emotional nature of humanity, the enormous pressure suggesting a purely materialistic reading of life, the vast conflict and disharmony among men themselves, the wide mental ferment which has made serenity almost impossible—all these constitute for an appreciable number of people the labour-bed upon which the infant of a divine intuition is being born. This intuition may manifest itself in different intellectual forms, but its essence is always the same: that life has a meaning and a purpose beyond the sensuous and the selfish, that it is ultimately spiritual.

49

You raise the question whether the present world conditions will not result in a quickened progress of seekers. I hardly think so. They will quicken the progress of humanity, as suffering, impoverishments, uprooting, and deaths will teach the old but ever-new lesson of inner detachment through the emotion of being tired of such unsatisfying life. But in the case of the few who have already been striving for self-enlightenment, the disturbed physical conditions and the undesirable emotional atmosphere will tend to interfere with their efforts. The seekers, however, will be able to progress quickly when the present upsets come to an end, as you will one day observe.

50

In the individual life it mostly happens that grace descends only after a period of great suffering. In humanity's life it is the same. Only when war and crises have run their course will new spiritual light be shed on us.

51

The kingdom of heaven will have to be established in men's hearts, for it can be established nowhere else.

52

All attempts to better the world which do not better the basic element in the world situation—the human entity itself—are narcotic drugs, not radical cures.

53

If it is a materialistic exaggeration to assert that social improvement is the *only* way to individual improvement, it is not less a mystical exaggeration to assert that self-improvement is the *only* way to social improvement. Both methods are indeed necessary.

54

The psychological forces at work in the crisis and the spiritual laws of life itself must be understood if the crisis itself is to be understood.

55

Without that perspective of evolutionary and karmic movement which the study of philosophy bestows, we look in vain for the deeper meaning of historic trends, crises, and culminations.

56

Every doctrine which disregards this human need of finding a relationship with what is beyond the merely human will fail to understand the present world situation, and every doctrine which repudiates this need will consequently fail to offer any real help in dealing with such a situation.

57

Other forces are operating in the world-crisis which are quite beyond the knowledge, experience, and perception of most people. They are certain spiritual forces of destiny and evolution.

58

The ancient attitude, still much alive in the Orient, ascribed the horrible results of famine, the dread travels of pestilence, or the bloodied course of warfare to the scourging hand of God. Where it saw the presence of a punishing deity, the modern sees only the presence of man's handiwork. But philosophy sees the presence and action of both.

59

Both destiny and man are back of the tremendous happenings of our times. Both superhuman directive and human will are working behind them.

60

A physical reconstruction which is rotten at its moral centre, try as it may, can never bring more happiness. It will succeed only in bringing more misery.

61

Our victory on the military level is a good augury for humanity's victory over the grave problems which present themselves with the coming of peace. But just as the military victory came only after critical hours when we skirted the verge of disaster, so it may well be that the other will take a similar course. Just as in World War II the collapse of France in 1940, the blitz over London, the approach to Moscow, and the naval destruction at Pearl Harbor in 1941, the cutting of England's sea lifelines, the invasion of Egypt, and the conquests in the Far East in 1942 were grave crises of great danger that did not prevent our eventual triumph, so the difficulties and defeats of peace are not likely to prevent humanity's victorious solution of its worst problems. It will be a fateful period, but there is reason to believe that the attitude of despair is unjustified. Thus the struggle against the forces of evil, aggression, violence, hatred, and selfishness may be severe, yet there is good hope for eventual triumph over these things. But in the end, humanity will not be able to evade the challenge of Jesus. There is no salvation ultimately except through the spiritual way.

62

"In all that he sees he beholds a preacher of God," wrote German Jacob Boehme. Note the word *all*. For in the most revolting personal crimes and terrible international or civil wars, he sees the negative results of godless, or pseudo-godly, living. In the benign philanthropies and tolerant sympathies of the benefactors of the human race, he sees the positive results of godly living.

63

A pretentious society whose members are fakes and phonies despite their wealth, a closed world where snobbishness and insincerity are rampant—in such a society and such a world there is no room for a genuine spiritual aspirant.

64

A world humiliated and chastened by world war may be more ready to receive the world teacher when he comes. That alone would be the appropriate hour.

65

If enough men and women were to try to better their characters and discipline their lives, we might expect a new and better world. Otherwise we shall have the same bad old world, if not a worse one, with nothing new except perhaps its political and social clothes. It is true that clothes influence the man, but they do not make him—whatever the proverb may say. If enough men and women could be aroused from the stupor induced by materialism, if a new reverence could be kindled in their hearts, then there would be hope. For a world governed by a working team of reason and reverence could quickly be made worthwhile. If the tragedies of two world wars and the distresses of two peace periods are not to go in vain, the human race must loosen its ego's grip. The harder it clings to its old selfishness, the worse its insanity will become. The madness which drove Germany and Japan on their self-destructive course was a direct consequence of their rabid defiance of spiritual laws. If the symbols of this madness, the Swastika or the Rising Sun, did not fly in every capital, this was only because the intuition of most other nations led them to respond, in varying degrees, to the new and higher ideal fate had set before them and thus to keep saner than the other. A shift of emphasis away from excessive egoism has become indispensable if humanity is to keep its balance.

66

The old doctrine of karma is quite correct in explaining present-day world suffering, but not all of it. The explanation is too complicated and must be left for the future. However, it may be said that the one lesson humanity is compelled to learn is that of its interdependence and hence of its ultimate unity. The sufferings and unsatisfactory conditions of one nation affect distant nations also. The sufferings of the world can be removed only by removing their cause. But ignorance of this condition is so widespread that it is a sign that there are practically no sages active in the modern world.

67

On *The Christian Paradox* by Cyril Scott: The theme of this book is that world conditions are the accumulated result of following principles at variance with those enunciated by all the great Sages of the past, especially by Christ. By restating the esoteric truths which the churches deliberately suppressed, he exhibits the teachings of Christ in a new light.

68

Not only is the whole world faced with eventual war but large areas are already threatened with the collapse of their social structures, the crash of their economic systems, the half-starvation of their peoples. The quest for salvation from these perils goes on but only momentary palliatives are found. Civilization is wearing a garment consisting wholly of patches. Nothing can save it from progressively falling to pieces except getting a new garment. Nothing can save it from apocalypse except bringing to the surface the hidden truth about itself. No economic reform, no political change can save the human race today. Those who believe otherwise have been disillusioned in the past and are being disillusioned today, even though they often fail to see it. The only salvation which will be effectual must come from within, must reform and ennoble character. It must change thought and rule feeling, for then only will conduct and fate also change.

69

We must view this episode in the wider perspective of philosophy. If we do this we may learn a most important lesson. It will then be seen that the law of compensation takes account not only of sins of commission but also sins of omission. For we were in the position of a man who could see from his window that a householder in a distant street was being attacked and robbed with brutal violence, a man who wanted to help the victim but hesitated to interfere because he loathed fights and wanted to live a peaceful life. Thus he sways between two contending emotions until one or the other finally overcomes him. We had reached the latter part of this internal conflict and would undoubtedly have yielded to her better self and gone to the rescue of endangered humanity before long. But we were moving a little too slowly, hesitating a little too much, and the karmic consequence of this was tragic. It was the terrible price which had to be paid for delay in doing the right thing. Other peoples had to pay karmically for the same mistake but they paid far more heavily because they made the mistake in too many directions and for too long a time. There was a clear duty in this inner-dependent age to *help* actively on the right side. The world distress is mostly due to karma. But we need a broader interpretation of this word. Many of us may be good and innocent but we have to suffer with all others, not for what we have done but for what we left undone. Today sorrow misses nobody. This is because humanity is completely interdependent. That is the lesson we have to learn; that we let others remain in woe or ignorance at our own peril. We are one.

70

Much of the pollution problem on earth and in air, river, and sea is blamed on technology. But the latter's expansion is itself in part caused by something else: namely, overpopulation. And not only pollution but also other evils derive from it, such as unemployment, violence, riots, food shortage, and insufficient income. The matter does not stop there. To what is overpopulation itself due? The first answer is not the only one: overindulgence in sexual relationships, whether within or outside marriage. There are also some other causes. In the end it all sums up to spiritual ignorance.

71

In all parts of Asia until recent times the way of life for the masses was prescribed for them by authority, whether the authority of the state or of the church. They could not be kept forever at the same low level but have to grow up—and they have been growing and thinking, but only at a very juvenile level. They have still a long way to go in development. The violence and discontent and rebellion which we see in all parts of the world is a symptom, however unpleasant, of the beginnings of this growth. We see it also in the demands for freedom from those who are still too uncontrolled to have full freedom, but who need to be given a little freedom at least if they are not to be repressed forever.

72

What kind of a civilization do we have? It has become top-heavy, lopsided, unbalanced, and therefore dangerous to the healthy development of the human race. Its intellectual and technical advance is indeed tremendous, but faith, intuition, and the moral virtues do not find in this iron-hard framework enough freedom for their operation. Indeed, they are being stifled. Such a course if continued can only end in their complete suffocation. Man is in danger of becoming a merely mechanistic, merely physical, and merely selfish entity. This is not in accord with the higher meaning of his life, and since civilization does not give sufficient signs of its willingness or evidence of its ability to correct this unbalance, since the valuable services which it has rendered in the past are coming to an end, Nature is no longer giving it the protection which it might otherwise have had against the destructive forces within itself. Between the incessant turmoil, the incessant multiplication of wants, the incessant physical and intellectual activities, the incessant stimulation of emotional desire, and the constant appeal to egoism—between these things and the inner voice that calls men back to the deeper things of spiritual life there is a hidden conflict which really exists under the obvious one.

73

So long as man does not know what the world really is, he can hardly be expected to know what he is talking about. And so long as his word lacks truth, so long will society lack worth. Chaos abounds everywhere because nothing else need be expected from a race which knows much about momentary affairs and so little about the Real. Universal affairs must first be understood properly before human life can be made worthwhile.

74

Large groups in the human race are trying to continue the old life in forms that belong to outgrown stages of their development. The effort is a misdirected one and brings confusion, strife, or self-injury as the penalty.

75

Although all leaders admit the annihilatory character of nuclear war and agree it is unthinkable, yet their actions reflect nineteenth-century thinking, as if pre-nuclear conditions still prevail. With both sides spending more and more on defense every year, the situation becomes utterly illogical. The pity of it all is that despite these fantastic expenditures we are no nearer any real peace than before.

76

A social danger which should be foreseen and prepared for, because it hinders the onset of abundant living, is the uncontrolled expansion of population, more especially in the Far East. Such rapid growth will make the maintenance of peace between nations a harder task. It is ironical that the poorer classes should also and everywhere be the prolific classes! The less food, the more babies!—such seems to be mankind's strange maxim. It is still more ironical that the Japanese could have claimed that they needed more living space after having encouraged their people to be the most prolific in the whole world. With similar logic they tried the bandit-like method of stealing it by brutal violence. Less brutality and more birth-control would have been a wiser policy. While the human race persistently overbreeds itself, it will continue to breed some of the causes of war, unemployment, famine, and epidemics. With a world in such a tragic condition and such a doubtful future, it is hardly fair to bring more and more children into it. Both ethics and reason would indeed counsel that we bring fewer and fewer children into it. The notion that a people should breed prolifically was wisely inculcated by the religious law-givers of antiq-

uity when the race was still in its infancy and the land was sparsely inhab-
ited. But times have changed and such self-multiplication has become
senseless. If nations whose lands which are already swarming with men,
women, and children insist on increasing their number instead of decreas-
ing it, what other consequences may be expected except more disease and
more conflict? By reducing the size of their families, they will reduce the
discomforts and miseries of many parents and more children.

77

There is nothing wrong or evil in the development of Power, the spread
of Prosperity, or the fostering of Education. The wrong comes in when
these things are not utilized with wisdom.

78

Not to recognize his obligation to attend within his capacities and
circumstances to this higher purpose of life is a criminal omission. That is
why he is being punished so drastically in this century. He may have
sinned in this manner to keep his life simpler, less complicated by further
duties, as well as easier, less burdened by new disciplines. But he has failed
in obedience to the law of his own being.

79

The world has foolishly made a fetish of organizations and institutions
because it has undervalued the reality of thought, the power of character,
and the potency of truth.

80

What is the use of idealistically proclaiming the illusion that the world is
one and indivisible when everywhere we see that it is many and divided?
We should be better occupied in proclaiming the truth, which is that
humanity's real welfare is one and indivisible and that reason and circumstances are moving it in the direction of realizing this fact, but that it is still
at so low a stage of evolution as to be generally unready and often unwilling to resolve correctly the resulting mental conflict within itself.

81

In earlier times man had to seek and find protection from Nature. In our
own times he has to find protection from himself. His power is now too
frightening.

82

The misuse of Nature, the spread of materialism, and the upsurge of
negative emotion have led to our present plight.

83

The experiences which the human race has gathered during the past few
hundred years have supplemented its knowledge, enriched its culture, and

improved its environment. But they have done all this at a price. For they have increased its intellectual vanity, impoverished its religious feeling, and unbalanced its values.

84

So long as any civilization plays the hypocrite to its best beliefs, so long as the inner life does not matter while the outer life can give it all the satisfactions it seeks, so long may one predict with full assurance that the arc of its history will sooner or later take a downward plunge into disaster. Why this should be so is no mystery if one understands that God has set man upon this earth to fulfil and realize obscure higher purposes as well as the obvious lower ones. Man evades the challenge only at the risk of unwittingly calling into existence destructive forces that will terrorize his civilization and frighten him into remembrance of what these higher purposes demand of him.

Historical perspectives

85

The history of a nation is really a translation from the history of its soul.

86

History returns periodically to the same basic problems, the same fundamental crises. Where a whole people has failed to solve them, or tried to solve them in the wrong way, they are brought together again by reincarnation and presented with a fresh chance to make good or suffer the same consequences.

87

It is absurd to talk of humanity as though it presented a uniform psychological pattern. On the contrary, it presents a particularly uneven one. It is indeed a conglomeration of groups in various degrees of development. Some are intellectually advanced whereas others are intellectually backward. Some are very near to the noble in ideals whereas others are very far from them. All that can be said about their psychological situation is that the forward movement of evolution may be a halting and lagging one but it is a certain one.

88

It is a fact that all men are at different stages and see life in different ways or under different limitations. Their experience is always relative to their standpoint. Hence it is wrong to declare any man to be ignorant, for usually he does know what is proper to his own level.

89

Though I criticize our present age, do not imagine I would enthusiastically care to return to an earlier one. The few who talk about the good
old days are welcome to them! Those were the times when heterodox men
who dared to publish their free and independent thoughts were rewarded
with the rack and the thumbscrew.

90

In *The Spiritual Crisis of Man*, I put forward some arguments in defense
of older nations, peoples, or races who preferred a simpler life to the
technological civilization of the modern world—and especially the modern Western world. This did not mean—as I hope was made clear in the
book—that we, too, should revert to their attitude and become, as it were,
disciples of Mahatma Gandhi. No, I have always advocated that we take
what is useful from the past, what is wise and practicable for us, and leave
the rest. In short, I spoke more than once in favour of an East-West
civilization. I agreed with René Guénon that we had given too much
weight to a utilitarian civilization and too little to the higher forms of
culture, by which I mean philosophical, mystical, and the basic foundations of religion. Indeed, I criticized the ascetic regimes and asceticism
generally when pushed to extreme, and pleaded for the conveniences and
comforts brought in by modern ideas. But it is the extreme unbalanced
one-sided forms of either the simple life or the materialistic life which I
opposed. A sensible balance which enables us or rather helps us to keep
mental and emotional equilibrium, inner calm, is the desirable thing.

91

To turn our gaze to past times and look for similar situations in them
and then to observe what happened thereafter, will not avail us today. For
such a situation has never before existed. It is without historical precedent.

92

We do not reincarnate only to continue or finish learning the same old
lessons—much less to repeat them—but also to start learning new ones.
Life itself demands of us that there should be a definite progression to a
wider and higher level. Those who want blindly to imitate only what
people did five thousand years ago, show their ignorance of life's requirement. This earth exists to enable man to progress from lower to higher
levels and from narrower to wider areas.

93

The planetary spirit is accelerating its own development and this necessarily accelerates the development of all living creatures—plant, animal,
and human—which dwell upon it. This is why man's experience crowds
into one life what formerly he crowded into a few, and why world history
crowds into one year the events which formerly took several years. If this

increase in tempo has also accelerated human suffering by crowding it more closely together, it has also paradoxically increased human pleasures.

94

The era of dynamic democracy is at hand.

95

If you look back over the tremendous change which has come about in human society and civilization through the activities of science, invention, exploration, commerce, manufacture, and art, you will find that the period covered is roughly about three hundred years. The movement for religious freedom started about the same time, after a thousand years of religious straitjacket upon the human mind. Such freedom became necessary to prepare the way for the next great religious teacher, and his coming would be useless if men did not have enough chance to seek truth and enough freedom to choose their faith.

96

We have entered a period rarely seen before, a period that comes cyclically about every two thousand years. Great changes accompany it, on physical and cultural levels: it is also an avataric period.

97

It is an old doctrine among most of the Orientals and even among the early Greeks as well as the Roman Stoics, that the world comes to an end at certain long intervals of equal duration. This periodical death, which is always followed by a rebirth, is held accountable for such catastrophes as the sinking of Atlantis and the destruction of Lemuria. When the earth's axis last moved its direction to the one it now occupies, bringing an end to Atlantis, the length of the year was changed in consequence by an additional five days. According to this doctrine, these great changes in the global crust are due to a declination of the plane of the ecliptic to the plane of the equator—that is, to a change in the angle which the plane of the ecliptic makes with the plane of the equator. The larger this angle formerly was, the warmer were the polar regions, so that there was once a time when human and animal beings were living there in numbers and in comfort. As the planet moves in its curved orbit its cosmically preordained destiny moves on with it.

98

Ideas which belong to an age that is passing away are themselves doomed to pass away. They become barren and ineffective. We must try to unlearn them. Even certain mental attitudes which suited past epochs have now become retrograde. Emotional reactions which were correct in primitive peoples have now become impediments.

99

The procession of false prophets, self-styled Messiahs, and publicized Christs who have come and gone since the last century have served but to add to the bewilderment and uncertainty of the age. The confusion arose simply because the seekers after a spiritual prophet have tried to find him in a human form, and also prematurely. The true saviour was then and is still to be found only in the inner sanctum of men's own hearts. Christ—the true esoteric Saviour—is, since the death of the earthly Jesus, no man, but the divine self in every human being. Hence men who look outwards for him, whether in so-called reincarnations, organizations, or buildings, look in vain. He is not there. Nor is there any other way to look inwards than the way of the mystic quest. On the second count, that men are expecting him prematurely, it is true that we are approaching the end of an era, the close of a long cycle. The signs of this transition are everywhere around us. They are as vivid and pointed as they were when the last great era closed with Jesus' coming two thousand years ago. However, the destined hour when the next major prophet is to appear among us has not yet struck—indeed will not strike in this century. Certain events have to happen first, events involving tremendous changes in the life of earth and man. Not before the middle of the twenty-first century will the proper conditions exist for his coming. Meanwhile, minor prophets will appear and are appearing. Humanity, so far as it must seek outwards because it is unable to seek inwards, may and should draw what comfort and guidance it can from them.

100

One great error which is found alike among the Christians, the Jews, the Muhammedans, the Buddhists, and other religionists is the belief that the next avatar will appear only to enable the dogmas, hierarchies, and institutions of their particular religion to triumph over all others. The avatar is never exclusively their own because he always comes to bring a fresh message and sow new seeds. This was always historically true but it is most emphatically so today, when he has to speak to the whole world.

101

Where so many creatures are at early stages of descent into ego-experience and ego-development, it is foolish to expect them to respond to teachings suitable for advanced stages alone—where the need is for growing release from the ego. The first group naturally and inevitably has different, even opposing, outlooks, trends, ideas, beliefs, inclinations, and desires from those of the second one. It wants to fatten the ego, whereas the other wants to thin it down. To condemn it as wrongly directed is ignorant, impractical, and mistaken. If the history of mankind has teemed with war and bloodshed in the past, part of the cause can be found here. But that same history moves also in cycles. We stand today between two cycles, two eras, two cultures. The next one will not only be new; it will also be brighter and better in every way.(P)

102

While the race was still infantile, both intellectually and ethically, it had to be instructed in a kindergarten method. Truths had to be explained in a picture-book manner, spiritual instruction given through symbolic plays, through rites, processions, and ceremonies to appeal to the show-loving childish imagination. But now that it has grown up into adolescence it is ready for a higher kind of religion.

103

A new religion will be born in this century because it is a historical necessity. It will grow and thrive at the expense of the older religions. And all indications point to the fact that it will be born in the West and thence spread to the East and over the whole world.

104

Religion will always remain. It is only the ecclesiastical bonds on us which may have to be loosened or even thrown away.

105

The priest will not disappear altogether in the new age but his status and duties will be transformed. In the past he claimed to be a mediator between God and man. Now he will be content with the less ambitious role of a teacher of men. In the past he exercised power in the government of society. Now he will be satisfied with demotion to being a counsellor of society.

106

We of the modern world have a cultural inheritance which takes in the religious, artistic, and intellectual products of all historic periods and all continents. The sane reaction is to accept it; the insane one is to reject it.

107

All the world's literature is now before us. What men have found, seen, reasoned, what has been revealed to men whose different levels of understanding and character stretch from the primitive to the profound, is now accessible to all seekers.

108

The human situation is the final resultant of various forces whose play and counterplay make it up. It is packed with complexities. The doctrinaire who oversimplifies it does so at the price of imperilling truth. Let us note two out of the several factors which control it. If every event were to be completely predetermined by karma, there would be nothing for us to do. But if every event were to happen exactly as we willed it, the universe would become a chaos.

109

All rules and institutions, habits and traditions should be adjustable if they are to remain relevant to actual needs.

110

Though the modern mood is impatient of theological theorizing, it nevertheless accepts the emptiest of all theories—that Matter is the be-all and end-all of life—and it indulges in the most superficial of all speculations—that which puts the world of the Skin far above the world of the Spirit. As a result, we witness Europe and America hanging the names of their politicians high in the heaven of emulation, but thrusting their mystics behind the hedge of contempt.

111

Not until the modern era were those who wanted freedom from tradition able to seek it so freely and find it so easily.

112

If men will not break away from what is *bad* in their past—as, for instance, the fear, suspicion, and distrust which develop between two races or two nations through their historic relationship—then Nature (that is, God, Life, call it as you like) will do it for them forcibly and violently through natural disasters (such as earthquakes, floods, climatic extremes, drought) or through merely presenting them with the fruits of their own thinking crystallized on the physical level—that is, with their karma in the form of war, revolution, and so on.

113

Progress seems to carry both good and evil along with it. If philanthropy now takes more numerous and thoughtful forms, so does crime.

114

The present revival of church-going religion has its parallel in the thirteenth century's vast increase of world-renouncing European monasticism on account of the end of the world being then expected. The same threatening situation existed in the fifth and sixth centuries, when thousands upon thousands joined the monkish ranks for the same reason.

115

Abraham was told that if only ten good men could be found, the civilization of Sodom and Gomorrah would be saved from destruction. This word "good" must be interpreted aright if the promise is to have any real meaning. For only men in whom the higher spiritual nature was sufficiently active and dominant to attract supernormal forces could bring about such a result.

116

So long as a nation does not accept the guidance of inspired or intuitive individuals, so long will its history repeat the age-old blunders.

117

It is more useful to follow the history of ideas than that of persons.

118

Some cynic has said that we learn from history that we learn nothing from history. This is because our cynical friend's knowledge of human history is too short. The few thousand years about which our scholars can talk—what are they in comparison with the millions of years during which man has played his little game on this planet?

119

History's first task will be to get a group of superior men who are dependable enough to carry out these aims faithfully and who are disinterested enough to carry them out selflessly. It is from such a group that there must arise educators of future generations.

120

There is a ridiculous notion among some mystical circles that new spiritual faculties are being unfolded in our time. The truth is that there was, proportionate to total population, a larger number of spiritually perceptive persons in ancient times and even in medieval times, than there is today. This was inevitable because external conditions were simpler and less filled with allurements and entanglements, and because intellectual development was in harmony with and not, as with us, away from the inner life. What, however, might be stated with verifiable truth about our own times is that a new kind of mentality is being evolved. We shall synthesize and harmonize the scientific, the metaphysical, the religious, the mystical, and the practical without falling back, as the ancients did, into monasticism and asceticism.

121

Formerly it was right and proper for man to think exactly as his ancestors thought. Today it is right and proper for him to think independently, as an individual.

122

We must be careful not to confuse inevitable developments with evolutionary developments, events that just have to be with events that better the preceding ones.

123

A trend of world history may be powerful and triumphant. Its consequences may be undesirable yet seem inevitable. But this does not mean that they must be God's will in any other sense than a karmic one.

124

The Greek states saw the value of arbitration not less than the World Union, and provided for it in their treaties. Yet it failed to keep the peace between them and broke down as a means of keeping out war. The trouble then was precisely the same as the trouble today. It was not in defective arrangements but in defective character. It was moral.

125

Those who, like René Guénon, nostalgically advocate a return to "tradition" usually mean a return to the social cultural and religious life of the Middle Ages. They do not see that such a return could only be possible by including the obsolete economic environment of the Middle Ages also. Consequently it would mean the reappearance of such social relics as feudal lords and feudal serfs, the disappearance of machines and the electric powerhouse, the reversion to an agricultural and pastoral activity, the use of simple methods of production and primitive methods of exchange. Much the same diagnosis and remedy as René Guénon's were put forth by T.S. Eliot in the world of poetry, but with more success and with the emphasis on mystical religion rather than on metaphysics. Eliot deplored the chaotic plight and sinful condition of modern society, the exaggerated individualism of modern literature. He demanded a return to tradition, a recovery of the sense of history and community, a submission to the Church in culture and morality. Granted that the unsatisfactory spiritual conditions of today point to the necessity of moving out of them, but the Guénons and Eliots seek to escape them by moving backwards. The wiser ones seek to overcome them by moving forward. The first group find comfort in a decayed past because they lack vision to enter an unknown future. The second group accepts the duty of hard pioneering and labours to create a new and better kind of life for humanity.

126

If it be asked, as I am often asked, how it is that the Japanese, a professedly Buddhistic people, could have taken to such un-Buddhistic ways, it must be replied first, that all institutionalized religions are nowadays largely rendered ethically ineffective because they have become matters more of social convenience than of personal conviction, and second, that after the great historical revolution of 1868, when the entire feudal system of government was abandoned, Buddhism also was largely abandoned with it. The new government disestablished it as a state religion, took possession of thousands of Buddhist temples, stripped them of their Buddha-images, and turned out their priests. Thus Buddhism, a religion of earthly renunciation, was discarded. A religion of earthly aggrandizement, combining feudalistic Shinto Mikado-worship with a feverish industrialistic ambition, replaced it. With this death-blow, the seeds of potential spiritual greatness were cast out and replaced by the dry-rot of a materialistic ambition. With it was lost the opportunity of becoming the torchbearer of a new and dynamic reform for the backward countries of

Asia. This was because Japan, of all the Oriental nations of that time, was the only one wise enough in her unique religious vision to take the serenity and mind-control gained in inward contemplation and express it in the outward version of inspired action. The Japanese were provided with this striking opportunity during the nineteenth century to rejuvenate the vast continent of Asia in the right way and thus become its recognized leader. This would have prepared the way for the introduction of that new East-West spiritual-material civilization of which the whole world is unconsciously or half-consciously in desperate need. Had they lived up to this opportunity Japan would quite properly have earned our profound respect and all mankind's gratitude. But unhappily for themselves and unfortunately for us, the Japanese lost their moral and mental balance in the vast turn-over which they carried out and became the votaries of sordid materialism and ruthless militarism instead. The purifying fires of self-earned suffering became their lot for failure to grasp this grand opportunity and accomplish a truly divine mission. Prior to the transformation of which we speak, the ancient Japanese conception of life possessed a virility all its own. It was infused into the Buddhistic wisdom which they absorbed from India by way of Korea, because the negative quietism, trance-seeking yoga, and sepulchral asceticism of India did not suffice to satisfy them as a complete goal. They used these things, therefore, and refused to let themselves be used by them. They brought the study of truth and the practice of meditation into relation with the need of practical life and social existence, which meant that they brought these treasured gems across the walls of cloisters within which they had previously been confined into the wider world. With them, penetration into the deeper significance of human life ceased to be a preoccupation for lethargic monks who lacked the opportunities to put their learning into practice, and became the *inspiration* of active men engaged in the work and turmoil of earthly existence. They turned a metaphysic which usually ended in logical abstractions into a gospel which ended in inspired actions. They made bodily experience, rational thought, and aesthetic emotion combine to proclaim truth with united voice. This was the gospel of Zen, as it was called. But alas! we speak here of old Japan, of the land which had not yet been opened to the West and not yet been dazzled by its industrial prosperity and material achievements, a land which has vanished and now exists no longer.

127

In a world where no great event happens by chance, where even the tiniest seed sprouts under an all-governing law, the destruction of a whole continent such as Atlantis is full of significance for humanity. It means that

Nature, which is but another name for God, could not proceed farther with its evolutionary purpose for the inhabitants of that continent without a fresh start, without a clean break from old ways which had exhausted themselves.

128

If you wish to study history properly, you should first study human nature, of which it is partly a reflection.

129

History brings many changes in the course of time, many new developments, many displacements of settled persons and a coming to the front of fresh ones. The same happens in structures, organizations, geographical situations, and even climatic ones. We must beware of making custom habit or convention too rigid a thing. For if this epoch particularly shows anything at all it shows that the world moves on, that change never ends.

130

It is the principle that is more important, not the event. For the latter passes, the former remains.

131

I like to reckon time as a wise history reckons it, not by the meaningless counting of calendared years. I look for the rise and fall of civilizations, for the birth and death of races, and above all for the grand manifestations of Himalayan men.

132

Nietzsche put Emerson's idea in another way. He wrote that a whole nation is a detour to create a dozen great men.

133

Such being the actuality of present conditions, the opening of a new channel between finite man and his infinite source has become essential. This means that a new religion must be born. The war and its aftermath have created conditions suitable to the establishment of a new faith. Therefore, if it be true that a sudden and widespread revival of the old conventional dogmatic beliefs after the war is unlikely, because orthodox religion in its present familiar forms has lost the inspiration and purity necessary to make it effective, it is equally true that with the coming of peace there will be more people ready for a new religious revelation than there have been at any time during the past hundred years.

The intellectual and spiritual requirements of one epoch are historically different from those of others. Human society changes, evolves or degenerates: it cannot stand still for long. Hence, it finds for itself in every epoch either a modification, alteration, and adaptation of traditional systems, or—if it is sufficiently creative at the time—gives birth to entirely new systems altogether. The truth of this statement has been attested to by every age of mankind and on every continent from ill-fated Atlantis to thriving America. To hold, as the representatives of vested interests and orthodox institutions usually hold, that a particular system is suited to all the needs of all humanity for all time and therefore cannot be replaced or should not be replaced by another system, is to write a full stop to human evolution. It is a senseless view, as historically unjustified as it is philosophically untenable. No revelation is or can be the last one, nor the exhaustive one. Now that we live in a time when so many of the old systems have exhausted their best possibilities and fail to meet our newer needs, those who have turned aside from them yet are unwilling to remain spiritually unnourished should not be blamed if they are willing to enlist as followers of a more vital, more timely, and more satisfying faith.

A divine man, born to fulfil a large and special religious mission, a man like the founders of the world-famed religions, not only has this educational task but he also reveals the Karmic will and expounds the evolutionary standards set for the coming age.

All civilized societies and all cultural forms of the past have shown that they are inexorably subject to a rhythm of birth, growth, and decay. They have their ardent springtime, their luxuriant summer, their cold autumn, their withered winter. Today, we witness the same storms of destructive events and the snows of miserable failure. Those who are not too timid to face the unpalatable truth know that this has only one meaning. We are at the end of an epoch. The old world is dying before our eyes. But death is only a transition—the joyous springtime of vital renewal always follows the freezing wintertime of outlived forms. A new epoch is indeed at hand, with fresh ideas to lead us and fresh ideals to sustain us. Only the mentally blind now fail to anticipate it.

It was a new comet which came to warn mankind that the old era was about to be liquidated and it was another comet which came to notify them that the new era had begun. This was no more a coincidence to those who understand the hidden workings of Nature than was the fact that all the three leading Axis powers—Germany, Italy, and Japan—started their nationalistic careers in the same year: 1871. The first harbinger appeared in the skies in the autumn of 1929. When the great economic blizzard hit America and thence spread to the whole world, it forced millions to realize that the old order was exhausted. Every country was affected by economic troubles with all their political, social, and cultural consequences. None escaped. Each reacted in its own way. Japan's reaction was shortly to plunge desperately into international robbery by invading Manchuria. If with the facts now at our command we think back, we shall realize that the

Second World War really started in 1931 with this invasion. For the line of continuous fighting against Japan in China down to the time of America's involvement after Pearl Harbor was paralleled for three years on the other side of the world by the civil war in Spain, where not only the Spaniards themselves but also Nazi Germans and Fascist Italians battled against Red Russians.

Thus, the earlier comet indeed prognosticated the coming world war, and the second comet, which showed itself towards the end of 1942, heralded its closing. The military turning point of the world war was coincident with its appearance. For the great series of democratic nations' military victories began about this time. But the second comet's special association was to act as the harbinger of a new age. These victories not only brought about the external liberation of millions of people from militaristic oppression, but were the prelude to the entire liberation of all mankind from every form of social and cultural oppression by the past. The new age could not fail, therefore, to be a new religious age also. Thus the new universal spiritual enlightenment was dated by the second comet. Whoever perceives this cannot but believe that when the need is so great, the yearning so widespread, the urgency so sharp, the divine wisdom which holds this earth within its grasp will not fail to inspire the most evolved human being available with a universal Messianic mission of up-lift, instruction, healing, and awakening. And nobody less than such an august being could undertake the responsibility of so tremendous a task, which will specifically be directed towards the masses, towards millions of people. Nothing truly great can be done without great men.

There must be a visible focus among us, even for the boldest of ideas. There must be a great leader. The spectacle confronting us today is the spectacle of a planet that is spiritually leaderless. We are told, "The hour produces the man." The hour is here, we believe, but we look around and see no Man. Spirituality is waiting to find its voice. Its reality is here, but its spokesman is not. Every half-baked cult and worn-out creed possesses its ambassador, but the ineffable divinity remains unvoiced. Nevertheless, we wait patiently for that one to come who shall utter anew the Christ-message to mankind. And his voice will not be as yours and mine, but will be a regenerative force which will startle the sleeping world. The world is in upheaval for a deeper reason than it suspects. For at a time of religious chaos and popular bewilderment, of world agony and human distress, such as the present, his coming is in perfect consonance with the fact that supreme intelligence rules the cosmos, that truth shall be uncovered once more for the sake of those who need it. However, it is not through any one prophet alone that the new dawn will be ushered in but through a plane-tary outpouring, which flows through every useful channel it can find. In this complex epoch, its manifestations are as complex and varied as are the needs of mankind. There will be different prophets bearing different messages to differently-delivered groups of people, but all will be inspired by one and the same timely power.

The human race has long been preparing for manhood. The end of war marks its crossing of the threshold. Now it must exercise manhood.

134

If the progressive character of the reincarnational chain be true, then we must grant that there are men half in and half out of the animal kingdom. They are clanking reminders of all that still has to be done still before a deep spiritual awareness of its best self becomes natural to the human race.

135

In the old days barbarians came down to civilized cities on foot or horse. Today they still come, but in machines.

136

We moderns have discovered how to release atomic energy. The ancients always knew, as the mystics still know, how to release spiritual energy. History will show those who cannot otherwise learn, which discovery is more important and most beneficial to mankind.

137

The Middle Ages of Europe produced many more saints than the modern epoch has been able to produce.

138

Those who refuse to turn the mind towards the centre of harmony within themselves do so because their experience of what is without is not full enough nor reflective enough.

139

Lao Tzu lamented the fall from simple living into extravagance and luxury during the period from primitive Chinese history until the highly civilized China of his own days. Juvenal criticized the same deterioration among his fellow Romans. Does this not illustrate two things: first, the inventiveness of the human mind, and second, the desires of human nature? These are innate, and will last as long as history itself.

140

It is somewhat ironic to write that what we regard as medieval, so far off in time as to be a museum-piece, was regarded by its own contemporaries as quite up-to-date, the very latest in thought and fashion! Erasmus, writing in 1514 about the various early Church Fathers' Greek sermons, commented, "Ambrose is not altogether appropriate to modern times"!

141

The longing for the triumph of goodness in world history is in most hearts. We may translate this as we wish.

142

The Oriental mystic is indifferent to world history because he is indifferent to time.

143

It is doubtful how far we have progressed, and even whether we have progressed, in the art of living, despite all our science and knowledge. We have only to remember those Greek colonists in Italy who banished all noises from their city to raise this question.

144

History traps the individual in its implacable movement.

145

There are occasions when the corruption of society is so high, its values so low, that the prophet must make a stand and challenge it.

146

Ancient cataclysms have buried whole continents, engulfed entire races, and hidden the evil horrors of man's own making.

147

The progression of human intellect is attended by the regression of human character.

148

It was not possible for earlier generations to crowd so much experience into so short a period of time, so much compulsory thinking about events into so many events themselves. Those alive today have the chance to make more quickly a forward move in spiritual growth, to learn certain lessons in which they have been laggards, but which Nature is determined to enforce.

149

Here and there doors are being opened through which the light needed by our darkened times is beginning to flow in.

150

Considering the world's nature and man's character, there has not yet been and there is no likelihood of ever being a Heaven on this earth. But much can and will be done to improve the one and exalt the other.

151

As he lay dying, H.G. Wells discarded his belief in the inevitability of progress and even felt that everything might end.

152

History is both a record and a confirmation of the transience of men, of the immutability of their civilizations and the evanescence of all their other creations. If there is any moral to be drawn at the end of every history book, it must surely be the old Latin one, "Thus passes the glory of the world."

153

The mastery of philosophy increases the capacity to interpret history correctly.

154

Because the social strata were too rigidly organized, because they did not permit the upward passage of worthy or gifted individuals, they provoked resentment and, in the end, rebellion. Democracy became the karma of aristocracy.

155

In this democratic age we preach equality but continue to practise, if and when we can, the contrary. We can hardly do otherwise. Social distinctions appear because there are differences of economic background, of upbringing and ways of life, because refinement does not easily mix with vulgarity. If each is the end product of a series of reincarnations, the differences in nature and experience are certain to show themselves, giving rise to social differences. But this is no excuse for exploitation and snobbishness in the more fortunate levels of society, or for rancour and class hatred in the less fortunate ones.

156

The hierarchical marks of class patterns, the differences of caste quality, the contrasting grades of status, prestige, culture, value, and refinement are blurred today, mixed up.

157

The philosophical group may have wisdom and character but despite this they are a small factor in such a large situation, being hopelessly outnumbered by all the others.

158

The philosophic minds are so heavily outnumbered that the world's fate is decided by the others.

159

The sage kings assumed the prerogative of their office not by heredity but by inner worth. They were kings of the mind before they became kings of men.

160

Neither historians in the Near East nor writers in the Roman Empire showed the slightest recognition of the coming power and eventual significance of Christianity during its first century of life. Is this an astonishing fact?

161

The Roman legions fought their way across Europe not merely to aggrandize the power and wealth of a city on the Tiber River, but unwittingly to lay a path through which the message of Jesus might spread.

162

The new religion should speak to the masses with more clearness and more common sense than the existing ones.

163

When we consider that two discoveries alone, electricity and the petrol engine, have shaped entirely new environments for the human being, we may well marvel at the kind of world in which mankind will live a hundred years from now.

164

These ideas are becoming vivid in the minds of so many persons not because of the activity of one man but because evolutionary forces from within and environmental ones from without have prepared and developed these persons to receive and appreciate them. Had this man never lived, they would still have been received and appreciated. Nevertheless it is also true that such a man brings the movement to a clear head and provides it with an impulsion along a definite road which he cuts for it.

165

The advent of a new era is now inevitable but the advent of a better one is not.

166

This dread of humanity's future spiritual destiny, this fear that without a powerful religious recall it is doomed, this belief that a lame external activity is needed to bring about such recall, this desire to set humanity on a quest beyond its own wish and strength—this is unfaith and unwisdom.

167

In all the history of man was there ever a period like this? Yet, although man has changed himself and his environment in every way, he has failed to change in the most important ways—morally and spiritually. Who has the hardihood to declare—in the face of the bestiality and cruelty which have appeared during this generation—that there is less evil abroad in the world now than formerly? And who has the equal hardihood to declare—in the face of the religious, mystical, and philosophic testament in writing which has come down with the centuries—that we have more intuitive knowledge of the eternal truths, more personal communion with the spiritual self, than the men of antiquity?

168

Unfortunately the land which produced a great psychologist like William James and a grand mystic like Ralph Waldo Emerson seems to have exhausted its resources with them. Its materialism has stemmed from the early needs of the nation, the inexorable necessity of firmly establishing a physical civilization before a cultural one could be established, the gathering together of ambitious, optimistic, energetic, determined, and enterprising men and women from the Old World. There are repulsive features in its culture still, and grave problems to be solved.

169

The human race has evolved to a point where its condition of receptivity to these teachings is more favourable than at any previous time.

170

New viewpoints develop among humanity as it passes through different historical phases. Sometimes they are merely revisions, developments, or improvements on the old viewpoints, but sometimes they are really fresh and notably different from the old ones. When we compare the earlier mental condition of mankind with that which prevails today, we are immediately struck by the enormous increase in the opportunities of the masses for education and enlightenment, together with the advance in knowledge of every kind. The result is seen in the changed outlook upon several departments of life, the widened views which have come to us. The contrast between human life of today and human life of a single century ago is vast and startling. In clothes, food, fuel, light, homes, cities, and social conditions on the external side; in literacy, journals, books, art, entertainment, discussion, standards, and intellectual development on the internal side, we see that an era of ferment has really come upon us. New ideas in religions of an advanced and idealistic character which, a generation ago, were furtively discussed only by a mere handful of people are now freely and widely discussed.

171

It is not the funeral of civilization that we are witnessing but the funeral of an outstanding phase of civilization.

172

The belief that the human race is improving requires careful definition and particularizing, for it is certainly retrogressing in some ways even though it is improving in others.

173

Before we can properly understand this we have first to understand a fragment of a theory which was held by the ancients throughout the world. This is the theory that history moves in rhythmic cycles of alternating life and death. This theory likens evolution to the course run by a new seed as it grows into a tree and yields fruit: it sheds its leaves and becomes barren in winter, but in the spring new green buds appear and the same course is run once again. According to the classic Chinese wisdom, every empire and every civilization passes through the varying situations of a periodic cycle whose turning begins with peace and unification, passes to prosperity and culture, moves with increasing age to decline and degeneration, and ends finally in disorder and disruption. Thus, the same wheel which lifted Rome to the height of her power and set her armed legions in control of Europe, North Africa, and the Near East dropped her, on its descending arc, prostrate at the feet of Huns, Goths, and Vandals. The rhythmic return to which this doctrine refers does not mean that epochs occur again exactly as before; for then existence would be meaningless and evolution a figment. It means that they occur in a similar yet more evolved way than before, as the twists of a spiral cover the same two dimensions of breadth and depth again but rise to a new third dimension of height. Karma has to find the best available human instruments, however imperfect they be, to carry out its will. Remove these men and you are left with steam hissing aimlessly into space, whereas they are like the piston of an engine which concentrates and applies it. Thus Alaric, Chief of the Goths, told a monk that he felt a secret and supernatural impulse which impelled his march to the gates of Rome. Accordingly, he descended on the Roman provinces when the fourth century had almost closed, and moved in triumph until his firebrands lit the proud palaces of Imperial Rome. "This may be considered as the fall of the Roman Empire," is the verdict of Gibbon upon Alaric's achievements. It is at the behest of karma that these Alarics, whatever such men may themselves superstitiously believe, have arisen to encourage mankind. Lenin, with all his distorted intellectual greatness, could only spend his powers impotently in Switzerland, unable to lift a little finger to effect the revolution he craved. He could do nothing until destiny stepped in and permitted him.

174

That prehistoric cataclysm—the sinking of Atlantis and the swallowing of its millions of inhabitants—affected the human race psychically and mentally.

175

We live in a word-culture where meaning does not sink deep enough to give inner experience but remains shallow and fugitive.

176

We have only to probe the truth out of history—a feat which requires almost philosophic impersonality and impartiality and research—to find that stupidity too often masquerades as patriotism or religion or some other unquestioned tradition or modern belief.

177

We complain about the disorderly conditions prevailing today. We do not realize that they would be considerably worse if the wise, the saintly, the inspired, and the prophetic had not lived among us. In this context, we may remember the words of a Chinese, Mo Tzu: "To give peace to the world is a function of the sages."

178

It would be more correct to talk of historical movement rather than historical progress.

179

The movement has always been slow, often erratic, with many relapses and much hesitance; but taken as a whole it has nevertheless been a forward one.

180

The old way of evolution led through a blind self-interest. The new way will lead through an enlightened self-interest. There is a vast difference between the two.

New era in evolution

181

All this unrest, disturbance, and violence which is going on in the world is a symptom of discontent with the kind of life into which materialism has precipitated so many members of the human race. It is also a symbol of the settling of karmic accounts which happens during the transition period in history from one zodiacal sign to the next.

182

It is true that the destruction, violence, and upheaval which have marked the last half-century are signs of the liquidation of the old era. This may be painful but at the same time heralds and overlaps the rise of a new era, the Aquarian age.

183

With the appearance of the atomic age it is not only the Christian era which is coming to an end, but also that of the Hindu—and all the others—as well.

184

The world crisis will not come to an end for some years. The whole religious outlook, as well as the cultural and institutional order of modern civilization, will be changed during this century. Only after these changes will the new spiritual forces become manifested.

185

It is not however the mechanistic nightmare which Marx dreamed of, nor the diabolic one which Hitler patterned, nor is it going to conform in the end to either. Both these men were too lopsided and too devoid of philosophical perspective to comprehend the proper significance of the mighty universal change whose coming they saw and sensed but whose meaning they grotesquely misinterpreted.

186

Mankind's spiritual forces could not be genuinely mobilized under the old order, which was mortgaged to antiquated theories and which could not struggle on indefinitely under such a burdensome load.

187

As we approach the close of this epoch, the tempo increases, the chaos spreads, the egotism waxes, and the face of evil smiles more and more triumphantly; but like the intersection of two arcs, a new epoch opens. If exhaustion and darkness have spread over the world scene, they have not spread alone—mingled with them are the beginnings of anticipation and light. If materialism has soaked so deeply into mass thinking that men and women tremble for their own future, spiritual truth has entered the minds of some who have resisted it, but because the old epoch has been with us so long and the new one is just being born, these latter form at present only a negligible group.

188

This condition of destructive criticism and hostile denunciation, of general tearing-down, exists partly because we live in an end-period, in a time of liquidation.

189

The end of a vanishing old arc is crossed by the beginning of the uprising new one. Hence the few hopes amid the many despairs, the few lights amid the wide darkness. Alas! it is not a new age that is here, not even its beginning, but only the dawn before the beginning of its beginning.

190

The great changes in human thought and society which marked the birth of the Christian epoch in the West, find their parallel in the great changes that are even now beginning to mark the coming birth of the next epoch. The labour pains have already begun, but actual birth will not take place until the next century.

191

This evolutionary change, this redirection of the ego's forces reflects itself in the chief events of the world crisis. But it would be naïve to expect such a colossal change to mature and bear all its fruits within our own lifetimes. It will need a hundred years at least for even the first small fruits to appear and ripen.

192

Both the opening of such a transitional era and its close are marked by a stupendous crisis. With them, not less than with the whole stream of events between both, the law of consequences punishes wrong-doing, expiates sins, strikes balances, and grants justice.

193

Thirty-three years ago, in *The Hidden Teaching Beyond Yoga*, it was said that we were living in a period of accelerated change. The acceleration has been plainly visible and increasing ever since. It is going on not merely in one particular department of existence, but in all departments in all ways.

194

The nations are faced with the challenging sword of repentance. They will eventually accept it and be blessed, or reject it and be struck down. Meanwhile, the business of the mystically sensitive is to open themselves up by prayer, meditation, study, self-improvement, and surrender to this divine force, not only for their own spiritual benefit but also for humanity's benefit. Their thoughts and deeds must bear witness to the fact that they are seeking to respond to its holy presence. These are assuredly the "last days" of which the New Testament speaks. The opportunity, choice, and responsibility which lie before us are all highly critical and decisive.

195

An all-around overnight moral change in human nature seems highly improbable. But if these divine forces are really in our midst a quickened moral development in human nature is not at all improbable.

196

The point now attained in human evolution by the ego offers us the key to a correct understanding of the world crisis.

197

The human entity's present evolutionary position is just about midway in the whole journey through its own kingdom.

198

Although it is true that humanity is everywhere found in different stages of spiritual evolution, that some peoples are more advanced and others more backward, it is also true that a broad band of average condition comprises the greater part of those incarnated today. And it is this general average which will be most affected by the ego's cosmic change.

199

The important change will not be undergone by all the egos but only by the general mass of them.

200

There are, of course, in every land a few who long ago passed this point in their development and more who have recently passed it. They are the pioneers, sensitive to spiritual ideals and struggling to follow them. But now the challenge has been issued to humanity as a whole. Its unseen guardian has issued an ultimatum. It must make the passage and will not be allowed to delay any longer.

201

If, with ordinary sight, we look at the contemporary scene, there is little to keep us from despair. But if we look with philosophic sight there is nevertheless something to give us hope. The terrible curse of the war may be converted into a blessing if it arouses man from materialist pursuits and turns him to the quest of the eternal intangibles. The fatuousness of seeking for true and lasting happiness in the unstable affairs of material life is being etched deeply in his heart. He is being taught the wisdom of seeking to live in the consciousness of the Christ within him.

The notion that humanity will have bought a new and better world at the heavy price of the tragic war years is true in the sense that an unheard-of opportunity has been presented to humanity to make a new and better world. That some advantage will be taken of this opportunity is certain, but that sufficient advantage will be taken of it to create a vastly different world is quite uncertain. The selfishness, the greed, and the hatred which hinder human advance are not likely to disappear overnight; despite the forced social adjustments of the war period, we have a very long way yet to travel to catch up with the golden rule. I do not therefore share the intemperate enthusiasms, opalescent visions, and unrealistic hopes of well-meaning political, religious, and mystical reformers. Neither do I say that we should all sit down with folded hands and wait a few more million years while evolution does its grim work of instructing men through constant suffering to cease their conflicts. If a perfect new age is far from fulfilment, an imperfect new age can, nevertheless, be had. Let us have it, then, by all means. For unless we strive to move even one inch forward we shall not move at all. We must set up ideals and we must work for their realization. We must try to make even a little part of our visions come true. If we take a pessimistic view of the possibilities of elevating mankind, then no effort will be made and no progress can be expected. But if we make a start and do what little can be done then some progress will be made. There will be this difference, however, between us and the impractical idealists, that whereas they believe all their visions can be materialized today, we are more prudent, more scientific, but nevertheless not a bit less visionary. The difficulties of making a new and better world are frighteningly formidable. But the difficulties of carrying on the old and bad world are also frighteningly formidable. If the sufferings of war awaken the conscience and purify the desires of mankind, its leaders may endeavour to atone for their errors and omissions of the past. Thus only can they go forward to meet the coming age and open a path to a better life for all mankind.

202

The spiritual possibility of man's improvement will be realized through the pressure of forces working both within his entity and within his environment. But it will not be realized smoothly. There will be lapses, setbacks, and retrogressions, albeit temporary ones.

203

We are passing through a disheartening period of violent and unprecedented storms, but if we have learned the single lesson of hoping on and holding on, we shall win through into clear weather.

204

The world's need is not new doctrinal fads, but new life, new inspiration, and a new heart.

205

It is clear that the crisis will not be overcome unless we acknowledge the worth of moral values above those which have hitherto reigned in actual practice rather than in hypocritical theory. That such an acknowledgment has begun to shine in the hearts of some powerful leaders is good, but it will have to shine in the hearts of several more if a successful result is to be attained. A section of people has vaguely felt this already, but it will become creative in their minds and lives only when it is clearly formulated. This century will not have much use for any gospel which keeps the worldly life and the spiritual life mutually exclusive.

206

It is a good thing in ordinary times to go back to the past for its spiritual treasures casketed in fine books. It is then a privilege and a satisfaction to find that they have come down well-presented and quite safe through century after century. But these are extraordinary times, urgent times, filled with pressure and crisis. The voices we most need to hear are living ones, speaking from out of the same circumstances as those amid which we dwell, continuous and contemporaneous with us.

207

If God can speak to one man he can speak to any other—if to Jesus' and Muhammed's times, then to our own times also; if in Palestine and Arabia then in Europe and America also. Help for modern man can best come from those who understand the modern mind. Man's environment alters with the course of time and so does man's mentality. A simple repetition of what he was in former centuries or a mere revival of what he knew in former centuries is not efficient today. There is no traditional form of this teaching which will hold good for all time. This is always true but it is particularly true today, when we live in the middle of a general transition from the separative cycle of evolution to the unitive. During the period of human evolution in which our generation lives, it is unwise retrogressive and inexpedient to look only to ancient sources for inspiration knowledge and revelation.

208

The inner wisdom itself, being out of time and space, does not and cannot vary, but the outer forms under which it is found do vary. This is not only because of the geographical and historical differences which condition those forms, but because an evolutionary development is also affecting them. This is an important reason why the coming era must find an inspiration adequate to its more progressive needs, must add new truths to the old ones.

209

Only that nation will act wisely in this critical phase of human history which acts on the recognition that this is not the medieval world, not the antique world, but the nuclear world. This is a new era which demands a transvaluation of values, method, and even men!

210

Humanity still clings much too strongly to its egoism in most matters, despite the tuition of war crisis and upheaval; this is the very standpoint which must be abandoned, or at least markedly modified, if humanity is not to pass through further large-scale suffering. And this in turn must itself be the fruit of an awakening to the higher purpose of earthly life—it does not matter whether or not such an awakening takes place through or outside the church. After the war's end, we had to wait a couple of years for the situation to clarify itself and for the uprising tendencies to show themselves.

211

Those who insist on this excessive adherence to materialistic thought and refuse to recognize the new evolutionary current of stimulated intelligence and spiritual individualization are trying to live in the modes of the past and have failed to find the purpose of their present incarnation.

212

Such is the swiftly moving time-spirit. It will not be denied, none can successfully impede it, and it must be accommodated. It is a challenging demand that human life be deliberately hooked to a better ethical basis, that the continuance of materialism is insanity.

213

The only effectual way to meet this crisis is the way of recognizing that an era of materialist error and extreme selfishness has come to an end, the way of wiping the slate of old wrong-doing quite clean, the way of making a complete break with the past, the way of doing the large and generous deed as a start-off for the new era.

214

There is no third way open to us. The world is rapidly moving into a new age. We may either cling to the remnants of the age that is vanishing or we may meet the age which is coming. We must make our choice. We have had enough and more than enough of the high-sounding platitudes of babblers. We need now some concrete expression that will be more truthful and less talkative. For the problems will stand squarely confronting them and cannot be avoided or evaded as lesser problems have often been.

215
If the crisis can force enough men to acknowledge their own insufficiency, if it can bring them to recognize that the old ways of living have led to a dead end, and if it can arouse them to search for higher values as well as newer paths, it will be passed successfully.

216
If enough people in positions of power and authority were persuaded that a change of direction must be taken, the solution would be simple. Or if enough of the masses were persuaded of the same thing, here again the solution would be simple. In both cases, the risky path of new direction would have to be accepted. In practice we know what to expect of the rulers and politicians of today. And we know what to expect of the multitude also.

217
There is little room today for servile accommodation to conventions. Necessity forces us to rip through red tape.

218
A colossal revision of attitudes is called for, an abandonment of outmoded ideas which belong to the story of the nineteenth century and which create self-deception when carried into the mid-twentieth century.

219
Ideals must still be given to the world, even if they seem quite impractical and even if the giver is crucified as Jesus was, or shot as Kennedy was. They are needed to offset the egoism and materialism which come so much more easily to most people.

220
Struggling students must make the best of this dark age, and while deriving inspiration and guidance from the texts of dead sages learn to think and act for themselves as children of the twentieth century should think and act.

221
It would be foolish to turn our backs entirely on the past. And it would also be foolish to fail in the comprehension of what we have to learn from it. But this does not mean that we are to live in it. Not to feel the clamant urgency of the present is to fit one's eyes with blinders. There is only one

way whereby we can bury the troubled mental pictures of an unhappy past and an uncertain future, and that way is to create a worthwhile present. It is needful to comprehend that there is no other way open for humanity except to make the creative effort needed to start a genuine new life. If it starts a pretended new one or a camouflaged old one, then all the troubles which it is seeking to escape will once more descend on its head. To look backwards for guidance will be to look for trouble. The old passé point of view was good for its period but has now fulfilled its function and lost its creativity. It must be displaced by a timelier one. Humanity must look forwards and let the dead bury the dead if it is to save itself. The problem today is not how best to return to the customs and complexes of a past phase which was long ago finished with, but how best to advance to the creations and visions of a new one. Humanity is called upon to keep in mind the inner developments, the outer events, and the spiritual signifi-cance of what is happening everywhere. And this can be done only by appreciating the inner significance of this sensational epoch. It provides an opportunity for mental expansion which may be accepted comprehend-ingly or rejected ignorantly. Acceptance may be a bitter drink at first but will be sweet in the end, whereas rejection may be sweet at first but will certainly be bitter in the end. That is why humanity must be realistic while not renouncing its ideals and must do the utmost that can be done under the circumstances, fortified by the knowledge that an upward movement will quite quickly attract divine support. Indeed, it is moving at a speed that makes a dramatic and dynamic changeover in this direction from materialistic ideas urgent and imperative.

222

The picturesque or exquisite survivals of a feudal age may continue for longer periods here or shorter ones there, but change is working and necessity is pressing: they will crumble away.

223

The old formulas will not fit the new conditions. Renaissance, not retrogression; forward to new achievements, not back to old decadence. Mankind must be flexible and adapt themselves to new times, accommo-date themselves to new necessities, or else they will suffer. There can be no creeping back to the ignoble. The powerful tide of evolution will catch and drown all those who make such a foolish attempt. It is cowardly to flee backward into the familiar past because the present is too hard for our weak souls. It is foolish to lag behind the century's needs. It is courageous to move forward into the unknown future.

New age directions

224

In *The Wisdom of the Overself* it was briefly hinted that the twentieth century was the era of universal human enlightenment. I have been asked to expand upon this point. Just as the nineteenth century was the era of scientific enlightenment, so our own is the century of universal enlightenment. This is taking three forms. First, general education, intellectual knowledge, and scientific discovery will continue to spread throughout the whole world and will not reside mainly in the West. Second, they will become available to all classes and not be confined mostly to the middle and upper classes. Third, religion, mysticism, and metaphysics will reveal their realities and shed their superstitions, will be made more rational and thus will no longer be regarded as being displaced by science but rather as being necessary to complete it. Furthermore, the philosophy of truth, which is the highest kind of enlightenment possible to mankind, will become as easily accessible as it was remotely hidden in former centuries. Because we are at a cyclic turning-point, this is the century when truth will be let loose on the world. Not only ultimate truth which philosophy reveals for the few but also political, economic, social, religious, and scientific truth for the many. The falsehoods which dominate human society, the illusions which individuals and groups hug so fondly, and the lies under which society lives are being—and, we venture to predict, will be still more—shown up for what they are. This is one reason why we saw the phenomenon of a Nazi falsification of every branch of cultural and practical facts on a scale unheard-of in history. For it represents the scum which rose to the surface so that it might be cleared entirely away, the night which attained its darkest pitch just before the first ray of dawn. It also explains why we are seeing a second and similar falsification being attempted by the hierarchs of Communism. It is certain that if the Nazis had conquered, this world-wide illumination could not have spread but instead humanity would have been plunged into a new dark age far worse and far more materialistic than anything it had hitherto historically experienced. The danger of falling into spiritual eclipse was therefore real.

225

We moderns have striven for power. We have gained it but lost peace. Even the power itself has run riot in our hands and half-destroyed our lives, our cities, and our societies. If we are to restore contentment to our hearts, we must restore balance to our strivings.

226

The time has come when education should re-educate itself, when medicine should give Nature's herbs their due and demand that all foods be rid of their added poisons, when the body-soul relationship should be correctly revealed by psychology and psychiatry, when for their health's sake and their soul's sake human beings should stop devouring corpses. The events and changes which have come on the world scene since the turn of the century stagger the mind, but those which will come before the end of it will be even more startling.(P)

227

The sooner utopian dreams of perfectibility of the human race are dropped, the less disappointment there will be. The sooner we find out what measure and what kind of transcendence we *can* realize, the more contentment we shall attain. The first is an unanswerable question because at that level there is no individual.

228

To reject modern civilization and its culture utterly—to condemn its faults, sins, errors, and evils to the point of refusing to have anything more to do with it—is to end in nihilism. This helps no one, not even the nihilist. Nor are sensualism, drugs, or suicide ways out. Those who say that a man cannot keep his moral integrity, cannot honour his conscience and still take part in the present culture, are not right, though they are not entirely wrong.

229

A mystical purpose must be introduced into our common life to balance the mechanical principle that now sways us. Then the State will become a sacrament. This is not to say that we need a new state religion. The less the state tries to impose a religion on the people, the better for that religion; it will then have to develop a real life of its own from within. This is simply an intimation that the ordinary institutions of our society should be so arranged and so balanced as to permit men to face Mother Earth, Nature, more often, and to enable them to turn their minds towards the couch of repose more frequently.

230

Twentieth-century man has to find a way of solving his problems, not of evading them.

231

It is not only capitalism which is being seriously threatened by its own defects or deficiencies, but also Communism. Both must not only reform themselves, but also modify one another, if they are not to break down.

232

It is true that a state which combines the practical, the modern, and the scientific with the spiritual (by which I do not mean the ecclesiastical) has yet to rise and seems unlikely to do so. But that is no reason why it should not be tried. The beginning can best be made by a few pioneers, on a small scale, and in the relative freedom of private effort.

233

The kind of unit which philosophy advocates in the political and economic, the national and international realms is a co-operative and not compulsory one. The higher ideal of complete world unification is beyond the understanding and hence the practice of humanity at its present stage of evolution.

234

Man's dependence on the earth for fuel such as wood, coal, oil, and gas, will give way in the future to dependence on the sun. Its rays will give him all that he needs for this purpose.

235

The world could be improved but it could not be turned into a Utopia. As Ramana Maharshi once said when dissension arose within his ashram, "There will always be complaints!" But let people try. They may make things a little better, but fundamentally they must make themselves better first. History alone teaches that. Hope easily deludes us, especially the idealists and optimists. In the end we must work on ourselves. As we grow better the world can get better.

236

An ideal solution would apply only to ideal people.

237

All external attempts to unite the different sects within a single faith are a pitiable confession of their failure. Such an artificial federation will not achieve much. Union must come naturally and spontaneously from within, from the innermost heart, or it had better not come at all—and because religious organizations are basically in competition with each other, this will not happen.

238

The keynote of yoga for this coming age should be divine immanence—that which is in oneself, in others, and in Nature. Democracy—the unification of society—will triumph. The opportunity to acquire knowledge will be freely available to the lowest. This includes mystical and philosophical as well as worldly knowledge. The racial prejudices, the political separativeness, and the religious preferences which assisted human progress at a former level of evolution but which now hinder it and cause strife and conflict will be broken down.

239

Destiny is compelling us to think internationally, which is the way a philosopher always thought without destiny's grim compulsions.

240

The problem of a common world language is an interesting and important one. Out of the crucible of war only two of the existing languages will emerge with any likelihood of leadership. They are English and Russian. And of these two, English will count most in a general reckoning of their pros and cons—chiefly because it is already in world-wide use. Therefore it would seem a safe and sound counsel to affirm that in addition to his or her mother tongue every pupil throughout the world be taught English as a secondary and universal one. But the matter is not so simple as that. For an age when so much will have to be constructed anew and when so many defective ideas will have to be replaced by better ones will find it more profitable to construct a better means of intercommunication also. Such an endeavour must be made. For the foreigner finds certain avoidable difficulties in his way when he seeks to learn English. These difficulties can be got rid of if England has the courage to cast convention to the winds and boldly inaugurate some much-needed changes in its tongue. English must first be simplified, regularized, and phoneticized. Such an auxiliary language will then become the supreme medium for international culture and commerce, travel, and conference. Books and magazines of planetary importance will appear not only in the language of the country of origin but as quickly as possible, if not simultaneously, in the language of the whole race too.

The chief advantage of Esperanto over English as a means of international intercourse is that it can be mastered in one-twentieth the time. This is a tremendous advantage. Those who have seen at first hand what difficulties foreigners encounter in the study of the complexities and confusion of English can alone appreciate it.

The twentieth century will assuredly see one language chosen to be universally spoken and written and to be taught as a second tongue among all the peoples of the world.

241

This opening up of old mentally shut-in states, this dissolution of long-standing bigoted sectarianism, will increasingly be one characteristic of the age. They are being brought to pay, by attack from without and disintegration from within, for the falsity they contain. It is true that in the course of time, human nature being what it is at the present degree of evolution, the new conditions that will replace them will become as shut-in, as bigoted, and as selfish as the earlier ones. When that happens they too will be called to an accounting.

242

The belief that this new shrinking of the planet, this closeness of peoples heretofore alien, this multiplication of transport and contact, would bring about universal brotherhood is a self-deceptive one. Propinquity of bodies cannot create propinquity of hearts and minds.

243

Sri Aurobindo's hopeful view about the establishment of a perfect society on this earth is one which, I must humbly say, does not seem quite in accord with realities. I wish he were right and I were wrong, for it would be delightful to expect such a Utopia to be realized one day. But the raising of human consciousness to the level of superman will not guarantee unity of outlook and attitude. Differences in these respects and, consequently, differences in action will still remain. Take, for example, the difference in attitude towards the world war shown by Sri Aurobindo himself, Sri Ramana Maharshi, and Swami Ramdas. If unity is to be really attained it could only be attained by evolving to a level even higher still than that of superman. And this indeed is the ultimate goal. But there is a further reason for the difficulty of realizing Utopia. When such a goal has been attained there will be no need to reincarnate on this earth, which is, in some ways, a purgatorial planet. That is to say, it is the natural residence for imperfect persons and not for perfect ones.

244

In the coming age, nuclear energy will be brought to the service of creative peaceful purposes. Its concentration on destructive military ones will be brought to an end.

245

A new and higher epoch in our history will come by divine cyclic law: nothing and no one can prevent its birth. And that will occur through the incarnation of spiritually intuitive men born for this special purpose. It is such an epoch alone which will witness the realization of dreams of world peace and justice, dreams whose failure of realization by political, military, and other means will force by necessity the attempt through the last and only effectual means—moral and intellectual renewal.

246

Those propagandists who eagerly use recent history to foretell the advent of a society which will be completely materialistic are completely wrong. For a world where everyone rejected the idea of a soul in man and God behind the universe would not last long. Such atheism is a sin against the Holy Ghost, and would be punished accordingly.

247

It is correct to say that one consequence of this evolutionary development will be the achievement of emotional harmony among mankind through mutual goodwill. But this is not the same as the achievement of intellectual unity, of perfect identity in view and attitude. This is impossible and unattainable. Each human ego has its own peculiarities, its own unique experience and its own psychological differences. No two are the same. Harmony as an ideal relation and ethical goal, yes, but unity as a necessary prerequisite of it, no!

248

Humanity will need more mental resilience, more readiness to accept change, reform, betterment, or sacrifice, and less of the inveterate idolatry of custom. It will need more imagination, intelligence, and intuition if it is to understand the pattern which the coming period is certain to assume. Those who suffer from stiffened mental arteries, who are incapable of profiting by past failures, of re-adjusting themselves to these changes and of meeting the new problems, will blunder badly. Whether they like it or not, whether it be for better or for worse, the fact stares them in the face that they are witnessing tremendous disruptive forces at work. They must understand what is happening and be courageous enough to accept intellectually that this is really a period of dramatic upheaval. To scrap old ideas which can have no place in the coming age will prove more profitable in the end. Those who remain foolishly purblind or selfishly prejudiced against what is happening all around them during this critical and swift transition cause themselves unnecessary suffering. They persist at their own peril in the delusion that the old materialistic ways which seemed to suffice before will continue to suffice in the future. For if a sufficient number of people do not accept a readiness to change, sufficient to influence the general social condition, then the entire fabric of society will bring down upon itself the terrible nemesis of violent destruction. Modern civilization as we know it will come to an end, self-liquidated by its own blindness. But its disappearance will be only to clear the ground for the arisal of a new and better one. Thus the coming era will assuredly bring mankind a better world. But whether it arrives at this happy goal through disaster and depopulation or through reason and peace is an unpredictable matter at the moment. It depends on the factor of free will which exists in a man's make-up. The time grows shorter for a conscious selection of the higher concerns of life.

249

I agree with H.G. Wells that science and technology have altered man's environment too completely to allow him to follow antiquated social and economic ways. I agree that the world could be organized to give a more abundant material existence to the masses of poor, underpaid, or unemployed workers. I agree that the lack of applied intelligence in the present social structure is appalling and that failure to adapt society to altered conditions is a menace to us all. I do not agree, however, that the icono-clastic and swift solution of these difficulties depends on the formation of a "world university" to collect and utilize all available knowledge. It de-pends, and has ever depended, on the discovery and application of the philosophic and ultimate truth about life, a truth which is not a totality of separate facts but a single central principle of being.

250

How is the human race to recover these truer instincts, these holier intuitions? The change required will be required in all the parts of the human being—thought, feeling, and body. Physically, there will be the need of counteracting a hostile environment and a wrong diet. Retreat from the cities to the country and great reform in the selection and prepa-ration of foods will be indispensable as a groundwork for the mental training. The first need is to abandon chemically poisoned, denatured, and devitalized foods, to leave the air of cities rendered impure with soot and filth as well as harmful with gasoline fumes, and to indulge in short one- to three-day fasts during the four equinoctial days marking the changeovers of the seasons.

251

We cannot reject the special needs of our century but we need not be enslaved by them.

252

If one thing is clear about the coming age, it is that henceforth a brusquely awakened humanity refuses to drift helplessly but intends ener-getically to give a positive direction to its fate and fortune.

253

Hitherto, developments naturally tended to centralize industry in huge establishments. This was absolutely necessary to heavy industries such as steel manufacture. It was done to reduce cost, but it was also done irre-spective of the human factor involved. It promotes neither mental nor physical health for people to live dreary diurnal lives under a smoky sky and work in factories where giant machines pound at their nerves. The owner-worker—that is, the little capitalist who labours for himself, the workman who prefers independence, and the peasant with a small land-holding—each of these has a right to exist. Under a wiser arrangement he could still do so without having to compete with the owners of factories, for he could collaborate with them.

A nation ought not to abandon itself to the hypnotic glamour of giga··-tic factories for the mass machine production of huge quantities of goods. On the other hand, it need not abandon such factories for the medieval notion of making everything by hand. It could make in factories whatever is best made there, such as automobiles and pencils, but it ought to encourage hand manufacture wherever that will serve best. A balanced industrial economy is ideal and will require both the big manufacturing, assembling, and distributing units in cities and the decentralized cottage crafts in villages. Small parts such as components and accessories can be made in the village workshops, and larger articles such as heavy goods and mass productions in the former. If the old idea was to take the worker to a machine in the factory, the new idea will be to take the machine to a worker in his or her home. The principle of mass production can still be employed, the most modern machinery may still be used, and yet the worker may have his freedom and retain his individuality by making part or all of an article in surroundings and under conditions where he can still be himself. This has indeed been done for many years in Switzerland, where village workshops carry out many of the processes needed in that country's famous watch and clock making industry. Such a scheme, of course, could be applicable only where the worker lived in a cottage or house of his own and not where he lived in an apartment or tenement situated in a building housing several other apartments or tenements. It would be ideal for "garden cities," which ought in any case to represent the type preferred in future town planning. Small-scale industries should be regarded as complementary and not contradictory to large-scale ones. The value and practicability of this arrangement have been well demonstrated by wartime experience, when a great diffusion of subcontracting enabled stupendous programs to be completed on time.

Why should not the towns themselves be converted into "garden cities" where every family has its own little house and its own little garden surrounding that house? In the garden city, beauty and use have demonstrated under the test of time a happy and successful marriage. Nobody who has seen Letchworth and Welwyn in England, understood their significance and appreciated their worth, would again be satisfied with disorderly drift. There should be a feeling of space and air, a presence of green grass and leafy trees in the modern town. The garden city idea, which balances industrial, residential, and aesthetic needs, is the best for dealing with the problem of placing manufacturing plants and housing their workers. The Lever Brothers at Port Sunlight and the Cadburys at Bournville have shown how clean, artistic, individuality-preserving, and kindly the factory system can be made when those who administer it have taste and heart as well as minds.

Metropolitan towns exist already, however, and have become too indispensable a part of each nation's economy to be eliminated. The solution of the problem they pose is to turn part of them into a group of connected garden-city units, arranged like concentric circles around a common centre.

A metropolis like London or New York needs at least half its population transferred to a dozen different newly built garden cities set in the clean healthy spaciousness of the green countryside. When the size of towns is kept moderate, their streets will be quieter and the health, happiness, and outlook of their inhabitants better.

A proper relation must be found between town and country life, between existence in the large factories and in the little workshops. A healthy modern society will be neither excessively industrial nor exclusively agricultural. A well-balanced society will enable its members to choose their work from a wider set of activities than merely industrial or solely agricultural ones. The worth of a sane equilibrium between such antithetical factors of life as machine toil and hand toil needs remembering. The decentralization of advanced countries is only part of the answer to the evils associated with their present industrial economy. We must think out an economic structure which will still make use of people as human beings, even while they themselves are making use of machines.

254

There is no reason why village handicrafts and cottage light-powered industries should not be encouraged alongside large-scale mass-production in factories. An avenue should be developed which combines the merits of modern mechanical production methods with the merits of medieval hand methods. Cheap and widespread electric power, small and easily manipulated machines, local centres for the supply of raw materials and the purchase of finished goods—all these will combine excellently with the "garden city" plan for urban workers and also furnish profitable winter employment for agricultural workers. This factor must now be taken into account.

255

Where a family wants particularly to keep all its members together during all the working day, it should be provided with a small agricultural property or a small workshop, which are better suited to such a purpose. It is desirable that small-scale industries should exist alongside heavy industry, and cottage industries diffused alongside factory ones. There is plenty of room for mass-production and there is plenty of room for individual production. The mass production of automobiles brought within the purse of the middle class what was before within the purse of the rich alone. It is in the making of common necessities especially that mechanical mass-production has an impregnable case. But even here the mechanic may and should work in co-operation with the artist. Much material could be fabricated in little one-room workshops and then sent to the central assembly depots or chief finishing factories.

256

Between the sentimentality of theosophical "universal brotherhood" and the sometimes callous rigidity of an aged caste-system, whether Eastern or Western, there is a sensible middle way.

257

The collisions within a family, an institution, a nation, all humanity, show how hard it is to make this dream of universal brotherhood a fact.

258

Only when the best in science and industry blend with the best in spiritual and artistic culture shall we have a civilization justifying the name.

259

Wendell Wilkie's book *One World* is in harmony with the philosophical position. I think that the author would have modified his views a little if he had known Asia for a longer time and in a deeper way. Humanity is not emotionally ready for the world-state, which would be the only way to implement his ideals with 100 percent efficiency, but it certainly is ready for an association of nations more advanced in its form and stronger in its power than ever before. Co-operation is perhaps the proper keyword to present problems; union must come later. However, in the consideration of all political and social problems, we have to return again and again to the human problem. The spiritual darkness of the human race is the real root of its external troubles. Only its spiritual illumination will really remove those troubles permanently. Until that happens we must necessarily alleviate the situation, so far as it can be done, by utilizing external methods. The result will never be quite satisfactory but it can be progressively so. The same applies to the settlement of internal social and economic problems.

260

The coming age will arise, phoenix-like, out of the destruction and violence of the dying one. It will, by reaction, be a constructive and peaceful one. The spectre of war will be exorcised. Mankind will learn to inhabit a peaceful planet.

261

Who can study recent history and not perceive that the world is being forged with relentless finality into a single unit, into a consolidating reconstruction which is long overdue?

262

To be a neighbour does not necessarily make one neighbourly. Modern

transport and communication have brought the most distant nations together. Yet they have still to learn to live in peace. And this would be the
result not of human engineering but of human understanding.

263

If we create a more generous and better-enlightened environment, it
will better serve mankind during the new upward twist of the evolutionary
spiral. Warned by our dangers and illumined by our sufferings, relaxed
from hesitancies and relieved of complexes, we should not find this tremendous task beyond our capacity.

264

It is undesirable for the capital of a country to be situated in a mammoth
industrial city. Those who govern a nation ought to reside in a small city
set by the sea or in the green countryside. A rigorous process of liberating
millions of industrial and commercial workers from the clutches of mammoth cities must form an essential part of the new program.

265

What groups are most unlikely to attain wholesale may be quite possible
for individuals to attain singly. This is the fact behind the utopia theory.
Here and there, uncommonly, a man detaches himself from the herd and
climbs to the mountain top. But the herd is satisfied to remain below.

266

The Oriental belief that former golden ages were necessarily happier,
wiser, and better ones than ours is true only in a superficial sense. While
the people of those times were still primitive and had only partially developed their latent possibilities, the character of mankind was only partially
developed for evil, too. But since then, they have had to evolve the powers
of intellect applied to practical life and to individualize themselves out of
tribal dependence. The consequence has been less communal spirit and
greater personal selfishness, less response to spiritual intuitions and more
reliance on materialistic sense promptings. Again, while the planet was still
thinly peopled, the struggle of man against man was less, hence the call on
his evil propensities was less, too. Actually, we have all lived through this
or other planetary evolutions before and therefore have all possessed those
manifold qualities and characteristics which belonged to the men of those
earlier ages. If they were happier and better, then so were we. Those
qualities and characteristics are still within us, but they have been over-
shadowed for a time by the other ones which evolution has since stressed.
Lapsed for a time they may be, but lost forever they cannot be. Evolution
does not discard its former gains but takes them up into itself, preserves
and transmutes them while it moves onward.
Empires built upon pyramids of skulls and rivers of blood rise but to

fall. Where is the Assyrian Kingdom today? The Greek might has cracked
and dwindled. The broken clay bricks of vanished Babylon afford fit
haunts for spiders and cockroaches. But the Assyrians, the Greeks, and the
Babylonians themselves have not vanished. They are with us today, albeit
in different bodies and in other lands. The law of physical rebirth has
brought them back to the school of life, either to learn fresh lessons or to
re-learn the old ones which were insufficiently mastered. Hence we have
within us today the stored experiences, the unfolded capacities, and the
accumulated knowledge of all the previously born races of mankind. Only,
some of them are temporarily overlaid or temporarily neglected or even
temporarily inaccessible. But they are there. We have to recover or express
them alongside what we have additionally gained since then. Over-con-
centration on the intellectual-physical phase of life may have made us
materialists, but the shift of emphasis which the tide of evolution has now
to bring about will make us something better. The time has indeed come
to restore the balance, to realize that what we once were in the distant past
we still are and much more besides, to open out all sides of our nature to
fullest bloom in equal measure. In an age which has experienced awful
disintegrations, we should begin to integrate ourselves. Such a rich integral life was not possible in primitive times. History has made us more
ready for such a fuller quest than were earlier races. That is why we of this
century must have the boldness to be ourselves and not pale imitations of
the men of the distant past. Every historical period must find its own
outlook, work out its own world-view afresh. How much more must this
be the case in a period of such unique character as the one in which we live
today!

267

The notion that we shall enter a marvellous new age when the lion will
lie down with the lamb is an idle one. Human nature would have to alter
first and it does not ordinarily alter with such excessive speed. But the
notion that we can have a better age than the wretched one which is dying,
is a sensible hope.

I dedicated *The Wisdom of the Overself* to the pioneers of a nobler epoch.
Does that mean I believe such an epoch will soon begin? My answer is that
I do believe it will begin but not necessarily soon. The arrival of a nobler
epoch, in the sense of one that will witness society being organized for the
material benefit of the masses rather than for the benefit of the few, is
becoming obvious to all. But a society organized for the spiritual benefit of
all classes is very far from obvious and I do not at all see it coming soon.
We are indeed a very long way from it, as I stated in the preface to *The
Hidden Teaching Beyond Yoga*. If anything may be predicted of the age

which we are entering, it is that the tempo of change will be tremendously accelerated, and that new inventions and new ideas will come quickly and plentifully to the front.

268

The interdependence of mankind was not understood through the logic of philosophic reflection, so it had to be understood through the logic of terrible calamities. Thus Soviet Russia and conservative England were forced by bitter necessity to make a military alliance. And what began as a war in one continent, Europe, ended by having repercussions on the whole world. For more than two hundred million people in a highly civilized continent like Europe could not proceed along a road without the rest of mankind having to follow in the same direction to some extent. This is a lesson in human interdependence which history has never before given. Thus the need of a long interlude of peace will enable the leading states to modify their self-sufficiency and take to some form of world-union and thus to become eventually a single unit.

The Belgians, who brutally enslaved the unhappy inhabitants of the Congo, were themselves twice enslaved by the Germans. Can nobody see the hand of Karma here? Life has taught us severe lessons by the sheer compulsion of events. The first and foremost of such lessons is that no race, no country, no class, and no individual can afford to stand aside in callous indifference to the welfare of other races, countries, classes, and individuals or in narrow nationalist isolation. The war showed up the interdependence of peoples as nothing else did. The British failure to respond to India's natural need of liberty sent thousands of Indian soldiers to death through the temptation thus given to Japan to pretend to "liberate" India, while the Indian failure to respond to the Cripps offer sent thousands of British and American soldiers to their graves. The truth is that humanity is even now secretly becoming, and must one day openly become, a great family. Such are the sufferings and upheavals of this unique period that men have been compelled under their duress to look the real issues at last in the eye. And those issues are primarily moral and mental ones. We may see in the miseries of today a powerful testimony to the moral degradation of yesterday. The tragic misunderstandings of mankind which fail to recognize this are deplorable but repairable.

269

It would be absurd to attempt to change mankind overnight. Human character and human outlook are produced by the course of evolutionary experience during immense periods of time. But if we ought not to embark on such a futile task we ought to embark on the nobler and wiser task of making the knowledge of Karma available to all. Then, if people continue to injure others, they will at least know that retribution must eventually come to them. To remove their ignorance and to increase their comprehension of truth is our clear duty. To act towards their neighbours with goodwill, will then be theirs.

To the profound thinker, the history of the last hundred years plainly evidences the existence of a higher power which is guiding the destinies of mankind no less than it evidences the existence of a karmic law which is tying pain to wrong actions. The careful study of history by a mind which is not only capable of independent thinking but also able to bear the consequences of such thinking, and which is equipped with a knowledge of the law of Karma, will lead to significant results of a most philosophical character. In this connection, Buckle's *History of Civilization in Europe* is a book worth reading even though its author had but an unconscious knowledge of the truth of Karma. We may learn therefrom that societies, like men, rise to their zenith and fall into their decline through their own moral and mental defects.

270

The Coming of a New Era

The amazing inventions and technological advances which the liberated intellect of humanity has developed open up an era of plenty, prosperity, leisure, and comfort for all. The Machine Age is ousting the Muscle Age. People today use less bodily energy for daily work and living than their forefathers ever did. Consequently, they ought to have more leisure for higher tasks. If, as is the case, they haven't such leisure, it is not the machine's fault but society's. Electric servants and other mechanical aids to living will do much to lighten even the domestic labour of the new age as they have already lightened its industrial labour. They will cook, sew, wash, carry, clean. It is not unreasonable to expect that at least one-half of the human effort expended in the operations involved in industrial, mining, and agricultural processes will become quite unnecessary. The Machine Age has made possible the Leisure Age. Individuals, for the first time, may work less and produce more. We are on the threshold of an era of unheard-of plenty, leisure, and culture, not for a few, as in the past, but for all. We can cross that threshold as soon as we reorganize society. Culture for all and not merely for the few may come into its own. Record players, for instance, are today grinding out the art of the few in the homes of the many. Once the struggle for bare existence is over, once men are able to give themselves less to the day-long drudgery of physical work and more to leisure-hour mental education, once we take full advantage of the machine's potentialities and make its benefits freely available to all, a big step forward in the possibility of human liberation will have been taken.

The inventions and innovations, the new discoveries, materials, and processes which will begin as a trickle during the opening years of the twenty-first century will pour out as a flood before the closing ones. The wars have given the sharpest stimulus to this development so far, but the real peace to come will complete it. The impetus of technological development in our own century has already become so swift and its inventiveness so enormous that the entire economic and domestic life of humanity will in the next century be magically altered. The first significance of this is that it will give both men and women more leisure; the second, that it will give them less labour. It will then be not beyond human intelligence and human goodwill to make the leisure and luxury that could emerge from a more effective use of the machine serve hapless millions. For too long, life for them has been too hard a struggle merely to exist. The lowliest man will share in a minimum of comforts and conveniences which the labour of the scientist, the power of the engineer, and the knowledge of the chemist will bring him. Scientific progress is multiplying the wealth of man. It can and will be converted into economic plenty. Modern power productivity has rendered more easily attainable the realization of idealistic dreams of economic betterment. It may be said that when James Watt sold and set to work in 1776 the steam engine on which his fame rests, he inaugurated the era of applied science. From that epochal year, men were able to manufacture goods with a swiftness and a plentifulness previously unknown.

There is no scarcity in Nature. It is simply a matter of competently mobilizing, by machine power, what she is willing to give us. It is not wrong to take advantage of new inventions and human ingenuity to give the body more comfort and the mind more freedom.

Those who are frightened by what the machine has done in the war may be cheered by what it could do in peace. Anyway, it is here and they'd better accept it. For so long as man's mind functions, so long as his thinking process continues, so long will the process of inventing new or better machines go on. The only way to eliminate their destructive use is not by eliminating the machine but by improving man.

The machine was born to help humanity. In the next century, it will help so amazingly and so widely that it will provide sufficient food, goods, and services to banish poverty and eliminate the jungle-like struggle for existence. Science has shown the way to enormously increased productivity. The inventive power of man has constructed wonderful machines, devised amazing techniques, developed extraordinary skills, created new materials, and made possible astronomical production figures. It has begun to make it possible for him to extract enough food, clothing, fuel, and shelter from the earth to give a worthwhile existence to all the members of his species. The multiplication of his power on earth is becoming a tremendous actuality. The human being stands behind the machine. He invented it, he exploits it, he must partake of its products. The sight of starving, ragged people could, in the next century, everywhere disappear. The degradation of slums could be wiped out once and for all. There would be no need for continuous class wars, no necessity for endless capital-labour struggles.

The amplitude of choice in attractive new materials and gleaming new colours which are available for manufacturing and constructional purposes are nothing less than amazing. Architectural beauty and practical utility meet and marry as they could never before. Utter cleanliness and dignified simplicity become possible for enrichment of the poorest home. Efficient accomplishment and aesthetic charm may join to satisfy everybody's everyday needs. All this casting aside of ancient limitations, crudenesses, and inefficiencies tends to change the stuff, the utility, and the appearance of our environmental forms and to change them greatly for the better. Life in the external physical sense could become better worth living for the toiling classes as it has always been for the sheltered few. Easily controlled temperatures in homes and vehicles could defy the worst inconveniences of arctic snow and tropic sun. The new materials of the coming age, the lighter metals and the stronger plastics, would alone make possible a productive transformation which could raise living standards, improve construction possibilities, and provide better opportunities and better employment. These materials will reflect the dynamic spirit of this age. Instead of waiting a whole lifetime for timber to grow, we can wave a wizard's wand over milk or grain or chemicals and compress the result into an instantly available substance which can be used in most of the ways that we have hitherto used wood. The most revolutionary invention of the century has yet to manifest itself, however. Steam changed the industrial character of the nineteenth century. Petrol and electricity have already changed the transport and domestic character of the first half of the twentieth century. But a cleaner, cheaper, safer source of power drawn from the air itself could yet immeasurably change its closing decade. Thus the setting of man's bodily life could be radically altered and rapidly evolved in the twenty-first century, both to express and to stimulate the alternations and evolutions of his mental life. New ideas and ideals will move in a flowing stream across the world. New patterns will spontaneously shape themselves to reflect and promote them.

It will be the business of the community to ensure that every member is able to earn a livelihood, to give him work that will support him, or, if it fails to do so, to supply him with the food, goods, and services which he needs. This will be regarded as not only ethical duty on its part, but also economic wisdom. A public dole system of relief is a confession of failure; a public works system, of half-failure. Such systems are bred by minds steeped in a psychology of scarcity. Success lies with an expansionist outlook, a full-employment policy, and a higher standard of common living. In this machine age, it is not production but consumption that lags behind. The equilibrium between the two must be maintained if economic health is to be maintained.

If the working masses could be delivered from the worst extremes of their economic servitude, they might begin to benefit by and even contribute towards the spiritual enlightenment which is historically due. This indeed is one of the main hidden reasons why destiny has decreed the immense economic and social changes happening today.

When economic anxieties, pressures, or deprivations absorb men's minds to the extent that they are unable to find the will, hope, time, or energy for spiritual studies, then the form of society which creates such a condition is harmful and undesirable. The toiling masses have had little time to think of spiritual truth in the past, much less to undertake its conscious and independent investigation. Hence, they have had to accept ready-made religion from others—mysticism and philosophy being so remote from their lives as to be almost non-existent for them. Thus, by promoting their exterior welfare, we shall not merely provide for the demands of social justice but also surround the masses with conditions more favourable for their progress spiritually. Physical well-being and worldly security are a necessary part of any economy which is to provide expression for higher values. Those who are interested only in their own comfort and security may not be interested in any altruistic proposals for the uplift of the underprivileged, but those who acknowledge an interest in the spiritual advancement of humanity cannot escape their responsibility in this matter.

We have, on the one hand, the machinery, the people, and the techniques whereby immense quantities of consumable goods and foods could be produced. We have, on the other hand, an immense human demand for them. But what prevents us from converting this potential demand into an actual one? For the transformation could be made if a great change of heart and a little change of head could be brought about. Society has ceased to desert and begun to accept its responsibility for the individual. Many of the overworked objections about the so-called impracticability of ethical and social idealism have been disarmed and disproved. We are ruefully waking up to the fact that the mentality which begins by imagining rigid restrictions on what can be done to construct a better world, ends by imposing them. We had to wait for the terrible stimulus of war before beginning to make needed reforms and overdue changes. Wartime necessity has shown that abundant production can be successfully achieved; peacetime events will one day show that abundant consumption can just as successfully be got, too.

When the world changed over from manual to mechanical production, it began to change over from feudalistic to modern ideas also. The twenty-first century will complete the process and apply it to the financial sphere, too. The twirling of a knob on a radio set and the touch of a control on an airplane switchboard—simple physical operations such as these, for instance—have twirled and touched a new order of financial ideas into actuality. Consider how the so-called bankrupt Germany which Hitler took over was able successfully to finance its gigantic preparations for the greatest war in history. It could not have done this if it had followed fear and tradition and limited itself to "bank wealth" or to the full backing of its paper currency by metallic reserve in gold and silver. It departed from the classic traditions of political economists with their mesmerisms of "sound" monetary equilibrium, economic cycles, and the law of supply and demand, knowing that the State's prestige assured the circulation of its paper. It went ahead with full confidence in the principle that there was no real bankruptcy while there was a sufficiency of labour, machinery, and materials—the rest was a matter of organization.

Only in this way can we advance at last to social sanity. If and when it comes, with the twenty-first century, we shall see the co-partnership of co-operative classes replacing the menagerie of conflicting ones. We shall see that nation greeted by history which knows how to serve best, not how to grab most. We shall see the stronger races, groups, and classes using their strength not to oppress the weaker ones, but to lift them up. We shall see a world of diverse peoples who have ceased trying to impose their will, their creeds, their trade upon each other and have learned to live and let live. We shall see public life converted from a wrangle for prizes into a field of constructive service. We shall see a world where the children of the lowest classes can share freely and adequately in the fruits of the highest education.

Such an order will bring out the best possibilities, as Communism brings out the worst. And instead of inducing men to struggle against each other, it will induce them to co-operate with each other. The principle of co-operation will help to crush individual and national selfishness and thus tend to promote ethical progress.

Role of philosophy, mysticism now

271

In his humbling discovery that for all his physical vigour and intellectual power he is still spiritually weak, contemporary man is discovering the need of religion, mysticism, or philosophy.

272

The crisis in the world today is such that straight answers must be given to straight questions. In former eras it was possible to accommodate the truth to the level of understanding of those addressed, to clothe it in symbol and allegory or to hide it behind enigmatic puzzling and obscure words, phrases, or sentences. But today there are ominous clouds in the sky which ought not to be ignored, and because of them the risk must be taken that those who cannot now understand may gather at least something, some part or some hint of the truth.

273

In ordinary times, when a new idea has to be introduced amongst a conservative people, it is best introduced by easy stages. Its advocates must seek out what is immediately practicable. But if many hindrances in the way of spiritual advance do exist, if progress must be proportioned to human receptivity, it is also true that we live in exceptional times and that a whole cycle of civilization is coming to an end. A new one is struggling to be born. Hence a definite speeding up of the tempo of progress will be right and successful just now, because it will be helped by karmic forces and evolutionary trends. Such a conjuncture of events and influences provides not only the opportunity to serve humanity spiritually as never before, it provides also the obligation to do so. We might have been quite content to wait for the vindication of the overwhelming rightness of philosophy, because events themselves have been contributing to our work for us. But they have been doing it slowly and cautiously, little step by little step. Now civilization's danger of collapse has come near enough to make us less patient. It is because we live in unprecedentedly troubled days that the light of philosophy is so needed. The more distressing the time in which we live, the more necessary is the quest for what will raise us above all distress. The critical changes and unprecedented events through which we are passing today call for a correct lead. It is an inescapable duty and sacred responsibility on the part of those who have the requisite knowledge to provide such a lead. The obligation to help the birth of a better world is both a moral and a practical one; it is now paramount. It is one of the philosopher's functions to reveal the true meaning of this world-experience, to explain the deeper causes of its chaos and turmoil, and to point the way toward a better life for mankind. His duty lies therefore not in making propaganda but in letting people become aware that the knowledge of truth does exist among men, that it is available for whoever seeks it earnestly enough. The gospel which humanity needs for the healing of its frightful malady already exists within its midst. But its existence is known only to a few.

274

Mystical culture must now reconcile itself with the new era's demands, must deepen its thought and widen its attitude.

275

In our epoch, when business enterprise is supreme, the need of fitting these doctrines to practical uses is also supreme.

276

It had to come, with history moving as it has done. The ferment of ideas, of minds provoked to seek truth, brought it on. This democratization of knowledge is happening in every other branch. How long could it have been avoided in this one?

277

We live in a time when mysticism *must* come out of the ashrams and monasteries and get to work in the marketplaces, the college halls, and the householders' abodes.

278

Philosophy is naturally best expounded out of gaiety of heart at the universe's wonderful meaning; but its lessons are best received, and its discipline best enforced, in the sadness of mind which comes to thought over the conditions of life today.(P)

279

The threefold ideal of rational religion, practical mysticism, and livable philosophy should be better appreciated in these times than ever before.

280

The psychoanalysts who assert that those who turn toward mysticism or philosophy to escape from the large-scale dehumanization, chaos, disorder, and tension of our times are taking an easy way out which lets them avoid facing their problems, are asserting what is true of some persons but quite false of others.

281

The more brutal our times become, the more does a sensitive soul long for the kindly peace which meditation affords.

282

It is now possible, because of the momentous evolutionary change which is marking out our epoch as one of the most important ever known to history, for a larger *individual* adherence to be given to philosophical

mystical doctrines than in former epochs. The blind slavish *tribal* adherence of patriarchal times to revelatory religious teaching is quite a
different thing.

283

The education of human intelligence, the culture of spiritual intuition,
and the ennoblement of character are necessities, since it is they, together,
that stand between mankind and catastrophe.

284

In this situation of world crisis, intelligent mystics should feel no longer
able to support the traditional policies of inertia, indifference, and escapism. They should be interested in humanity's present upheaval and future
direction. They should be thinking about how they can contribute something—however little—to help it go upwards out of this terrible trial to a
higher life and not sink downwards to a lower one.

285

If he remains completely preoccupied with his personal salvation and
tries to ignore the destruction and suffering rippling through the world,
that is his own affair. He is entitled to do it. There may even be nothing
else that he can do. But the falling bombs will break into the quiescence of
his meditations.

286

Only wisdom can keep its serenity and look behind the horrible events
of yesterday and beyond the chaotic events of today. The unpurified heart
and unequilibrated mind of the unwise confine understanding to the
short-range point of view, limit perception to the surface of things, and
agitate feeling within the immediate moment.

287

There is developing in the contemporary world an increasing sympathy
with mystical attitudes and an increasing realization of the insufficiency of
intellectual ones.

288

The world crisis has not only made it possible for these ideas to penetrate minds which were formerly indifferent towards them, but also to
show their immense value when practically and personally applied.

289

Those of us who are driven by troubles, disappointments, or frustrations to seek solace in mysticism do well. Nevertheless, we do not understand that the inner peace it will yield us is after all an intermittent one.
Only from the philosophical standpoint will we be able to find an enduring peace. Those of us who started to endure the wartime horrors with
such a standpoint were able not only to maintain but also to fortify it.
After the violent stresses of war, we shall need constructive principles to

guide our disturbed thoughts and mystical practices to steady our disturbed emotions. Only such principles can remain unclouded by the happenings of a world in crisis. The message philosophy proclaims, with its balanced estimate of fundamental human nature, brings tranquillity to the heart depressed by grim appearances to the contrary.

290

Mystics may disregard the events of their time but philosophers cannot.

291

Philosophy today represents a refuge for those suffering from the hatred and strife in the world as well as a source of goodness and wisdom for those who seek to permeate their lives with meaning.

292

Through the efforts of pioneers and the evolution of thought, there has unquestionably been some awakening in many countries, particularly European countries, to these new-old teachings and practices of a mystical or Oriental character. They are no longer so startling or so unfamiliar as they formerly were. This awakening has been greatly accelerated by their presentation in a modern form, however primeval they are historically. The need for them was very real as a necessary counterbalance to the contemporary tendencies, and as a self-protective reaction to the contemporary helplessness.

293

When we consider such a situation and ways to remedy it, it is noticeable that people who are limited by merely intellectual views are impatient and want to get quick results. They offer methods which will supposedly bring them quick results. But the fact is, all they can get are either imperfect or even bad results. The other way, the philosophic way, works in a deeper realm, sees quite clearly more of the basic factors, the real character, and is consequently more patient. It penetrates directly through the formal appearances of the situation to its fundamental realities. Therefore it can render better service to humanity by pointing out these realities than the most well-meaning statesmen who blindly grope their way round and round can render. Its counsel hacks at the single roots of all our troubles instead of hacking at a thousand branches.

294

The writings of the wisest spirits of the modern era are in their hands, the records of the great mystics of the medieval era can be consulted in their libraries, and the literature of the sages of the antique era has been translated for their benefit.

295

Philosophy knows well that it could contribute worthwhile ideas towards the easing of humanity's hard situation. But it believes that its voice would be a whisper crying in the wilderness, that too few would listen to it to make any effective difference. If it is pessimistic about the outcome of present tendencies, that is because it perceives, from abundant evidence provided, that their conflict with the divine plan can only end in their own destruction.

296

The need today is for Christ militant, for the spiritualization of life in the world, and not for flight from the world. The appearance in our own time of anti-Christ Communism is itself suggestive of this necessity.

297

For those who properly understand it and faithfully practise it, philosophy stands amid the uncertainties and threats of our time as a secure citadel. In it one finds assurance for heart and mind, and will find safe guidance for one's body.

298

Ought we to congratulate ourselves that in these days the sages appear within paper covers on the same shelves as the popular entertainers and romanticists?

299

It is not to be expected that the mass of people, with their weak moral and mental capabilities, could accept and follow the philosophic ideals. This was true in every past century and it is still true today. But never before has so widespread and so devastating a peril threatened mankind. It may be that a certain number of persons who might otherwise have passed the philosophic revelation carelessly by will feel the pressure of the times sufficiently to take warning and to take more heed for themselves.

300

Religions must rise and fall, change and die, because men's beliefs must change with the changing times. This is why I see in the higher philosophy of Truth the only enduring hope for a peace on earth which will be unbreakable, and the only charger for goodwill towards men which will survive as long as this planet survives.

301

How emotionally refreshing, how intellectually valuable, and how practically applicable are the certitude, the clarity, and the insight of philosophy at a time like ours of confusion and doubt, uncertainty and despair.

302

Men's lives are so disoriented in this age, their minds so confused and their feelings so frustrated, that the spiritual truth—could they only appreciate its worth—would be accompanied by proportionately more solace now than it was at other times in the past.

303

Can anyone escape the tension, the disturbance, and involvement in the world crisis today? Even the fact that Tibet—the hermit country—could not do so is both a symbol and a warning.

304

The custodians of the higher philosophy will not waste their time by engaging in futile activities. They recognize the psychological fact that only those people who want higher spiritual help will be prepared to accept the higher philosophical teaching. When dissatisfaction with the orthodox teachings is present and inability to find another to replace them is also present, and when the proper moral intellectual and intuitive capacities also exist, then there will be favourable ground for the reception of such philosophy—but not before such conditions do exist.

305

It is because painful experience has combined with scientific discovery to teach mankind that human resources unguided by divine revelation are not enough that mankind will have to listen to the voice of philosophy in the end.

306

A Prayer For The World:

In this time of confusion and anxiety, of strife and trouble, it is our holy duty to remember our dependence on Thee, O real Governor of the world!

We realize that the darkness in the world today has come because so many have forgotten their dependence on Thee.

Those whose positions of power or influence have placed them in the nations' councils need, in their grave responsibility, the help of Thy communion and the benefit of Thy guidance as never before, that they may not stray into error or weakness.

Therefore, we shall daily pray for them and for ourselves, in minutes of private worship or silent meditation, that all may regain the feeling of Thy presence. We shall constantly confess our shortcomings and faults, but we promise to strive to better and ennoble our lives. We shall endeavour to cast out all evil thinking and materialistic belief.

Our need of Thy mercy and grace is vast. Show us the way to win them, O Infinite Father of all beings, Whose love is our last resource.(P)

Need for wisdom, peace

307

The twentieth century must bring forth its own prophets, the West its own appropriate wisdom.

308

Every prophet or prophetic writer who arises for the guidance of erring humanity is only a secondary help on the path of life from ignorance to enlightenment. The primary guide must in the end be humanity's own intelligence, as it develops itself through growing experience. At first, when misdirected by appearances, it makes many mistakes and humanity suffers as a result. But later, tutored into the seeking of realities, it becomes wiser and plays its proper role.

309

The present awakening of the nonwhite races is full of significance. We hear much of the barbaric cruelty and savage violence accompanying it, but not enough of the saintliness which occasionally flashes across the black man's sky. Martin Luther King, for instance, now as I write a Nobel Peace Prize-man, comes closer to the character of Jesus than the vast majority of white men. The spiritual future of this planet may hold surprises and one of the greatest could well be the appearance of the next great prophet in the despised body of a dark-skinned man. No divine law has prescribed seership as a white-fleshed thing only, nor established the bringing of spiritual balm as a white monopoly for all time. This is mere human opinion frozen to the past by its own historic past. But the past becomes musty, faded, and has to give way to the new forces now pressing for entrance.

310

There is such a confusion in contemporary human affairs, such a threat to human nobility from its physical environment, that ordinary rational knowledge proves insufficient to carry the thoughtful human being through a serene and peaceful day-to-day existence. Only a super-rational and mystically revealed knowledge can provide the added elements necessary to such an existence.

311

The need today is for compounds of inspired visionaries and determined workers.

312

Is there any single source to which we can track down the entire multitude of disturbing events which continue to afflict the nations year after year? Is there one fundamental explanation which will explain all the other explanations that are constantly being offered us? For our answer we must go to those who possess no accredited position in the scheme of things today, whose very existence is largely unknown and whose voices are so quiet that they are seldom heard above those of the multitude which come to our ears.

We must go to the men of deeper insight, clearer vision, and impersonal outlook. Truth is a shy goddess and reveals herself only to those who court her in the right spirit, ready to crush all personal prejudice and to put aside all other desires at her bidding. Such men are rare and therefore the true understanding of life is equally rare. The eyes of such men are really open because they are no longer blinded by self-interest.

313

The philosopher who has opened his mouth too freely and frankly, told what he has foreseen in the belief that preparation for the worst offers some protection against the worst, soon learns to shut it tight again. For he learns that if it is unpleasant such truth is unwanted, and also that he is dangerously misunderstood as regarding as desirable what he merely regards as inevitable. During the First World War a few illumined seers, both Oriental and Occidental, knew how it would develop and how it would end. Before the peace treaty was signed they knew that a second war would break out about twenty years later. As early as 1942 they knew both the outcome of that conflict as well as the course to be taken by the peace to succeed it. They knew then the general direction of world events, for the following years confirmed their understanding, which did not come to them by reasoning or by calculation but by revelation. Where it could serve a worthier cause, they passed on fragments of this knowledge to responsible leaders during both wars, to sustain and inspire them. So long as the seers could give a message of hope, their words were welcome. So soon as, with the first years of peace, they gave a message of warning in both cases, their words were unwelcome. Because man is inwardly free however outwardly bound, free in his spirit but not in his ego, their prophecies were always conditional upon his rising to fulfil his spiritual possibilities, when they would necessarily have to be entirely changed. This was the unknown factor which made and makes perfect prediction quite impossible. But the likelihood of its fulfilment has become thinner with each year; the most crucial and fateful period was the eighteen months following the second war's end. Its failures point the way to the realization of forebodings, to the fulfilment of doom.

314

They foresaw the crisis and the war, knew that the entire planet had begun to spin in a whirlpool of increasing disaster, but they were helpless. They did not count in the conventional social world. Whatever they could do would be a mere drop in a bottomless bucket of planetary tragedy. All that they can do nowadays is to fashion, each for himself, an attitude which shall be resistant to the corrosive cynicisms around them and which shall be immune to the dark impurities beneath.

315

We need to employ but little reflection to perceive that the religious enthusiasts' dream of an absolute and sudden conversion of mankind by the millions is contrary to possibility, is in fact but a piece of wishful thinking. It dare not be said that it will be an era of renascent spirituality. Is the whole expectation of such an era merely a piece of wishful thinking? Not that the ultimate destiny of every living creature is inglorious: the eventual awakening of its individual mind into the universal divine self is indeed as certain as the dawn of the next day's sun, but truth can be understood only by those who are willing to accept the atmosphere of eternity.

316

It is not without worth to humanity that in a transitional era of catastrophe and violence, in a society of superficiality, neuroticism, and insanity, there should be some men and women who can act as direct links, as it were, between it and the divine world, as shining lighthouses in the darkened sea of their time. Only the mystical philosophers possess the essential knowledge of all the forces which are active behind the leading episodes of the world scenes, because they alone possess insight. And only the mystical philosophers estimate those episodes adequately and accurately, because they alone possess enough selfless impartiality and inner freedom to do so aright.

317

It is a characteristic of human groups that they cannot keep their foothold continuously on lofty moral heights through successive generations, but sooner or later sag and weaken. Religion, as the fountainhead of morals, advances but to decline and eventually exhaust itself. Hence inward renewal is needed, and hence new inspiration-bringing prophets must periodically appear. The task of a prophet today differs from the tasks of all other prophets who have hitherto appeared amongst mankind. For whereas they came for the benefit of some particular area or some definite race, he must come for the benefit of the whole world and all races. Where is the God-inspired soul who can inaugurate such a world-wide religion and who is conscious of being invested with such a divine world-encircling mission? We may search far and wide and yet find him not. Where is the beacon on the spiritual horizon? Where is the sign that humanity is about to witness the arisal of a prophet who will lead it out of this dangerous chaos? Where is the ground for hope that God-guided men will soon appear, ready to place their light and power at the service of their groping fellows? We must sadly confess that the sign is absent, the ground lacking. He who is to bring a new spiritual dispensation to humanity is still invisible. But his coming is certain. He will come to uplift the millions who have fallen into the abyss of despair, hopelessness, and misery. The war was an awakener. It is bad enough that we have forgotten our divine self. It is worse that we have forgotten that we have forgotten it. This is why the work of an awakener has to precede the work of a teacher. The proper time for the Messiah's appearance will be in the chaos after the third postwar period. For humanity must again go through the purifying and educative fire of wartime agonies. He will bear an unusual message and bear it personally to the whole world through travel—which no previous teacher has done, not even Baha'u'llah, who claimed to teach all nations.

318

The world's urgent need is more peace. But peace can come only out of goodwill if it is to last for any length of time. Therefore the world's real need is more goodwill. The individual's need, however, is not the same. It is for more truth.

319

Confusion and disorder rule the postwar world. This is inevitable because they already rule the minds and hearts of men. Human thought projects itself upon its environment. The mental confusion of our times prevails in every department of the inner life. The need for spiritual principles, clear thinking, and consistent analysis, if much more desirable here, becomes much less attainable. There is all the more need, therefore, for an illuminating knowledge which can act as a pathfinder through the confusions, a bestower of peace amid the disorders.

320

Ideals of spiritual excellence are a necessity if society is to survive and not destroy itself.

321

However grave the events of contemporary history may appear, one may draw strength and courage in the knowledge that Infinite Intelligence is always behind them, directing things.

322

The modern world has rightly sought and attained knowledge. Now it must quickly seek and attain wisdom, the next higher octave of knowledge, or it risks losing its gains and destroying itself.

323

What can even the most enlightened man do in these circumstances other than to withdraw into a retreat where he may help by meditation to purify the polluted mental atmosphere and bide his time?

324

The talisman in these difficult days is to hold to a sense of spiritual proportion, for to surrender to the suggestions of environment is no cure but only makes the trouble worse.

325

The dearth of sages in our time is ominous for the destiny of our time.

326

Even though it has taken such an unattractive form, there is a spiritual opportunity in the world crisis. For whom is this crisis? It is for the ego. But who is *he*? He is infinite being and timeless. So he puts Appearance in its proper place, stops being hypnotized and victimized by it, and remains in the Real, indestructible by war, imperturbable in its own sacred stillness.

327

We are not here offering likely speculations or problematic probabilities. We are trying, with guidance higher than such merely intellectual guesswork, to hold a flickering match in the awful night which surrounds us.

328

There are great truths which the world needs today but which the world is not consciously seeking for and therefore will not readily accept. Those who have found these truths, tested their correctness and worth, are consequently not willing to engage in the futile path of aggressive proselytizing. They quietly make the truth available to whosoever is willing to take the trouble to seek it out.

329

One prediction may be safely made. If a new saviour of humanity really does arise and *does* something to save humanity instead of merely talking about it, he will definitely not arise from any political party.

330

Amid the confusions and dangers of today, this faith in a divine plan of the world can support us like a rock.

331

We are men in the hard grip of adverse fate, who struggle even when we fear we cannot win, who go on and on like the heroes of Greek tragedy, despite frustration and defeat.

332

Amid the babel of passion-led or self-interested earth-limited voices which we hear today, we listen wistfully for a truer voice speaking with a new accent. We are waiting piously to hear the divine Word. Some suppose it can speak in Sanskrit and will echo forth only from the Himalayas.

But they are wrong. It may speak in English or Dutch, may echo forth in Arizona or the Hague. Who knows? Let us commit ourselves to no narrow doctrine of spiritual monopoly, be it Hebrew or Hindu. Some think it must speak resoundingly and masterfully, like a missionary. They too are wrong. It may speak quietly gently and humbly, like a mystic.

333

It is not only a real solace to have the reassurance that a higher power supports the universe and a higher intelligence sustains its operations but, in this period of widespread calamity and evil, a vital necessity.

334

The enormous danger of this situation is not to be met with escapist apathy and alarmist fear.

335

The world's need is silently crying out for inspired and selfless people who will awaken the world's attention to spiritual values. There is little need today for a philosophy which is merely academic, or mostly antiquarian, or utterly antediluvian.

336

It was this same High Lama whom I met at Angkor who foretold that the world's spiritual enlightenment would next come through a Western channel. The fulfilment of this prediction cannot be far off now.

337

We must begin to see what the philosophers have long ago seen—that, psychologically, the maladjustments, the frustrations, and the spiritual impoverishments of modern man are the root causes of his outer troubles, that, given the right atmosphere of co-operative goodwill and creative intelligence, all practical problems involving human relationships will soon solve themselves within it. That most strife-breeding political, economic, and social questions would vanish altogether if we could create this new atmosphere, this new spiritual outlook, has become quite evident to them. The widespread exclusion of higher principles and ethical considerations from the ruling policies of modern states is something that has brought its own Nemesis upon the modern world. Only when the world will consent to become inspired by higher principles can it hope to find the real solution of the multitude of economic, political, and social problems that face it. All solutions which lack these principles are but paint and varnish which hide but do not change the real problems. Only by raising the public conscience through the efforts of inspired individuals and true religious teachers will real change come about. The higher executive posts in every country throughout the world should be filled by individuals who are as spiritually minded as they must needs be practically minded, if mankind is to make true progress. Such individuals should be put at the head of the social pyramid, as was formerly done in the prehistoric times under the system of king-sages, or spiritually minded advisers should be put at the sides of those in authority to ensure wisdom in action.

338

No true reform is likely to be created by a committee. It is the single uncommon outstanding person who is usually responsible for bringing it brilliantly about. A committee can also achieve results but they will be of a mediocre kind.

339

Someone must give a lead, must initiate the higher development, must create the first new way. Until then the world remains what it is.

340

What cannot be achieved by all mankind as a whole, since their negative conditions are too deep and too widespread, can still be achieved by those individuals who are less caught in such conditions and more responsive to right ideas.

341

In a world subject to change there are no lasting solutions to its problems. But to the extent that individual men stop making further problems for themselves and others, and reduce old ones by changing themselves, they can better the world situation. For without some knowledge of the World-Idea and the higher laws, how can they act wisely in matters concerning their personal lives and relationships, their surroundings and their people?

342

The prospects for mankind are materially very unpromising. However, it is through every kind of experience that the species has to grow and learn its lessons, and ultimately acquire understanding and goodness. Meanwhile, the individual can still build his own independent inner world for himself to some limited extent.

343

The clear Stoic perception of Marcus Aurelius Antonius lamented, "Rome is dying because Rome has nothing more to live for." But the awakened persons of today who refuse to yield to the animality and materialism of their epoch have something tremendously important to live for. They have escaped conquest by it because their own escape is to be the first fateful step towards achieving the future world-remnant's survival and escape. In doing so, in making their lone stand against this inner peril, they perform a valuable service of defense against the outer one.

344

It is not enough to ask for help from Heaven. Mankind is in the throes of leaving adolescence and approaching maturity. Consequently Heaven wants it to stand a little more on its own feet, make its own choice, and learn to be more like men. It must do this of its own volition.

345

Wherever the fortunes of life may take you and whatever the dangers it may bring you, I hope you will always keep the thought of the Divine Overself as the best talisman to cling to. It is in these terrible times that you may come to appreciate more than ever the value of faith in divine wisdom behind life and assured immortality after death.

346

What is the use of philosophy in a social situation that is hopelessly imperilled, in a struggle that moves before our eyes to the anguish of defeat? Its acceptance by a few individuals cannot change the situation itself, cannot save civilization from the doom it has brought upon itself. What philosophy can do is to help the individual, both in the privacy of his inner life and in the reactions to his outer fate. In a desperate situation such as we have confronting us today, philosophy bids him remember that this reaction offers him the chance of rising swiftly to a higher status, the opportunity to be ennobled rather than crushed by disaster. It reminds him of what is, after all, the higher purpose of life—the building of character and the pursuit of wisdom. It bids him develop the spiritual hero in himself and face what must be faced with serenity and reflection. If such advice seems too high for his modest powers, it is nonetheless practical. For even if no one could live up to it—which is untrue—anyone would be better able to cope with fate if he tried to.

347

He soon sees that although there is really nothing that he can do about humanity's dangerous situation, there is something that he can do about his personal situation. He may try to put his body into surroundings more attuned to, and expressive of, his ideals, and he may try to put his mind into a state more imbued with, and fortified by, those ideals.

348

Governments may prepare systems of defense and rescue, of protection and relief, but the only adequate form that will save half their peoples is outside their capacity and beyond their courage. They are too hypnotized by the past to be able to rise abruptly out of it and meet an utterly different kind of future. It is for the individual who does not want to die prematurely to prepare now with the work of saving himself. This is neither a selfish nor an antisocial course to follow, for in doing so he will best be able to help and save others. It is the only practical thing he can do and it is a duty which he owes himself and his family: to refuse to hang onto the coats of helpless leaders who are being driven toward the edge of an abyss. There is nothing wrong in practising such self-preservation, and any real service that he can render to humanity will only become possible through it.

349

What is the hope left to a man in such a frightful historical situation? In terms of direct effort he can do much for himself but little for others. He can resolve to clear his own spiritual darkness and correct his own graver weakness.

Forebodings

350

If we insist on looking at the world's worst, we ought in fairness to couple it with the world's best. Only then can we get a clue as to the world's trend.

351

Nothing here written should be read as a prediction; everything should be read as a warning only. Humanity as yet is on trial and no verdict has been finally given.

352

Powerful forces in the heaven worlds are gathering for a transmission and will enter our world at an appropriate time, which is fixed and measurable within this century. These forces will stimulate new thoughts and new feelings, new intuitions and new ideals of a religious, mystical, and philosophic kind in humanity. It will verily be the opening of a new epoch on earth, comparable to that which was opened 2000 years ago by the coming of Christ. The impulse will bring science into religion and religion into science: each will sustain the other and both, purified and vitalized, will guide humanity to a better and truer life. Insofar as science is an expression of man's desire to know, it is in perfect harmony with the highest spirituality. Only when it is unguided by his intuitive feelings, his heart, and put at the service of his animal nature alone, does it become anti-spiritual and bring him self-destruction as a punishment.(P)

353

Suffering is not leading into world despair but into world hope. Mankind's crisis has been fateful, but it need not be fatal.

354

Many sensitive persons suffer on account of their awareness of humanity's tragic suffering. But they must realize that life is still in God's hands and will assuredly remain so. The human viewpoint receives only a limited fraction of the whole picture. God's love is greater than ours has yet shown itself to be, and it is infinitely wiser. Despite the activity of evil forces and the horrors of the contemporary scene, this is nevertheless a dominant fact.

355

Postwar economic difficulties afflict practically all the countries of the world. It requires not only genius to handle them, but a mind awake to the fact that a new era is dawning for mankind, a mind unhampered by past prejudices or limitations. But just as serious is the spiritual crisis, for Nature is demanding a choice of roads and destinations also. After all, we are here on earth not just to bake bread in order to keep the body alive, but ultimately to use that body to effect spiritual salvation. If the response to this crisis is not right, then our economic geniuses will not be needed, for the planet will simply shake her back and swallow up millions of people and their economic systems. It would be pleasant to look the other way and be blandly optimistic, but experiences of the past few years incline those who understand, more and more towards pessimism.

356

The refusal to recognize the obsoleteness of war, the inability to change a point of view with which men have lived until now, will in the end destroy those men and liquidate their civilization. There is no possibility of escape by mere drifting and no evasion by mere ignoring of the challenge. Time is short, the decision must be made now. The correct one will necessarily be also a humbling one. It is a crisis in human affairs such as human beings never formerly dreamed possible. More than that, it is an unprecedented spiritual crisis of man. He is being put to the ultimate test. For if we study the history of evolution we shall have to note the implacable fact that those creatures which could not adapt themselves to altered conditions could not survive. They perished, and their forms perished with them.

357

If nations have suffered appalling wars in our time, and if, to the consternation of the thoughtful, even more appalling ones are still possible, let them learn that there is no real preventative while they continue to rebel against Truth and reject its messengers.

358

Enthusiastic dreamers know no balanced factual appraisal of the world's spiritual situation. Either they declare mournfully that we are all doomed to cataclysmic self-made destruction or they assert joyfully that the perfect millennium will shortly dawn. The truth is that men are too good and too sensible to fall into the first fate but they are too wicked and too foolish to deserve the second.

359

Some have heeded the message and will receive its protection. But most have not. The response is sadly insufficient to prevent the doom which menaces contemporary society.

360

If men and women have to move once again through the whole cycle of war and chaos, tragedy and suffering, before they will be willing to listen to a true prophet, then they are unlikely to be deprived of the experience.

361

That we must expect the advent of immense renovations in religion and vast innovations in thought can be reasonably denied by nobody. The forces of retribution or reward, which are adjusting all accounts and which are now operative in all departments, are too impersonal in their purpose, too universal in their scope, and too powerful in their character to be ignored or resisted successfully. The twentieth-century world cannot escape from its extraordinary destiny. It is for them to see that it is no longer a question of their private ambitions or wishes and personal interests or leanings. It is a question of whether they are willing to bend before the storm or else be broken by it. For the new forces of enlightenment tread on the heels of the Four Horsemen. If history is forcing these changes into human understanding today, it is doing so at a heavy price in untold agony. Are we to have further necessary ideas taught us in the same way or are we going to embrace them consciously deliberately and willingly?

362

Is this to be the inglorious end of the human race, to be melted down to a whiff of powder? Was it all but an empty and useless experiment?

363

In the *Anguttara Nikaya, Chatukka Nipata*, Buddha says: "When the rulers or their representatives become unrighteous, the Brahmin householders become unrighteous; when they become unrighteous, men in the towns and villages become unrighteous; when they become unrighteous, the influence of the sun and moon becomes poisonous. The planetary influences become bad, the days and nights are affected, the seasons are changed, poisonous winds begin to blow, the roads become impassable, the gods become angry, the rains do not fall regularly, the corn-fields become impregnated with poison, and when people eat the produce of these fields, they become weak and many diseases attack them."

364

If we make a comparison between our times and the conditions which preceded the destruction of the Greek and Roman civilizations, and if we note the chaos, dissension, strife, and violence which then prevailed and now prevail, we shall be forced to regard the future of our own civilization with apprehension.

365

That the world's peace will eventually come we may believe, but it will come only after receiving a further experience of suffering, since humanity does not heed sufficiently spiritual messages from its teachers.

366

The world may have to undergo another war. Life, like Nature, teaches at times by harsh violence without sentimentality. If the good suffer with the bad, it is because of their ignorance. They too must wake up and acquire knowledge of the truth. They also must grow. There is a threefold evolution going on separately: physical, mental, and spiritual. We suffer through, and because of, their ignorance on these three levels. They are not here on this planet only for enjoyment of the animal urges or satisfaction of the ego-pressures which drive them, but for the purpose of growth in all three of these evolutions. "We are not here for Bhoga [pleasure], but for Yoga," said an Indian holy man to me. Each movement must go on, heedless of personal feelings or thoughts. Despite its largeness and grandeur, the World-Idea has already mapped out each individual course of growth among myriads.

367

The opening postwar period will be the hollow of the world-crisis wave.

368

That a new age will come, and come in this century, is surely written in the stars. But whether or not we shall have to pass it over the bloodsplashed route of a third world war, a large depopulation of this planet, and a virtual collapse of our civilization, is within our own power to choose.

369

If the modern world's descent into extreme violence, aided by the skill of science, is not to be utterly self-destructive, it must be stopped at some point. How near or how far we are from that point is visible enough to the seers. This is certain, that we shall reach it and that if no other way is effectual by then, we shall reach it with a shock so great as to affect the nervous system and mental outlook of the larger part of the human race. That will be the historic moment when the West and the East will begin their upward climb once again toward Spiritual values, although each hemisphere in its own way.

370

"The will of God which is revealed through prophets, holy men, should be received in humility," the old Chinese *Book of Changes* warns the present-day inhabitants of Cathay, but we also must heed these words. I am neither a prophet nor a holy man but I feel very strongly and know very deeply that it is the divine will for man today for him to put the violence of war aside by a certain date, or else be punished *terribly* for his arrogance and obstinacy. *There is a time-limit.* Those who give no heed to these warnings will later have to bear the severer whippings of self-earned destiny.

371

Those who know what will be the true outcome of these world events are not yet permitted to make any prophecy: they are permitted only to utter the warning that mankind is in a position of extreme danger, a position from which he can free himself by one means alone. He cannot save himself by military, political, or economic means; he can save himself only by spiritual means.

372

I do not say that war *must* come. I say only that another crisis, as desperate as war, will arise, that a tide of catastrophe will break suddenly over the world.

373

The crisis gives us a last opportunity either to arouse our consciousness of life's higher purposes and orientate ourselves to a life closer to them or to stay in the old ones and wait inert, unhoping, for the end.

374

If we do not succeed in solving these problems, we shall tremble on the verge of perils as immense and deadly as the war itself: economic disaster, social cataclysm, famine, pestilence, the general dissolution of religion, morality, and civilization, with a fleeting reversion to barbarism as the end of it all. Only then, only after whole countries and continents have been largely depopulated through tasting the extremes of suffering, will the scanty remnant of people find their way back to a new and nobler and healthier way of life than that which prevailed before. It will surely come, even at this fearful price, because it must come. It was hinted in two earlier books that if our civilization does not better itself, it will have to sink and make way for another one. And we have hinted also that humanity is walking on the edge of a precipice. But this does not mean that our failure will necessarily result in a total lapse into barbarism. Rather will it clear the way through wide depopulation and sharp anguish for the coming of a nobler and more advanced society than the present one. The sins and sufferings of our generation cannot destroy the faith of the philosopher in humanity's nature. He knows that its better nature will triumph in the end, even though the price of that triumph may be an utter destruction of all its civilization and a fresh start after still worse suffering. For it faces the necessity of giving up the materialistic outlook which brought it into such catastrophe. There is no escape from this necessity.

375

No one knows with any certainty what is to come out of such a desperate world situation, what future mankind has amid such conflicting forces.

376

Prophets have often been wrong over every Armageddon date they were incautious enough to give us. The fateful day or year has usually arrived only to depart and be forgotten. These failures may serve a good purpose if they serve to warn the next batch of prophets to keep dates out of their prophecies!

377

A near-miracle like this arrest of the drift toward war would not be credible to those who do not know the power of the spirit in man's personal life. If it can do that for *one* why not for two billions?

378

There comes a time however when catastrophe cannot be averted, when both self-amendment and sincere prayer are fruitless to alter fate's decree.

379

None of us in this generation will live to see spiders spinning their webs across atomic bombs or ballistic missiles, but no prophecy is more certain to be fulfilled in the lifetime of a later generation. For suffering will force its lesson home on the unwilling minds of reluctant pupils, new egos will incarnate with more receptive hearts, and the World-Idea will impose its rule under an iron law.

380

There is an old Buddhist prophecy that this planet will split apart, that the great roaring explosion will tear the mineral world and the mountain ranges into dust. But before this event, a Buddha will come, full of loving kindness, to show us the way of salvation.

381

In the twelve months between the full moons of May, 1956–1957, the world will take or miss its most important chance to appreciate or ignore these teachings. Inner decision and outer destiny are here locked together.

382

The world's fate hinged on those eighteen months after the second war, as it did again on that year of final choice and chance—1959.

383

The war is not at all inevitable; it is preventable, but neglecting to take the prescribed and proper course will render it inevitable.

384

The world situation is worse in some ways since the great crisis of 1962, but in more ways it is better. The outcome is at present quite unclear and only a rash person would venture to make any dogmatic positive announcement. The war risks still remain, but in a somewhat mitigated form.

385

Nostradamus predicted that art and religion would dominate the coming era (the twenty-first century onwards) and that wars would no longer be waged.

386

While mankind will be driven to take eventually the only practical means for its self-protection against war, which is the creation of an international form of association with a single international police army, such an external means would in the end not be enough if it were not accompanied by an internal means, which is the casting out of those antisocial aggressive or destructive lower forms of thinking and feeling which it has brought over from the animal stage of existence.

387

In the very week that Hitler started his invasion of Russia, I told India, in a Bombay newspaper interview, that it would end in disaster, and why. Events confirmed that prediction.

388

Further sorrow awaits modern society unless it can produce a finer quality of thought and a better way of living. It has reached the parting of the ways. Only a recognition of this fact can save it from further blunders and consequent disastrous suffering. It will be compelled by events themselves to face the issue which cannot longer be postponed. We approach the zero hour. Procrastination will gain nothing but lose everything. For if it does not end materialism, then materialism will end it. The human race walks on the very edge of a yawning chasm. If it misses its step or takes a false one or loses it balance, it may fall and this civilization will reach its terminus. Unless it can bring less blind selfishness and less materialistic prejudice into its view of the world, its civilization will not escape its final Nemesis. Modern man must rediscover these higher truths or his civilization will perish with him in a holocaust both man-made and nature-made to which the past has no parallel.

389

Is it too late to overcome the tragedy in which the world is so deeply involved? The answer is that if enough people and if enough leaders of the people gather around the standards of a genuinely spiritual ideal it would not be too late. The likelihood of such an event seems remote, yet it is the adoption of these ideas and attitudes, these ideals and practices which is absolutely indispensable to overcome this tragedy and save humanity.

390

Can we be saved from going headlong over the dangerous precipice which we are skirting so uncomfortably? Out of this world catastrophe there could have emerged an era dedicated to truer religious ideas and higher social forms. But instead the war years have brought to many people a degradation of outward circumstance and, what is much worse, a degradation of inward character. It has brought out bad instincts like hatred, violence, brutality, lust, greed, and envy. Suffering has taught them the wrong lessons. It has made them more materialistic instead of more spiritual. If civilization is destroyed, such people will be largely to blame. Our generation has been given its last chance to survive. At present utter collapse is merely possible. But if wiser principles are not adhered to or if their acceptance is too long delayed, then utter collapse will be sadly inevitable. If humanity cannot or will not respond to the call of this evolutionary voice, then its civilized life will collapse in a new Armageddon followed by devastating famine and widespread disease. Only after it has lost everything in unheard-of sufferings will the remnant that will be left alive after the inevitable interval of anarchy realize the need and have the will to make a fresh start in a nobler direction. There is sufficient reason to support the hope that a total collapse is unlikely. The human race will not wholly perish, although much in it that deserves to do so will perish. A remnant will emerge alive and pass into a new and better phase and a purified form of its evolution.

391

The road to the salvage of civilization is still open to us, but it will remain open for a shorter period than the twenty years which separated the two world wars. The situation is tense; it may become grave; it may even end in the utter disaster that so many fear—but it will never end in the defeat of the divine plan. That is impossible. We may lose this world battle, the forces of destruction may burn down all that we see around us, humanity itself may perish in the titanic holocaust, but human life will return, will go on and slowly rebuild its house again. But, humbled a little or purified by its suffering, it will build more nobly next time.

392

Nothing is gained by letting the wish for peace override the certainty of war. Since it is now too late to avert the latter, all hopes and thoughts, projects and plans for the future ought to be nurtured with this tremendous and terrible ultimate development in mind. Since the warnings which I gave many years ago when the tide might have been turned remained unheeded, all reckonings concerning the next few years must include this Armageddon which will terminate a whole cycle of human materialism.

393

If men insist on bombing each other out of existence—which will not happen even though the attempt will—this does not mean that the higher power must abandon its higher laws, deprive them of the full result of their insistence, and maintain an enforced peace among them.

394

Operation W.W.3: Its object is not to benefit certain persons while others, equally meritorious, remain unbenefitted, but to guard the higher philosophy and to preserve the Quest's practices and disciplines for generations yet to come. The benefit to individuals is incidental and due in most cases to favourable karma created by devoted service.

395

That the war's end will bring a new trouble—namely, a condition of chaos—should not seem surprising but a logical corollary to the tremendous devastation which will characterize this new kind of war.

396

The refusal to recognize and apply this truth, that man is divine in essence and evolutionary goal—let alone its complete rejection—must bring disasters in the end, must provoke raging storms from time to time.

397

When this atomic nightmare will have passed and the anarchy which it brings about will have ended, humanity will pick itself up again and rebuild its civilization in a new way. Warned by its own sufferings and by the devastation of its environment, it will surrender to the unavoidable and make higher principles the basis of communal life.

398

Karma has determined to shatter to pieces the obtuse conservatism which clings to disguised materialism and camouflaged immorality.

399

If civilization falls, it will not be utterly obliterated. Something will be left, some scattered remnants of population will here and there gather up its shattered fragments and slowly, arduously begin the work of reconstruction.

400

Civilization will be terribly wounded but not mortally wounded. The larger cities will suffer destruction but here and there a remnant of people will remain.

401

Karma is not and can never be a merely individual matter. Society as a whole creates the slum which creates the criminal. If society calls him to account for his crimes, he may in his turn call society to account for making his criminal character possible. Consequently society must also share with him, if in lesser degree, the karmic responsibility for his misdeeds.

402

For no nation can escape collective responsibility for its acceptance of the codes and policies, the ideas and actions, the standards and loyalties that bear its name.

403

If it be unpleasant to accept the grim inevitability of world disaster, it is better than hiding from it. For at least we shall thus give ourselves the chance to meet the thought with proper preparedness every time it harasses us. By learning the art of thought-control, by studying the higher laws that govern life, above all by seeking out the true self within us, we shall be able to create enough mental peace and emotional courage to make the best of the worst.

404

The world does not need a change of head so much as a change of heart; it needs newer attitudes rather than newer ideas.

405

Einstein thought that an atomic war would destroy ninety percent of mankind. We doubt that but we do not doubt that it would destroy at least half of mankind. Yet we do not think that it will be either the explosiveness of the bombs nor the radioactive emanations which follow in their wake that will be so responsible for this result, as the consequent breakdown of the highly centralized form of civilized living which has been developed in modern times. For with it will come the disorganization of city supplies and the temporary paralysis of country farms, the disappearance of orderly government, the moral chaos and gross selfishness that will manifest themselves during the anarchic struggle for survival, and the inability of city-dwellers to endure and adapt themselves like pioneers to the primitive conditions with which they will abruptly be faced.

406

We have said for years that the atomic war is inescapable and that the planetary devastation consequent upon it is unimaginable. But because of its very nature, it can last only a short time. What will last comparatively longer is the period of chaos and anarchy which will succeed it. During that period, more people are likely to die than during the period of bombing itself. For the great centres of population, where millions of people are now cooped up in towns and cities, will either be destroyed by the actual explosions and their inhabitants by the radioactive emanations left by the explosions, or if not destroyed they will become paralysed and unable to supply their inhabitants with the necessary food and materials wherewith to live and carry on their vocations. The entire commercial and industrial system of today is so centralized and so complex that the means of supporting those people will be absent. The system itself will be disastrously disorganized. The transportation and distribution of food and goods will cease for a period of time. It is during that period, which in some cases may be only a few months but in others as much as a few years, that the difficulty of survival will be most pronounced. The sensible thing to do is to prepare ourselves for it and to learn how to keep ourselves fed, sheltered, and alive until the reorganization of communal existence and the beginnings of normal living return again.

407

The problem of preparing to meet the onset of war and its destructiveness has never before had to be met in such a way and on such a scale as it will have to be met in the impending future. Only an ostrich-like attitude or a paralysis induced by fear will refuse to admit it into consciousness as a problem that must be thought about and whose solution must be sought. Those who dislike giving it such thought in advance will not have the time to do so when the terrible actuality does arrive. They are making a grave mistake. Everyone knows that the first places to receive bombs will be the metropolitan cities, the centres of government, the industrial towns, the ports and junctions, the military bases and aerial fields. Is it not practical wisdom therefore for those who can to withdraw from them and for those who cannot to explore every possible means to find a way out, making every possible sacrifice to do so rather than waiting passively until the fatal day? It is a tragic irony that most explosions and destructions will certainly happen in the temperate zone, where people are least fitted for primitive forms of living, whereas the least will happen in the tropical and semi-tropical zones, where people are better fitted for such living and better able to endure and survive the breakdown of civilized existence. Therefore the first physical preparation is to accustom ourselves to a simple hardy life and to train ourselves in the techniques of pioneer living.

408

In view of the immense hardships and difficulties that will face us after the war, part of the advance preparation for this period should be the building up of bodily health and strength, endurance and robustness. Another part should be to learn how to live simply with a few things and without luxuries, how to live in and with Nature by our own labour. Thoreau's book *Walden* is very relevant today.

409

Anti-escapism: It is a fallacy to believe that there are any special zones which are not danger zones. Therefore it is a wrong course to emigrate anywhere expecting that such a place will provide safety and security when destruction and poison fall upon the globe. Running away is no way out; whatever place you run to remains as dangerous as the place you run from. It is better to go into the silence and find your protection there. Then, if the higher self directs you in or after meditation to move to another zone, you may accept its guidance. The removal will be a right course, because intuitive, whereas the other is dictated by the blind intellect's cleverness. This is another way of saying, "Seek ye first the kingdom of heaven, and all these things [including protection] will be added unto you." In his 1962 book *Witness*, J.G. Bennett confirms this. He writes: "The group of people working with me was very little affected by the war. None was killed or seriously wounded. This was done without deliberate withdrawal from war activity, and it appeared to be the consequence of having set ourselves to serve an aim beyond our own welfare . . . those who are called to serve a great purpose." He also says: "If the leaders of mankind were so lacking in responsibility and understanding, and the masses so passive and inarticulate, what could the future bring but new and more terrible wars?"

410

With each war cumulatively worse than the one which happened before, humanity hardly dares imagine the horrors of this latest and worst war which menaces it. Its work of self-destruction will be assisted by Nature, who will not herself remain idle. She too will scourge the world with flood and famine, pestilence and earthquake, storm and upheaval. Such a universal catastrophe will be more than civilized society can bear, more even than man's will to live can endure. Great destructive forces will be used by mankind in its process of self-annihilation. All this planet's people would not be destroyed by these forces, but the greater part of them would.

411

The physical condition of the civilized world, the mental condition of civilized mankind, and the moral condition of all mankind will be, after such destruction, so deplorable as to stagger the imagination.

412

Those who look for and those who expect a millennium of spirituality and justice, of goodness and truth—or even the beginning of such a millennium—as a result of the spread and acceptance of some cult, have always been disappointed in the past and must be so again in our own time.

413

We live in the last days, not of the world but of an age.

414

Historical disaster and outward catastrophe might destroy civilization but could not destroy humanity. Its inner life will go on.

415

Western man has touched the low water mark of his ethical materialism; he will fall no farther. Henceforth he will begin to rise toward the realization of his nobler possibilities.

416

Just as the pendulum swings farther backwards if it has first swung farther forwards, so the human being rises to the loftiest heights of spiritual consciousness only if it has first sunk into the blackest depths of materialistic ignorance.

417

We see every indication around us that the old order of foolish ideas and self-centered ideals is undergoing its last stages of existence. Its cultural possibilities are close to exhaustion.

418

If the opportunity which existed during the one-and-a-half-year period after WWI had been properly appreciated and used, today's menaces would not have come into existence.

419

Many people in different parts of the world escaped being disturbed by the first world war. Some people in some parts escaped the second world war. But no person in any part of the world will be able to escape the planet-circling atomic forces of the third world Armageddon.

420

Those who are destined to survive the ordeals of this crisis will also survive to confirm the truth of these dismal warnings of inescapable challenge and verify the accuracy of these hopeful predictions of general enlightenment. Only a minority will escape the general catastrophe. Out of this remnant a new and spiritual race will develop. The war of bombs and shells will be displaced by a war of ideas. Men's minds and not their bodies will clash against each other. If conflict will not come to an end, at least bloodshed will. The steely clash of arms will give way to the verbal clash of opinion.

421

What does the future hold for mankind?—this is a question often asked and variously answered. One of the answers is given by Hinduism which says that the present period is the Kali Yuga—that is, the iron age—when life is at its darkest, man more corrupt, sinful, and wicked than ever, spirituality, religion, morals at their lowest ebb, sufferings, catastrophes, diseases at their highest tide. Moreover it says we are only at the first quarter of the iron age and we still have the other three quarters to go and that as we go farther into Kali Yuga the conditions will get worse and man more wicked. However Hinduism also says in its scripture the *Bhagavad Gita*, through the person (mythological though he may be) of Sri Krishna, that the Avatar—one who descends from a higher plane into human incarnation to bring in a new and better period—will come near the end of the iron age and use his power and knowledge to usher in the reign of goodness and righteousness, Truth, and above all Peace. Everywhere throughout the world today we see violence, agitation, and destruction, and this too, according to Hinduism, is to be expected in the Kali Yuga. Therefore attempts to end war are unlikely to meet with much success until the Avatar comes. If however we go not to Hinduism, but to the astrologers and ask for their predictions, the story changes, brightens, and becomes full of hope, for they say we are entering the Aquarian age, the age which spreads knowledge, goodness, harmony, and peace. It might be asked, "What does philosophy say?" The answer is that there is something of truth in both the Hindu and the astrological prognostications. First the evils of war, violence, destruction, and so on, will come to a climax with the materialization of nuclear war. Too much has been created on the mental plane and is being created not to find its way back to earth again in physical explosion. Only after a nuclear war with the major part of the human population wiped out will it be possible for a new start to be made, will mankind have learned the lesson of substituting goodwill for ill will. Secondly, philosophy says that there are ages within ages—that is to say minor, lesser, and shorter periods within the great period—and we will after the nuclear war and after the chaos it brings enter one of these better periods.(P)

[*Editor's note*: With the exception only of the last para in this section, we know neither the dates nor the historical sequence of when this predictive material was written. We do know, however, that para number 421 is the most recent, and that it was written in the last year of P.B.'s life.]

Good will ultimately prevail

422

Those of us who are the humble spokesmen of philosophy neither seek cheap triumphs nor expect swift victories. We know where human nature stands today. We are resigned to accept whatever results may come because we are convinced that the forces promoting human moral and mental growth are irresistible, that however slow and long the human journey may be, its final arrival at Truth and Beauty and Goodness can never be prevented.

423

It is pardonable and natural to take short views of life and Nature, and consequently to become impatient of long views. Yet the short one reveals horrors and evils that are often unreconcilable with the belief in a beneficent and omnipotent Power, whereas the long one reveals both ameliorative adjustment and an emerging significance, a unifying World-Idea which gives a place and purpose to all things.

424

These men, the scientists and technicians of our time, the businessmen and engineers, the professionals and lawyers, need their opposites, the prophets and mystics, to remind them of life's deeper side, to warn them of the incompleteness of their own lives, and to impart to them some appreciation of subtler and finer states of being where the promises of all that is best in religion and philosophy, art and culture, become fulfilled.

425

Somewhere between a roseate optimism and a gloomy pessimism, truth hovers. It does not stand still. For each person touches it at some point predetermined by his own personal experiences of life.

426

No aspirant need be distressed because so few accept the higher teaching. Religious prophets and mystical seers arise in different localities to take care of the others, those who lack the subtlety of perception and the refinement of intuition to respond sufficiently to it. All aspirants have to acquire something of the immense patience of the sages, who know that evolution is always in progress and that Nature takes her time. But along with that patience they have constantly to suffer the remembrance of a terrible fact—a crisis in human history has been reached and failure to return to a truer spiritual basis for life quickly enough will bring terrible catastrophe. Nevertheless all events will be used in the unfoldment of the World-Idea and all will work out for good in the end. They must trust the divine wisdom. It never makes a mistake and its hidden purpose is utterly beneficent.

427

It is inevitable that during the uncertainty and danger of war people often turn for help to God, but after the war there is a reaction away from God. This has usually happened throughout history. However, there is very little that an individual can do about the world's spiritual condition, but there is a great deal that he can do to improve his own. The more he can understand the universal laws by increasing his knowledge of them, the better he will understand that even in the darkest times, when evil seems to be triumphant, still that is only temporary and limited because only the good can triumph in the end.

428

Humanity is not likely to remain impervious to the call of intuition forever; and even now we may see, especially in the Western world, signs of a silent gathering up of spiritual forces which will lead, when it finally erupts after the next Armageddon, to a tremendous renewal of the inner life of mankind.

429

This is the future of the human race—that all its traits of character, all its faculties of mind, all its activities of feeling and body will one day be unfolded into happy equilibrium.

Part 2:
THE ARTS
IN CULTURE

Art brings beauty to the body's senses, yet if we wish to pursue it farther we must withdraw from them, inwards, keeping the mood they started, etherealizing and developing it until we penetrate to its abode. There, under enchantment, we *are* beauty.

1

APPRECIATION

The arts and spirituality

Beauty has its own holiness.

2

A life devoid of the contributions which the arts can make is an arid life. Aridity is not the same as simplicity.

3

Philosophy includes no narrow type of asceticism. It does not reject, like some of the forms of religious mysticism or Oriental yoga, but gratefully accepts the ministrations of Nature's beauty and man's art. It knows that what calls forth our attraction toward fair scenes and our appreciation of lovely sounds is, at its final degree, nothing other than the exquisite beauty of the Overself. Therefore the productions of talented artists are to be welcomed where they are true responses to this call, true aspirations to answer it, and not mere representations of the artist's own diseased mind. For the same reason, the introduction of art into the home and of artistic design into industry is also to be welcomed.

4

I cannot separate, as the old Greeks could not separate, the love of beauty in Nature and art from the love of Truth in thought and experience.

5

Art and Nature may so be used as to enlarge us, to give us less egoistic ideas and greater hearts.

6

Aesthetic appreciation of art productions, no less than harmonious rapport with Nature, leads us nearer and nearer to the divine in us, until our inner being is wholly absorbed in its ecstatic joy or unutterable peace.

7

In our own era many people are unable to come to Spirit through religion but are able to do so through art.

8

I believe, as the Platonists of Alexandria believed, that "beauty nourishes the soul." But we may need to learn what is really beauty.

9

Any creative art which opens up an entrancing world of beauty to us, if it refines and uplifts us, opens up a spiritual path at the same time.

10

Anyone who is susceptible to beauty in music or place has a spiritual path ready-made for him.(P)

11

The cultural arts offer a path to reality, whether one can actually create or can only enjoy their products. Through good inspired drama, painting, writing, poetry, or opera, there is the possibility of achieving contact with its transcendental source.

12

To bring man to the Real, art must become more and more refined.

13

It is the higher, more refined forms of art which at times reveal this authentic note of inspiration. The low forms lack it because they belong to the grosser, more primitive cultural levels where mere physical activity is the prime concern.

14

Although it is true that aesthetic appreciation is relative and not absolute, it is also true that the process of evolution has set up standards within us which are progressive from a lower to a higher, a vulgar to a finer one.

15

Art opinions and reactions are more than just a matter of personal taste. They are also indicators of evolutionary status.

16

It depends on a man's taste, which in turn depends on how mature he is, how rich an experience garnered in former lives he possesses, how developed and balanced is his judgement, and, lastly, how refined are his feelings.

17

Only out of a beautiful heart or mind can a work of true beauty be produced.

18

The first test of a piece of art is, "Is it beautiful?" Many minds today, especially the younger ones, will vehemently deny the truth of this statement; but that is because they do not know who they really are, what the universe really is, and why they are here at all.

19

The stage epitomizes and dramatizes human experience. This offers us the chance to draw some of its lessons. Serious literature interprets human life and offers some of its meaning. Music's incantation can draw us up to exalted levels, and the other arts can show us a beauty which refines feeling and uplifts emotion. But all these possibilities can be realized only if the creators of these productions are themselves open to true inspiration.

20

The refined works of art come out of the refinement of the artists. The coarse, crude, and materialistic workers in this cultural area are simply that—manual workers.

21

There are moods when the aesthetic feeling in some individuals rises to the surface and expresses itself as the beauty of lofty aspiration or the beatitude of nurturing reverence.

22

In scholarship, in the arts, in precious classics of poetry and literature and music, wide-ranging over the entire world and back to ancient eras but not deserting the latest knowledge of science, he will find nourishment for his mind and feelings. Culture, real education, makes man *man*, puts him over the animal.

23

Despite all the degradation which art, literature, and music have suffered in our time, their work will be carried on by the sensitive. They will continue to use imagination to create beauty or to copy Nature and, with its help, to refine human beings, to draw them away from and above the beasts.

24

Art cannot be expelled from human culture, any more than thought. Just as all attempts to stop the followers of religion from exercising the faculty of reasoning do not succeed in the end, so all attempts to stop them from making sacred figures likewise fail. The first Buddhists were without statues for at least two hundred years. The first Romans did not venture to carve figures of their gods for the same period. The Muhammedans still do not dare to imitate sacred sculpture—neither Allah nor Muhammed is ever depicted, so fierce would the opposition be—but their artists put their skills into geometrical patterns to build mosques of striking beauty. Art cannot be dismissed as mere embellishment. It answers a human need. As Plato saw, the search for the beautiful is only another aspect of the search for the true and the good.

25

He will be told by the ascetic-minded that he will have to shed the arts on his upward way because simplicity of possessions and freedom from desire for outward things are essential. This is true. But he can learn to shed them inwardly by becoming unattached. If he does this then he may accept them into his life again. The cult of ugliness is not a necessary part of the spiritual existence.

26

Culture rebelled against those ascetic doctrines and fanatic teachers misusing the virtue of simplicity for the propagation of hatred for beauty.

27

For us it is not enough to search for reality. We search also for the Beautiful Reality. We need its presence as enjoyably visible here and comfortably felt now.

28

A creative work of music, pictorial art, or literature which kindles an inspired mood in the audience, the beholder, or the reader has justified itself. It has made a contribution to humanity not less valuable on its own different plane than that which is made by the engineer or the builder.(P)

29

No nation can call itself truly civilized which does not encourage the teaching, the practice, or the appreciation of the arts.

30

A country without culture, without music, painting, poetry, drama, and literature, is a country without a soul.

31

If more persons can be stimulated to create these works, and more beholders encouraged to view and appreciate them, the country benefits.

32

Beauty is as much an aspect of Reality as truth. He who is insensitive to the one has not found the other.(P)

33

We must call in the services of art to give religion its finest dress. Music must show its triumphs in the individual soul, architecture must create the proper atmosphere for communion, painting and sculpture must give visual assistance to the mind's upward ascension.(P)

34

Judge a work of art by analysing its effect. Does it leave you feeling better or worse, inspired or disturbed, calmed or restless, perceptive or dulled? For every opportunity to behold great paintings or listen to inspired music or read deeply discerning literature is itself a kind of Grace granted to us.(P)

35

When art or literature inflames negative passions, it renders a disservice; but when it purifies, redirects, and exalts them, it renders not only a cultural service but also an evolutionary one.

36

A gracious and refined style of living might be disapproved by those of ascetic tendencies and even decried as materialistic. But aesthetic feeling can be quite compatible with spirituality.(P)

37

One of life's objectives is to develop in us these aesthetic feelings, for they lead to the Overself.

38

Why should culture be abandoned at the bidding of a harsh, anti-intellectual, anti-aesthetic asceticism? It need not be so. One can become spiritual, detached, and even enlightened without depriving oneself of those enrichments of mind and heart which culture can bring.

39

A work of art which awakens in its beholder or hearer or reader a deep feeling of reverential worship or inner strength or mental tranquillity thereby gives him a blessing. It enables him to share the artist's inspiration.(P)

40

To the extent that the beholder immerses himself—that is, concentrates on—a work of art, to that extent he partakes of the artist's inspired state.

41

The inspired beauty to which a true artist introduces the world is an aspect of the same power to which a true priest introduces his flock.(P)

42

A philosophic temperament, well-developed and sufficiently rounded, has little taste for the ugly bareness propagated in the name of simple living, or for the dreary denial of the beautiful arts in the name of anti-sensuality.(P)

43

Tolstoy, in his ascetic recoil against his own handiwork, called art "a beautiful lie." Well, it often is so. But it is quite often not so. It can arouse either devilish or divine feelings. It can lead men to that higher beauty which, Keats saw, is one with truth. Whenever its influence is bad, it is the artist who is to be blamed, not art.

44

A mind caught up with spiritually significant meanings, or attentively held by highly beautiful sounds, is a mind that one day will respond to Truth.(P)

45

Beauty is one side of reality which attracts our seeking and our love. But because it is so subtle and our perceptions are so gross, we find it first in the forms of art and Nature, only last in the pure immaterial being of the intangible reality.(P)

46

The way to benefit most by an inspired production is not only to recognize it for what it is, but also to greet it with love.

47

If it is an inspired, worthwhile piece of art—whether it be music, composition, or painted picture—it will be able to shift one's attention from other and personal things to itself and hold that attention, however briefly. In short, it helps him to forget the self and to become the other. Now if he could make that same transition from the self to a higher level of consciousness where the highest part of his being resides though it is seldom brought within the circle of consciousness, he will achieve the greatest blessing he could give himself.

48

If a work of art or a piece of writing cleanses the heart or stimulates the search for truth, it is worth what it costs if you have to pay for it, or worth your time if you do not.

49

Art should evoke an atmosphere. It should transfer an emotion; if it merely transmits a thought, it is but half art.

50

It is true that we get experience at second hand if we get it through art, but it is also true that we are then able to get experiences of a kind that otherwise we would never have had at all.

51

True art is successful to the extent that the artistic production guides the listener's, reader's, or viewer's thoughts into the mood in which it was itself created.

52

Creative art demands concentration if it is to be taken seriously. This is achieved by entering at least a half-meditation.

53

The need of aesthetic surroundings which once was felt by few is today felt by many more. With the democratic spread of education this is as it should be; this is an evolutionary gain. This is one area where the craving for beauty can satisfy itself. What is still needed is a refinement of this craving, of the taste it engenders, to the border of elegance. With the desertion of vulgarity and grossness must come the appreciation of quality and refinement.

54

The interest in making or in seeing good paintings among classes previously indifferent towards them is in a way a symptom of everyman's search for spiritual integrity; it is another signal of a half-aware dissatisfaction with a merely materialistic life. Beauty in art and Nature is one side of spiritual appearance which, through the ages, has in poems, stories, paintings, drawings, and sculptures attracted man. But because it is so subtle and our perceptions so obscured, we find it first only in the forms of Nature, then in the forms of art, and finally in the intangible experiences of the deepest feeling.

What calls forth man's attraction toward fair scenes is in the end nothing other than the exquisite beauty of the spiritual link which he there has with God. This is why the productions of talented artists are to be welcomed and valued, but of course only to the extent that they are responses to this inspired call from within.

55

The difference between creative art and the sterile copying of art is to be learned in sitting humbly at the feet of the higher self.

56

Beauty of form without nobility of soul misleads its beholders.

57

Art is the culture of the Beautiful. Yet there is no art greater than that of living.

58

The Beautiful necessity is not only an aesthetic demand but also a practical asset.

59

Men follow the vision of beauty because it is an attraction of the Divine and not, as they believe, merely because they happen to like it. Art can be used to ennoble and inspire man, and to revive divine memories in his mind.

60

To deny spiritual worth to art because it is created to meet physical sense is shortsighted. It starts with the physical response but, in its highest form, it transcends that level. Beethoven set as his loftiest mission the exaltation of man to a harmony with sacred ideals, to joy in the triumph of good over evil, to peace and goodwill on earth. Bach comes near him in certain works which are more specifically concerned with religious themes, whereas Beethoven was more favourable to humanitarian ones.

61

However enjoyable an aesthetic experience may be, its possibilities are limited by the presence or absence of inspiration in the artist who made it possible. If his own creative work failed to lift him, its result will fail to lift others, too.

62

It is true that men learn through disappointment and develop through suffering. But this need not cause us to forget that they also learn and develop through joy and beauty.(P)

63

It is too much an Oriental tendency to regard suffering and unhappiness as the principal causes of turning to the quest. We Westerners must put a better balance on this idea. The love of beauty can also be a step towards the quest. This love can express itself through an ever-increasing refinement of manners or appreciation of nature, and through art and poetry.

64

Why are so many so attracted by the beautiful in Nature and Art, in creatures and ideas, and so repelled by the ugly in form and thought? Did Plato the cultured Greek and Baal Shem-Tov the unlettered Hebrew share the same truth when they asserted that beauty, rightly understood and properly regarded, could lead us Godward? For different persons react to the Divine differently, because it has—like themselves—different aspects or attributes. If some are attracted to the Truth-side and others to the Love, why not also to the Beauty?

65

To live with inner death all the time, as unfeeling asceticisms and dried-up metaphysical systems would have men do, did not appeal to the ancient Greeks. Their attraction to the arts, to culture, and to philosophy prevented that. Perhaps that is why their contact with Asia gave those beautiful figures of the Buddha to that vast continent but did not give Greece the *fakirs* in exchange.

66

The interest taken by the young people of today in the various arts, both creatively and publicly, at exhibitions and in galleries, would be a good sign and one beneficial to their evolution if the object of their admiration were really worthy of it. But too often this is not the case. We find productions which are senseless, almost insane, or ugly and sinister or sensual and degrading.

67

Goethe discovered during his Italian journey that the common people seldom had what he called "disinterested admiration for a noble work of art. It was utterly beyond them." Just as Emerson was left quite unimpressed by the uniforms and ceremonials of the religion he found in Italy—a "mummery" he called it—so was Goethe, who wrote of his stay in Rome and visits to the churches: "I felt that I am too old for anything but Truth. Rites or processions, they all run off me like water off a duck's back; but Nature like the sunset seen from the villa or a work of art like my revered Juno leaves a deep impression."

68

Through art man can create images of those qualities and attributes he finds in the Overself: its beauty, its order, its intelligence. Whether these images come through the medium of music or painting, of sculpture or poetry, they may bring their audience into a mood, a glimpse, or a thought closer to their source.

69

Why should the enjoyment of beautiful surroundings, things, clothes, music, poems, and moods be sinful, as they are to puritanical minds? Is not the infinite Being the hidden source of the True, the Real, the Good, and the Beautiful? To the philosophic mind their blessings and inspirations are bestowed on man.

70

Where the faith in, or feeling of, God's reality does not exist, then morality, art, metaphysics may be taken up instead.

71

The Moors put only a single rug on the floor of a room, as the Japanese put only a single picture on a wall. The aesthetic effect is at its highest when attention is concentrated; but at its lowest when scattered.

72

The concentration of attention instead of the dispersal of it—this is the guiding rule which is behind the Japanese custom of displaying a single picture for a period of time instead of several competing with one another. There is a precise remembered effect in the first case but a confused one in the second.

73

Just as art when applied in one's own personal life, environment, and work is an expression of the person himself, so can art also be used as a kind of therapy to refine taste, harmonize character, and uplift moods. So, too, can even a useful craft like handwriting and penmanship be used for the same higher purpose. To turn a clumsy, ugly, half-illegible script into a symmetrical, graceful, easily read one needs good observation, self-discipline, and careful training.

74

He should refuse to crush his aesthetic instinct.

75

There is the heat of rapture, the feeling of ecstasy, when we touch this Spirit of Beauty that draws us through and beyond all beautiful things.

76

Correct taste is more easily and correctly formed if we deliberately seek for the best and continually ignore the worst—that is, if we discriminate under proper guidance.

77

Art is at its best when it is adventurously creative, but it still serves useful purposes when it is imitative.

78

Let him expose himself to the *best* influences in art and spirituality. If they are not available in persons, they may be in books and periodicals, in pictures and statues, in records and concerts.

79

Art may be the mere embellishment of a drab human existence, or it may become a veritable approach to divine existence.

80

I am old-fashioned enough to believe that beauty ought to be the aim of art.

81

It was not all Greeks who were deeply sensitive to beauty, but only the educated ones.

82

A man may possess metaphysical wisdom yet truly lack aesthetical taste.

83

If through lack of faith people cannot bring themselves to look upward to the Higher Power, or inward to the spiritual self, and if the experiences of life are not interpreted as exhortations to do so, then the other means of reorientating them which is still left is art.

84

The lack of artistic taste is not a thing to be proud of: yet when it appears as ascetic indifference to beautiful things, it is considered a virtue!

85

The practice of art requires qualities which the discussion of art does not. In the first case, we get actual knowledge whereas in the second we get only mere opinion.

86

For the majority, Art ought to be a path toward a higher level of being, and for the enlightened an expression of it.

87

The writer who has something worthwhile to communicate, the artist who has an offering of beauty to contribute, blesses his world, but the other kind pollutes it.

88

Even Buddha never condemned art; that was left for his misguided followers to do: he even recommended, as one exercise to help attain goodness, "the contemplation of the beautiful."

89

He is thankful for the crocus's purple or mauve colours, for the thrush's song, for the inspired poems and the uplifting books. He appreciates them all the more because he is well aware of the evils and shadows, the horrors and uglinesses.

90

To recognize, appreciate, or create beauty is to bring gladness into life.

91

There was a professional landscape gardener (he is not now alive but his work is very much so) who laboured in a public park for thirty-five years. His toil was his spiritual path, a karma yoga. It gave him inner satisfaction, and gave us who visited that park a chance to share it. He was a true artist, with a pure love of Nature.

92

The leading fashion models show the kind of female beauty admired today—high facial bones, deep eyes set wide apart, slim bodies. The ancient Greeks admired this kind, too, and added the straight line along forehead and nose.

93

It is better to make efficient yet beautiful things than those which are only functional, better to provide serviceable yet handsome towns than those which offer shelter alone.

94

If an artistic style makes great ideas seem greater still, let us honour it for the enrichment given us.

95

We have only to compare a muddled, bewildering statement of truth with a clear, carefully phrased one to learn the value of verbal accuracy. We have only to put a prosaic record of inner experience written by an ascetic side by side with one written by an artist—that is, one devoid of all distinctive style and beautiful form alongside of one that possesses them—to feel which is more likely to stir emotion, inspire action, or affect thought.

96

He may find beauty in the productions of man, as in the graceful architecture of Muhammedan lands, the elegant harmonious temples of Greece, the prints of Japan, the crafts of China, and many pictures of our own

Western painters. He may find it in the music of the Viennese trio—
Mozart, Haydn, Beethoven—and in scintillating gems of the poetic art.
He may find it in Nature, what she has to give through the season,
through a day even, through the forms and colours she shows.

97

The beautiful symmetry of the public and esoteric buildings put up by
ancient Greek architects fulfilled that part of their purpose which was to
create a certain high atmosphere. This also happens with the finest artwork
of any era or country.

98

Any piece of musical composition or literary material which has inspiration will also have impact. But not all the hearers or readers will feel this
impact. Some amount of sensitivity is called for in those who would
patronize the arts, as well as in those who would work creatively in them.

99

He will achieve at best what the artist or author has himself achieved in
the production placed before him, but only if he can put himself in the
mind of its creator.

100

Art is a help to spiritual perception.

101

The man who has discovered the mentalistic source of beauty does not
need to disdain its physical expressions. He can accept them because he has
adjusted his life to the practice of inner freedom in the outer world.

102

He does not have to be a creative artist to possess the pure love of
beautiful moods. They may come to him from admiring landscapes, listening to music, appreciating decorative things. But they may also come
entirely from within.

103

The love of Nature and the appreciation of art follow easily from, or
equally lead up to, Philosophy.

104

Let those who want a bare ascetic spirituality have it. But let us inheri-
tors of the culture of the whole known past enrich our lives with their arts,
their literatures and music, their educational knowledge.

105

But however much we appreciate aesthetic feelings or cultivate artistic
talents, we must also recognize that we cannot stop with these activities. It
is not enough to paint pictures or play music. We must still rise to our
godlikeness.

106

Inspired art should carry one upwards, should enable the soul to soar to higher levels of feeling and thought.

107

All rare and inspired art is to be received as the Overself's voice uttering a message and calling us back to our true homeland.

108

Feeling refines itself if he pursues the true ideal of art, until it attains a delicate exquisite grace like a ballet's in its best moments.

109

A man may welcome and enjoy any aesthetic enjoyment obtained by the physical senses from Nature's beauty or art's creativity. But if he stops there he serves the body only; it is not enough. What about the soul?

110

They insist on looking at the shaded side of life—its brevity and instability, its infirmity and mortality—and then assert that there is no joy, no happiness in it. But the man who has risen into the consciousness of beauty through art finds the clue which can one day lead him to these things.

111

When Nature's beauty or man's art moves you deeply, be grateful for their help and appreciate their service. But do not stop there. Use them as aids to transcend your present level and come closer to the god within you.

Value of aesthetic environment

112

The closer he draws to the Overself's beauty, the more will he feel the necessity of linking it with his physical circumstances; the more will his taste, senses, outlook, and desires become refined. His home and clothes, his furniture and speech, even his diet, will begin to improve aesthetically and be touched by a delicate grace. An environment that is dirty and ugly may be an ascetics's delight but it will not be his: it will, in fact, affront his finer feelings.

113

The intimate association which is built up with a beautiful environment satisfies the finer instincts. And if the objects in it are themselves associated with spirituality, then higher instincts are encouraged. Moreover, to the extent that the creator of a decorative scheme or work of art possesses a measure of mystical experience or intuition—or, rarer and even better, philosophic insight—something of this quality may be seen or felt in the production.

114

A beautiful home helps to introduce beauty and refinement into thought, feeling, and even character.

115

The use of pseudo-antique furniture and classical reproductions today in architecture is a tragic sign of bankrupt artistic creativeness. The use of newly designed furniture and contemporary architecture, of up-to-date materials and methods and inventions, is a praiseworthy sign of true inner vitality. Modernist home, office, factory, and public buildings, furnishings, decorations, fitments, appliances, and machines are strong in their own right because they have stemmed from modern developments in thinking, feeling, and living. The antiquated past products, with their fancy decorations rather than functional design, were useful and attractive to former generations but have now fulfilled their mission. Today their imitations sound futile and untimely notes, whereas the twentieth-century creations, styles, and productions are harmonious parts of the symphony of our very existence in this twentieth-century world. Nevertheless, they too fall into a one-sidedness which is the defect of their own virtue.

The modernist architecture and merchandise, furniture, airplanes, and automobiles, which express themselves in streamlined but plain clean-cut forms almost entirely devoid of ornament, do so in the belief that the purpose of a structure should dictate its form and that the mechanical function of a household article should govern its appearance. This leaves little room for aesthetic feeling. These designs are highly efficient for their purpose. But does not integral living call for something more than such monotonous efficiency—something more than such severity? What harm is there if a touch of the picturesque is introduced? The cold bare undecorated lines of modern productions are as extreme as the tropic ornate lines of baroque architecture. The one seeks comfort and utility, the other grace. Why not combine both in the philosophical manner?

116

An artistic and refined environment is a dispensable luxury to those of coarse unevolved stuff, but a spiritual necessity to those of sensitive evolved fibre.

117

Will it make a sensitive man more dull if he lives in a dull surrounding? Will it increase his desires if he shapes and colours it to suit a refined taste and puts comfortable furniture inside it? Will a plain and homely hut conduce to greater so-called spirituality? Will the daily rendezvous with his higher self through meditation be adversely affected one way or the other by the amount of money and care he spends on his environment? The answers must depend on the kind of man he is, not on other people's opinions.

118

To surround oneself with beauty in materials and designs, in clothes and carpets, in pictures and decorations, is not necessarily to be snobbish and ostentatious, nor is the cultivation of taste and refinement necessarily accompanied by revelling in luxury. And to assert that elegance and quality and beauty must be abandoned for the simple life when one enters the path of spirituality is to raise the question: what is simplicity? Is it utter barrenness, the caveman's life? Is it mere ugliness? Is it squalor and dirt? Is it discomfort? And further: How many could agree on the basic needs of a simple life? In any case, let us not force all spirituality into a single groove. The philosophic way is to seek a quality of consciousness which transcends the ordinary, which is enriched by one's spiritual development and not impoverished by it. Both thought and feeling must be able to meet in the Silence, bow down and worship It. Both of them should enter into this final act as a consequence of their own growth and creative fulfilment.

119

Refined and gracious living is an expression of refined taste. It does not necessarily need great wealth to support it, for even within a modest income it can still be expressed in a modest way. A few plants, soft lights, fine porcelain, pleasantly patterned carpet, brightly coloured pictures, and a minimum of decorative furniture will give a man comfort and beauty.(P)

120

The home, be it room or house, is both an extension and an expression of oneself. It tells, to some extent, what one has made of oneself.

121

Small narrow minds find fit expression in cramped living quarters, but spacious refined minds need spacious and beautiful homes if they are to feel at ease.

122

A dingy room in a squalid slum will not obstruct the saint or sage in feeling the Spirit, but it is hardly inspiring to less evolved persons.

123

Two hundred years ago life was dressed in colours, and a walk through the town's streets was like walking through a fancy dress parade.

124

Drab, tasteless, and mediocre rooms do not contribute toward spiritual uplift merely because they cost less to decorate and furnish. A refined sensitive nature will feel depressed rather than uplifted in them.

125

Bright colours in a room where cheerfulness, warmth, and vitality are needed are most apt decoration and furnishing, as soft pastel hues fit better to one where quietude is desired.

126

The human being is played upon by various influences at various stages of his life in the body. We all know what climate and music will do to create different moods, but one factor often not understood or neglected is the influence of colour. It is always there in our surroundings, in a room, apartment, or house, in our clothing and in our furnishings. It can contribute towards health or take away from it; it can cheer or depress the emotions; it can invigorate or devitalize the body; it can give pleasure to the eyes or irritate them. Red, for instance, colour of the planet Mars and associated in astrology with war and anger, can be stimulating and life-giving if it is in its pure clear form. But in its undesirable darkish shades, it simply stimulates the lower desires, the animal feelings. However, it is a warm colour and for those who are old in years and in whom the circulation of blood is poor, the presence of pure red in the decorations and furnishings will help to keep them warmer. Orange will give the beneficial side of red and less of its negative side. Yellow is the colour of reason and helps to lift a man above his lower desires. In its pure golden sun-coloured phase, it is the colour of spiritual attainment, of the master who has achieved rulership over his emotions and body and passions. Green, which is Nature's colour, is restful, soothing, cheerful, and health-giving. The pure azure blue of Italian skies is associated by astrology with the planet Venus, the star of art, beauty, and sympathy verging almost on love. In its purest form it denotes devotional love, spiritual aspiration. It is not enough to know the meaning of colours; one must also know two other things about them: first, how to blend different colours and second, how to contrast them.(P)

127

A view which offers pictorial pleasure helps to give those conditions which favour meditation.

128

The craving for a little natural beauty in their home, a flower, a tiny garden, which the humblest of families may have, is subtly nostalgic. Through Nature it is an echo of longing for the spirit.

129

Any object of decoration, furnishing, or other figure in our surroundings which helps to remind us of the Unchanging Goal in this changing world is desirable.

130

Why should the wish to live in physical comfort be opposed to the wish to live in mental calm? It is indeed a blind form of asceticism which does not see that the two can be kept in a harmonious equilibrium.

131

If the philosopher—in contrast with the ascetic—calls for beauty, refinement, even elegance in his surroundings, this is not a weakness for luxury or a pandering to vanity. It is a genuine response to aesthetic feeling, a sense of its value.

132

A refined, artistic, simple way of life, such as the more cultured Japanese have practised for centuries, is a fitting accompaniment or prelude to the philosophic way.

133

A simple environment, even an austere one, is understandable and acceptable in the case of those who have outwardly renounced the world, as well as of those who try to live in the world and yet be inwardly detached from it. But an ugly environment, even a drab one, is neither understandable nor acceptable in the case of those who profess to worship the Spirit. For its attributes are not only Goodness and Truth, among others, but also Beauty. To cultivate an indifferent attitude toward material possessions is one thing, but to show an insensitive one toward beautiful creations and to feel no repugnance toward ugly ones is not a spiritual approach; it is anti-spiritual.(P)

Sacred mission of art

134

When, as often, I mention art as having a high mission, a sacred one, I do not necessarily mean the portrayal of anecdotes from the history of any particular religion.

135

The mission of the artist is to admire and embody the beautiful, so that others may be brought into the admiration and appreciate the beautiful too.

136

There is a two-way possibility in art. It can lay a pathway to the divine for the untalented seeker, and it can become a manifestation of the divine in the hands of the talented artist.

137

The technique of art is important, but the mission of art—to communicate and awaken the intuitive feeling of Beauty—is still more important.

138

It is the business of an artist, poet, or writer (of the more serious kind) to lift a man out of himself, his little ego, by presenting beauty, truth, or goodness so attractively that the man is drawn and held by it to the point mentioned—of forgetting himself.

139

It is the proper business of an artist to find the highest beauty in Nature and then to reveal it, through his medium, to others. But this he cannot really do until he has first found it within himself.

140

The higher mission of art can only be fulfilled by a higher calibre of artists. They must look to something more than skill for results, must prepare themselves to be worthy of being used as channels.

141

Those who are able to bless society with a talent or gift which is truly inspired and uplifts people are themselves blessed in its use and uplifted in turn. With this comes a responsibility to purify themselves and thus bring the work to a higher level.

142

The artist may work to earn his livelihood. But if he is also to consult his conscience, he must at the same time strive to become a servant of the Holy Spirit.(P)

143

What is the final call of true art? Not to the work which expresses it but to the spirit which inspires it, the divine source of which it reminds us.(P)

144

Ever since art separated itself from religion there has been confusion about art's relationships. Ought it preach, teach, propagate a message, be moral, be amoral, or only stand aloof from these things? The answer is that it can do or be any or all of these things, so long as it does not forget that primarily it is art, wedded to the Beautiful, and only secondarily, indirectly, concerned with religion, morality, and the other things. Let people make their own sermons from the mental pictures they are presented with, draw their own morals from the stories they read, and provide their own religious moods from the musical sounds they hear. Such work the artist ought not do for them.

145

Whether it be applied in the home (furnishing and decorating), expressed through sound in music or paint in pictures, in poetry or prose, drama or dance, the mission of art is to create images of beauty which attract man to refinement ever-increasing.

146

An art production whose form derives from spiritual tradition or symbolism, whose content derives from spiritual experience or understanding, is at least as worthy of veneration as a religious relic.(P)

147

When they fulfil their highest mission, painting and sculpture try to make visible, music tries to make audible, prose literature tries to make thinkable, poetic literature tries to make imaginable the invisible, inaudible, unthinkable, and unimaginable mystery of pure Spirit. Although it is true that they can never give shape to what is by its very nature the Shapeless, it is also true that they can hint, suggest, symbolize, and point to It.(P)

148

Art can take the place of and be a substitute for religion only when it is truly inspired.(P)

149

If art has only an ornamental value, if it is merely something with which to decorate our clothes and our homes or to titillate our senses of sight and hearing, or if it is an escape in order to forget the burden of our cares, it has justified itself. But it has not found its highest mission, which is achieved when men are so affected by it, by the feeling of refined beauty which it awakens, that they accept the clue thus offered them and follow it up until it leads them deep within to their higher Selves.

150

Art, like spiritual cults, is infected with charlatanism. The truly beautiful in art and the really noble in cults are too often missed because the quacks are more aggressive.

151

The inspired mission, the higher purpose of art is not only to create in us the heavenly mood, but also to celebrate it, not only to tell, but to tell joyously.

152

Art is a channel to the lower or the higher, to ugliness or to beauty, to the gross or to the spiritual. When inspired, it is at its best level, but it can not be self-sufficient. Even art must fit into a place in the Whole, must not remain the sole fulfilment of life.

153

It is open to the artist, as also to the man of thought, to use his work to uplift himself—quite apart from the question of what it may do for others. When he was twenty-one years old, and as he prepared himself for his first post as a minister, Emerson wrote in his diary, "My trust is that my profession shall be my regeneration."

154

Whoever accepts the higher mission of art and comes nearer and nearer to it through his creative activity, will then go on from art to the Spirit deep within his own self.(P)

155

Art and poetry must rouse the most delicate feelings, must enchant us, if they are to fulfil their highest mission. For the highest state of man's nature is a mysterious feeling, blended though it is with understanding, knowing—that is, intelligence. But when art and poetry titillate only the sensual side of man they fail to render this service.

156

Art succeeds in its true mission and highest objective when its quality is technically developed enough to induce concentration in the recipient, and spiritually profound enough to awaken inspiration in him.

157

Only those artists and writers, priests and gardeners who are authentically inspired can give us real beauty. Only work born from such a state of grace fulfils art's loftiest mission.

158

The artist, and especially the writer, who is sensitive and talented to a high degree will have to choose between working to please the mass taste or working to please his highest idea of art and literature.

159

It is sometimes said that the artist who clings to his ideals and refuses to degrade both his aims and his art at the bidding of a harsh commercialism will most likely find scorn and starvation for his lot. I am not inclined to accept this statement, although I know well that it is partly true. It is not fair to make such a hasty, all-sweeping generalization. I think it fairer to say that the genius often has to content himself with some crumbs gathered by working for the appreciative few, rather than earning a better subsistence at the expense of the wider clientele which naturally prefers mediocrity. Nor is the latter always to be blamed.

160

The inspired artist, the inwardly-led writer, does not have to see the effect of his production upon others. It is really enough that he has brought this addition to the world's cultural wealth into being. But if these others feel this effect, and if some among them recognize its beneficence, they will be willing to pay for the service rendered—and thus help to keep him alive for further work!

161

Art is a form of communication; it is not and cannot be (if it is true to itself) an end in itself. It is a way of imparting to others what one thinks or feels about anything. Whether it be music or poetry, sculpture or literature, art presupposes an audience.

162

Wallace Stevens once wrote, "I am the necessary Angel of Earth, since in my sight you see the earth again." He thus unconsciously described the mission of philosophically inspired educators, composers, artists, poets, and writers.

163

If an artwork engenders some kind of elevation, if it extends the recipient's consciousness, it has fulfilled art's highest purpose.

164

The artist who has left his audience, beholders, or readers as much the victims of their little personality as they were before, may have amused, interested, or titillated them, but he has not rendered them any higher service by the capacity in him to create.

165

Whoever produces an idea which penetrates another man deeply and brings him a new sense of harmony and peacefulness is one of that man's benefactors. But this can only be so if the idea is a true one, not a misleading fantasy ending nowhere or, worse, a mischievously false one.

166

The picture in art and the word in literature may be dark hindrances to truth or real helps. It depends on how much illumination, or how little, there is in the artist or writer.

167

We may find that the arts too may enlighten our way because they may give us glimpses and not just bring everyday life to its full refinement of culture. And out of these glimpses—with the purification and uplift they give—we may be led to the supreme way of liberation, redemption, and peace.

168

A composition—be it written or painted, played on instruments or carved in stone—has done its most vital work if it opens our hearts to the rare feeling of tranquil harmony.

169

Behind the work of a poet or composer true to art's higher mission is this hidden power of his own higher self. It bestows the inspiration which permeates his work.

170

Only as art lifts man to higher concepts of beauty does it fulfil its best service to him. For it then lifts him to spirituality too.

171

The artist susceptible to fine shapes and lovely colours or to whispering, melodious, and exultant sounds, or to words which transform the mind by alchemy, fails himself, his best self, unless he rises to this high service of holy communion with Overself for us all.

172

To be creative, to bring something new, better, or worthwhile into the world, is the privilege of inspired persons. To bring something beautiful into the world is the inspired artist's mission.

173

In the squalor of Verlaine's personal life and the beauty of his poetry we see a startling contrast. It illustrates the need to remember that however grand the higher mission of art is, it does not quite attain the goal of human existence; it does, however, rise to the level next below that goal. It is a genuine spiritual path but not the ultimate final one.

174

The real worth of an artistic production, a piece of writing, a painting, or a song is attained only if it succeeds in giving others a Glimpse. Otherwise it is merely a form of entertainment, a passing pleasure, or an escape to kill time.

175

If art fulfils itself when communicating beauty, it transcends itself when the communication lifts a man into ecstasy.

Criticism of "modern art"

176

The new modes in art have attracted and excited some people, especially younger people, but others have found them ugly and undisciplined and repulsive. Is modern art as insincere as its critics claim? Is it pseudo-art? Whatever else it be, it certainly shows the spirit of ferment in this period.

177

Those artists who are truly dedicated and occasionally truly inspired will not be found in the contemporary mass movement of those who mistake their bizarre subconscious nonsense for sublime creation, their excessive mercenary motives for an authentic mission.

178

It is not abstraction itself that is objectionable and insufferable but ugliness and meaninglessness.

179

Ill-informed persons or those with confused minds have produced pieces of work under the heading of abstract art or of avant-garde poetry which they allege to be mystical productions following a tradition of Chinese, Japanese, and Indian mysticism, when in fact they are nothing of the sort.

180

We may grant that colours have their own independent offering to make to us. We can understand that, in a search for being different, forms and images derived from the world are rejected and that, in a revolutionary protest against enslavement by the past, chaos and anarchy seem preferable, even though most of us would emphatically disagree. But who can understand why so many people have come to accept and live with modern abstract art in the numerous instances where charlatanry and commercialism masquerade so blatantly under this title?

181

We are promised a meaningful intellectual perception and an emotional experience if we continue to study these spatterings which pass under the name of non-objective or abstract pictures. We are told that the intuition will be awakened, since the painter created his or her work by intuitive direction, and we shall receive even a mystical revelation. But although all this would certainly be true if the painter were actually illumined and inspired by the Overself at the time, it is quite untrue if he or she were not. The fact is that almost all these artists are undeveloped souls with confused minds, quite incapable of receiving inspiration because unfit for it.

182

The "art for art's sake" school wanted beauty and form even when they rejected intellectual meaning and spiritual purpose. But today's abstractionist school wants none of these.

183

Most of this modern abstractionist painting is done from the head and not from the heart. Its claim to be uncontrolled subconscious automatism is a self-deluded one. Its ugly splashes and smears, its crude splotches and stains fitly belong to the machine age, but totally lack the symmetry, the rationality, and the elegance which are not seldom found associated with the modern machine.

184

When song and melody go out of poetry in the name of liberty for the poet, of freedom from rules, laws, and systems, poetry itself becomes a half-mute, its spell half gone.

185

With all their insanity and futility and ugliness, these modern movements in art possess a dynamic spirit, a youthful vigour, a readiness to discard the debris of the past, a forward-looking attitude which knows that the artist cannot remain creative if he or she stops rigidly with the copying of old petrified forms.

186

The aesthetic aberrations which are offered to the public as works of art show, first, a misuse of language; second, a blatant commercialism; third, a soulless materialism; fourth, an affinity with lunacy; and lastly, a cynical contempt for all the finer ideals of humanity.

187

Painters who reject all the training of the schools but make no effort of their own to replace it are like pianists who reject the mastery of their instrument. The confused noises which would be played out by such pianists' fingers are paralleled by the absurd pictures such painters offer.

188

So much modern art lacks both design and beauty, that its frequent failure to command respect is understandable.

189

The free creativity which may follow inspiration will be none the worse if it is expressed through a training in the art concerned, if it is disciplined by traditional forms. It need not be limited entirely by them, but it cannot do without them without losing its power of proper communication. Those who reject such education entirely not only reject art itself but exhibit a touch of madness. There is a case for pointing out the danger of inspiration's being suffocated by too much pedantic and academic erudition, but the young rebels not only overstate the case and make it sound ridiculous: they destroy it.

190

Abstract art, which reproduces nothing to be found in Nature, or represents no meaningful concept, may have its place. But it is not exempt from the primary responsibility of all art: to lead mankind along the path of beauty. If abstract compositions are ugly they no longer come under the category of art. They belong elsewhere.

191

It is true that interest in bold new ideas and experimentation with daring new procedures have accompanied the artistic and intellectual work of our time. But they have also accompanied its disintegration and deterioration.

192

Those modern artists, writers, and composers whose productions seem utterly senseless confound the irrational with the inspirational. They regard the two terms as interchangeable.

193

It is a common mistake among artists and writers to regard inflammation as inspiration, and to take inflamed feelings for inspired revealings.(P)

194

An art which, in the name of intuition, non-objectivism, and non-representationism, substitutes meaninglessness, chaos, anarchy, and ugliness and rejects form, order, beauty, and discipline is only a pseudo-art.

195

We may say of this kind of pseudo-art what Santayana said in another context: "It is not true that deformity expresses the Spirit."

196

Be original, yes, be creative, but not at the price of becoming insane and spreading insanity.

197

Why go back to the primitive peoples for models to copy or to be inspired by when they were either the deteriorated remnants of earlier Atlantean-Lemurian races or the beginnings of our own later ones—both living in Nature like half-animals or semi-savages? Why ignore all the creditable history of art, culture, aesthetic taste, refined perceptions, and intellectual quality which has been our glorious possession and memorial through the work of seven thousand years? If some of this new art led to a higher degree or a further improvement of what we now have, it would justify its existence. But instead we see only a horrible deterioration. Its fruits are ugly monstrosities which can have only a bad influence on its beholders. Let us welcome the less advertised but more sincere work of those among the moderns who, while remaining faithful to art's lofty mission as illustrated in so many classics, yet have not hesitated to let the spirit of the times touch their hand, throw out the unsuitable debris of the past, and open their eyes to fresh visions which shall guide their creations.

198

The modern Western art movements such as cubism and non-objective painting have used geometrical forms in an ugly way. If anything attractive has ever appeared in their pictures, it has come through the colours used. The Oriental Muhammedan artists and architects have likewise used geometrical forms, because this was the restriction laid upon them by the prophet Muhammed; but they have used them in a beautiful way. A mosque is a thing which is a joy to see whatever one's religion may be. What further comment need be made?

199

Whether it is a book, a landscape, or heard music, whatever it is it provides us with an opportunity to discover our own higher self—but it can do so only if it is itself functioning on that higher level. This is why so much of modern art, most of it in fact, fails to fulfil the best mission of art. Nature's value to us as observers depends upon our reactions to it. Feeling is as necessary as thinking, but it must be positive or intuitive feeling, not negative or materialistic.

200

I have tried to indicate the importance of art and to plead for the artist; but in these days not so many know what art really is, nor do so many who claim to be artists understand what they are claiming. At the very best most of them are craftsmen, technicians, even mechanics, but this is not the same as being artists. At the worst they have no technique, no talent, no sanity.

201

Let these new art forms take their place for those who are attuned to them, who want them; let these forms coexist with the older ones. But let not the Good, the True, and the Beautiful in the past be thrown aside and trampled on by intolerant innovators.

202

If the art forms of today contain much that is worthless, they will pass away unregretted with time. If there is excess and absurdity in them, there is also vitality, youthfulness, and often colour.

203

Those alleged artists who are interested only in technique and not in content, whose avoidance of representation has become an obsessive mania, whose horror of meaning has run so far as to run into madness may, if they are sincere, which many are not, be experimentalists or technologists—but they are not real artists.

204

The freedom which allows greedy, mercenary, or sensualist persons to poison literature, theatre, and other arts by stimulating lust, is unethical and unhealthy. Its victims, whether young or old, are stupefied by their own animality.

205

Modern art has exiled beauty and forgotten, not fulfilled, its mission.

206

Much modern art and poetry, music and literature is derived from sources that have nothing to do with genuine art. Neuroses, psychoses, imbalances, and decadence itself are often its roots.

207

Those composers, playwrights, novelists, and painters who use images of other people's horror render a disservice to their audience. The result is a harmful flow back into their own selves.

208

When unpleasantness is called entertainment, when excessive sadism, extreme violence, murder, homosexuality, promiscuity, adultery, and pornography are the nourishment of leisure hours, then values are very low. Audiences demand such strong sensations, the purveyors claim: they are uninterested in moral innocence and find no attraction in calm characters. But it is not less true that the entertainers deliberately set out to stimulate these decadent attitudes.

209
The artist, the poet, or the musician who gives nothing beautiful to the world may give everything else, may titivate, excoriate, narrate, or adumbrate, may entertain or thrill, but he has failed to fulfil the higher in the mission of art.

210
Note to PB: Investigate the possibility that the hidden and real origin of abstract art—where it is genuine and drawn from the Unconscious as is usually claimed, where it is not produced by the ordinary conscious methods to profit financially by a current fad—is in past evolutionary prehistoric periods, especially those which Subud meditations and LSD drug-taking reveal.

211
The artist who degenerates into a sloppy, dirty, and slovenly way of living which he or she calls "bohemian" possesses no aesthetic sensitivity, no refined feeling, and is unworthy of the name. True art requires a feeling for beauty which in turn requires the artist to follow a finer, more fastidious, way of living than the average. Filthy surroundings, a dirty body, and soiled clothes are not the appurtenances of such a way. True bohemianism is simply the disdain for the conventional pursuit of money and luxury at the cost of higher ideals. It is the willingness to live a simple life rather than sacrifice those ideals.

212
Those among the surrealist painters and poets of last century and the non-objective artists of this one who wanted to break away from the materialist representations of their time merely discarded what they found: their approach was negative and destructive. They could not arrive at the farther step because they lacked the vocation, the dedication, the character, and the knowledge. They could not enter the real source of inspiration and beauty, the abode of authentic silence, but only too often the drug- or alcohol-born caricatures.

213
To call such ridiculous productions art is to misuse language and misguide the young. They are more properly called non-art, even anti-art. They display a complete failure to understand the purpose of art. It would be a waste of time to comment further upon them were it not for the unbelievable number of spiritually minded persons who have been falsely led to regard them as manifestations of the spiritual intuition! They are as miserably negative as a true art is firmly positive. A single painting of a countryside scene by Constable, derided as being "representational" by talentless pseudo-artists, will be esteemed and honoured long after their worthless productions are thrown away into the rubbish-can where they belong.

214

We have heard much of the polluting effects which applied science and technology have brought into modern life. We have heard less of the polluting effects which television's portrayal of violence, the theatre's portrayal of sexual animality and perversion, and literature's portrayal of all these, have brought into mental life.

215

Poetry without rhythm, music without melody, prose without meaning, non-representational pictures without form, and everything without beauty grace or charm never touch the source of inspired art.

216

Contemporary artists, writers, and poets who violently reject the old forms and denigrate the great names of the past, who find wisdom and beauty and genius only in their own times (and even then only in their own particular coteries and partisan movements), are merely trying to be different, and to be themselves. That is, whatever their physical age may be, this is really one part of their general attempt to assert their freedom from adolescence. They are emotionally young and intellectually immature persons who lack the experience and balance to form sound judgements.

217

Writers and painters, musicians and sculptors who are devoid of craftsmanship, technique, skill, care, and training take eagerly to these contemporary movements which reject the need of such things. Consequently their works lack form, orderliness, rationality, meaning, health, beauty, charm, melody, and sanity.

218

An art which does not open the fountains of beauty but instead releases decay, violence, destructiveness, negativeness, nihilism, sickness, nastiness, and disease has missed its way, has lost itself.

219

Far too much of modern artistic production finds its ultimate roots not in inspiration of any good kind, but in deliberate commercial greed. Even the discussions, arguments, and interviews purporting to expound the theories of the various groups have a hollow insincerity behind them.

220

Even the untalented, the semi-literate, the incapable, the untrained avoid the necessary disciplines of art and literature on the excuse of completely free self-expression. This is mere verbiage.

221

What contemporary thinkers like Jean-Paul Sartre say about "the loneliness of man" refers to there being no God to keep him company, which is a false belief.

222

There is no attempt to evoke beauty, simply because there is no capacity to do so.

223

The contemporary impertinence which flouts Nature in order to present its own repulsive ugliness, which rejects the Real in favour of the insane, will and inevitably must pass away into oblivion, as it deserves.

224

Abstract painters lack direction yet glory in the lack. Where this is just a means of hiding their lack of skill, it is understandable but unpardonable. Where they have the skill, which is uncommon, it is to be deplored as a surrender to unbalanced or unworthy influences.

225

Much of this pseudo-art suggests not the primitivity which is perhaps intended, but a kind of insanity!

226

The false feminine prettiness which cosmetic manufacturers and considerable advertising have created, the pretense of beauty where there is little or none, is another symptom of the sickness of our era.

227

Out of African jungle-orgies there came to Europe by transmission through, and modified by, Harlem and New Orleans a dance or symphonic music which was intended to arouse erotic impulse, which was a vulgar aphrodisiac.

228

To look at the pictures of criminals on television or cinema and to follow their doings, just as to read about them in novels, is to associate with them. To do this day after day is to keep company with low debasing persons.

229

In these days when so much of art is nothing of the kind at all, when true aesthetic and poetic inspiration becomes rarer and rarer, it is more needful not to desert the best of the past while welcoming or seeking fresh living creativity in the new.

230

Out of the gutters and sewers of human existence has come a generation of writers, mostly working-class, who were never taught any better because their parents knew no better, who take delight in using filthy language or telling dirty stories. They reproduce in literature and drama the only kind of society—quite a low kind—which they know. There are unpleasant necessities connected with animal bodies, such as that of excretion. The proper way to deal with them is taught in private to properly brought-up children. They are not openly referred to in public among adults with the slightest claim to manners. Yet these novelists and play-wrights, who degrade the name of artist, constantly use in literature words which pollute it by their coarseness, vulgarity, and ugliness, or oaths which "take the name of God in vain." Restraint, refinement, and good form are personal qualities unknown to these writers. They claim to make transcripts from life. But to picture the lowest levels of life serves no good purpose, only bad ones.

231

When artistic taste and human dignity are missing, we are left unmoved or unhelped.

232

It is all to the good that the younger writers and composers, painters and sculptors seek to produce new and different work. But when they have to force their technique into unnatural arbitrary and senseless forms, the result is only new and worse work from which a sensitive taste must turn away in disgust.

233

How far down has that man himself sunk whose work is intended to stimulate animality, shock conventionality, or propagate hostility, who has lost sight of the higher mission of art, which is to uplift and not to degrade mankind.

234

It is not art but a trick: each tries to outdo the others in devising new tricks.

235

Art ought to be conducive to beautiful feelings, graceful living, and sensitivity to Nature. If we do not find much of this in modern art, we must look at the artists themselves to understand why this is so.

236

The exclusive concern of so many writers and dramatists, novelists and film-makers, with sexual looseness and perversion is unhealthy. The effect upon readers or audiences can only be to breed unhealthy emotions lead-ing in some cases to undesirable action.

237

A production which carries aesthetic irritation to those who behold it is not a true work of art.

238

Mixed-up and confused as the minds and feelings of so many artists are, the meaninglessness of their productions may yet be a far-off precursor of a newer and truer art to come.

2

CREATIVITY, GENIUS

Creativity

The true self is the creative centre within us.

2

The creative mind brings forth the Eternal Present out of the unlimited; the ordinary mind brings forth mere echoes out of its limited past experiences alone.

3

A work is creative if it is originally conceived, that is, if the process of giving its basic and fundamental ideas birth is an intuitive, illuminating, and inspirational one.

4

It is a mistake to believe that this creativity comes only by a sudden flash. It may also come by graduated degrees. The difference depends on the resistance met.

5

The original creative mind initiates its own ideas, but where do they come from? You might as well ask where does all inspiration come from. There are deeper levels of the human consciousness which feed the inspired person at times. It is beyond emotion and beyond thinking, although we express its promptings through these things.

6

No artist really creates anything. All he can do is to try to communicate to others in turn what has been communicated to him.(P)

7

If he succeeds in transmitting through the medium of his work something of the inspiration he receives, be he priest or artist, he is truly creative.(P)

8

A true artist will search for forms worthy of his inspiration, its beauty and power.

9

Those who write, paint, draw, compose, and sculpt should bring their creations from spheres of inspiration which are radiant with light. Yet too many do the very opposite and present us with misshapen figures, patterns, poems, and musical pieces which nullify hope, meaning, and order and enshroud gloom.

10

The creative power of man, working through imagination or sensitivity, has brought to birth the musical composition, the painted picture, the written novel, and other great forms of art. They are the forms which move feeling and inspire action.

11

The artist who is inspired by nothing higher than the thirst for dollars and cents, fame and notoriety, power and influence, will never produce the highest possible art.

12

It is the task of a creative thinker to give out new ideas.

13

The creative faculty should be cultivated and developed as both a great aid to, and an expression of, spiritual growth.(P)

14

The processes of meditation are analogous, up to a certain point, to the processes of artistic creation.

15

The need of self-expression in creative effort is paramount with the artist. His job is his joy. This inner relationship to his work is important and satisfying.

16

It is not enough for the writer, the poet, the painter, or the composer of music to be original, for some men have found original forms of murder and of robbery. Moreover, insanity has not seldom passed among the artists for originality. Also it has been associated with exhibitionism and with neuroticism, with the desire for publicity, to draw attention to oneself. In short, it can be a malady of the ego. He who is truly original learns to think for himself and especially to be aware for himself—resisting the influences, the suggestions, and the pressures of his surroundings. All human beings are destined to develop until they acquire this kind of originality, for then they will come close to the fulfilment of the main purpose of human existence.

17

Originality is certainly and eagerly to be welcomed, but when it means sacrificing everything worthwhile, when its revolution is aggressive only in order to surprise by its ugliness or shock by its coarseness, when it becomes meaningless to the audience and insulting as a so-called artistic production, it ought to be firmly rejected.

18

Why should we not give a great genius a little extra latitude to break society's rules? In a few years he will be gone forever but the power of his work will continue to impregnate so many minds for so long a time. And it is this that really matters to us, not his brief peccadilloes or shortcomings.

19

For the sake of a few possible geniuses who might appear among them, the hordes of pseudo, mediocre, uninspired, or untalented artists have to be endured. Alas! we wait and wait for their masterpieces. Most perhaps have a shallow sincerity, being young and lured to art as a seemingly easy means of making a living or acquiring fame; but they have too little knowledge, no real creativity at all, and only a capacity for imitation. This explains why their work lacks quality and will pass away: an imitated eccentricity is not fresh discovery nor true vision of the universe's order.

20

Their self-conscious attempts to appear original may justify criticism but at least they show appreciation of the idea that originality is creative, is a ripple from the higher levels of our being, is something to be admired, valued, and sought for.

21

To be creative in the full sense it is not enough to put the thought into words: the picture must summarize and suggest it. Both must go deep down and touch, even disappear into, the Stillness.

22

To stimulate his creativity in whatever field he engages in, he should bring a more loving interest into it. For instance, the artist who loves his work is likely to be more creative than the one who engages in it without such feeling.

23

The two things which anyone needs to become creative, whether in any of the arts, sciences, or crafts, in professional skills, or even in the art of living itself, are first, the instrument, and second, the inspiration. Technique, talent, ability are not enough. Originality, freshness, great power, genius come from above.

24

The artist, the writer, or the composer who feels that he is getting into his stride on a piece of work, feels also an exultant joy.

25

An artistic production that is really inspired must give joy to its creator at the time of creation equally as to its possessor, hearer, or beholder. If it does not, then it is not inspired.(P)

26

The imagination can people a man's atmosphere with creations that are devilish or heavenly, can draw other men downward or lift them upward. Being a creative artist does not entitle anyone to complete licence or justify his claim to being the highest type. There are other considerations.

27

His art is made out of his inner life. If that is crooked, insane, or horrible, if thoughts and feelings are in a tangled mess, then the poems, pictures, or music will correspond to it and be just as distorted or unbalanced.

28

Let a man withdraw far enough from the active world and the impetus for creative work will withdraw with him. For, belonging no more to that life, he loses interest in it.

29

It is not only the mystic and the meditator who may pass through a dark night of the soul, but also the artist. He may find that his creative faculty seems to have deserted him. Either he will do no work at all or discontinue what he has been trying to do and change to a different work in which he can summon up an interest. He knows that one day the phase will pass and this may be in a matter of days, weeks, or months.

30

Another cause of unequal value in productions, of deterioration in form and spirit, is that the artist or writer may outlive his creative powers.

31

Those sterile weeks are known by every artist, when words are dragged out from the pen as though they were teeth, and when inspiration turns disappointingly into a mirage.

32

Most of us know that inspiration flickers—or it simply dries up. At such times the object is usually put aside until the light returns. This procedure is quite sensible from a practical working standpoint. However, it ignores the fact that there are layers of consciousness, and that when one layer dries up, it's worthwhile to penetrate the deeper one—for it exists.

Genius, inspiration, technique

33

Genius flashes from facts to conclusion, while argument slowly labours step by step in sorting them out.

34

What is it that manifests itself during the creative moments of genius? A current of force from the Overself! Its inspiration acts as a catalyzer, that is, it releases the creative imagination, which sets to work to provide an appropriate form for its manifestation.

35

It is from this level of consciousness just before that of the Overself that all great art and all great ideas derive, presenting themselves to the conscious mind as inspirations or intuitions.

36

All great drama did not die with Shakespeare, and all great philosophy has not perished with Plato. Perhaps there are brighter souls than theirs waiting to be born during this century. The infinite storehouse whence genius draws its wealth is not less infinite in the twentieth than it was in the sixteenth century.

37

The genius is both receptive and expressive. What he gets intuitively from within he gives out again in the forms of his art or skill.(P)

38

The most valuable contribution which any artist or writer can make to the world is to let himself be carried away by inspired moods when he can give utterance to the Overself's voice, radiate its beauty, dispense its wisdom, and show its benignity.

39

The artist must raise the cup of his vision aloft to the gods in the high hope that they will pour into it the sweet mellow wine of inspiration. If his star of fair fortune favours him that day, then must he surrender his lips to the soft lure of the amber-coloured drink that sets care aflying and restores to the tongue the forgotten language of the soul. For these sibylline inspirations of his come from a sky that is brighter than his own, and he cannot control it.(P)

40

The inspired individual does not need to rehash and deliver other people's ideas. His power is creative; through his medium, truth or beauty is born anew.

41

He creates, not to express his small personality as so many others do, but to escape from it. For it is to the divine which transcends him, which is loftily impersonal, that he looks for inspiration.(P)

42

The inspired man does not work in order to submit his pages to the fine taste and delicate nose of the literary critics; nor does he write to entertain the bored or to provide fresh subjects for the tittle-tattle of parlour and club. He writes because he MUST.

43

The supremely gifted artist who works primarily out of pure love of his art—whether it be writing, painting, or music—rather than out of love of its rewards, sometimes approaches and arrives at this same concept through another channel. Such a genius unconsciously throws the plumb-line of feeling into the deep mystery of his being. He is lifted beyond his ordinary self at his most inspired moments. He feels that he is floating in a deeper element. He receives intimations of the pure timeless reality of Mind, whose beauty, he now discovers, his best works have vainly sought to adumbrate. The flash of insight is granted him, although if he is only an artist and not also a philosopher he may not know how to retain it.(P)

44

The actor who never loses his own ego in the personage he is portraying may be a man of much talent, but he may not be a genius.

45

The artist has this advantage over the intellectual, that he recognizes sooner, obstructs less often, and obeys more quickly the intuitive prompting.

46

If the artist becomes truly inspired he will not seek to bring horror to men but rather beauty. This will be so whatever way it shows itself—colour, sound, word, or form. The final step is not with beauty for its own sake but for what it points and leads to—the beautiful Consciousness which awaits man, the inner beauty.

47

If he composes, paints, sculpts, or writes as the light within shows him the thing or thought to be depicted—not as opinion, bias, or untruth urges him—he will be truly inspired.(P)

48

There is this quality about an inspired work, that you can come back to it again and again and discover something fresh or helpful or beautiful or benedictory.(P)

49

Such an inspired production gives out a form of energy which makes those who can receive it with enough sympathy feel and see what its creator felt and saw. There is an actual transmission.(P)

50

The inspiration will come to the extent that he lets go of himself when he opens the piano, to the degree that he forgets that he is the artist, the writer, when he takes up the brush, the pen.

51

Perhaps it is a matter of sustained power of concentration. Perhaps the genius has this ability to maintain steady and unbroken concentration upon the part played without a break so that thoughts of self-consciousness or of what the audience is thinking do not have the power to enter in. Therefore, the artist who has successfully mastered the art of meditation should be able to transfer the qualities so developed to the work of creation or of composition in his art and thus attain a state of genius. For to sit without moving, intensely concentrated, held completely by the object of concentration, is one way of providing part of the necessary conditions for artistic creativity.

52

His objective is to receive a communication whose inspiration remains pure, uncoloured, and undistorted, whereas too many others use their art as a pretext to put forward the twisted constructions or illusory imaginations of their own little egos.

53

He will express himself and his aspirations fully only when he, his body, and his thoughts are unified.

54

It would be hard to find and state new metaphysical or spiritual truth at this late date of human culture. But a brilliant mind may state it in such an unexpected and perceptive way as to give it the force of a new revelation.

55

Artistic composition and production, aesthetic style and method, involve the artist's freedom if he is to do really worthwhile creative work originating in his own deepest inner life, that of his secret spiritual identity. He must be determined to keep uncommitted.

56

If imagination is permitted to wander unbalanced, unchecked, totally free, it may lead to genius, inspiration, or to lunacy, disorder.

57

Sensitivity and passivity are needed to absorb inspiration. If they are not inborn, they will have to be studied and copied for a long while before they can appear of their own accord and be truly personal.

58

The creations of inspired art deserve appreciation for that which is beyond their technical excellence.

59

He is ever alert for that faint but fascinating beginning of an intuitive thought.

60

Those art productions which emerge from this higher state of consciousness have a quality which the other kind lack.

61

Whatever medium an artist works with, whatever sounds or words or sights, and whatever technique he develops and applies, he still needs both concentration and inspiration.

62

A pet cat often settled on the long and broad cuff of Muhammed's sleeve when he was writing, thus interrupting his work in Arabia, but a butterfly occasionally settled on the pencil of W.H. Davies, the tramp poet, and perhaps assisted his verse-making in a little Kentish cottage. Yet who knows, the pauses of inaction may have allowed Muhammed to relapse into meditation and thus, indirectly, assisted or enriched the subsequent writing.

63

The singer gifted with a voice which can exalt and inspire men, the artist endowed with a talent which compels them to pause and behold, may each be used as a channel for the Overself.

64

The quality of sublime inspiration distinguishes the true artist from the mere technician.

65

Even the most inspired mystic needs technical skill and developed intel-
lect to convey his message adequately to his readers. The more he lacks them, the more inarticulate will he be—no matter how strong his inspiration. The more that adequate experience and competent technique are missing from his equipment, the more will he fail to fulfil his own intention and the less will his readers be able to gather in whatever values he represents to them. To know is one thing; the talent to present what you know is another.

66

It is true that education gives a man the power to express in word forms or artistic productions what he thinks or feels. It is also true that an uneducated man may have a far deeper content much more worth express-ing. But unless the latter is able to radiate some of this content by silent look, glance, or touch, he will actually not be able to give others as much as the former.

67

The artist, the craftsman, or the writer who has mastered his profes-sional technique remains a workman if he stops there. But if he learns to enter into the spiritual part of himself, if he practises going into its creative quiet before he begins producing anything, he becomes something more and his production becomes inspired.

68

In matter and manner, in content and technique, in substance and style, the productions of the faultless artist who is only technically competent will never equal those of the faultless artist who is also spiritually ma-ture.(P)

69

The creative mind needs several conditions to promote its work. Among them secrecy during conception and solitude during inspiration are help-ful.

70

The creative poet, writer, or artist who meditates, even for a short while, before his work begins gains proportionately in the visible results.

71

The creator of inspired music, poetry, pictures, and books must work alone if his production is to keep its high quality. If he works in a group he has to struggle to keep his inspiration, as well as to avoid distraction.

72

The skill of the artist, craftsman, poet, painter, composer, or whatever must meet and unite with the inspiration of the glimpse: then there is true creativity in his work.

73

The artist has two functions: to receive through inspiration and to give through technique.(P)

74

Inspiration for a writer does not necessarily mean that the sentences come tumbling through like poured water, or for a painter that the brush-strokes rush across the canvas. It may, but also it may not. What it does mean is an inflow from a deeper source, neither a calculation by the intellect nor a movement by the egoistic emotion. Its first sign is that it is really a smooth flow, whether slow or rapid or waited for. Its second sign is a freedom from doubts, the presence of certainty, sureness, and a sense of rightness. Its third sign is the quiet joy which either accompanies or ends the work, for it is truly a creative act.

75

The author who asks for light on the subjects in his book, who prays for guidance in the writing of it and for inspiration in the doing of it when the little ego cannot see its way, can gain truth and power from on high to do a really outstanding creative job if he knows the technique of inducing the "Interior Word" to speak within Him. This Voice, heard in meditation, is so compelling and so inspirational that it will provide all that he seeks.

76

The superior artist in China is more of a mentalist than his Western equivalent. For he does not just sit down and paint what he sees, whether model or landscape. He sits down quite a few times but makes no attempt to record what he sees. He lets his mind's eye do that. When the time comes to paint the picture, he remains alone in his studio and transfers the mental record.

77

For an aesthetic work to be born, one should first turn the mind inward, get it quiet, and then let the mind go back and let the senses reveal what they can of full and real beauty.

78

The happy and unusual satisfaction which the creative worker of any kind—and especially the artist or writer—feels when he has become deeply immersed for hours in a particular piece of work is a remote ripple of the bliss in which the second self is always itself immersed and to which his prolonged concentration brought him nearer. Again and again through this concentration he stumbles against and unwittingly opens a door in his mind which gives access to the ante-court of the Overself. In the creative experience he begins to find fulfilment but in the spiritual he completes it.

79

What he feels is one thing; what he can express is another. The distance between these two depends on his command of technique not less than on his receptivity to inspiration. The great artist is great in both these respects.

80

The way a thought is expressed, the style in which a teaching is conveyed, possesses a value which is highly exaggerated by the intellectualistic or the artistic but highly undervalued by the mystic and ascetic.

81

Although technical equipment is not all there is to the practice of art, it must be mastered. Without it, inspiration suffers from a faulty or deficient medium.

82

Creative work, insofar as it truly touches the depths and heights of inspiration, takes our minds out of our personal troubles and thus gives us temporary peace—for it brings the impersonal Overself into contact with our troubled person and the contact provides us with a higher point of view. Those moments of artistic inspiration when the mind becomes almost incandescent are always moments of intense concentration and rapt absorption. "It is from this condition of their being (trance), in its most imperfect form, that Poetry, Music, Art—all that belong to an idea of Beauty—take their immortal birth."—Lytton's *Zanoni*

83

Inspiration gives a man the strengthened faith and virile force to work; but he himself must find the words or sounds for the results—the written poem or musical piece.

84

Creative inspiration can charge words, sounds, paint, or stone with magical power.

85

The composition is technical but the inspiration is mystical.

86

Skill with the use of an author's pen does not necessarily indicate a higher consciousness.

87

Buddha says in the *Lankavatarasutra*: "Mahamati, it is like the mastery of comedy, dancing, singing, music, lute-playing, painting, and other arts, which is gained gradually and not simultaneously; in the same way, Mahamati, the purification of the Tathagata of all beings is gradual and not instantaneous." Years of practice give the sculptor or the painter a dexterity of the hand which is a marvel for witnesses of his work.

88

A genius who possesses poor technique and deficient mechanism will never be a complete master of his art. His productions will always be imperfect ones.

89

He who puts his skills as a craftsman, an artist, or a public servant to the service of his essential self, his diviner self, puts them to the best use.

90

Good art is not complete unless it has *both* praiseworthy technique and inspiration, form and content.

91

A writer's or artist's value depends not only on his technical equipment but also on his being manipulated by the Overself.

92

If he lacks this inspired creativeness he will produce mere toys to entertain people, not spiritual treasures to enrich them.

93

The true artist—that is to say, the inspired artist—must necessarily be sparse in his output. So alone can he keep up the choice quality of his work.

94

The truth can be put in short plain words and short easy sentences or it can be put in polysyllabic words and long winding sentences. It is not the higher power which uses the one kind or the other, but the author himself.

95

The inspiration comes from beyond time; the formulation in thought, picture, pattern, or sound takes place in time.

3

ART EXPERIENCE AND
MYSTICISM

When creative art is truly inspired, it comes close to being sacramental.

2

There is a path to mystical intuition and sometimes to mystical experience in the beholding of Nature's beauty. There is another through the listening to musical beauty.

3

Only truly inspired geniuses of art and intellect, and those members of the public who appreciate their productions, understand that religion has to a large extent appeared in different vesture to this generation.

4

It is inevitable that inspired art and illumined writing should arouse the beginning of mystical feelings in the hearts of those prepared and sensitive enough to appreciate mysticism. But even in hearts not so ready, the dim echoes of such feelings are often aroused. This is particularly true of music.

5

If he can lay himself open to the power of beauty in art or Nature, letting it get deep inside him, he may receive an intuition or attain an experience as mystical as the meditator's.

6

Where literature, poetry, music, painting, or other real art is truly inspired, it comes near to religion and nearer still to mysticism. Those persons who cannot find any affinity with these last two may get their spiritual aid from the arts. Respectfully approached, properly used, and correctly understood, these too can be sacred, as the ancients well understood. If today art has been dragged into muddy gutters and mad encounters, if it has been squalidly commercialized and deprived of purpose, meaning, form, or Truth, that is because the invaders are not artists but barbarians.

7

Religion and art, liturgy and sculpture, prayer and poetry, come together as relatives when inspiration touches them.

8

Through the practice of art a man may come closer to soul than through occultism.(P)

9

Is the artist's and the mystic's experience identical? Sometimes it is but more often not at all. The times when the artist, the writer, the musician, or the poet touches the same level as the mystic depend partly upon his ability to forget himself in devotion to his creation, partly on other things.

10

The ecstasy of the mystic is psychologically akin to the ecstasy of the artist. It is not metaphysically the same, however. For the mystic, inasmuch as he has been prepared to renounce all external things in its pursuit, is freer and has gone farther. He has not to depend on such things as a stimulus to his effort or as a focus for his method.

11

The practice of the artist is one level below the practice of the contemplative.

12

The artist uses a medium *outside* himself to effect his own personal approach to the ecstatic state of ideal beauty as well as to inspire the appreciators of his artistic production. The mystic uses no external medium whatever, but makes his approach to the source he finds *inside* himself. Although the mystic, if he be blessed with intellectual talents or artistic gifts, can project his ecstatic experience into an intellectual or artistic production when he chooses, he is not obliged to do so. He has this internal method of transmitting his experience to others through mental telepathy. Hence mysticism is on a higher level than art. Nevertheless, art, being much easier for most people to comprehend and appreciate, necessarily makes a wider appeal and reaches hundreds of thousands where mysticism reaches only a few.(P)

13

The artist, the musician, or the writer who uses his art as a spiritual path must one day come to the point where he finds that it is no longer sufficient—that he must go beyond it, or rather, transcend it and find entirely within himself and without this outside means the uplift and the exaltation that he formerly got during the minutes of composition or creation. In the end, we have to look within because there alone is the real being, the soul. Art can lead us to its very border but art is still something that works upon the senses, and these senses have to be transcended, the senses of the body, the five senses.

14

Art succeeds in its finer and fundamental purpose if it succeeds in inducing absorption in the theme to the point of self-forgetfulness. Then the higher nature can come through and permeate the man's being with joy or truth, hope or strength, and whatever attribute is suggested by the theme itself.

15

The question whether art alone is enough may be answered affirmatively by the artist only until one of two things happens. Either he is confronted by a shattering event in his personal life or he is confronted by an uncommon one in his inner life. By the latter, I mean a descent of grace with no external cause or with one in human or nature form. This confrontation with an enlightened person may act as a catalyst, or this blessed gift of mountain-sea immensity or forest peace may touch him more deeply than earlier experiences. It is then that he understands that the importance of art can be exaggerated, that there is another level of being for which it can prepare him, or to which it can lead, but which it cannot touch because it is derivative—not direct, not immediate.

16

Human language is impotent to tell us exactly what this profoundest of all experiences is like, but it can give hints, clues. Human art cannot depict it in picture nor give it sound or music but can come near enough to excite or hush us.

17

With all its benedictory beauty, art alone cannot save a man. It can lead him to the very verge of ethereal moments, but not to the illumination which lies within them.

18

The release from care and repose after toil which the arts or Nature can give are more thoroughly given by mystical meditation, which has the further advantage of depending on no external person, medium, instrument, or vehicle. The way of art, being dependent on external forms although the goal itself is an interior one, has limitations which make it fall short of the way of mysticism. For if a man gets so attached and entangled in the attractiveness of those beautiful forms that his reactions to people and things constantly swing, pendulum fashion, back and forth between attraction and repulsion, then his aesthetic senses will no longer help but rather will hinder him from attaining the goal.

19

Those who find their fulfilment in any form of the arts and who look to it for their highest satisfaction may become, and often do become, attached to it in such a way that it blocks their way to the still higher level where all attachments, including this one, must vanish. For unless a man finds his higher self and values it above everything else, he has not brought his quest to completion. This does not mean he can throw aside all arts; they need not become obstacles in his way so long as he keeps them in their proper place and knows that they are on the step just below the highest one.

20

The creative artist is taken out of himself for a time and is serenely elevated, just as the meditative mystic is. But the two states, although psychologically similar, are not spiritually similar. For the mystic enters his elevated state consciously and deliberately goes in quest of his inner being or soul. He uses it as a springboard to escape from the world of space time and change. The artist, however, uses it as a means of creating something *in* the world of space time and change. Hence although art approaches quite close to mysticism, it has not the same divine possibilities, for it lacks the higher values, the moral disciplines, and the supersensuous aims of mysticism.(P)

21

Even the highest art is only a means to an end—it ought not to be made an end in itself. The inspired artist must in the end put aside his theme, his medium, his work and turn to the Divine alone, not to its expressions down here.(P)

22

That beauty in Nature which moves the artist to compose his piece, write his poem, or whatever, must in the end give place to the beauty in a glimpse, ethereal and elusive but more deeply felt than any other.

23

It is not only the workers in art who may get carried away by their concentration, but also the laymen who become the recipients of their productions and put themselves under their charm with a similar degree of concentration. In both cases—in the artist who creates and the layman who contemplates—there is an approach to the borderline of yoga. If it is pure beauty which calls forth their adoration and not some lesser thing, they may indeed cross this borderline and find themselves in a yogic state. What is said here of art is true also of the impulses derived from Nature. If man would only take such moods more seriously and rise to the highest level towards which the mood can carry them, they may well return to ordinary consciousness if not with a glimpse then with the next best thing to a glimpse.(P)

24

Such mystical experiences are priceless to the artist. They give him the subtle but strong inspiration without which the finest technique is a half-failure.

25

Art is at its best and greatest when it is motivated by the endeavour to express such a glimpse.

26

Shelley called these glimpses "visitations of the divinity in man" and he called art "a record of the best and happiest moments."

27

The function of art is different from that of mysticism, but both converge in the same ultimate direction. Both are expressions of the human search for something higher than the ordinary.(P)

28

Chuang Tzu tells the story of a carpenter highly gifted in carving wood. When asked how he made such masterpieces, he said, "When I'm about to do this, I guard against any lessening of my vital strength. I first reduce my mind to absolute quiet. For three days, in this condition, I end up by forgetting any question of gaining reward. For five days I forget anything about getting famous. For seven days my skill becomes concentrated, all disturbing things from outside vanish. I see the form in my mind's eye and set to work."

29

The greatest Japanese master of camellia growing, arrangement, and art in our time, Cholaa Adachi, said to disciples, "You must give yourself over completely to the flowers. Look upon their beauty with a warm heart and devoted mind. You have to sit and face flowers silently for a while. Old Japanese proverbs say, 'A flower is a mirror to the mind' and 'Be beautiful and pure like flowers.'"

30

The dangers of a disequilibrated psyche are vividly shown in the lives of gifted artists and inspired poets. If we comprehend that genius in the arts is in essence a spiritual thing, we can comprehend too why the ruin that overtook Ernest Dowson and Paul Verlaine was equivalent to a spiritual failure on the quest itself.

31

A brilliant concert pianist, who was also a successful meditator, told me that the same feeling of being taken over by a higher power which came at a certain depth of contemplation, came also after a certain period of time had elapsed during her playing. Both experiences caused her to be suffused with Peace.

32

The artist or poet who is highly inspired has a chance to find God.

33

Let the intellectuals argue and debate: that is as high and as far as they can go; the thinking machine must continue to revolve its wheels. But let also the intuitive-feeling poets, the beauty-searching artists, and the inward-turning mystics have their say.

34

The indescribable mystical content of a poem or picture is given to the delicate sensitivity of the man who undertakes to provide the outer form which it takes. Without feeling it is nothing; without depth its measure is slight. And of course the whole result grows under the warmth of tender love.

35

In the admiration of Nature's beauty and the appreciation of art, music, poetry, and literature, the seeker can find sources of inner help and themes for meditation.

36

Art is a means of pleasantly enforcing meditation, of unconsciously leading the mind inwards, of transferring attention from the material thing to the immaterial idea.

37

The mystical intuition and experience can come to men solely through a practice or appreciation of the arts, and can also be given out through them.

38

In literary and dramatic works which rise to the higher planes of thought, creation, imagination or aspiration, there may be moments when some among the readers or audience are carried to experiences where the ordinary self is dropped and a nobler one takes over; where a rare peace holds the mind or ecstatic beauty suffuses the feelings, not for long perhaps but to be long remembered.

39

The ultimate result and worth of a work of art lies not in the immediate pleasure it gives, but in the far deeper feeling of fulfilment. For this in turn arises out of the divine stillness, which was momentarily and unwittingly touched, or which momentarily absorbed and held the satisfied ego.

40

Whether in the presentation of Nature's scenes or the productions of man's art, the beauty which attracts the best instincts is a faint reverberating echo coming down from the highest divine world.

41

The poet's appeal to feeling, the architect's graceful forms, and the composer's melodious music can be elevated from a merely technical level, dependent on talent alone, to one of jewelled inspiration if he lets himself surrender to this ethereal stillness.

42

The closeness of God and Light, Matter and Light, Mystical Experience and Light shows itself in the study of philosophy. It is not a surprise to find that painters of genius have been lured into working with light to find their highest appeal—beauty!

43

For some poets and composers the experience of Reality is almost within their grasp.

44

It is the superior business of an inspired work of art to bring out the best in us for a time. But it is our business to put forth the efforts needed to keep it active for all time.

45

The beauty of some scenes in Nature and some pieces of music—who that feels them, and reflects, can fail to be touched by sadness at the thought that they die all-too-soon, leaving him alone again *with himself*? In the end, he must find it there.

46

A piano student tried to find if music was used in India as a path to the philosophic-mystic experience. She found no such practice, but that it was used to stimulate religious devotion, which is not exactly the same thing.

47

Whereas the Buddhist tradition frowned on music and dancing, most in the Sufi tradition delighted in the first and those in the Dervish one delighted especially in the second. Where Buddha banned music as a hindrance to aspirants, Pythagoras and the Neoplatonic masters praised it as a help.

48

Beethoven generally looked to the nature of the feelings to be brought out by music. Thus someone else's genius, that of a Beethoven perhaps, may help us get the mystical glimpse.

49

A beautiful scene or piece of music stirs the mind to unconscious re-membrance of its own beautiful source. If this mood is sustained long enough then a kind of nostalgia develops.

50

The creative artist who has produced inspired work knows from his own experience that art can be connected with the higher development of a man.

51

He knows from the force of his own inspiration that there is a part of his being which transcends his normal level.

52

The inspired composer of music or painter of pictures may be so carried away by the beauty of his inspiration as to be lost in it. He then forgets himself, undergoes a temporary loss of ego.

53

If the artist could only learn to be as inspired in his life as he is at times in his work—that is, as elevated and idealistic—how quickly would he realize the quest's highest state!

54

Goethe knew, and said, that if he could find out why an artistic production interested and impressed, excited or fascinated him, he could advance another step forward towards saying the Truth.

55

Through these beautiful forms our feeling is aesthetically pleased, but through its own higher evolution it is merged and rapt in the spirit of Beauty itself. In this matter the thinking of Plato coincides smoothly with the knowledge of philosophy.

56

An inspired work is always fresh, for it always comes of a man's own deep spirit.

57

That which is most evident and attractive and inspiring in what the best artists and composers give us is not far from that which is given in thought and feeling to others who have felt the Presence.

58

The philosophic search for enlightenment and the artist's search for perfection of work can meet and unite.(P)

59

The artist whose first impression of philosophy is a false one may believe that he has nothing to gain from it. The fact is that he can discover much in it—beauty, inspiration, support, a sense of art's real mission.

60

The admiration felt for a work of art or a piece of music, an inspired poem or a mountain scene, should be turned into something more than brief enjoyment. This can be done by entering more deeply and more quietly into the experience.

61

Plato saw what the inspired artist discovers in the end, that beauty of form and shape is only a lead to the formless beauty of Overself.

62

The classical arts and crafts of several Oriental countries served a double purpose for their better practitioners. They were a professional means of earning a living. They were also part of a spiritual path. The craftsman who gave weeks or even months to finish a product gave it also considerable concentration. When he turned away to spiritual exercises, he brought this power quite naturally into his devotional prayer or meditational inner work.

63

A poem or a piece of music fulfils its highest purpose if it leads reader or hearer beyond poetry or music. Art is not the end of living: the beauty to which it points must be found *in* man himself.

64

Art in its best moments tells of a supernal reality. If it can lead him to look upon the face of that reality, he can then dispense with art.

65

It is possible to combine the artist's search for his highest self-expression with the mystic's penetration into his self-ground.

66

As he yields himself to this admiration for nature, to music, to art, more and more he will find on specific occasions that a kind of stillness settles down over him when he is engaged in this attitude.

67

This faculty of admiration, properly used and rightly directed, may become a way of inner communion. Music, sunset, landscapes are, among others, fit objects.

68

When the beautiful thing has led to the exalted thought, when the mind is lit up by the glimpse, then the work of art or Nature has rendered its service of acting as a springboard and should be deserted.

69

When a piece of deep music or a chapter of illumined writing puts him under a kind of spell towards the end, when the aesthetic joy or intellectual stimulus of one or the other gives him the sensation of being carried away, he ought to take full advantage of what has happened by putting aside the thought of the music or book and remembering that he is at the gate of the Overself.(P)

70

If his affections are engaged and he feels the effect of beauty—whether in Nature or art—so deeply that admiration verges on worship, he would do well to take the next step and search for beauty's source.

71

It is a rare moment when he looks upon Beauty itself rather than upon the forms of Beauty.(P)

72

This meditation on beauty, which is practised by true artists and practisable by all others who are sensitive to Nature, can be stretched to a point of full absorption. The meditator is then lost in lovely feelings where the holy trinity of Greek worship—goodness, beauty, and truth—fuse as one. He rises from it as an inspired man. The beautiful object which was outside his body kindled the spirit of beauty inside his heart. The visible led, by adoration and concentration, to the invisible. It is then possible, while this influence lasts, to carry it back again into outer life.

73

From the attachments to beautiful forms, sounds, phrases, he has been set free by Beauty itself. He may still enjoy them, but no longer depends on them, just as he may still use a candle but worships the sun.

74

The arts may be used to approach the verge, the very edge of "nowhere and nowhen," but philosophy is needed to go beyond.

75

The artist's productions may be most inspired; he may glorify art and put it on a pinnacle as the noblest and loftiest human activity when at its best. But it is still a manifestation of man's ego, the finest and final one. He must transcend it in the end. Like yoga, it prepares the way, is a step not a stop.(P)

76

He is a philosopher first, an artist second. This is the order, the hierarchy, by which he lives; yet this does not render him any less appreciative of a poem, does not stop him enjoying music to its fullest.

77

The artistic experience provides something of a foretaste of the philosophic one; there is something of the mystical glimpse in it, too: but because it depends on an outer stimulant, it passes after a while and leaves the experiencer bereft. But it refines and exalts feeling.

78

The glimpses produced by the arts, and especially by music, are only brief and slight ones. They cannot equal the measure or quality of those produced by the Quest's more direct techniques.

79

Words give us the idea of things, sculptures and paintings actualize their pictured forms, music renders sound-effects, but none of these has ever evoked the Real. For that everything else must be banished—only the Void, Silence, and Stillness may Be; nothing to see or touch.

80

Art can be a path to spiritual enlightenment but not to complete and lasting enlightenment. It can be born out of, and can give birth itself to, only Glimpses. For art is a search for beauty, which by itself is not enough. Beauty must be supported by virtue and both require wisdom to guide them.(P)

4

REFLECTIONS ON SPECIFIC ARTS

Writing, literature, poetry

Writing can remain a way of expressing the narrowest and basest parts of the ego, a stimulant to violence and coarseness and animality. Or, in the hands of a more evolved person, it can become a source of uplift to others and, like any other art, even a way of development for the writer.

2

When writing achieves importance through style or effectiveness of expression or beauty of form, it has attained the level of literature.

3

If the writer is to come to inspiration, he should not be aware of any audience: the only reader must be himself. Otherwise he does not do his best work, for the self-conscious ego is behind it all, puffed up with its own importance.

4

The creative writer must give his topic an inward-turned concentration as if he were listening to a mental voice speaking within himself. The concentration must be absolute, without distraction; it must not even be shared with any background music.

5

Wisdom is all the better when it is likewise witty. Raise a laugh while you lift a man. Mix some humour with your ink and you shall write all the better. Sound sense loses nothing of its soundness when it is poured into bright, good-humoured phrases. Truth is often cold-blooded and a bath in warm smiles makes it the more attractive.(P)

6

The writer may set down whatever word comes into his mind to express his thought in order not to lose the thought, but later he should not hesitate to come back and examine what he has written and ruthlessly to change those words or to throw them out altogether if his meaning is not expressed with sufficient fineness.

7

Keep on writing no matter what it is—put down whatever comes into your head; in this way you develop fluency. The criticism and crossings out of what has been done can follow at a later time.

8

The notion that the effects of inspiration should not be handled by the labours of revision is a wrong one. This is so, first, because few artists ever achieve a total purity of inspiration—however ecstatic their creative experience may be—and, second, because even if achieved it is still limited by the personal nature of the channel through which it flows. The writer who refuses to touch manuscripts again or to correct proofs displays vanity or ignorance or both.(P)

9

We who work in literature or poetry must learn to put images of truth or beauty into the minds of readers. The sensitive person is too often cowed by the prevailing materialism in the society around him and particularly in its way of life—cowed to the point of falling in with this way and doing what the others are doing. This is weakness and cowardliness, the surrender to external suggestion.

10

It is the business of a philosophic writer to put a moral value and metaphysical meaning into life for those who can perceive neither one nor the other in it.

11

The author who puts pen and paper into fruitful conjunction is stating a message for others. Does he recognize in the depths of his being, his soul, his conscience, that he has a certain moral responsibility there?

12

I feel that it is a writer's duty to write about the best, the highest, the truest things he knows and then only to communicate these thoughts to others. Only when I can see them quite clearly and am convinced of their correctness, ought I to start to turn to others.

13

We who write have a responsibility for the thought-forms we create and let loose in the world.

14

We should remember that a piece of prose which uplifts the reader and gratifies the writer is the work of his best moments. What does he do with his lesser ones—for he must be humble enough to accept that they are there. If he is wise he will accept the Pythagorean advice to work upon himself. He will do more than well to transfer activity from unresistant white paper to obdurate negative tendencies. The reshaping of the self is not pleasant and not easy but it is rewarding.

15

When the presence of the Real is so ineffable, its secret so incommunicable, how can any writer—no matter how deft and experienced—put a correct picture of it in a book?

16

A piece of writing which lacks literary form does not have the power over readers of one which does have it. Two men may utter the same truth but one will have many more hearers than the other. Style still counts.

17

The best service a writer can render is to seek and find divine inspiration and true thinking, and then to offer the result to his fellowmen.

18

No man who has seen his soul's grandeur and felt its sublimity could write in a dull dreary inartistic style about it.

19

In this matter of communication he must be contemporary, producing work of and for his own time, current and therefore resultful, alive and therefore able to reach the living more closely and more personally than a dead person could reach them.

20

Sentences free from voluble overdecoration, almost as nude as they are noble; ideas phrased with verbal thrift so that meaning is kept clear and communication is as explicit as can be—this ought to be the modern idea. There are not many countries left today where such open speech about religion—Jewish, Christian, Islamic, or otherwise—will be punished by execution or persecution for heresy.

21

Playing with the power of words to give new forms, new expressions, new images, and new mantrams for the spiritual revivification of man, the writer of vision truly makes the Word become flesh. His gifts should be valued accordingly and received gratefully.

22

The nimble use of words is not alone a satisfactory substitute for the accurate use of facts.

23

A writer cannot work properly when surrounded by noise, when compelled to work at conventional hours, when society, neighbours, and would-be friendly persons intrude upon him.

24

When a writer feels that the flow of thought runs smoothly, he should not interrupt the work by taking to some other task temporarily or let anyone else interrupt it, but should take advantage of this peak period, as one might call it, for when he picks it up again the work may not run so smoothly, because the inner push is absent.

25

It is hard for an author to efface himself from his production. Not only is this so, but a one-pointed attention is also needed in the reader. He can do so only if he possesses the capacity to be so completely concentrated in the work as to forget everything else. This achieved, the personal ego will naturally be absent.

26

A budding author usually thinks his work to be far better than it really is, whereas the mature, proficient one is his own best critic—always ready to amend, revise, cancel, and change what he has written earlier.

27

One should be willing to examine carefully what he has said or done or written; and he should do it not to praise it but to correct or improve it imaginatively.

28

The value of documentation in a book, whether through footnotes or text, is that it answers critics or opponents holding opposite views, *in advance* with facts, and also that it helps to prevent the malicious falsification or distortion of history.

29

He should know that no man's work is so good that it could not be better. Save for the plea of lack of time a writer is prudent to revise sentences and even polish phrases. As soon as he assumes the mantle of vanity his work suffers.

30

When an author can effect contact with his Overself his writing becomes a spiritual activity. It inspires him, teaches him, uplifts him.

31

How often he will have to erase words and alter phrases and improve sentences, if his communication is to fit the thought which his intuition has given him!

32

Inspiration is more valuable than information. But the writer who can impart both to his readers renders them the best service.

33

Do not allow stylizing to usurp the throne of truth; do not let manner-ism get out of hand.

34

The same fact which, when presented drily and logically, leads to no result may, when presented vividly and imaginatively, lead to a stirring of the emotions. This, in turn, may lead the man to take action.

35

Technique does count. Sentences which are slipshod in construction irritate the reader, and phrases which are awkward in form obscure the meaning.

36

If his thinking upon this matter is logical and coherent, and if the expression of his thoughts is grammatical and accurate, then those who seek to learn from him will have less difficulty in understanding him.

37

The writer reduces life to words, that is, to mere symbols.

38

Write what can be useful to others, what will simplify the teaching for them, and what will lead them to seek the source within their own beings.

39

Even if nobody wants to read his books the author of concentrated, well-done, or finely inspired work benefits himself internally.

40

The poet who lives at times from this profounder self will link his words with words as others do, and his rhythms with rhythms, but the difference of level will appear in their effect.

41

When he writes at his best, what he writes may be on a higher level than himself.

42

If a writer can put his theme, case, statement, or argument only in shrill hysteric tones, you may be sure he is an ill-balanced person.

43

Complimentary letters from readers may fatten an author's ego if he is not careful. It is therefore good if there is a sufficient leaven of criticism, or even abusive letters, from those who dislike his work or who disagree violently with his ideas.

44

The equilibrium of a written piece may be upset and the meaning somewhat falsified by putting too much stress or according too little weight. A prudent balance is essential in expressing any particular idea.

45

Goethe on writing: "I have the whole thing in my head and only need the mood to write. I wrote down little or nothing until I had worked out most of it in detail in my head."

46

We must write from what we know, from our own experience, from what we observe as facts around us, but where we cannot do either we must state that a theory is only a theory, however plausible and good it may be and however worth our hoarding.

47

There are different ways of making notes and marking books. There are also different colours which appeal to some writers and not to other ones. Queen Victoria scribbled her thoughts or decisions, suggestions or comments on official reports submitted to her: all were endorsed with a violet-coloured pencil. Alice Bailey wrote her Arcane Teaching books with an ordinary black-lead pencil, never with pen-and-ink: she got inner contact either with her higher self or with her guru's mind that way, she explained.

48

Aldous Huxley has outgrown his merely rationalistic stage and begun to express mystical ideas. This is a most gratifying advance. But he has fallen into the common error which makes the quietist ideal the supreme ideal. He may try to refute this activist outlook as being mystical heresy. He may even write a whole book, such as *Grey Eminence*, to show the misfortunes brought on his country by a French mystic leaving his monastic retreat to meddle in State affairs. But Huxley's effort has been a vain one. It is just as easy to write another book showing the good fortune brought to her country by Joan of Arc, also a French mystic, through meddling in State affairs. In this matter, I would rather accept Plato's teaching, that true knowledge compels to action. And Plato's philosophy was surely a mystical one. But there are two facts which refute Huxley. First, there is no such thing as inaction. No man in his senses will spend every day every year in contemplation alone. He has to get up and do something, even if it be only eating his dinner. A life of continuous meditation, without any interruption, would be impossible and undesirable, impracticable and unbalanced. Everywhere in Nature we see striving and activity. For man to attempt to refrain from both (as if he really could!) in the name of an exaggerated unbalanced and perverted surrender to God is to misunderstand God's— that is, Nature's—working. Second, the refusal to act is itself a kind of action; the real available choice is only between one kind and another, between good action and bad action. Walking about in the monastic cell is as active a deed as walking about in the statesman's chamber. But whether we take a short or a long view of the matter it is a mistake to regard the worldly life as necessarily materialistic and sordid. Men may make it so or they may ennoble it. The evil or the good is in their thought of it, that is, in themselves. The notion that the quest of the Divine must necessarily lead to denying the social and despising the historical belongs only to an unripened and imperfect mysticism. The fact is that no mystical experience and no metaphysical idea can complete our duty towards life. They are no substitute for right conduct.

49

I agree with Israel Zangwill, when he remarked at a public speech, "It is always a mistake for a literary man to show himself in the flesh; the flesh is generally a little disappointing; an author should be a disembodied spirit!"

50

Many writers get into an excited state about the work they happen to be engaged in, but few have also gotten into a state of entrancement. In the latter case, the works produced seem to have had considerable effect upon the readers and made quite an impression upon their feelings. Three writings come to mind immediately: the first, Walt Whitman's *Leaves of Grass*; the second, Joel Goldsmith's first and most celebrated work [*The Infinite Way*—Ed.]; and the third, Allen Ginsberg's *Howl*.

51

Words are clumsy things with which to express these ethereal moods: a telepathic concentration on the one side and a passive meditation on the other would be better. But failing such silent inner contact, what else can we use but words, or music, or some other art form?

52

T.S. Eliot is too often a neurotic writer of the "precious" school, begetting muddled mystical nonsense. His reputation is overrated partly because of the portentous air he gives himself and partly because he is sufficiently incomprehensible to put himself out of the herd. But in *The Cocktail Party*, where he leaves verse for playwriting, he rises to a truly superior and truly mystical level.

53

When Wordsworth first saw that beautiful structure Tintern Abbey, he was uplifted to a spiritual plane. He put his feeling into a poem which those who could not visit the Abbey could read. A glimpse which inspired one art-form was transferred to another.

54

There are those who claim the poetic value to be as important as any other; who make poetry synonymous with spirituality; who rank it at the head of all the arts. "When I read poetry there is evoked in me a sense of beauty. My feelings, however, go deeper . . . I approach God through poetry. This is the true experience of a deep-searching person." These lines were written by Ryosen in the first few years of this century. He was a leader of the young intellectuals in Japan but died in his thirties. He began as a devout religionist, became a sceptical rationalist, but in the last few years of his short life moved over into mysticism.

He later explained the above quotation: "The sphere of truth and the sphere of poetry are from the outset different. . . . To the extent that we penetrate to the innermost part of human life, truth and poetry draw close . . . now in harmonious union."

55

I consider poetry to be a grand form of human culture but poets to be, quite often, victims of their own conceit, emotionalism, hallucination, and wishful thinking. Plato severely criticized them. Muhammed wrote harshly in the Holy *Koran*: "And as to the poets, those who go astray follow them; do you not see that they wander about bewildered in every valley? And they say that which they do not do."

56

Plato banished poets from his ideal Republic but nevertheless he crowned them first. By doing so he acknowledged poetry's well-deserved prestige but also its danger. For poets are more tempted, because more responsive to feelings, to exaggerate or sometimes even to falsify in their attempts to weave an emotional atmosphere and create an influential effect upon the reader by using metaphors and figures of speech. Of course that would not mean a deliberate falsification but rather a carelessness about truth. Unfortunately, truth was Plato's primary value. Take the famous and beautiful line: "A rose-red city, half as old as time." Note the exaggeration concerning time.

57

I am not alone in regarding the mystical deliverances of poets with special caution. Quite unconsciously, and because they are carried away by emotion, their sense of truth becomes impaired, their capacity for judgement imperilled. Moreover, poetry is concerned with personal feelings; prose can ascend higher and express the impersonal and the universal. Hence the poet is so often an egotist whereas it is easier for the prose writer, so far as his work goes, to be an altruist. Newman, although himself a Catholic, criticized Faber's writings in favour of Papal Infallibility as follows: "Judicious people think them crude and young, perhaps extravagant. He was a poet."

58

Poetry is akin to music in that it appeals more to feelings, and feelings in the end are so important that they push us into actions and deeds. But feelings can also mislead us and endanger us; therefore they need to be brought into equilibrium with reason and even more with intuition. Hence a poem which combines wisdom with its beauty, thought with emotion, will serve its auditors better in the end than one which does not.

59

An author is not always to be judged by his books. Sometimes he is much better than his writings; sometimes they are much better than he. The reason is plain. Inspiration raises the writer to a higher level of being; his inspired moments represent the peaks of his character, but afterwards he must fall back into everyday normalcy.

60

An autobiography can be and most often is what Guide, the English Victorian novelist, now so forgotten, called a degrading form of vanity— which he refused to write despite the request of publishers. But it can also be a work of utility to those who read it, even of wise helpful instruction to the younger people who have to find their way through the difficulties of early life and the deceptions of later life.

61

When will people understand that they come closer to a writer by studying his ideas rather than by meeting him in the flesh? Thoreau once said: "The best of me is in my books; I am not worth seeing personally."

62

All imperishable poems have this same quality—they worship beauty of the highest kind.

63

The Razor's Edge, by Somerset Maugham: The guru described in Maugham's novel is a compound of Ramana Maharshi and others, but the descriptions are fanciful and the events unreal. The ashram is greatly exaggerated and the young American rishee has not yet existed on earth. Maugham is a newcomer to these things, anyway, and cannot get even a quarter of an inch below appearances, while often soaking in clouds of self-deception. Nevertheless he has come out of agnosticism to this higher standpoint; it is good to know that he wrote this novel instead of concentrating exclusively on sex, as in his other stories.

64

The malign destiny which snatched the young Keats and Shelley from physical life, which kept the gifted Byron captive of his physical passion, deprived them of their chance to come to spiritual maturity, and the world of a greater deeper poetry.

65

Once W.B. Yeats wrote in admiration of Shankara's teaching. But in middle age he married and later revised his views and then wrote: "Ah, how many years it has taken me to awake from out of that dream!"

66

The poet should bring us to adore an uplifting beauty, not plunge us in a mad frenzy.

67

The sensual weaknesses to which writers like D.H. Lawrence devoted so much of their literary talent, instead of being regarded as morally undesirable, came to be regarded as praiseworthy virtues! It was forgotten that the prudent man will contain his desires within reasonable limits, if ideals and not caprices are to rule his life. It is true that Lawrence possessed ideals, even mystical ones, but lacked prudence. In short, he was unbalanced.

68

What D.H. Lawrence wrote in one of his private letters—"I feel sometimes that I shall go mad"—is the key to both the man and his work. One part of his being was, in his own words, "damnably violent" but another and—as he granted—a deeper part responded to "the kindness of the Cosmos." He was a disjointed disconnected man, a seer filled often with bitter spleen.

69

Leslie A. Fiedler, summarizing an article in "CEA Critic," May 1974, said, "Popular Literature—sentimental, horror, pornographic—titillates the emotions, releasing the reader from rationality and allowing him a moment of ecstasy. To define a true majority literature [i.e., low cultural—P.B.] we should evaluate a work not by ethics or aesthetics, but by the ecstasy it produces." Comment by P.B.: If a literature of refined cultural taste, mature intellectual statements, and civilized courtesy is to be rejected because it admires self-control, then we surely shall move backwards.

70

I do not understand much in modern art, modern poetry, and modern literature. When I hear on all sides, from professors in colleges and universities—more particularly, those in American institutions—when I hear them placing James Joyce's work (especially his *Ulysses*) among the creations of genius and fulsomely praising it, I am dumbfounded! I feel like Mansfield when, after trying to read this book, she wrote, "This is the future, and I'm glad I've got tuberculosis." As we know, she died from this dreadful disease. I do not take so black a view as hers because I believe the future contains positive as well as this negative material.

71

Shelley's death at an early age has often been lamented. Yet, leaving aside the elements of fate or karma, we may see how the negative quality of impatience contributed towards it. He had bought a small sailing vessel during his residence on the Italian coast. He went on a journey to purchase supplies and to tend to other matters and then was about to return to the residence, where his wife and child awaited him. It was only one day's sailing from where he was, but an expert seaman and also the lighthouse-keeper warned him that a storm was coming and that he would do better to postpone his trip until it had passed. He did not listen to them owing to his eagerness to return to his wife, and he sailed away. Within a very short time, quite short, the storm suddenly appeared. There were violent upheavals of the water, and the little ship disappeared beneath the waves. This is how he was drowned. Shelley was lost with it—at least the living Shelley, for his body was recovered later—and humanity was deprived of the products of his bright genius at a still more mature age.

72

The modern verse movement in the English language came into being largely through the pioneering efforts of T.S. Eliot and Ezra Pound. Of the first man I have little to say: he was a good man, a talented man, a spiritually sensitive man, but in this effort he was misguided, and would have done better for the world if he had never gotten associated with Pound, who was a bad influence on him.

73

It is pardonable for people to expect a writer to incarnate his own words. This would seem necessary if he is not to be a hypocrite. But they forget that his best writing comes out of his best moments, that such times come only at intervals, that such levels are inspired, hence beyond or above his ordinary ones, and that like all true artists he is used to paint ideals for the benefit of himself as well as other people. The ideal has its legitimate place even though there is a time-gap between it and the actuality. We need not be harshly over-critical of the writer who portrays it but is unable to live by its higher standard today. If he is sincere, he will arrive at it another day. If he is not, he still renders a useful service despite himself.

74

Those whose literary actions come not out of goodwill but out of hate hurt themselves as well as others.

75

There are pieces of prose which are almost pure poetry, and there are lines of verse which are almost pure prose.

76

It may be asked why Plato banned the poets from his ideal Republic. Is it not, perhaps, because poetry seeks to move the feelings of its hearers or readers and that feeling induced from outside, as by poetry, can be carried to an extreme point and sweep a man off his feet, as the saying is, so that he acts on impulse or from ungoverned emotion and passion?

77
The most intelligent of writers are sometimes the least intelligent of philosophers.

78
Nietzsche's distorted semi-mysticism set up before educated people the ideal of a barbaric Superman, and Oswald Spengler's distorted intellectualism led them to draw the false lesson from history that man is always a beast of prey.

79
Nietzsche was a lunatic who rejected Jesus but accepted Socrates, an ascetic who denounced hedonism, and a firebrand admired by the Nazis.

80
There is this weakness in the poet who is only a poet and nothing more—that he is likely to accept almost anything as truth, provided it be beautiful.

81
Whoever writes for publication is in a position of public trust.

82
The sculpted wood, cast metal, or carven stone image speaks instantly to all, but the written word only to those who know the language used.

83
There is a difference between those who report in their writings and those who create. The first are carried away by the moment's happenings, the second look deeper and find weightier things.

84
The poet's language is necessarily rich in metaphor and simile because he himself is rich in imagination.

85
Nobody could look less like a mystic than Walter Russell, yet his long poem *The Divine Iliad* is a kind of work we associate with hirsute, eccentric dreamers.

86
When anyone reads a book, he comes into mental contact with an author—that is to say, with a creature who is a part of a human being. But when one meets him in person he meets the other part. He will see the difference.

87
In biography and autobiography he will get something of the thrill of reading fiction yet possess the satisfaction of discovering truth.

88

Toneless verses fall somewhat flat in the ear. Meaningless ones offer no nourishment to the mind.

89

Shakespeare has been justly praised and admired for his extraordinary dramatic genius and for its unusual breadth of subject. "Unique!" we exclaim. And on the few occasions when he allowed a little philosophy to creep in and interrupt the story we begin to wonder whether Francis Bacon did write the plays.

How did the same man come to create so brilliant a play as *The Merchant of Venice* and then stuff it with such narrow, rabid, and unkindly prejudice? How could he fall into the common superstition which, for over a thousand years, led to widespread intolerance and persecution?

90

The key to Henry Miller's real character is plain from his own confession: ". . . the life of the streets, of which I never tire. I am a city man; I hate nature, just as I hate the classics." There is revealed all the commonness and vulgarity of his character, the coarseness of taste, the lack of true culture.

91

Norman Mailer has enormous creative powers; he is unquestionably a genius: but this does not stop him from being somewhat mad.

92

Wilde's highly coloured paradox-loving alliterative style degenerated from being a means into becoming an end. Truth was sacrificed to style.

93

"Elbert Hubbard had his moments before big business got him," is Stuart Chase's critical appraisal of this great American genius. Whether so or not, the wisdom expressed in his writings and the originality exhibited in his printings were inspired, as we might anticipate, by a living faith in the esoteric philosophy.

94

Of the five most famous Russian writers of the nineteenth century, Tolstoy was the most powerful writer of them all. He was also the most spiritual and most influential. But in himself he was an ill-balanced man. Dostoevski, who is usually praised as being the most spiritual, was the most religious; but he was an emotional psychopath in love with the idea of suffering. He needed straightening out. Turgenev was competent and talented but quite worldly. Maxim Gorki, although but a materialist, was fairly sensible and an excellent writer. It would not be fair to compare Chekhov with the others, because, although his work was always good, he wrote plays, which the others did not.

95

When we find that leaders in English literature like Somerset Maugham and Aldous Huxley, who received supreme homage from the most cultivated and sophisticated audience outside France, bravely turned from scepticism to mysticism despite the howling of disappointed followers, we find a phenomenon worth looking into.

96

Poetry provides images for the mind to dwell upon. If it is inspired, those images bring man to a higher plane.

97

Too much of modern literature has too little of greatness, let alone nobility or goodness. Where it is not morbidly pathological it is aggressively scatological; where it is not criminally violent it is absurdly trivial.

98

A printed page has served us well if it enables us to meet a finer character, a riper intelligence, and a deeper knowledge than our own.

99

Tolstoy, in the earlier period of his life, created some artistic pieces which gave him Europe-wide fame. But in the later period of his life, when a gloomy saturnine asceticism held his mind, he preached moralizing sermons instead and puritanically denounced art.

100

It makes all the difference possible if a man plows through twenty books in order to put out the twenty-first on the subject, or if he writes it out of direct firsthand knowledge.

101

The interest in physical adventure stories is a sign of adolescence and, when they involve crime, of undisciplined adolescence.

102

The work of Emerson's pen is excitingly inspired and serenely beautiful.

103

No boat from America brought the other four continents more inspired writings than that Argosyan vessel which left her shores with the first published work of R.W. Emerson. There are some of his phrases which hold the memory as in a vice! And Emerson's sky is always blue. However, I was not always in this perfect concord with the Concord philosophy. When I first came to Emerson's pages, as a green and guileless youth, I found the epigrammatic nuts of his wisdom too hard for the teeth of my understanding. So I put him aside for a few years, and then, with stronger molars, successfully renewed the attack.

104

A good book which revives inspiration or invigorates reason is as blessed to write as to read. Its cost is no adequate return and its author can never be adequately thanked.

105

Despite the volume and variety of Bertrand Russell's comments and considerations upon life, I have come across no interest in the appreciation or cultivation of beauty. Does this not help to explain his mystical deficiency?

106

On this topic of writing I would like to quote from an experienced writer himself—a man who wrote over one hundred books, though I doubt whether they are at all read today. I met him only once. He was a staunch Catholic, highly dogmatic, but very devoted to the values of contemplation even though he was too busy a man to practise them much. He was violently critical of most things and most leaders in society—so much so that he abandoned his membership in the British Parliament in disgust. His name was Hilaire Belloc and he wrote about writing: "The worst enemy of prose today is the snobbishness of rules and forms . . . the mumbo-jumbo of hieratic prescription."

107

The young writer has one great defect and one great lack. The defect is that he is irresponsible; the lack is that he is inexperienced. The mature, perhaps middle-aged, writer is much more cautious, much more careful of the words he uses.

108

D.H. Lawrence told a friend who was at the dying novelist's bedside that he could feel himself withdrawing from the physical body yet at the same time looking at the scene from outside as if he were floating away.

109

If both beauty and melody are removed from a poem, what is left? Call it what you wish but do not insult readers by calling it poetry.

110

The writer who continues civilized cultural traditions may also be a creator of culture itself.

111

Do not seek to meet the author of a mystic noble or wise book, for you may suffer disappointment. You expect to find him superior to his book but then he is revealed as inferior to it. (Not always.)

112

A book which evokes the intuitive in you, however briefly or spasmodically, or which awakens you to newer recognition or deeper perceptions is itself a guru to that extent.

113
What I appreciate about Cardinal Newman's personality and writing is exactly what repels others. I appreciate his aristocratic attitude, his refined speech, his dignity and quality.

114
I would like to give myself the pleasure of quoting here a writer whose personality I esteemed when he was alive and whose books I admire— A.E., the Irish poet.

115
Seventy years ago that versatile Irishman who used the pen name A.E. published his collected poems. He was a gifted painter as well as poet, economist as well as a prose essayist, clairvoyant, seer, and, when I met him, more of a sage. Looking through his verses, I select a few lines which impress me:

1.　The power is ours to make or mar
　　Our fate has on the earliest morn,
　　The DARKNESS and the RADIANCE are
　　Creatures within the spirit born.

2.　The Wisdom that within us grows
　　Is absolution for our sins.

3.　He does not love the bended knees,
　　The soul made wormlike in HIS sight,
　　Within whose heaven are hierarchies
　　And solar kings and lords of light.

4.　He felt an inner secret joy—
　　A spirit of unfettered will
　　Through light and darkness moving still
　　Within the ALL to find its own,
　　To be immortal and alone.

5.　Dark churches where the blind
　　Mislead the blind.

6.　Unto the deep the deep heart goes,
　　It seeks a deeper silence still;
　　It folds itself around with peace,
　　With folds alike of good or ill
　　In quietness unfostered cease.

116

It is a great and widespread error to identify the best modern poetry with the disciples of Ezra Pound, as the naïve Mr. T.S. Eliot, himself one of them, did. Perhaps we owe this bit of literary foolishness to the American professors of English Literature, not necessarily because Pound was also American but because they were too naïvely led astray by the editors—and editresses—of poetry's "little journals."

117

Ralph Waldo Emerson's intellectual way of life is a great standby for many. One could not wish for a finer example.

118

Some spiritual books are written in a dull, almost dead manner. The writers seem to believe that because perchance they are writing of an ancient wisdom, they must be dull and mournful, with no more joy in their work than there is in the rumble of a hearse.

119

Those who can only learn by trial and error will continue to do so. The results are important only to themselves, and to a few others in their orbits. But when the trial is made by writers and the error is passed on to numerous readers, the situation which develops becomes of wider importance.

120

Early in the nineteenth century a young writer unexpectedly broke in upon British attention, electrifying people with his thought and phrase alike. That man was Carlyle. Out of his hermit-like meditations upon his epoch, he emerged to peal forth in thunderous tones the plaint of a truth-seeker in an age of social shams.

121

Francis Bacon makes a new sentence hold a new idea. He requires an audience of busy thinkers, rather than mere readers. I refer of course to his *Essays*.

122

Some years ago a Czech writer, Karel Čapek, published a novel called *The Absolute at Large* in which he pictures an inventor who succeeds in utilizing the energy of the atom, not for military purposes but only for peacetime industrial purposes. In the same book, he imagines the effect of this discovery upon religion and metaphysics. Supporting the doctrine of pantheism and affirming that divinity is present in all matter, he pictures a divine by-product issuing from each atomic turbine. The consequence is that all the people in the neighbourhood of the turbine become spiritually minded! They begin to renounce the world, to talk inspirationally, to perform miracles, and to engage in revivals. The idea is a clever one, but is it a true one? How can spirituality be turned on by a mechanical instrument and let loose upon the people? The basic fallacy in Čapek's notion is that divinity is contained within the atom. On the contrary, philosophy says that the atom itself is in divinity, which requires no machine to release it. It is everywhere and always present and if it is to be released and communicated, that can only be done through a human instrument, not through an arrangement of steel and springs.

123

In Sanskrit formulations and analyses on the art of poetry, its place and purpose, its styles and techniques, the important thing is for its message to be implicit rather than explicit, to give hints and clues rather than revelations, to use suggestive imagery rather than to deliver plain statements—but, as with our own Western work, to use myth, metaphor, and symbol to arouse feeling and release emotion.

124

Poetry which gives no beauty to man or which raises him to no nobility has failed even to become itself, that is, poetical. But when it is mere disjointed gibberish, spluttering nonsense, then it is harmful to the orderly sanity of those who adore it.

125

What witchery is this which enables a man to take some words and connect them with other words, so that the result affects other people's feelings and minds?

126

A genuine aesthetic feeling shrinks from the crude filth and the vulgar four-letter words of some of these "in" young writers. They elevate the lowest as if it were to be admired.

127

The writer who knows no more of truth than what some guru—that is, what someone else—has told him ought frankly to say so to his readers.

128

The neurotic screaming of a D.H. Lawrence is seen for what it is: an adolescent's passional excited discovery of sex and his (Lawrence's) inability to get over it, his incapacity to grow up into an adult responsible and balanced view of it.

129

In his book *Between Heaven and Earth*, the late Franz Werfel wrote: "The stupidest of all inventions of nihilistic thinking is the so-called impersonal God. Confronted with this non-personal God, one is tempted to bless the personal non-God of the honest atheist; for the concept of a spiritless and senseless world created by nothing and by no one, and existing nevertheless, is for all its ghastliness, more acceptable than the idiotic notion of a kind of extra-mundane and autonomous power station that creates and feeds all things without ever at all having been invented or operated by a creative Mind. The impersonal God is the most wretched reflection of technologized and thought-weary brains, the modern old folks' home of senile pantheism."

These sentences betray such a misunderstanding of one of philosophy's basic metaphysical tenets that they call for a reply. We offer the most unstinted praise of Werfel's genius as a novelist and we consider his book *The Song of Bernadette* one of the finest permanent contributions to modern religio-mystical biography. But Werfel got out of his depth when he attempted to criticize this, the ultimate concept of all possible human concepts about God. For he brought to his thinking, albeit quite unconsciously, all the limitations of his otherwise gifted personality. We must remember that he was primarily a man of imagination, an artist to whom "forms" and "entities" are a necessity in the working of his mind. Consequently the idea of Void, which is Spirit in all its uttermost purity, remained impenetrable to him. To the philosopher, the privation of all things and even thoughts represents the only absolute emancipation from the limits set by matter time space and ego. Therefore it represents the only power which is really infinite and almighty. That is, it represents the only true God. Werfel unconsciously looked for a mental picture in his search for God because only such a picture, together with the ecstatic devotion it arouses, could give him, as an artist, the assurance of a real presence.

Werfel not only was incapable of accepting the concept of the Void but he also did not want to accept it. This was because he was, like so many artists, an emotionalist. Witness in proof of this assertion the three intellectually weak reasons he gives why a Jew should never become a formal convert to Christianity. When analysed, these reasons turn out to be nothing more than mere historical tradition-worship, passionate sentimentality.

Inspired revelatory writing

130

There are great books, call them scriptures, classics, or commentaries, which are vehicles not only of instruction but also of inspiration and enlightenment.

131

Ordinary writing is a process of the common intellect, whereas revelatory writing is a product of the inspired intellect. In the first state the intellect works by its own power and momentum, whereas in the second it works under the possession of the higher power and by a higher activity.

132

There is a style which is formed artificially and self-consciously by nimble, intellectual rhetoric. There is a style which forms itself unconsciously out of natural loftiness of character. Truly inspired writing and speaking come from the latter class.

133

The author who willingly and humbly gives himself up to such an inwardly guided mode of writing learns new truths from its results, just as his readers do.

134

A piece of writing which expresses the illumination of the writer has the possibility of initiating the reader. It is an echo or a reflected image.

135

In inspired writing you meet an individual worth meeting; you are taken directly into a mind worth knowing. You partake of communion with a being superior to yourself.

136

When the inspired sentence is read, the sensitive mind comprehends that it is no longer merely reading words. It is also receiving the grace of the Presence.

137

The effect of inspired writing is to arouse spiritual aspiration or provide spiritual guidance. This is its highest function.

138

What readers get from an inspired book depends on their own capacity. It can communicate the truth or beauty, the sublimity or goodness found in the inspiration only to the extent that the reader can feel something of such a thing himself. The better it is written, the more effective is the communication.

139

A spiritually inspired book must not be read too lightly or too quickly. The reader should try to penetrate deeply into the ideas on each page . . . so deeply that he comes out on the other side.

140

When writing of writers and their productions, Thomas de Quincey set forward an interesting theory. He divided books into two kinds. The first belonged to what he called the "Literature of Knowledge," and they were intended to give instruction or to present information. But such books would, from time to time, become obsolete and have to be brought up to date, or need revision for some other reason, or re-arrangement. But, anyway, they do not generally have permanency. The second kind, which he called "The Literature of Power," *did* have permanency because it moved: it had the power to move the heart, the feelings of people. And being what it was, written from the author's living experience or what he had himself seen, gave the writing a power which instructed works of information do not possess. In other words, the Literature of Power survives, whereas the Literature of Knowledge gets superseded.

141

Truth sits perched upon the pen of one who has surrendered his hand to the Overself. Hence his words endure and are to be found among the records that Time keeps in its treasury, whereas the words of egotistic and ephemeral writers are often thrown off into oblivion as soon as they are written.

142

The literary legacy of the modern world is nothing short of amazing. Although the wisdom of the Alexandrian Library was burnt down with it, I warrant we have today a fuller and more rounded record of human knowledge than the ancients ever thought likely. Yet withal the great secret eludes us.

143

There is a power in inspired writings and authoritative revelations not only to work upon the minds and hearts of their readers, like many other books, but also to work upon their intuitive natures. This is a far more valuable service than providing information or stimulating emotion. They start a process of fruitful thought or give glimpses of hitherto unperceived truth or formulate clearly and decisively what has been half-felt and vaguely known.

144

The writer follows a profession which is glamorous but hollow: he is merely a manipulator of words. But it is hollow only if his words come out of no facts, if they are nothing but babble. It is only when his experience of living is rich, wide, and vertically cross-sectioned, or when his mind touches deep sources by its power of concentration, that his words are loaded with content and his readers are enriched with inspiration.

145

It is for the reader successfully to recreate in himself the mood which inspired the writer.

146

You must look for meaning not only in the words but also in between the letters of the words, for such are the ways of the mystics and also of the writers of paradox.

147

The writer who engages the reader's mind and invites it to think renders an intellectual service. But the writer who incites it to intuit renders a spiritual one.(P)

148

There are phrases in the New Testament which must impress the mind of every sensitive person. These phrases embody truths but they embody them in language which carries added authority derived from the style. I refer to the King James version, the translation into English made in the seventeenth century and today replaced by several modern versions in plain everyday twentieth-century English. It is true that in the modern ones the ordinary person gets a clearer notion of the meaning and, therefore, for him the modern translation is undoubtedly more useful. But I wrote of the sensitive person. For him not only is the meaning clear enough in the old version, but the style, with its beauty and authority, makes the statements even weightier.(P)

149

The way to use a philosophic book is not to expect to understand all of it at the first trial, and consequently not to get disheartened when failure to understand is frequent. Using this cautionary approach, he should carefully note each phrase or paragraph that brings an intuitive response in his heart's deep feeling (not to be confused with an intellectual acquiescence in the head's logical working). As soon as, and every time, this happens, he should stop his reading, put the book momentarily aside, and surrender himself to the activating words alone. Let them work upon him in their own way. He is merely to be quiet and be receptive. For it is out of such a response that he may eventually find that a door opens to his inner being and a light shines where there was none before. When he passes through that doorway and steps into that light, the rest of the book will be easy to understand.(P)

150

A writer who gives out high ideals ought to be the first man to follow them himself.

151

It has been said that it is somewhat disillusioning to make the acquaintance of writers in person and that it is better to be satisfied with enjoying their work. This is less true of the general category of authors than it is of those who write upon religious, mystical, and philosophical subjects. Readers form preconceptions of what the authors of such books must be like personally and physically, but such pictures are based upon their bias, their prejudice, the limits of their reading and experience—especially social experience. So they receive a surprise, sometimes even a shock, when they find that the reality does not coincide with the preconception.

152

The spiritual author who conforms to his own teachings, who is as careful of his ethics, motives, actions, and thoughts as he is of his style, is a rare creature. There is not less posing to a public audience in the world of religio-mysticism than there is in the world of politics. The completely sincere may write down their experiences or their ideas for the benefit of others, but they are more likely to do so for posterity rather than for their own era. Their most inspired work is published after their death, not before it. The half-sincere and the completely insincere feel the need of playing out their roles during life, for the ego's vanity, ambition, or acquisitiveness must be gratified. The half-sincere seldom suspect their own motives; the insincere know their own too well.(P)

153

Most modern writers who deal with some aspect of mysticism, spirituality, and the higher consciousness generally have done little more than probe along the margins. This is true no matter how fluently or authoritatively or mysteriously or loftily they write. It is easier and commoner to enter the stillness and speak from its pleasant transcendence than to penetrate to its inconceivable core and achieve insight.

154

He who can put God's Great Silence into words renders a high service to his fellows. He is not only a revealer who opens doors in their minds; he is also a healer who relieves hurt places in their hearts.

155

The correct key to the meaning of Omar Khayyam's *Rubaiyat* is neither the literal nor the mystical one, but a combination of both. The Persian character and outlook are such that they can easily hold the sceptical analyst, the pious devotee, the careless sensualist, and the theosophical *fakir* under a single hat. Consequently some of the verses of the *Rubaiyat* are to be taken as they stand, but others must be searched for an inner meaning. And this meaning is openly hinted at by a Persian Sufi teacher, Sheikh Ibrahim, in a quatrain where we are told to weep in yearning for the divine soul and to give it our heart's love:

> The real wine is the blood of our hearts,
> Do not search for it in the bottle.
> The true pearls are the tears of our eyes,
> Do not look for them in the ocean.

156

A work which brings *true* faith and *reasonable* hope to hearts not only bereft of both but steeped in despair, has some usefulness.

157

A man's spiritual aspirations may remain asleep until he comes into contact with an advanced mystic or an inspired book. By marking out the path which his feet will have to tread as well as by showing its deviations and pitfalls, the man or the book may help him to tread aright.

158

Some of those ancient texts were written on so high a level of inspiration that one approaches them in awe and reverence. It is as if the Word was made script, the intangible given form to break through the limitations which shut man up in tight ignorance. The unnameable Godhead has used a few humans to tell humanity that it IS and that they are not alone.

159

A mere handful of words may contain the wisdom of a lifetime. A single page may teach a man much about himself. No one—even the mystic—need despise books, but they need to be kept in their proper place. Reading cannot supplant meditation.

160

To read inspired books is to live for a time with inspired minds.

161

You may test a piece, a book, or a passage for inspiration by whether or not it yields the feeling that a living person is speaking behind its words.

162

The idea may previously have come intuitively to them, but too weakly to have directly influenced them. Yet when they read it formulated effectively in words and put into print by someone who is expert in both writing and the subject itself, the likelihood of acceptance is so very much more that a result like conversion is not seldom produced. When the readers find their secret but uncertain thought openly proclaimed in the strong language of direct knowledge and personal conviction, they may submit to its authority in a single transforming moment.

163

Any piece of writing that can move men to seek the true and honour the good will have done more for them than if it moves them to join a sect or a cult.

164

It may not be important to arrange a lot of words on paper, but if those words convey intimations of an inner life that is more satisfying and less illusory than the outer life, then their writer performs a useful activity at least, a very necessary one at most. Even if his be only a voice in the wilderness with few or none to hear him, the tremendous importance of his message remains.

165

Those who lack the capacity to practise meditation should compensate for this by reading and studying the writings of the others who possess it.

166

There is a deep chasm between books written out of genuine knowledge and those written to advocate a point of view.

167

The beginner has little capacity to discriminate and seldom knows whether he is reading the work of a great mystic or only the imitation of such a work. What makes the situation even worse is that in addition to such copies there exist the mere imitations of imitations. Of course it is mainly the ideas themselves that are plagiarized, for the inspired presentation of them is not commonly within the compass of mediocrity's hand.

168

There is something like magic in the way a simple white sheet of paper can stir one man to rancorous frenzy, or another to delirious joy, if certain black marks are made upon it. But still more magical is it when the message contained in those marks induces a transcendental state.

169

The work of an inspired individual will always carry authenticity but it may not always carry style.

170

Light comes to us with certain writings; they make our mind fertile and our understanding clear. These are the great writings of the human race, whether they are known to it or neglected by it.

171

Poetry arouses feeling and this in turn, if lofty enough, can awaken intuition.

172

Words may give other persons their cue to start off in a new or higher direction, may encourage or inspire this move, but the inner work has still to be done by each person for himself. The words become more valuable as they lead the aspirant to absorb intuitions. This is their best service.

173

There are authors who get these inspired moments, who sometimes write better than they know, who have to wait—like their readers—to catch the high revelatory meaning of a piece they have put down as it flowed through them.

174

Ancient Oriental authors on spiritual subjects offered, in their first lines, their homage to their master or to their personal ideal—the purpose being partly to keep their writing free from personal distortion and partly to gain inspiration.

175

To sit there, spinning out the phrases which shall carry ideas to other men, is not less an act of worship or of preachment—if they be reverently composed religious mystical or philosophic ideas—than praying on one's knees or addressing others from a pulpit.

176

In the reading of these books, just as in the presence of the masters, we grow emotionally and are at our best mentally.

177

A word, a phrase, a sentence, or a paragraph may be enough to awaken a hundred sleeping minds.

178

A spoken word or a written book which reaches through a man's ordinary everyday character to his better self renders him a service which may be fleeting or lasting. The result will depend on whether or not he follows up the mood invoked.

179

It is not only that he is trying to communicate a message; the work does not end there: it is also that he is trying to move his readers to feeling and to action or, contrariwise, to a depth of stillness they do not ordinarily know.

180

Shankara of Kanchi: "The Hindu artist dedicates his work to God. By such dedication purity of mind arises."

181

In the symbolism of several scriptures, the Saviour represents the higher self and the seeker the lower one. Thus, in the *Bhagavad Gita*, Krishna is the divine soul, Arjuna the human ego.

182

To write noble and beautiful words constituting a message that will still be read eagerly a thousand years later and that will seem fresh and inspired is something worth doing.

183

Fine passages grow upon the pages of the olden seers as thickly as grass in spring. Where are such great and true voices as those today? I can hear the bleat of the lost sheep but I cannot hear such voices.

184

Style and its artistic function may have no place in the ascetic prophet's scheme of things. He may say what he has to say in the barest most unattractive way, or put it so clumsily that his hearers may have to interpret his meaning.

185

If any passage in his writing moves your mind or will in the right direction, it has served you well. Do not ask that it shall do more and solve your own personal problem directly and definitely.

186

These great minds actively live again in his own consciousness during the intent study of the ideas in their writings.

187

It is a useful exercise to memorize the most inspired or the most appealing passages in books written by masters of the spiritual or philosophic life.

188

The difference between inspired writing drawn from within by intuitive feeling and paraphrased writing drawn from without by omnivorous reading is always clear to a practising mystic.

189

Writings so inspired, so revelatory, exorcise the evil spirits of hate and anger from our hearts.

190

Coleridge's *Ancient Mariner* is a mystical poem. When he wrote it, he was plunged into the study of the metaphysical mystics such as Plotinus and other Neoplatonists.

191

If through a book we can associate ourselves with a mastermind, it represents an opportunity we cannot afford to miss.

192

Truth takes on flesh and blood in such inspired writings, embodies the bodiless Spirit and announces its own existence to a doubting argumentative world.

193

Some come among us commissioned with a sacred message.

194

If it is to be inspired work it will have to be written out of the fullest inner conviction.

195

The writer who lifts his readers to a higher plane, who makes them feel that spiritual achievement is within their reach, is as much a minister of religion as any ordained one.

196

These inspired phrases lure the understanding on to seek the seraphic Source whence they have arisen.

197

Through inspired documents and inspired prophets, people who are blind to this reality are enabled to see.

198

These passages seem to bring with them the higher part of the reader's nature. They not only stand for it symbolically but also deputize for it actually.

199

If I read a truly inspired piece of writing with all the attention and feeling it deserves, then I take part in a sacrament no less religious than the one in a church.

200

The permanent truths enshrined in inspired classics are to be loved, their good counsels deeply respected.

201

The words of a book may speak to an inner need which may be raging within him or which may not even enter his consciousness until that moment.

202

When anyone else utters for the ordinary inarticulate man, in words and with precision, what he feels vaguely and obscurely, he is helped intellectually and fortified spiritually.

203

Here are words aglow with divine ecstasy, ashine with divine truth.

204

Philo the Alexandrian tells of feeling so inspired that the ideas flowed of themselves effortlessly through his pen.

205

That book renders a real service which lets in light.

206

If the book is really inspired it will strike sparks in the reader's mind.

207

The songs of Kabir show what wisdom can go into an artistic form: the two are not necessarily divorced. The poems of Rumi perform the same function.

208

An utterance which is authentically inspired will leave its mark on someone.

209

A noble piece of writing can serve those who are receptive to its message by cleansing their hearts and uplifting their minds.

210

The translation of the *Bhagavad Gita* by Prabhavananda and Isherwood is one of the most readable, clearest, easiest to understand.

211

Much of Emerson's writing came from his intuition rather than from his intellect.

212

There are truths which do not easily declare themselves, which hide or resist so that they must be dug for. But that is precisely where an inspired book can help the seeker so much. And then when the discovery is made, when the jewel is found, it can be added for his greater enrichment.

213

That writer has fulfilled his purpose whose reader catches fire from his words.

214

Oratory is great when it gives its auditors more understanding, but it is greatest when it gives them a glimpse!

215

It is right to expect that a writer on the art of mental quiet will produce works which themselves bear a style and atmosphere, a content and message of quietness.

216

The book which prods us into finer thought or higher feeling or makes us live better has served us well.

217

A voluble tongue or a prolific pen is no evidence of an inspired mind.

218

In these pages they will find their half-held best hopes taken up and transformed into reasoned affirmations.

219

When you read such inspired works, it is not enough to read them with the eyes alone: you must absorb their contents into your inner self; they must penetrate you through and through.

220

A poem which stirs a young person to high aspiration has done a noble service.

221

To regard every part of a work as equal in inspiration, or even in value, with every other part is naïve. The artist or writer has times when he may be only half-awake, overtired, moody, and depressed, and his work is not likely to be then at its best.

222

These words evoke exalted feelings in the heart of a thoughtful, well-informed, and sensitive person, but is the same result likely to happen to a cynical, sceptical, totally materialistic person? Without some preparation of philosophy they may fail to take hold on a limited mind or a mainly selfish one.

223

He will love the writings of inspired prophets, illumined seers, or intuitive thinkers. The more they succeed in conveying the feeling of their experience of, or kinship with, the Overself, its presence and power, its beauty and peace, the more will he love them.

224

An artistic or literary product may be nothing more than the mere expression of a capricious mood, of a passing whimsy, something altogether insignificant; or it may be allied with great spiritual meaning, loaded with riches for beholder, listener, or reader, and finally metamorphosed into a ritual of high magic.

225

A deeper force is operating at such a time than either reader or hearer is aware of, but the result depends on whether the sensitivity, receptivity, and passivity are permitted to dominate.

226

The reader who joins his own with an author's mind gets a chance to go as far as the author has gone.

227

Lao Tzu's classic and only work, *Book of the Way and of its Merit*, tries to make its readers see values which only the sage ordinarily sees.

228

A wise and noble statement in an inspired book may come back to some reader's mind at a moment of great need when it will be meaningful to him and help him through a difficult period.

229

A few words may carry a man's mind to an uplifted state, may help to awaken a brief association with his better self, and may help him relate to a finer state of consciousness. But this depends on who uttered or wrote those words.

230

Is it possible that something of the writer's mind infuses itself in the attentive reader's? Why not, if the reader is also receptive? But the effect may be brief and soon fade out.

231

A single word or a short phrase may become so charged with meaning for him that, pondering upon it, enlightenment grows rapidly and the inner work progresses accordingly.

232

A writer in this field of study attracts the serious and earnest, the sensible and level-headed, but he also attracts the psychotics and neurotics, the mildly lunatic fringe who become a menace to his quiet industrious existence.

233

We all know that there is a dark negative side to life, with its miseries and sufferings, as we know that there are so many imperfections, follies, meannesses, and wickednesses in humans. But why should an author on spiritual topics depict them? There is not much in existence today to comfort and gladden us, so we look to such an author to hold up noble, beautiful, peace-bringing ideals, ideas, and experiences for our gaze.

234

Sometimes a single spoken or written sentence can reveal to the perceptive mind that the speaker or writer is, for those moments at least, an enlightened individual.

235

This literature has begun to familiarize them with the ideas and practices of mysticism, the lives and ways of the yogis. Ignorance must give place to acquaintance before it can give place to acceptance.

236

Wilhelm von Humboldt read Wilkins' English translation of the *Bhagavad Gita*, with the result that he felt bound to thank destiny for having left him life long enough to allow him to read the incomparable work, which he called "the finest philosophic poem that the literatures known to us can offer to humanity."

237

If we believe that the men who wrote scriptures were inspired and if we know our world literature, we must be very insensitive not to see that other men have written since then who were at least only a little less inspired than the scriptural authors and who wrote with a light and wisdom not their own.

238

Literature can be as much a spiritual force in these modern times as liturgy has been in medieval times.

Stage, cinema, dance

239
Ancient Greek tragedy plays, with their atmosphere of helpless and hopeless disaster, give truth only if they are countered by modern writings or speeches based on worship, personal optimism, and success stories.

240
If *The Tempest* was Shakespeare's final work, it was also his most philosophical play, neatly expressing his highest thoughts. There is less conflict and tragedy, more calm and dignity in it than in any of his other writings.

241
The theory of Tragedy, which developed out of the Dionysus cult, remained a spiritual thing for the Greeks. Aristotle considered that it aroused pity and fear for the hero and thus purged and healed the audience's emotions.

242
It is important to remember the power of suggestion when we examine the effect of a theatrical play on the spectators. This power can be used to harm them morally or to elevate them emotionally.

243
I have often asked people connected with the theatre whether they become the role which they play and entirely forget themselves; or whether they never entirely let their own personal identity disappear. The answers have been contradictory. There does not seem to be universal agreement upon this point. Some say they no longer identify with themselves, others say they always remember themselves. Perhaps the solution is that the very few who have real genius do succeed in letting go of the ego and becoming the character which they play, totally. Others, who may have good, real talent but not genius, will not be able to let go of their ego, will not be able to forget self, however well they may assume the role on the stage itself.

244
Was Salvini right when he said that an actor weeps and laughs on the stage yet all the while he is watching his own tears and smiles?

245
The people of Athens could think of no better honour for their tragic dramatist Sophocles after his death than to say that a god had lived with him as a guest!

246
We have gone far from the serious use of a play in the theatre. Shakespeare used it to help us get, for a couple of hours at least, a slightly more detached view of human existence than is possible normally. This might

help us to get a slightly better understanding of our own existence. But today criminals are admired by the audience and held up for admiration by the author. Sex without self-control is another praised theme for the titillation of audiences and the brisker sale of tickets at the box office.

247

It is risky to try to modernize Shakespeare's story and language unless great restraint is used.

248

The fictitious sufferings and joys enacted upon a theatrical stage may move an audience to tears or pleasure, but with its departure comes the awakening to reality, that knowledge of what *is* which is truth.

249

A play which carries something of the atmosphere of a religious ritual thereby brings the Theatre near to the Church.

250

If the audience reflects, either during or after the show, on the piece of life it has seen on the stage, it will have some higher profit than mere entertainment.

251

It is true that Shakespeare held a mirror up to the events, persons, and histories of his time. But it is also true that he inserted philosophical comments which carried force.

252

We may ask why Shakespeare has portrayed too many human faults and too few human virtues. But the answer can only be because he has gone to life itself for his sources, where human imperfections are all too plain.

253

I have known the man who was, in his time, the world's greatest screen comedian—Chaplin.

254

I go to the cinema partly to get the opposition which will in a mild but varied form test my ascetic indifference towards earthly attractions and partly to get vivid instruction in their deceptiveness and vanity. The very scenes which excite the sensuality of most beholders, I use, by a process of keen intellectual analysis, to excite my repulsion. Finally, I also go to the cinema simply to enjoy myself with comedies and laugh over them.

255

Too many films are turned out following a cheaply melodramatic or allegedly funny formula. Soon after the start of a picture one knows how it is going to unfold. It is inane, a denial of true artistry, a *false* escape from reality, a waste of time. One can attend cinemas only when they show versions of a good novel, a good play, or a worthwhile comedy.

256

The cinema is here to stay. Everybody understands its pictorial language. But like other forms of science applied to art, its powerful influence needs to be purified.

257

The cinema has over-exploited sex and over-pictured its saccharine sensualities.

258

The box-office success of the film *The Razor's Edge* is proof that there is a little room for something loftier in the entertainment world. Here is a story of a young war veteran whom Nature has made an individualist and whom experience has made reflective about experience itself. He begins a search for inner peace, which in the story is contrasted with a setting of continental worldliness and Parisian sin.

259

Rudolf Steiner compared the effects of cinema-going to those of a drug. Perhaps he would have included the entertainment side of television, the reading of light fiction, too. But if we analyse the pleasure which such attractive distractions yield, we shall find that they let us get away from the ego.

260

The dances used in connection with the ancient religions, and particularly those of the Near and Middle East, were not intended to offer pleasure or provide entertainment as most of our modern or Western dancing is. They had a sacred or symbolic meaning. At some stages they might bring the audience into chorus chanting or even certain movements along with the original dances.

261

Whatever the other reasons are for the tremendous postwar popularity of the ballet both in Europe and America, be they its colourfulness, its poetry, its vigour, its beauty, and its blending of different arts, there is one more, which is important: its other-worldliness. It answers a spiritual craving that does not know it is spiritual.

Painting, sculpture, architecture

262

The painter must not only have the talents of drawing and colouring, but also the bodily gift of seeing sharply and the mental gift of visualizing, imaging.

263

The light which informs and brightens the colours of the best medieval paintings is suggestive and symbolic. The artists worked often under inspiration got from mystical rapture, for they worked often with religious subjects.

264

The tiny figure of a Buddha appears in some Tibetan paintings or statuettes. It is a perfect replica of midget size placed in the heart or head. It is put in by the artist to show the unseen, the real Buddha within the outer form that is all most people see.

265

Inspired drawings may give as much a spiritual impact as inspired paintings.

266

Those pictures—Buddhist, Hindu, and Christian—which show the benedictory raising of a hand, show only one of the ideas which exist side by side in different religions.

267

Christian art was not the first to use a halo round the head when depicting holiness. Chinese pictures have used it too.

268

Some paintings of pop art seem to be scenes taken from the astral plane. They are more than mere imagination—extraordinary creatures or amazing monsters. They are mostly results of astral clairvoyance.

269

A painting which beholders find quite incomprehensible and whose maker boasts of its meaninglessness belongs to human pathology, not to human art. To him life itself is without meaning: his picture is a jumble because his soul is a chaos.

270

Those ultramodern artists who scorn to draw well because they cannot draw at all, whose slovenly productions and ugly colouring repel the seeker after beauty in art, possess neither technique nor inspiration.

271

Raphael, Leonardo, Michelangelo, Fra Angelico, and Piero della Francesca had unquestioned genius in art. But they belong to the old school, and modern youth craves the new, the different. The craving is legitimate but the acceptance of crazy nonsense merely because it is new, of untalented ugliness merely because it is different, must be rejected.

272

It may be that those whose taste has been formed around the modern expressions by contemporary artists will have some difficulty in adapting it to the completely different masterpieces of Byzantine art, and in appreciating them. Those who are confronted by them for the first time may need a sufficient period of adjustment to the highly ornamental character of Byzantine painting.

273

When we stand before one of the luminous dawns so frequently painted by the Frenchman Corot we feel peace-giving healing radiations.

274

Despite the fine work put forth by our European masters, Western art has yet to reach the level of vitality in colouring attained by old China.

275

In a painting of the Chinese master Chou Tun-Yi, the great philosopher is shown holding a sceptre. This is called "The Sceptre of Power." It stands for the masculine elements within the person. The sceptre being held within his hands shows that the masculine energy is held within his control, that he is indeed a master in this sense, a ruler of himself—for the sceptre is adorned with a diamond, hardest of stones.

276

In this portrait of Chou Tun-Yi which looks down upon me from the study wall, this great master is sitting in full robes holding the flat sceptre of authority at its lower end with his right hand and supporting its upper part with his left hand. This ceremonial sceptre is not only symbolic of high status on the worldly scene, but in his case is also symbolic of spiritual power.

277

Even if the simple peasant fervour of the figures appearing in medieval pictures may not be in accord with modern mentalities, yet the authentic inspiration is there; also admiration is due for the magnificent paintwork itself, the clear luminous colouring, and the skilled drawing of a Piero della Francesca or a Fra Angelico. Art was alive then, artists were creative, talent was visible, and training was fundamental. Today the contrast is saddening: pseudo-art flourishes, is well-paid, while the taste for the real thing is little.

278

The Chinese regard painting and calligraphy as the highest forms of their artistic expression.

279

Not the slow and patient building-up of a picture, as is ordinarily done, but the swift strokes, the decisive confident execution of the work in the shortest possible time and the least amount of effort: that is Zen artistry. It tries to take advantage of the inspired moments to give birth to memorable and exceptional drawing on paper or painting on silk. It is truly creative.

280

The icons of Greek Orthodoxy were highly stylized and tradition-bound: the artist was not free to introduce his individual variation.

281

What the painter puts with his brush and colour on a canvas becomes the medium of his own expression. If, in addition, he has become a vehicle for his higher self, then there will be a twofold effect, the one personal and the other inspired.

282

Calligraphy was placed as high among the arts by prewar Chinese as music and poetry have been placed by us. Handwriting and sign-writing were used not only to communicate but also to decorate, not only to express but also to give joy.

283

How inspired by the feeling for beauty are often those delicately painted scrolls on which Chinese artists put their impressions of pine trees set on mountainsides, leaping waterfalls, and quiet river banks.

284

The strength shown in Greek male statues, the gracefulness shown in their female ones are matched by the equipoise shown in Greek philosophy.

285

What the Asian adept pointed to, in a statue confronting us and which he called "the Angkor smile," could only have been chiselled by a skilled artist who was also intuitively sensitive to the profound serenity of his subject.

286

In a piece of Japanese lettering, the arch over a Moorish doorway, or an old Greek pediment, beauty naturally inheres. Each in its own way is symmetrical, balanced, a harmony of two opposite sides. In a sage's mind there is the same attractive equilibrium.

287

The solid balance and intelligent proportion which Greek philosophy admired and taught were expressed in the elegant pediments and colonnades of Greek architecture. The fervent devotion and direct simplicity of Muhammedan religion were brought into the tapered minarets and arcades of Arab architecture. From the thought and faith of a people came forth its art.

288

The superb balance and fine proportion of Greek architecture holds lessons for man, for his person as for his way of life.

289

It is one more sign of the unbalance of our times that architects overconcentrate on the straight line in their designs for the massive new buildings which appear in all major cities, and ignore its counterpoise the curve.

290

Too many modern buildings have the soullessness, the materialistic inner and outer nature, of mechanical constructions. They are not *growths*. This is why they lack beauty, grace, charm. Competent function only is their purpose. They achieve it. But they are monotonous barracks.

291

Buildings that are like boxes, without any identity or individuality of their own, show the decay of imagination and the mistake of letting the functionalist supplant the artist instead of working side by side with him.

292

The pillared arcades which transform a street, making it picturesque and giving it dignity, ought to be multiplied a hundredfold.

293

The dignity of Greek architecture, expressed in fine stately pillars, invites respect for the Greek mind.

294

The straight clean-cut lines of the exterior, the modernistic cubes and parabolic curves of their interior, are fit symbols of directness and newness; the sky-jutting spires are apt symbols of the altitude of achievement which beckons young ambition.

Music

295

Musical compositions which carry their hearers up into higher worlds of being are benedictions.

296

The miracle of musical beauty is to be experienced gratefully, not for the sensuous and emotional satisfactions alone, but also for the reminder to make all life beautiful.

297

Of all the arts which minister to the enjoyment of man, music is the loftiest. It provides him with the satisfaction which brings him nearer to truth than any other art. Such is its mysterious power that it speaks a language which is universally acknowledged throughout the world and amongst every class of people; it stirs the primitive savage no less than the cultured man of the twentieth century. When we try to understand this peculiar power which resides in music, we find that it is the most transient of all the others. The sounds which delight your ears have appeared suddenly out of the absolute silence which envelops the world and they disappear almost instantaneously into that same silence. Music seems to carry with it something of the divine power which inheres in that great silence so that it is really an ambassador sent by the Supreme Reality to remind wandering mortals of their real home. The aspirant for truth will therefore love and enjoy music, but he must take care that it is the right kind of music—the kind that will elevate and exalt his heart rather than degrade and jar it.(P)

298

Music can be a start along the Path the same as other arts, if it is used as a means of elevating feeling and uplifting oneself to the primal beauty of the Soul. It is itself a yoga path and can be not only a means of expression but one of lifting thought and feeling to the higher realm of illumination.

299

What man cannot receive directly through the intuition, he must receive in a different form through the physical senses. This is why music, for example, takes the place of a spiritual medium, as it can be heard by anyone, whereas intuition is unfelt by the insensitive.

300

Those who are insensible to the mystical in its ordinary form may be responsive to its musical form.

301

Music can express the mystical experience better than language; it can tell of its mystery, joy, sadness, and peace far better than words can utter. The fatigued intellect finds a tonic and the harassed emotions find comfort in music.(P)

302

Who can respond to the genius of Bach's *Saint Matthew Passion* unless some awakening of spirituality—however small—is in him?

303

We come to concerts and operas to hear music. Loud applause interrupting what we hear introduces the shock of noise. It spoils the atmosphere.

304

Music is still used, as it was for more than a thousand years past, by many Sufis to help bring on lovingly and devotedly the joyous abstracted depths of meditation.

305

Music like any of the intellectual arts may help or hinder this Quest. When it is extremely sensual or disruptive or noisy, it is a hindrance and perhaps even a danger. When it is uplifting or inspiring or spiritually soothing, it is a help.(P)

306

Warner Allen says he got, at the age of fifty, the mystic experience of timelessness, saw the Divine Light in vision, and felt one with God while listening rapt in Beethoven's Seventh Symphony. (I have heard it but only the second movement is mystical.)

307

If an inspired sonata by Beethoven brings you momentarily to the borders of heaven, do not stop with the enjoyment. Explore the glimpse afterwards for all its rich content, its immense meaning, its glorious revelation.

308

(1) Bach: the final chorus from *Saint Matthew Passion*, (2) Beethoven's last piano trio (*Archduke*), (3) the slow movement from Mozart's G Major Violin Concerto, K. 216—these three are spiritually inspired musical works.

309

Musical geniuses like Bach and Beethoven, Mozart and Brahms, Handel, Vivaldi, Puccini, Rachmaninoff, Schubert, and Wagner touched and drew from the Overself's inspiration, although in unequal degree. They gave their hearers higher values and even, in the case of the more sensitive and prepared ones, spiritual glimpses. Beethoven himself said, "I was conscious of being inspired by God." Brahms said, "When I reach my best level during the task of composition, I feel a higher power working through me."

310

Beethoven's music is not only melodious, which is common, but also charged with thought, which is not.

311

Tchaikovsky's Symphony no. 5 is a spiritually elevating composition.

312

The *Pastorale* Symphony by Beethoven is a call in music to our native spiritual homeland.

313

Even until a couple of decades ago the better class Indonesians would play one of their several native musical instruments after sunset as a spiritual exercise to refine, purify, and discipline their feeling.

314

Music receives a sacramental form when it is the expression of an inspired composer; it truly helps its hearers spiritually.

315

It is curious—this contrast and contradiction of Buddha banning music and Beethoven receiving divine exaltation from it. Buddha said it led astray; Beethoven said it led to God. But analysis shows that most people were too tasteless or weak or ignorant to be entrusted with such an influence and allowed to make their own discrimination between the degrading or exciting and the ennobling or calming, so it was probably safer to ban music altogether. Besides, their time as monks could be better used in reflections and meditations, studies and practices.

316

In the Persian Sufi book *Diwan i Shams i Tabriz* it is written: "We do not attend musical assemblies nor employ music. In our position there is more harm than good in it. Music improves the approach to the consciousness, if heard in the right way. But it will harm persons who are insufficiently developed. Those who do not know this have taken up music as if it were something sacred in itself. The feelings they experience from it are mistaken for sublime ones; sentiments are aroused, which is no basis for further progress."—Bahaudin Naqshband, leader of the Naqshabendi-Dervish Order

317

Sufi Teaching on Music:

(1) "Do not train yourself to music in case this holds you back from higher perceptions."—Ibn Hamdan (medieval)

(2) "They play music and cast themselves into states. . . . Every learning must have *all* its requirements fulfilled, not just music, thought, concentration."—Mainuddi Chishti, in a letter to disciples, referring to ecstatic states. The master explained further the fact that love of music was not enough, that emotional feelings produced by music were being confused with spiritual experience.

318

Play of the Soul and the Body—Cavalieri, born mid-sixteenth century in Rome, died 1602 in Rome, was General Director of the Tuscan Court in Florence in 1588. He belonged to the circle of "Camerata Fiorentina," which brought a great innovation in Western music: the "Nuove Musiche" (New Music), a special new manner which had a hypnotic effect on the whole audience. His *Rappresentazione* was performed twice in Rome in 1600. Fifteen Cardinals were present at the first performance. It was the first work written in a recitatio style. It is a religious play, related to the medieval "mystery plays," especially to the morality play *Everyman*. It is

Buddhistic in basic theme—the human soul, blinded by worldly life and deceived by pleasures, finally has a revelation of the transitoriness and shallowness; then it rises to the higher experience, the sphere of true happiness, of angelic hosts and eternal peace.

319

In 1822 Rossini visited Beethoven at the latter's Viennese lodging. Two impressions remained vividly and dominantly afterwards in the visitor's mind: ". . . the indescribable untidiness of the room and the indefinable sadness of Beethoven's features." The question arises: How could the creator of such joyous music appear so unhappy himself?

320

What Mozart expressed in his Fortieth Symphony was what, in a different way, Buddha expressed in many of his sermons—a melancholy, a sadness, a dissatisfaction with life amounting almost to rebellious protest. Yet in neither case does one leave it with a feeling of despair, as one does in the case of Tchaikovsky's *Pathétique* symphony. On the contrary, there seems to be a way of escape: with Buddha plainly stated as the "Noble Eightfold Path" to Nirvana, but with Mozart appearing only as the joy which is so fundamental in most of his other works.

321

Brahms got creative moods in the woods. Walking did not stop them from occurring, despite the body's movements, while the solitude combined with Nature to foster his inspiration. It was only at home that he put his composition into writing.

322

Mozart was able to compose and complete a whole symphony in his mind before he put it down on paper.

323

Wagner himself tells us that he composed *Parsifal* as an escape from the human evils of this world and as an attempt to picture a nobler one.

324

There are many passages, melodies, pieces of inspired music. These include parts of such works as *Saint Matthew Passion*, *The Magic Flute*, Haydn's Duet Song, and Bach's church music.

325

Handel's *Messiah* is as inspired a piece of music as any ever written. It is a communication from heaven to earth, from the gods to man. The machine has made it available on a scale and to homes impossible in the days when Handel composed it. All aspirants who need to cultivate the religious-devotional and reverential side of their nature should hear it from time to time.

326

"I've never seen him act like this before," said Handel's servant to a friend. "He just stares at me and doesn't see me. He said the gates of heaven opened wide for him and God Himself was there. I'm afraid he's going mad." But the fruit of this "madness," of these long hours when Handel refused to eat and wrote and wrote, was the greatest oratorio written during, before, or after his century—the *Messiah*.

327

The sensitive heart will feel inexpressibly grateful for the soothing melodies, the peace-fraught bars of such music as Bach's fugues. Life is temporarily glorified and redeemed under this spell.

328

Handel sat for three days *motionless*. Then, out of this physical and inner stillness there came to him the tremendously inspired, triumphantly majestic strains of the *Messiah*.

329

It was an ill and suffering Handel, an ageing and impoverished man, who gave the world its greatest oratorio. How did he do it? He sat immobile, staring vacantly into space until the inspiring choruses burst upon his inner ears, and then he wrote feverishly for hours at a time. This went on for three weeks. So was born the *Messiah*.

330

The unearthly beauty of Gregorian sacred chants must bring joy to sensitive ears, whether those ears are Catholic or Protestant, Hindu or Muhammedan, if prejudice does not intrude itself and block or distort the hearing.

331

Mendelssohn's Concerto for Violin offers not only beautiful sounds to the ear but also celestial peace to the heart.

332

The ancient Greeks gave more importance to singing than to instrumental music, for the reason that it was associated with words, and hence ideas.

333

I shall never forget the wonderful message which Ramana Maharshi sent me by the lips of an Indian friend (he never wrote letters). It was some years before his death and my friend was visiting the ashram preparatory to a visit to the West, whither he was being sent on a mission by his government. I had long been estranged from the ashram management, and there seemed no likelihood of my ever seeing the saint again. The visitor mentioned to the Maharishee that he intended to meet me: was there any communication of which he could be the bearer? "Yes," said the Maharishee, "When heart speaks to heart, what is there to say?" Now I don't know if he was aware of Beethoven's existence in the distant world of Western music, but I am certain he could not have known that the dedication to the *Missa Solemnis* was "May heart speak to heart." This is a work whose infrequent performance stirs me to depths when I hear it, so reverential, so supernal is it. Few know that Beethoven himself regarded the *Missa* as his greatest composition. It must surely be his most spiritual composition, a perfect expression of the link between man and God.(P)

334
It is said that Handel declared that he wished to make people better, not just to entertain them.

335
The witch-doctor who beats out a rhythm on his drum—or who has an assistant do the same—accomplishes a concentration of mind, a lulling of the senses, and a recession from the world for his hearers to a greater extent than they would have been able to accomplish for themselves.

336
Schubert was deeply affected by the beauty and tranquillity of eventide. His song "In Abendrot" expresses this mood, and how his complaints at life, his confusions in human relations fade away when viewing the sky's red glory.

337
In the choired singing of a Russian church, in the Sanskrit chanting of a Hindu ashram, the Soul of *bhakti* finds a magnificent outlet.

338
Art is not only here to embellish human existence. It is also here to express divine existence. In good concert music, especially, a man may find the most exalted refuge from the drab realism of his prosaic everyday life. For such music alone can express the ethereal feelings, the divine stirrings and echoes which have been suppressed by mundane extroversion. The third movement of Beethoven's Quartet in A Minor, for instance, possesses genuine mystical fervour. One may derive for a few minutes from hearing its long slow strains a grave reverence, a timeless patience, a deep humility, an utter resignation and withdrawnness from the turmoil of the everyday world.(P)

339
In Oratorio, music rises to its most spiritual height. It not only gives the joyous feeling that other musical forms can give but also a spiritual message.

340
Tchaikovsky's Piano Concerto is grandly beautiful, spiritually ecstatic, happy, elevating, other-worldly.

341
Refresh yourself at the end of a day's hard work with food and drink and then settle down to listen to a recording of Beethoven's *Emperor* Concerto. It will enrich and refine your feelings until, at the end, your mind will be well prepared and elevated to enter the state of meditation and attune itself to the infinite silence deep in the heart's core. Thus, the beauty of music can lead you to the beauty of the Overself.

342
In the greatest works of composers like Bach, Beethoven, and Vivaldi, we hear music which brings us as close to inspired moods as music can bring human beings.

343
A music which enchants the senses, refines the emotions, and temporarily dissolves some limitations of human existence must be an inspired one.

344
It is hard to translate these moments of uplift into music but, aside from and quite different from Beethoven's, Bach's, and Handel's most religious compositions, the music got by the Chinese from pigeons by tying tiny pipes to their pinion-feathers and then letting a flock of these birds take flight is most spiritually suggestive.

345
A man may enjoy listening to Beethoven; to that extent he appreciates music and derives pleasure from the physical sounds; but if this is as far as he goes he has not sounded art's depth.

346
Music fulfils its highest purpose when it honours the higher power in that aspect which is beauty.

347
Church music and choir singing may be helpful to put a congregation into a more receptive and worshipful mood; but when they are repeated too often, become too familiar, and are no longer spontaneous, there is the danger that they then become mere theatrical performances or musical shows.

348
Who has not felt the strength which some of Beethoven's music imparts, far profounder than the melodious rhythms of so many other composers' works, charming though they are!

349
Moved by the exultation of Beethoven's music, the intense passion behind it all, he can come nearer to the higher life.

350
Why is it that the divinest of the arts—music—is nevertheless the most evanescent of the arts?

Index for Part 1

Entries are listed by chapter number followed by "para" number. For example, 4.115 means chapter 4, para 115, and 2.129, 132, 314 means chapter 4, paras 129, 132, and 314. Chapter listings are separated by a semicolon. Please note also that, for the reader's convenience, the first number in the right-hand running heads throughout the text indicates chapter number.

philosophical mystics 2.391
plane of ecliptic 4.97
plane of equator 4.97
planetary evolutions 4.266
planetary spirit 4.93
Plato 1.329; 2.131, 368, 529, 546
 Republic 3.135
political leaders 2.504–506, 520, 534,
 537, 549, 553–555; 4.216
political party 2.556
politics 2.500–587
 fanaticism in 2.568
 and philosophy 2.581
 principle of adoption 2.540
pollution 2.136; 3.101; 4.9, 70, 250
poverty 2.304, 320–321, 324
prayer 1.198; 2.211, 214, 229, 261;
 3.113
Prayer For The World, A 4.306
predictions 4.18, 336
problems, guidance in solving 2.211–
 303
prophecy 4.313–314, 380
prophets 4.145, 307–309, 317, 360,
 376, 424, 426
 false 4.99
psychiatry 2.134; 4.226
psychology 4.226
puberty 3.19, 24, 75
public conscience 4.337
Pythagoras 2.368

Q

Qabus Nama 3.67
Quest of the Overself, The 2.499

R

racism 2.377; 4.238, 309
Radhakrishnan 2.87
Ramana Maharshi 1.365; 4.235, 243
Ramdas, Swami 4.243
Rasputin 2.580
rat race 3.46, 87
reactionaries 2.567

reform, *see* social reform
reincarnation 1.36–37; 2.16
religion 4.104
 ceremonies of 4.102
 new 4.103, 133, 162, 229, 282
 role of priests 4.105
religious devotion 2.103
residence, changing 2.371, 375, 377,
 382–385
revelation, modern need for 4.206–
 207
reverence, instinct of 3.29
revolution, violent 2.545
revolutionists 2.567
romance 2.456, 485; 3.41, 59, 69,
 72–73
Rome, ancient 4.139, 160–161, 173,
 343
Russia 2.87, 580; 4.133, 268

S

sadhu 2.383; 3.87
sage kings 2.542; 4.159
sages 1.357; 3.39; 4.31, 48, 66–67,
 177, 220, 316, 325, 426
sahaja 2.177
saints 1.424; 4.137; *see under*
 individual names
saviours 2.117; 4.35, 43, 64, 95, 133,
 164, 329
Schopenhauer, Arthur 3.190
Scott, Cyril (*The Christian*
 Paradox) 4.67
Secret Path, The 2.497
seminaries 2.650
service 2.426, 429–436, 439–440
sex 3.142
Shakespeare, William 2.25
Shaw, George Bernard 3.147; 4.31
sickness 3.135, 142
silence
 going into 2.218, 279
 mental 2.295

Index for Part 2

Entries are listed by chapter number followed by "para" number. For example, 4.122 means chapter 4, para 122, and 1.178, 180–183, 190, etc., means chapter 4, paras 122, 180–183, 190, etc. Chapter listings are separated by a semicolon. Please note also that, for the reader's convenience, the first number in the right-hand running heads throughout the text indicates chapter number.

L

landscape gardener 1.91
landscapes 3.67
Lankavatarasutra 2.87
Lao Tzu 4.227
Lawrence, D.H. 4.67–68, 108, 128
learning through beauty 1.62
Leaves of Grass 4.50
Leonardo 4.271
light 3.42
  in painting 3.42; 4.263
literary style 4.16, 18–19, 33–36,
  125, 169, 184
literature
  autobiography 4.60, 87
  biography 4.87
  Czech 4.122
  inspired 4.130–238
  Oriental 4.174
  Russian 4.94
Literature of Knowledge 4.140
Literature of Power 4.140
LSD 1.210
lust 1.204
Lytton, *see* Bulwer-Lytton

M

Magic Flute, The 4.324
Mailer, Norman 4.91
Mainuddi Chishti 4.317
Mansfield 4.70
Maugham, Somerset 4.63, 95
medieval painting 4.263, 277
meditation
  and artistic creation 1.52; 2.14, 51,
    70, 75; 4.50
  and beauty 1.127; 3.18, 35–36, 72
  and music 3.31; 4.304, 341
  and reading 4.159, 165
  memorization exercise 4.187
Mendelssohn, Felix (Concerto for
  Violin) 4.331
Merchant of Venice, The 4.89
Messiah 4.325–326, 328–329

Michelangelo 4.271
Miller, Henry 4.90
Missa Solemnis 4.333
modern art 1.176–238; 4.70, 126,
  268–271, 277
modernism 1.115
Moorish rugs 1.71
movies, *see* cinema
Mozart, Wolfgang Amadeus 1.96;
  4.309, 322
  Fortieth Symphony 4.320
  G Major Violin Concerto 4.308
  The Magic Flute 4.324
Muhammed 2.62
  on poets 4.55
Muhammedan art and
  architecture 1.24, 96, 198
music 1.227; 3.45, 47; 4.295–350
  in Buddhism 3.47; 4.315
  Chinese 4.344
  choral 4.302, 308, 325, 330, 337,
    347
  composing of 4.309, 319, 321–323,
    326, 328–329
  Greek (ancient) 3.47; 4.332
  Indian 3.46; 4.337
  Indonesian 4.313
  inspired 3.52; 4.307–309, 314–315,
    321, 324–325
  and mystical experience 3.67; 4.295–
    350
  opera 4.323–324
  oratorio 4.325–326, 339
  for piano 4.308, 340–341
  Russian 4.337
  Sufi teachings on 3.47; 4.304, 316–
    317
  for violin 4.308, 331
mystery plays 4.318
mystical intuition 3.37
mysticism, *see* Ch. 3
mystics 4.146

N

Nature 1.5, 54, 91, 96, 103, 128; 3.2,
  5, 15, 22–23, 40, 45, 68, 70
Nazis 4.79
Neoplatonists 1.8; 4.190, 204
  and music 3.47
New Testament 4.148
Newman, Cardinal John 4.57, 113
Nietzsche, Friedrich 4.78–79
Noble Eightfold Path 4.320

O

Omar Khayyam 4.155
opera 4.323–324
oratorio 4.325–326, 339
oratory 4.214
originality 2.16–17, 20, 23
Overself
  art leads towards 1.37, 111, 171;
    2.78, 82; 3.69; 4.341
  as source of art 1.68, 107, 112, 169;
    2.34, 63, 91

P

painting 4.262–283
  Buddhist 4.264, 279
  Byzantine 4.272
  Chinese 2.76; 4.267, 274–276, 278,
    283
  colour used in 1.180; 4.263, 274,
    277
  French 4.273
  Greek 4.280
  inspired 2.74; 3.42, 52; 4.263, 277,
    281
  Italian 4.271, 277
  light portrayed in 3.42; 4.263
  medieval 4.263, 277
  modernist 1.180–181, 183, 187,
    212; 4.268–271; *see also* modern art
  Tibetan 4.264
  Zen 4.279
paradox, writers of 4.146
parks 1.91
Parsifal 4.323

Pastorale Symphony 4.312
Pathétique Symphony 4.320
Persian poetry 4.155
Philo the Alexandrian 4.204
philosophical insight, expressed in
  art 1.113
pianist 3.31
piano music 4.308, 340–341
pigeons 4.344
Plato 2.36; 4.48
  on Beauty 1.24, 64; 3.55, 61
  on poetry 4.55–56, 76
Platonists, *see* Neoplatonists
plays and playwrights 1.19; 2.44;
  4.89, 94, 239–252, 318
Plotinus 4.190
poets and poetry 1.73; 4.50–124
  Irish 4.114–115
  Japanese 4.54
  modern 1.184, 212; 4.72, 116
  Muhammed on 4.55
  Persian 4.155
  Plato on 4.55–56, 76
  Sanskrit 4.123
  spiritual 4.40, 50, 53–54, 62, 96,
    115, 190
  surrealist 1.212
pop art 4.268
Pound, Ezra 4.72, 116
Prabhavananda 4.210
Presence 3.57; 4.136
priests 1.157
Puccini, Giacomo 4.309
Pythagoras, and music 3.47
Pythagorean advice 4.14

Q

quietism 4.48

R

Rachmaninoff, Sergei
  Vassilievich 4.309
Ramana Maharshi 4.63, 333
Raphael 4.271
Rappresentazione 4.318

The 28 Categories from the Notebooks

This outline of categories in *The Notebooks* is the most recent one Paul Brunton developed for sorting, ordering, and filing his written work. The listings he put after each title were not meant to be all-inclusive. They merely suggest something of the range of topics included in each category.

1 THE QUEST
   Its choice —Independent path —Organized groups —
   Self-development —Student/teacher

2 PRACTICES FOR THE QUEST
   Ant's long path —Work on oneself

3 RELAX AND RETREAT
   Intermittent pauses —Tension and pressures —Relax body,
   breath, and mind —Retreat centres —Solitude —
   Nature appreciation —Sunset contemplation

4 ELEMENTARY MEDITATION
   Place and conditions —Wandering thoughts —Practise
   concentrated attention —Meditative thinking —
   Visualized images —Mantrams —Symbols
   —Affirmations and suggestions

5 THE BODY
   Hygiene and cleansings —Food —Exercises and postures
   —Breathings —Sex: importance, influence, effects

6 EMOTIONS AND ETHICS
   Uplift character —Re-educate feelings —Discipline emotions —
   Purify passions —Refinement and courtesy —Avoid fanaticism

7 THE INTELLECT
   Nature —Services —Development —Semantic training —
   Science —Metaphysics —Abstract thinking

8 THE EGO
   What am I? —The I-thought —The psyche